THE COMPLETE BOOK OF
Scriptwriting

J. MICHAEL
STRACZYNSKI

WRITER'S DIGEST BOOKS
Cincinnati, Ohio

The Complete Book of Scriptwriting. Copyright © 1996 by Synthetic Worlds, Ltd and J. Michael Straczynski. Printed and bound in the United States of America. All rights reserved. No part of this book may be reproduced in any form or by any electronic or mechanical means including information storage and retrieval systems without permission in writing from the publisher, except by a reviewer, who may quote brief passages in a review. Published by Writer's Digest Books, an imprint of F&W Publications, Inc., 1507 Dana Avenue, Cincinnati, Ohio 45207. (800) 289-0963. Second edition.

This hardcover edition of *The Complete Book of Scriptwriting* features a "self-jacket" that eliminates the need for a separate dust jacket. It provides sturdy protection for your book while it saves paper, trees and energy.

Other fine Writer's Digest Books are available from your local bookstore or direct from the publisher.

00 99 98 97 96   5 4 3 2 1

Library of Congress Cataloging-in-Publication Data

Straczynski, J. Michael.
    The complete book of scriptwriting / J. Michael Straczynski.—[Rev. ed.]
      p.   cm.
    ISBN 0-89879-512-5 (alk. paper)
    1. Playwriting. 2. Television authorship. 3. Motion picture authorship. 4. Radio authorship. I. Title.
PN1661.S75   1996
808.2—dc20   96-30630
                                                                          CIP

Edited by Jack Heffron and Roseann Biederman
Designed by Jannelle Schoonover and Angela Lennert Wilcox

ABOUT THE AUTHOR

As Creator, Executive Producer and Head Writer for the Emmy-winning
series *Babylon 5*, J. Michael Straczynski has written over 150 *produced* television episodes, including half-hour, hour and two-hour programs. He has
served as writer/producer on such series as the top-ten rated *Murder, She
Wrote*, as well as *The New Twilight Zone*, *Walker Texas Ranger* and *Jake and
the Fatman*, among others. He has also story edited nearly half a dozen
animated series, and is the author of numerous plays, radio dramas, nonfiction articles, short stories, and two novels, *Demon Night* and *OtherSyde*,
both published by E.P. Dutton.

Straczynski currently resides in the Los Angeles suburb of Sherman
Oaks, writing between 2,000 and 3,000 pages of published or produced
material every year.

PREFACE

Don't be afraid. That simple; don't let them scare you. There's nothing they can do to you . . . a writer always writes. That's what he's for. And if they won't let you write one kind of thing, if they chop you off at the pockets in the market place, then go to another market place. And if they close off all the bazaars then by God go and work with your hands till you can write, because the talent is always there. But the first time you say, "Oh, Christ, they'll kill me!" then you're done. Because the chief commodity a writer has to sell is his courage. And if he has none, he is more than a coward. He is a sellout and a fink and a heretic, because writing is a holy chore.
    —Harlan Ellison, *from his anthology* Dangerous Visions

Up through about 1987, when the press of work made it too difficult to continue doing so, I taught seminars on scriptwriting. The students invariably came from all walks of life—housewives and college students, mechanics and poets, retirees and a few people who couldn't have been more than eighteen. There were always members of the local literati who figured they could sell a script or two in their spare time (since it can't be that hard, after all) in order to sustain their efforts at *real* writing. There were those from the local script group whose members gathered monthly to read their scripts aloud to one another—and did little else with them. There were those who had never seen a script; those who had written dozens of them, trying desperately for years to sell their ideas to the motion picture and television industry, without success; others who simply wanted someone credible to reassure them that they had talent; and a few with fragile talents and delicate sensibilities, to whom criticism or rejection is the creative equivalent of a diagnosis of terminal cancer.

In any such group, you can usually figure out pretty fast who belongs to which group. What you as a teacher end up looking for are the dreamers, the craftspeople, the prophets and the illuminators of the eccentricities of the human condition, for whom a place in the scriptwriting universe is always reserved but to whom the practice of professional scriptwriting is as unfathomable as the Dead Sea Scrolls. Talk to them and you'll find that while some of them have been discouraged by brief and unsuccessful forays into telescripting and screenwriting, the majority have had no experience in trying their craft and don't even know where to begin. For these people, the process can be depressing and frustrating in the extreme.

In the years since, I have continued to run into people like this. They send letters and e-mail, asking "How do I get in? What do I do? Am I doing the right thing? All the other books can tell me how to write a script, but nobody tells me what to do when I'm finished with it." Simple questions, but there are no simple answers. Doing the job right would require an entire book—just like the one you're holding in your hands.

On the one hand, this book is written for all these people, to try and make some sense of the creative, business and craft-oriented aspects of the scriptwriting business. At the same time, in a strange way, I'm writing this for my own benefit. I wanted to write the kind of book I wish somebody had written when I first started in this business. Like everyone else, when I first began selling scripts, I had no clear idea what I was doing. I was doing *something* right because I was selling what I wrote, even seeing it produced. But there was so much I didn't know, so many things that, until now, could only be learned through trial and error. I had to fall on my face a lot in order to learn what it was I should be doing. It was painful and difficult, but I learned a lot. Much of it is in this book. I can't save you from all of it, but with luck, I may be able to shave off a little of the grief along the way, to help you learn what you need to learn—not just to write scripts, but to write *well*, to *sell* what you write and to *survive* the process by knowing the system and understanding how it works.

Knowledge is power. Nowhere is that more true than in the life of the average scriptwriter. From markets to methods to agents and new technologies, the more you understand the field, the better your chances of surviving the attempt to write for it.

QUESTIONS, QUESTIONS

But it's impossssible to sell scripts without an agent, and you can't get an agent until you've sold something! Wrong on both counts. You can become an active, selling scriptwriter even without an agent. It's harder, no doubt, but it can be done. You'll learn how in the pages that follow. Can an agent make the process simpler? In general, yes, though they're not the ultimate guarantor of success. So this book will also help you understand how to find, evaluate and secure an agent for your work, even if you're unproduced and unpublished.

But I can't even get my script in the front door at a movie studio or a television network. No problem. We'll examine the techniques for tracking down a producer and getting him to look at your script with the hope of purchasing it. We'll discuss where you should look and where you shouldn't look, and thus avoid wasting precious time chasing down dead ends.

But I've never even seen a script! In the following chapters, you'll find samples of every kind of script currently in use in every medium, along with the specific typographical format required for each of them.

We'll examine everything from the physical packaging of your script to the marketing process. We'll look at the creative end as well, including directions on plotting, characterization, pacing, camera angles, blocking directions, dialogue and so forth.

But I'm unfamiliar with the terminology. Every reference is carefully explained; a glossary of film and television terminologies is also included.

In addition, each chapter examines the history of each medium, explaining how that market came to be the way it currently is, discusses how it is likely to change in the next ten years and analyzes how those changes may affect those writers working to break in.

There are, however, two things this book will not do, and will not even attempt.

First, it wil not teach you "the formula" because the formula doesn't exist except in the minds and workshops of those who stand to profit hugely by convincing you that it *does* exist. After all, could one reasonably charge three hundred dollars for a weekend workshop whose main lesson was, "Write what moves you to passion?" Of course not. To sell you on the idea that there is a formula, they have to make it as complex and rigid as possible. So they tell you that you *must* have the climax by page 82, that you *must* have a reversal on page 64, that your characters *must* have certain characteristics common to similar characters created earlier by others. If there wasn't a formula, they would have nothing to sell.

When the first edition of this book was published in 1981, there were maybe a handful of popular scriptwriting books. A recent survey of my local bookstore yeilded a total of forty-five such books. The business of teaching scriptwriting has become a cottage industry unto itself, rife with different schools (Truby vs. McKee vs. Straczynski vs. Froug), written by consultants, specialists, psychologists, studio execs and even the occasional writer.

The authors and lecturers behind these books and workshops generally approach their subject with one goal: to get you to write like everybody else. Surely this is a good thing, right? After all, since everybody else is successful, why not try to be more like them, to write like them?

Because if you study to write just like everybody else, you probably *will* end up writing just like everybody else.

There's only one problem.

We already *have* everybody else.

So why should we hire you?

As a story editor and a producer, when I look around to decide which writer to hire, I look for someone who brings to the work a unique and personal perspective. You don't get that out of mass-market approaches to writing. That is as heinous a concept as the books published for neophyte romance writers that provide boilerplate plots, prefabricated characterizations, even dialogue snippets to plug into the novel at the correct moments, "Oh my darling [insert name], how I've longed to see you again."

Blech.

So if you're looking for that sort of thing here, you won't find it.

I believe in the Socratic method. I will ask you questions, challenge you, involve you. I will ask you to think about *what* you write, about *how* you write, and give you some suggestions on how to improve your writing *without* changing the unique approach that you take to your work, which, in the final analysis, is all a writer has to sell.

Second, this book cannot teach talent or persistence. You've either got those two essential elements or you don't. There's no middle ground. You can take any group of unpublished, neophyte writers and bring them up to a certain level where they can sell. I've done it; so have others.

As an experiment, while teaching a basic-level creative writing class at San Diego State University, I wanted to see how many students could actually publish something—an article, a poem, a short story—by the end of the semester, with proper training. Publication in a legitimate magazine or newspaper meant an automatic A for the class. Nearly 75 percent of them had done so by the time finals rolled around, and another 5 percent managed to publish in the first few months thereafter.

They had written—had even sold. But most of them would tell you quite freely that they wre not writers and did not consider themselves to be such. Writers *burn*. They hear the music. It isn't just a creative exercise; it's their life.

So this book is directed toward a certain kind of writer, the type best described by Mignon McLaughlin when she said, "Anyone can write. The trouble with writers is that they can't do anything else."

Which is not to say that writers are incapable of doing anything else, like changing tires or extracting troublesome molars. It's just that writing is the only thing they can do for an extended period of time without chewing on the furniture or checking in for therapy. It makes them happy. It fills a need, whether that need is a longing for self-expression or a quest for immortality through the written word.

Dilettantes, curiosity seekers and literary sightseers are encouraged to apply elsewhere. I am of the personal belief that there is somthing unique about writers that prepares them from birth and propels them throughout their lives toward this most remarkable of professions. Most of these writers are unstoppable. Throw as many obstacles in their way as you like, and still they persevere toward their goal, often with nothing more than a vague idea of what that goal might be. Nothing, not even the most severe rejection, can impede the progress of such a writer.

But a little help is always a good thing. So if the new edition of this book can be of use to even one writer in his progress toward professional scriptwriting, it will have been an unqualified success.

J. Michael Straczynski
Sherman Oaks, California
January 3, 1996

INTRODUCTION

Begin at the end; end at the beginning.

It was 1988 and the absolute dead of summer. The Writers Guild of America (WGA) was on strike. It was a terrible time, six months of walking sidewalks in the stifling Los Angeles heat in a last-ditch effort to convince management that we would no longer take cuts in previously achieved territories at a time when the studios were showing record profits. Our demands were modest and reasonable, tied to the cost-of-living index. After accepting cutbacks in the last two contract negotiations, it was no longer a case of asking for more; we simply refused to accept less. So there we were on this particular summer day, out on Pico Boulevard in Los Angeles, picketing Twentieth Century Fox in the killer heat. I was walking with friends, as one tends to do when there's nothing else to do for hours at a stretch except hoist a picket sign, walk around in circles and drink Gatorade. Beside me in a little group were Harlan Ellison, Walter Koenig, David Gerrold, Ed Asner and a few others, all of us trudging along and checking our watches to see when we'd be allowed to escape the heat.

As we turned the loop to begin another pass in front of the studio, somebody jumped out of the other side of the line and came rushing over to me. "Are you J. Michael Straczynski?" he asked.

I hesitated, but after noting that he didn't *look* armed, and since insofar as I knew I didn't owe anybody money, I allowed as how I was.

"Hey, great," he said. "I just wanted to let you know that I got into the Guild about a year ago, and I've got your book to thank for it. I followed that thing like a bible, underlined huge sections of it, did what it said step-by-step and it paid off. I sold a feature, and I'd just started on staff on a series when the strike hit."

Then he thanked me again and rushed off to rejoin his companions on the line.

David nodded in the direction of the other writer. "What'd he want?"

I hesitated again. "He was just saying hello," I said, and I shouldered my picket sign and continued walking.

Why didn't I answer him more accurately?

Because I flinched.

I've flinched a lot since this book came out.

Not at first, mind you, and not all at once.

And not that there was anything wrong with this book, which was first published in 1981 by Writer's Digest Books. It's just that I'm a perfectionist, and as 1981 faded into the coming years, I grew more acutely aware of the things that could have been included to make the book even more than it was, to make it better.

As originally written, this book was as good as I could make it at that time. Since then, however, I've written over 140 produced scripts and story edited another 200. I've worked in syndication and for networks, for independent producers and major studios, writing half hours, hours, two-hour movies and four-hour miniseries. Along the way, I've learned and grown more aware of areas that need to be addressed in a book like this: changing trends, new markets, useful techniques of style and dialogue and characterization. I also received tons of letters through my "Scripts" column, which ran in *Writer's Digest* magazine from 1981 until 1991. Those letters gave me a better sense of what information readers wanted most, items that hadn't occurred to me while writing the first edition because we hadn't yet been introduced.

Like I said—I'm a perfectionist.

So perhaps you'll understand why I flinched when I learned that this book had become one of *WD*'s top ten all-time sellers and that it had become a standard text at over half a dozen major universities and I don't even *know* how many more regular colleges and junior colleges. I flinched, as I did when mail came from readers extolling the virtues of this book and when I ran into WGA members who said they broke in because of my book.

At conventions and seminars, people would compliment the text. "Yeah, but there's nothing in there about animation," I would say, or "Yeah, but the whole spec screenplay market has changed," or "Yeah, but jeez, I spent so much time on the practical side, I should've spent a little more on the theory of writing."

I found that I could "Yeah, but" myself right into a blue funk that would go on for days. Finally my spousal overunit would ask what the heck was wrong, and I'd tell her that somebody said something nice about my writing book . . . and she'd nod and tell me not to move while she made a few phone calls, they're nice people, just put on the jacket, yes, we know the arms are a little long, but it makes them easier to tie in back. . . .

I'm not an easy man to live with.

I probably would've gone off the deep end altogether if not for my *WD* column, which allowed me to drop in the material that, in retrospect, I would have included in the book. I wished, on more than one occasion, that I could somehow merge the column and the book, update it, take out the parts that were no longer as relevant as they were when the book was new, add a few chapters, tighten the screws and toss out the ballast.

Now imagine my reaction when the mail brought a letter from Bill Brohaugh, my editor at *WD* magazine for eight years, now the Chief Mojo at WD Books. He thought it might be a swell idea to update the book for a new edition, add a few chapters, merge the columns into the text, on and on . . . and would I be interested in taking on the task?

I don't think I've ever before fired off a reply that quickly. Acutally getting the book out the door has been a slightly longer task, in part due to the fact that I've been working almost nonstop in the script field, writing and producing television series and other projects and in part because I kept revising the chapters over and over, trying to get it *all* in there. There were moments I wanted it just to *go away and leave me alone.*

After about two years of this, Bill Brohaugh flew out to Los Angeles and we had dinner at Ma Maison, just between Beverly Hills and Hollywood. He said Writer's Digest was content to wait as long as necessary to get the book in-house and publish it. He said that they weren't about to let me off the hook, and they were all very excited about doing it—however long it took.

The man hates me, I concluded. That's a terrible thing to tell someone who's subconsciously looking for any excuse at all to get out of a responsibility that has exploded into a massive job of rewriting. So I continued revising and expanding and researching until I finally called Bill and said he'd have the new edition by the beginning of 1995.

Okay, so 1995 rolled into 1996; I had some nifty new elements to discuss in the growth of CD-ROM movies and DirectTV and laser discs and . . . and. . . .

"Art is never finished. Only abandoned."

The book you now hold in your hands is the result of several years of rewriting. It's as exhaustive and inclusive and timely as conceivable, because if it isn't—if it doesn't serve your needs as best as humanly possible—what's the point?

My intent with this new edition is fundamentally unchanged from the first version: to write the sort of book I wish someone had written when I was first starting out. The scriptwriting field is unpredictable and potentially hazardous to your sanity, chockablock with all the paraphernalia of warfare—booby traps, blast craters, land mines, poison gas and agents. Your best hope of survival is to begin the journey with as much information as possible about the landscape and the strange people who live hereabouts. Because, while there are certainly those among us out here who'd as soon shoot you as look at you, there are just as many others happy to give aid and comfort to a weary soldier.

You just have to know how to tell the one from the other.

So with hope for the future and for warm meals beside great fires, I present you with the only gift I have to give. It is, I believe, the most comprehensive book ever written on this particular subject.

At least, as of this moment.

Check back with me in another ten years.

With luck, I won't flinch.

One final thought—to end at the beginning, as promised.

After the first edition of this book appeared, it was pointed out to me that it would've been helpful to have a little more in the way of biographical material, for reasons that should become apparent quickly enough.

I don't come from showbiz stock. I came to Los Angeles without the benefit of friends or family or "contacts" in the industry. Though I've lived all over the country, I'm basically a New Jersey street kid, in the most literal sense. I've lived in houses without roofs, without proper heating, going from school to school, in a family that, for most of its history, could be described as lower middle class if one was being charitable, upper lower class if one was not. I got my education in the mean streets of Newark and Paterson, sandwiching schoolbooks between stickball and street fights. I attended half a dozen grade schools, four high schools, three junior colleges and one medium-size university; I didn't major in telecommunications or film or study theater at one of the major, prestigious film schools. I got my degrees in psychology and sociology and related fields. I cut my teeth on little community theaters, local newspapers and radio stations.

In short, I'm not much different from you, the person reading this introduction, who maybe didn't attend the best schools, who doesn't have pull in the scriptwriting business, who, as a kid, used to stay up all night watching movies and TV, lost in amazement at strange tales from distant places, wondering what it must be like to make magic out of phosphor dots and possessed of the silly but increasingly irresistible notion that maybe, just *maybe*, we had something important to say, a story to tell.

But everyone knows that people like us don't make it in Hollywood. Your parents, your friends, your teachers, meaning only the best for you, hoping to save you from disappointment and pain, will offer that piece of advice, repeating it over and over until you either accept it or go mad. Sitting at a restaurant counter in Cincinnati, standing in a bus chugging down El Cajon Boulevard in San Diego, you, the person reading this book, glance around. The people around you will take one look at the book in your hands and shake their heads. What a dreamer. No offense, but folks like you just aren't the *type* to make it in Hollywood, to see your name on the screen or the television tube in front of millions of viewers. Please. Get real. It doesn't happen that way. *Everybody* knows that.

Except . . . except for one little truth, which is at the core of this book, the one singular and important truth you must keep close to your most secret heart, the truth I learned, the truth I hope to pass on to you.

Here it is. Ready?

Everybody is wrong.

Keep writing. Keep fighting. Keep dreaming.

Because sometimes, every once in a while, the dream really does come true.

Even for folks like us.

PART I

Television

The writer is a special angel or in league with the devil, depending on your view. The writer is a prophet or a colicky infant. But either way, the writer is to be indulged, spoiled, cultivated, especially if he is a comedy writer, since there are never more than fifty good ones on the planet at any one time. Everything begins with words on a page. Good scripts make good shows. You must pray for good writers as fervently as for salvation. If it ain't on the page, it ain't on the stage.

—Bob Shanks, The Cool Fire

Chapter One

A Brief History of Television

I
f you want to get technical about it, television dates back to 1915, when
Guglielmo Marconi—who in 1894 transmitted the first radio signals—
predicted the rise of "visible telephones," devices that could transmit
pictures over the air or through wires for great distances. This was the
first credible prediction of television from a member of the scientific community, although writers of the fantastic had long speculated on the transmission of visual images. Even Mark Twain, in 1886, wrote in his journal
that he foresaw a day when "portraits and pictures transferred by light
accompany everything. The phonograph goes to church, conducts family
worship, teaches foreign languages, pops the question, etc."

In 1923, Marconi's words were borne out when Russian-born American
physicist Vladimir Zworykin applied for a patent on his latest invention:
the iconoscope camera tube, a predecessor of today's cathode-ray tube. The
patent application was complicated by the existence of competing designs
and other legal maneuvers that were taking place at the same time, all in
the interest of being the first to come up with a patented television receiver.

It was not until January 1, 1939, eight years after the first experimental
television signal was broadcast, that the United States Patent Office
granted Zworykin a patent for his iconoscope camera tube.

But time, television and lawyers wait for no man. Even as Zworykin's
litigation dragged on, progress continued to be made in television technology, based loosely on his work. In 1927, the first television program was
transmitted by wire from Washington, DC, to New York City, an event
heralded as final proof that commercial broadcasting was technologically
feasible. But *feasible* is not always the same as *practical*. At first, it was
thought that this new technology would be far beyond the price range of
individual owners, due to the expense involved in sending television by
landlines leased from the phone company (which at that time was the only
reliable form of transmission). The general consensus at the time was that

each community and town would have a "theater TV," where customers could come to see television the way they went to the movies. Instead of seeing newsreel accounts of boxing matches and other major events well after the fact, customers would pay a small admission price to see it live on theater TV. It's interesting to note that we have come full circle on this idea, which was essentially an early form of pay-per-view cable. And while there are plenty of TVs in American households today, it's not uncommon for people to gather around the local bar or club that has a satellite TV or cable to watch an exclusive event they can't afford to purchase at home.

EXPERIMENTAL TELEVISION

Recognizing the tremendous potential of television, the National Broadcasting Company (NBC) and its parent company, RCA, applied for permission to open an experimental television station as an extension of its radio broadcasting facilities. Permission was granted on October 30, 1931, and W2XBS-New York went on the air, broadcasting from the Empire State Building on an irregular basis.

NBC initiated the first daily schedule of television programming on May 1, 1939, a year in which the network provided 601 hours of programming, and became the first broadcaster to use telephone lines to relay television signals.

Realizing at last that television was not going to go away, that it was not a fad, despite the predictions of experts, the slightly more conservative Columbia Broadcasting System (CBS) jumped in with its own television stations. The long overdue move by CBS was hampered by the fact that NBC had greater physical resources; CBS was only one network, while NBC actually consisted of two radio networks, the Red and Blue Radio Networks, which gave NBC a wider range of technical support and expertise in making the transition.

Ironically, this dual networking became a liability to NBC rather than an asset when in 1941 the Federal Communications Commission (FCC) decided that "No license shall be issued to a station affiliated with a network organization maintaining more than one network." The FCC felt that such an operation constituted a monopoly not in the public's best interest. Within the year, NBC sliced off its Blue Network with its 116 radio stations and put it up for sale. The $8 million price tag was paid by Edward J. Noble, founder of the Life Savers candy company. Eventually, this new network became the American Broadcasting Company (ABC), a name originally owned by radio station WOL-Washington, which sold all rights to the name for $10,000.

Between 1941 and 1945, the FCC gradually began to set standards for television broadcasting. Transmissions were set at thirty single frames per second, with each frame consisting of 525 individual lines. Accompanying sound was to be transmitted along designated FM frequencies. The FCC allocated thirteen VHF (very high frequency) channels for use by commercial television. (One of these channels was later taken back for use by two-way radio, leaving us with the currently available broadcast channels 2 through 13.) At the time of this decision, July 2, 1945, there were only about 16,500 television receivers in the United States.

ABC didn't begin broadcasting until April 19, 1948, through its recently acquired affiliate, WFIL-Philadelphia, but it didn't take long for the new-born network to start picking up additional affiliates. There was a rush to sign on board this shining new television era, a condition that persisted for all of about six months.

THE PLOT THICKENS

Suddenly, on October 4, 1948, the FCC surprised industry analysts by declaring a five-year freeze on television licensing, the process by which affiliates are added to a network. This move effectively left ABC in the cold, stuck far behind its competitors while the FCC pondered what to do about the television stations that had been eliminated by returning channel 1 to radio.

But this move didn't just affect ABC. Many of the movie studios in Hollywood were at that time going through tough times. From their all-time high in 1946, box office revenues and film production had fallen precipitously, creating the biggest destabilization of the motion picture business since the Great Depression of 1929. Warner Bros. Studios virtually stopped all filmmaking activity from November 1948 through February 1949. Compounding this problem was the fact that, under the studio system at the time, the major studios had high-ticket actors and directors and writers under yearly contracts, and they had to be paid. This was a massive drain on faltering studio resources at a time when there was no other revenue coming in.

So now television came along, and for many of these studios it represented an opportunity to create work for the talented people they had to pay anyway, and, not coincidentally, generate some badly needed income.

Prior to the licensing freeze, major studios, such as Twentieth Century Fox, Universal, Paramount and Warner Bros., rushed to get into television and radio. Since radio was then the primary means by which one built a foundation for television (eventually transferring radio station licenses or adding onto them), Warner Bros. purchased two stations, KFWB in Los Angeles and WBPI in New York City (the WB standing for Warner Bros.), and entered into a joint venture with Paramount in a failed effort to purchase one of the radio networks. Twentieth Century Fox, RCA and Paramount tried to get into the theater TV business, even going so far as to build massive projection systems used in various test demonstrations, including a live broadcast of the Joe Lewis/Joe Walcott prizefight at the Fox Philadelphia Theater in June 1948. The FCC's freeze order came just as the studios were ready to make their leap into television. By the time the freeze was lifted four years later, it was too late for the studios, which were relegated to *producing* television programs rather than *owning* networks. But their desire to create their own television networks never went away, as we'll touch on in chapter five, "A Look at the Future."

So who benefitted from the freeze? The executives at CBS and NBC. Between their larger base of TV stations and nearly a decade's head start, they had nothing to fear from the studios, and they were confident that ABC's days were numbered.

And they might have been right had it not been for a legal decision that at first seemed to have nothing to do with the networks, but ended up blindsiding them on *both* sides of the issue. Under the Sherman Anti-Trust Act, Paramount Pictures was ordered in 1949 to divest itself of its theater operations and create a separate corporation for it having no connection to its film operations. (For further details on the impact created by this landmark decision, see "The End of the Studio System" in chapter six.)

After the decision, Leonard H. Goldenson, head of the newly formed United Paramount Theatres, a group consisting of the actual theaters themselves, not the studio, decided upon a merger with ABC, a decision approved by the FCC on February 9, 1952. The infusion of new money helped sustain the fledgling network until the FCC finally lifted its freeze on station licensing. New stations built in the intervening years, and those frozen out by the removal of channel 1 would be given access to the UHF (ultrahigh frequency) channels.

Seventy of these UHF channels (numbered 14 through 83) were subsequently allocated for commercial use. Broadcasters who had been awaiting the decision were justifiably unhappy with it becuause very few television sets at the time were equipped to receive UHF transmissions. It would be many years before there were enough properly equipped sets available to the public for UHF broadcasting to be profitable.

ONE SMALL STEP FOR BROADCASTING . . .

The 1950s were a landmark in television history. ABC, which had until then been referred to as "fourth in a three-network race," was finally on sufficient financial footing to challenge the superiority of CBS and NBC, even though it would take nearly twenty years for ABC to creep up toward the number one spot. The 1950s also saw the official introduction of commercial color television, although color signals had been broadcast on an experimental basis as early as 1940. After examining various competing color systems, some of which could only be received on a "color equipped" television, the FCC finally approved RCA's "color compatible" system, which allowed color programs to be received on black-and-white sets without distortion.

In addition to technological advances, the first twenty years of television saw quite a bit of innovation and experimentation. CBS and ABC were particularly noted for trying new concepts. Exciting ideas popped up every day as producers, performers, writers and directors looked at this brand new medium and asked themselves, "What if. . . ." Television was a toy, a magic box whose limitations had not yet been set and in which the rules changed with the sweep of the second hand or a new line dropped into the middle of a live broadcast. This emphasis on innovation led such performers as Ernie Kovacs to push the artistic potential of television to its very limits, often with surreal results, and gave Milton Berle a forum to revive vaudeville and imbue it with a sense of immediacy and vibrancy that reached across the "cold fire" of the television screen to warm households across the nation.

WRITERS, ACTORS AND CENSORS

A roll call of shows created during these ten years, often referred to as the Golden Age of Television, reads like a Who's Who of the medium: *Your Show of Shows*, with Sid Caesar; *The U.S. Steel Hour*; *The Colgate Comedy Hour*, with Donald O'Connor; *Kukla, Fran and Ollie*; *Make Room for Daddy*, with Danny Thomas; *The Honeymooners*; *Lassie*; *This Is Your Life*; *Sgt. Bilko*, with Phil Silvers; *The Ed Sullivan Show*; *Playhouse 90*; and, toward the end of the decade, Rod Serling's *The Twilight Zone*.

In producing these programs, television culled its artists from radio and the stage, enlisting such notables as Jack Benny, Groucho Marx, Ed Wynn, Edward R. Murrow, Perry Como and Jack Palance. Then, as now, it was understood that the easiest way to sell a sponsor, a network, a studio or a viewer on a new show was to attach a star to the project. In order of importance after the star, the most valued commodity on the market was the writer. Television scripts were then tele*plays,* and the networks, whose creative centers and production were based then in New York, treated the writers much the same as the playwrights they encountered locally. Radio dramatists and playwrights were recruited for the new medium. Television plays were reviewed in major newspapers, and the writers were always recognized, whether panned or praised. A writer of television had visibility. Rod Serling once said of that period, "I don't suppose anything ever made writers so famous so fast as that so-called Golden Age. Names like Reginald Rose and Paddy Chayevsky and Tad Masel and mine became household words overnight."

Part of this freedom came from the fact that television programs were fairly inexpensive to produce. Where a motion picture in 1952 might cost $1 million to produce, a half-hour television series cost only $25,000, and hour shows went for approximately $65,000. By contrast, in 1994, the majority of TV hour-long shows cost well in excess of $1 million—sometimes up to $1.9 million in the case of some heavy-action or special effects series. Compared to movies, which, in the same year could cost as much as $75 million, television is still a bargain.

Writers who could produce quality programs were given the opportunity to pursue their own vision. They were put in charge of whole series and given considerable artistic freedom. Anthology series like *Playhouse 90* and *The U.S. Steel Hour* highlighted the power of the written word (if only because the technology and budgets of the day left them with little in the way of grandiose visual effects). Writers were allowed to explore different topics each week, examining social issues and the human condition as deeply as was possible within the carefully defined parameters of what was socially acceptable on television.

And it was in this arena that, eventually, these writers ended up in conflict with the networks, who wanted programs that would not offend consumers. Not even Serling was above their machinations, as he discovered during the production of his script "Noon on Doomsday," when he was forbidden by the network censors to identify a Jew as a Jew.

Many of the restrictions then imposed on writers seem downright peculiar when viewed from a contemporary perspective. When Lucille Ball became pregnant during the run of *I Love Lucy,* she and the rest of the cast were forbidden to use the word *pregnant* in any of the scripts, even though by the eighth month she was very obviously so. They could only say she was "in the family way."

Sex was a constant target for network censors. It was against the rules to show married couples sleeping in the same bed; only single beds were allowed. And if they should by chance sit on the same single bed, there could be little touching, and both actors had to keep at least one foot on the floor. In a scene from a dramatic program that called for the simulation of a Catholic mass, the censors refused to allow a reference to "the Virgin Mary," because the term *virgin* was unacceptable.

Another classic example of network censorship came during the production of "Thunder on Sycamore Street," by Reginald Rose. The story examined the conflict that results when a black family moves into an all-white neighborhood. The censors felt that the tensions such a program would provoke were too extreme. As a result, the script was rewritten over Rose's opposition into a story about the problems faced by an ex-convict and his family when they move into a middle-class neighborhood.

Thus it was that television writers learned an important strategy that's sometimes necessary in dealing with networks: You have to fox them at every turn. You don't lie outright, never that, but you obfuscate. Delay. Mumble. Double-talk them to death. Bank on their constant confusion and lack of memory to get what you want.

Network executive to writer: You know that first scene, where the burglar comes in through the front door? I want you to rewrite that so he comes in the window instead.

Writer to network executive (two weeks later): Remember that first scene, the one where you said I should have the burglar come in through the front door instead of the window? Well, you were right. It works a lot better that way.

Fortunately, the technology and hectic pace of live television often played into the hands of writers. Commented Martin Manulis, producer of *Playhouse 90*: "Sponsors and network brass never got around to reading the script until a couple of weeks before it went on. Then they would scream from New York, 'You can't do that!' I would tell them that we were so far into rehearsal that either we did that script or they had ninety minutes of blank air."

Later on, he said, "You do the show, you watch it on the monitors for the East, you go home and watch the replay (on kinescope) for the West Coast, you cut your throat and go to bed."

In all fairness to the networks, such mandates very often didn't sit well with the very censors forced to deliver them. There were outside forces to contend with, in the form of advertising agencies, who functioned as front men for the sponsors who at that time often financed entire series and thus exerted tremendous influence. During the production of a Chevrolet-sponsored western series, the sponsors requested that a line containing the words "ford a stream" be deleted, on the grounds that they didn't want to plug the competition. In retribution, a show financed by Ford deleted a shot of the New York skyline featuring the Chrysler building.

At about the same time, *Playhouse 90* was producing a drama featuring actor Charles Bickford as the captain of an 1850 whaling ship. One scene called for the character to shave with a straight razor. Unfortunately, the sponsor for that particular program was a manufacturer of electric shavers, who insisted that if the character was shown shaving, then he must use an electric shaver. The fact that such devices didn't exist in the 1800s was beside the point. Rather than slug it out with the networks, the scene in question was simply dropped.

In an attempt to eliminate the influence of advertisers on television content, the practice of one sponsor underwriting an entire series was eventually discontinued. It was hoped that this would allow greater creative freedom. But as the costs per minute for commercials rose under this new arrangement, the power of advertisers only increased.

The threat of removing one's advertising remains a formidable ultimatum even today, when advertising agencies and sponsors are targeted by special interest groups promoting one agenda or another. Threats of boycotts and letter-writing campaigns (one recent show logged over thirty thousand letters per month because of an organized campaign) have modern advertisers leery of anything considered too political or sexual or "in contradiction to accepted norms" (whatever those are). That this continues despite the fact that not one boycott has ever been successful in removing a show or seriously eroding viewership is one of those astonishing displays of fear devouring sensibility that's so prevalent in American business.

As a result, network television has gradually become more regimented. No longer can a writer/producer concern himself only with what makes good drama. As television series have become more expensive, leading to heated contests for ratings and the advertising dollars they bring, networks feel they can no longer trust their futures to the predilections of any one person. So where once there were only a few people at the very top of the network structure making decisions about what would and would not go on the air, now regiments of executives have begun seeping out of the catacombs of corporate structure. There were vice-presidents of specials, vice-presidents of development, vice-presidents of programs for either coast, vice-presidents of business affairs, vice-presidents of comedy, vice-presidents of dramatic programming . . . and with each vice-president came a cadre of advisors, flunkies, plenipotentiaries and yes-men whose purpose was to monitor the pulsebeat of the viewing public and react accordingly, sailing with the wind of popular opinion wherever possible.

Granted, the networks have an FCC-mandated order to function "in the public interest, necessity and convenience." Granted, they can properly ask of a program, "Is this objectionable?" But the trap is sprung when that question metamorphoses into, "Is it possible that this might offend *anyone* out there, any group or individual, even those whose perspective is so distorted that it fails to touch reality at any two contiguous points?"

The severity of this problem depends on whether a network is in a high- or low-ratings cycle. Lower-rated networks are often willing to experiment with new concepts and risk offending a few people if it gets them (1) good press and (2) ratings. After all, if they're already in the cellar, what do they have to lose? A number one network, on the other hand, afraid of jeopardizing its comfortable status, plays it safe. What results is a cycle: The network that offers innovative programming begins edging out the established networks. But as that network begins to climb toward the top, it becomes increasingly less willing to try new things, as opposed to the former number one network, which is now willing to try innovative programs in order to regain its throne.

Everything you need to know about the inner workings of a TV network you can learn by watching *Hamlet* or *Oedipus Rex* or *A Day at the Races*.

Chapter Two

The Writer, the Language, the Formats

As television continues to evolve, the public demands more and different programs. Who can give you those programs? Writers. What do writers want in exchange? The same things the networks want: money and power, usually in that order. This has led to the growth of writer/producers, often called "hyphenates." Your basic low-level hyphenate is given the title of producer and some additional responsibilities, even though his main job is to write scripts, rewrite freelancers and sit in on casting sessions. At the top is the executive producer/writer, or "showrunner," someone who can create a show, write a show and usher a show through the production process.

At the other end of the spectrum is the freelance writer, who moves from show to show, selling scripts and getting residuals on those scripts. To clarify a common misperception about residuals, they are not a bonus, not a gift. They are nothing less than a form of deferred pay. A television series can bring in a huge amount of money over time, or it can die within weeks of its debut. Writers share some of the risks through the residuals process; if the show is a hit and runs forever, the producer continues to get money from it, and the writer gets a piece of it. After all, the show wouldn't have succeeded if it was poorly written. If on the other hand the show fails, then the producer gets nothing, and neither does the writer. It would be possible, I suppose, to negotiate one huge flat fee, but in the long run, residuals *favor* producers and networks by spreading the risks around a little.

That's just a little something to remember the next time you read in the newspaper about Hollywood writers going on strike. Writers *do* share the risks, and when you consider that the top five studio executives in town earn, between them, more than all members of the Writers Guild put together (there are over nine thousand), it tends to put such things in a different light.

On balance, television writers today are the highest-paid practitioners of the literary profession in history. But mark the phrase *on balance.* If you can sell two one-hour scripts per year, which is a pretty good average for a freelance writer, that's about $40,000 per year, before taxes. That figure is comparable to or less than the yearly salary of elementary school teachers and considerably less than plumbers. The majority of working writers fall into this financial category. It's only when you get to the top 5 to 10 percent that you find the writers and hyphenates who routinely earn six figures a year or more. So if you come out here for the money, think twice. The odds of hitting six figures per year aren't great. If you like teaching or fixing pipes more than writing, your interests are probably better served there. That said, it's important to make clear that the odds aren't impossible, either, and the chance of being the one who breaks through is a powerful attraction. It was sufficient to draw me to Los Angeles without contacts, without friends in the industry, with nothing more than the dream that you, gentle reader, probably share. I encountered pretty much the same odds, the same risks that you will. Unless you're the son of a major star—and regardless of what you hear, that's more the exception than the rule—it's the same process for all of us. By all rights, breaking in should be impossible. But strangely enough, sometimes it actually works out.

But the rewards sought are not (and should not be) only financial. There's a thrill that comes with seeing your work brought to life by professional actors, directors and support personnel and knowing that tens of millions of viewers will be watching something you wrote in the solitude of your home or office. Television writing is heady stuff, leading to the creation of television writing curricula in creative writing and telecommunications departments at colleges throughout the nation. Nearly every professional writer, no matter what genre provides the bulk of her income or reputation, toys at some time or other with the idea of writing a television script—"But just so I can have the money to write what I *really* want to write, you understand."

Or its bitter, unfortunate consequences.

As a new writer, however talented you might be, you must realize that you are one voice among many, all crying out like eager children, "Look at me! Watch me! Pay attention!" You must somehow distinguish yourself from all the others—from the dilettantes and the amateurs and the hustlers and the all-talk-no-action crowd.

The only way to distinguish yourself from the rest of the pack and draw the attention of the industry is to demonstrate a wealth of talent and a surplus of professionalism. Many people can be talented but lack the ability to present themselves in a professional manner, antagonizing those they're trying to impress. One would-be writer, believing himself to be vastly talented, unwilling to go through the same process as everyone else because that was beneath him, parked himself beside the gate at Paramount with a sign that read "Future Emmy-Winning Writer." Suffice it to say, he never got inside. Another stood outside NBC Burbank every day wearing a sandwich billboard (earning the nickname Billboard Man on the *Tom Snyder Show*) and proclaiming his comedy screenplay the funniest thing in history. Every month, ads appear in *Daily Variety* and other industry publications from unknown writers hawking their unpurchased scripts, offered as though they were doing the industry a favor. At seminars I've attended, I've had people in the audience decry all television as garbage, then turn around and offer to sell me a script on the grounds that *they* could do better and save the industry from itself.

Professionalism and discipline are the elements that most profoundly separate the wanna-bes from the real writers. Wanna-bes nickel and dime you and want you to do the work while they graciously offer to split the resulting money with you fifty-fifty. The real writers are out there pounding out script after script, learning their trade and getting better at it every day, honing their skills until they are sharp enough to cut through any resistance. Wanna-bes don't write scripts; they try and get into meetings where they think they can sell their ideas for millions of dollars, see their names on TeeVee and retire to Hawaii. They don't want to write; they want to be famous. Big difference.

If you're serious about writing for television, and if you carry nothing else from this book when you are finished with it, remember this: To have an idea is not enough—no matter how good the idea is.

You have to write a script. Preferably more than one. You have to be willing to do the work.

Period.

As a story editor or producer, my job is to deliver 22, 24 or 26 episodes of a television series to the network or, in the case of syndication, the studio. I am allocated *x* dollars with which to purchase scripts.

If my writers are late or turn in scripts so awful they cannot be salvaged through revision, I will quickly go over my budget. Sets, locations and stars who have been contracted for that episode may have to be jettisoned. Long nights may be spent rewriting the script in-house. This takes away time from my own scripts or from such other producer duties as screening dailies, taking part in scoring sessions, editing and casting. If the script can't be saved, and we're in a deadline crunch, I may have to write a whole new script overnight. I might have to postpone shooting or even temporarily shut down, at a cost of $45,000 or more per day. The responsibilities resting on the producer's shoulders are enormous.

So before I can trust *any* writer with an assignment, I require concrete proof that she can deliver. To do otherwise is to abrogate my responsibility to the series.

And a sample script is the only bellwether that any story editor or producer can trust.

THE LANGUAGE OF TELEVISION WRITING

Peculiar as this may sound, writing for television is at once the easiest and the most difficult branch of scriptwriting. Easy in that many factors are predetermined: the length of the script, the number of acts, the range of permissible topics and the characters you'll be dealing with. The schematic has already been set down. Your task is to plug your own ideas into that context, which for some writers is where the process becomes quite difficult. You're required to work with characters created by someone other than yourself, structure your story around commercials and other artificial timing devices, set aside your ego when the producer says, "Our character wouldn't do that," and limit yourself in the number of sets and the types of situations you can develop into story lines.

To the *literati* who turn up their collective noses at the idea of such restrictions on the muse . . . *every* form has its restrictions and its rules. Sonnets, haikus, stage plays . . . you either play by the rules or you don't get to play. Whether the convention at hand is an act break or a set number of stanzas or the use of iambic pentameter, you work within the limitations of the form while trying to extend your craft to the very edges of that form.

To establish the rules of telescripting, we'll start with the basic terminology, beginning with the structure of a television script, which consists of the following items in varying configurations and combinations.

A *teaser* is a brief, opening segment, usually running two to four minutes, that introduces the characters and the action to follow. A teaser can be a significant introduction to the story that follows, an off-topic aside or a collection of shots from the story prefaced by "Tonight on [name of show]."

The best kind of teaser is one that is linked to your larger story, that dramatically sets events in motion and prompts the viewers to stick around at the pivotal top-of-the-hour slot when they're most inclined to channel-surf.

The *tag* is the flip side of the teaser, a brief segment at the end of the show that wraps up the action in a nice, neat and sometimes humorous package. A tag can also be effectively used to create a character moment after the main events of the story have reached their conclusion.

An *act* is the body of the story, the stage on which your characters interact, the plot is revealed, the bad guys are punished and the good prevail. Each act begins on some element that draws the viewers smoothly into the story and ends on something that makes them come back after the commercial break.

For now, those are the only three terms you're going to have to know. There are plenty of other terms used in the offices of story editors and television writers—terms like *laying pipe, putting in a trap door, walk 'n' talk* and others, usually metaphors borrowed from the construction industry—but for the moment, we'll focus on the terms and rules required to get into those offices in the first place.

The specific rules of television writing depend in large measure on the area you choose to pursue.

Episodic Comedy

Thirty minutes long, an episode consists of two acts or a teaser followed by two acts or two acts followed by a tag. Usual length: 26 pages for a show on film, 42 for a show shot on tape. For first-run syndication, sitcoms often run three acts to allow for an extra commercial break. On pay cable shows, there are no commercial breaks, but the two-act structure is usually followed anyway in order to expedite syndication once the show leaves pay cable.

Episodic Drama

Each episode is sixty minutes long, consisting of four acts or, in some cases, four acts and a teaser and/or a tag. Syndicated hour dramas can have as many as five acts and a teaser, again to allow for more commercials. And because there are generally more commercials in syndication than network, the dry time (i.e., minus commercials) of a syndicated show is about a minute or two less than network shows. Average length 48 to 54 pages.

Ninety-Minute Dramas

Forget it. The ninety-minute episodic drama has all but gone the way of the trilobite. With the exception of variety programs, specials and the occasional miniseries, like PBS's landmark *Tales of the City*, the berth previously occupied by the ninety-minute program has subsumed into the sixty-minute drama and the two-hour television movie.

Movies for Television

Also known as Movies of the Week, often called MOWs in television parlance, these are 120 minutes long, generally consisting of six to eight acts of equal length. Usual length 101 to 110 pages, film format.

The number of movies made for television has dramatically increased in recent years at the broadcast and cable networks. In a typical season, one of the major basic-cable channels purchased and produced nearly sixty MOWs. Such movies can also function as backdoor pilots for series, allowing networks to test the water with a concept before committing to a full series. They are growing in popularity because in many cases a network or studio shares in the ownership of the MOW and can benefit from foreign distribution, videocassette sales, laser discs, books, sound tracks and other ancillary merchandising. If a series is on for one season, gets limited ratings and is canceled, everyone loses; there isn't enough to syndicate, and the studio can write off all hope of ever recouping its investment. But even a low-rating movie can, over time, recoup its budget through creative distribution methods.

Another reason for the growth of TV movies rests with the often exorbitant prices asked by studios for a first-run theatrical release; in many cases, it costs a network less to produce its own movie than to purchase the television rights to a hit theatrical motion picture. They can also control the language and content of these movies, which they consider very important. Often a broadcast network will spend substantial amounts of money to acquire a hit film, only to be in the improbable position of being unable to show the entire film without substantial editing for language, nudity and graphic content. In essence, the network buys the movie at an exorbitant price, then ruins the film it spent all this money to acquire through cuts and other "massaging." This is, by contrast, one of the elements that has led to the growth of pay cable. Most people who want to see a movie the way it was made will watch it, uncut, on cable. So by the time a gutted version of the motion picture finally airs, the core audience has already seen it, which further erodes viewership.

True stories. In the last few years, the major growth in television MOWs has been in the "based on a true story" category. Stories of controversy—the Menendez Brothers' killing, the O.J. Simpson story—are often put into production while the core controversy is still going on. Producers were shooting a MOW based on the Waco, Texas, standoff between a cult and the police even as the place was burning down, rewriting along the way as the tragedy unfolded in real life. If you don't have access to someone's true story, for which you'll have to pay lots of money, there are other stories of controversy that are matters of public record. These may have taken place ten to fifty years ago but can be turned to dramatic purpose if you're willing to do the research.

While the broadcast networks tend to concentrate on the true story MOWs, fictional movies are far from moribund. The cable networks are far more inclined to fictional MOWs because they're evergreens, they don't rely on contemporary headlines to fuel ratings and they can be aired year after year. Many of the major studios, including Paramount and Universal, have programs whereby they produce MOWs for $3 million and under that are then sold to cable networks and foreign distributors or are sold directly into video stores for sale or rental on cassette. It's not uncommon for American-made TV movies to show up as feature films in many smaller countries—all of which makes it fairly easy for the studio to recoup the small initial investment.

But although networks will continue to produce MOWs, their main business remains the production of comedy and drama series.

WRITING THE EPISODIC PROGRAM

The single most important rule to follow before writing a script for episodic television is to study the series you intend to write for. Don't laugh; you'd be surprised at the number of scriptwriters who submit work having researched nothing more than the synopses that appear in *TV Guide*, without having actually seen a single episode. Shortly after finishing production on the pilot for my series *Babylon 5*, I received letters from writers stating that they had completed spec scripts for my show—which at that point had not even *aired* yet—based only on what they'd *heard* about the show and its characters.

That doesn't mean you have to be a fan of a show to write for it, only that you should proceed with a baseline amount of necessary information to competently handle the series's characters, format and story range.

Once you've selected your target series, you should keep a notepad beside you while you watch. Recording it on videotape is also helpful since it allows you to play back the episodes and study them in greater detail. Write down everything about the show and its characters. Note their attitudes, habits and eccentricities, the use of colloquialisms and any nicknames they may use for one another.

This study process becomes more important the newer you are to television writing. If you've been working within the conventions of television for a long time, you can thumbnail or fudge things a little. In 1989, for instance, I was bugged mercilessly by my agent to go in and pitch on *Jake and the Fatman*, a highly rated CBS series. I had never even seen the show. But after she set up the appointment, I scrounged up five or six episodes on tape from friends, bummed some sample scripts from the show's secretary, and was able to get a decent mental picture of the series in the week I had prior to going in. I then took that information, combined it with what I already knew about the hour drama form and went in sufficiently well prepared to present a credible pitch.

Know Your Characters

You must familiarize yourself as much as possible with the history of your characters, both the series's regulars and the characters you will create for your individual episode. If you want to sell a story in which a series's main character falls in love, it helps to know that he was married once before, that he blames himself for the split and that he doesn't entirely trust himself in a new relationship. That has a *major* impact on how you structure your story and saves you from that awful moment in a meeting when the story editor stops you midpitch and says, "Sorry, our character wouldn't do that." The more you know about your characters, the easier the writing and plotting process becomes. And, again, remember that you're trying to sell this idea to someone who knows the show far more intimately than you ever will, so the closer your vision of the show resembles hers, the better the odds of selling your story.

Here's a hint for how to make your characters realistic and true to who they are: Think of your best friend for a moment. (If you don't have one, borrow the best friend of the person sitting next to you.) Now visualize your friend, and place him or her in a darkened living room. Have your friend walk across the room and suddenly bang his shin on the coffee table. Knowing your friend as you do, you know *exactly* what your friend will say at that moment of excruciating pain. The same principle applies for the characters you create. You must come to know them so well that you don't have to work at making them speak and move. You then drop them into a difficult situation, stand back and let your intimate familiarity with the characters ease them naturally into the flow of the story.

As a story editor, I can't tell you how important it is to have your characters flow smoothly from one action, scene or situation to another, riding on logic and characterization. The time that I lose interest in a pitch is when the writer suddenly makes the character behave in unnatural or stupid ways, just for the writer's convenience. During a story meeting I had with a freelance writer on *Murder, She Wrote*, she described a moment in the plot when, after a murder, amateur detective Jessica Fletcher remembers that a box arrived the day before, one of many delivered to a big party. Suddenly concluding that the box has an important clue, she requests all of the suspect's credit card slips.

"Why *that* box out of so many?" I asked. There was no reason given to suspect *that* person more than anyone else, there was no indication what was in the box and there was no connection established between that box and the murder. The response I received was, "Well, that's where the clue is. She has to go there." Like many new writers, this one simply moved the characters around like chess pieces, putting them where needed, regardless of whether going to that place made any sort of story or character sense.

Convenience is the enemy of all writers, but it's easily the number one enemy among television writers.

Ancillary Issues

In your analysis of the series, you should examine the social underpinnings of the program. Is it realistic or lighthearted? Does it deal with important issues or avoid them? If the former, does it deal with issues head-on or by metaphor? On *Murder, She Wrote*, we generally avoided social-commentary stories because we knew that's not what the show was supposed to be and not what the audience really wanted to see at that time (8 P.M. Sunday).

Ask yourself as many questions as possible about the show, and dig out the answers:

- Is each episode focused exclusively around one plot (the A-story), or are there subplots (B-stories) that fill out the hour?
- Who is the show aimed at? What age range, social level, educational level and sex?
- Are there any themes or aspects of character growth that recur throughout the course of a given season?

Physical Constraints

As well as the specific rules of any given show, there are generics that pertain to the form itself: situation comedy vs. hour-long dramas. In sitcoms, it's important to restrict the number of sets required by your story. Most sitcoms are limited to just a few sets: the *primary set*, such as the living room/kitchen in *Dinosaurs* or *The Cosby Show*, and a couple of *supporting sets*, which are often specific to the script in question—a classroom, for example, or a meeting hall. Some situation comedies have access to a slightly larger number of sets, usually called *standing sets*, that are used when required. There are also *swing sets*, used rarely, but which are stored for those occasions when they might be needed. This is referred to as a fold-and-hold. A larger number of sets is most associated with ensemble shows, where we follow the various characters as they go about their business outside the home.

If the program you choose to write for has many standing sets, feel free to use them when and if required by your story, not just because they're available. You should avoid introducing more than one new set in your script. This may seem an arbitrary decision by the producers, but each new set constructed to be used only once drains the production budget. Scripts have been known to be rejected or massively rewritten because they required too many sets.

But sitcom writers aren't the only ones who make this error. Dramatic writers new to the business can do the same, lining up a series of distantly related incidents that don't culminate in any kind of satisfactory resolution and calling it a story.

The characters must strive to achieve something, or to avoid something, and as the writer, it's your job to come up with obstacles to throw in their way as they pursue that goal. In a sitcom, that goal can be anything from one character trying to get another character to go out on a date with him to throwing a surprise party or avoiding an audit. The humor results from sabotaging your character at every possible turn until it looks as if her entire life is about to go down the tubes, at which point you save her from utter destruction. But not too easily, and not without a few pounds of flesh being extracted in exchange for escaping the wrath of the gods.

The best example of this kind of writing—and, not coincidentally, perhaps the funniest sitcom ever produced for television—is the British series *Fawlty Towers*, starring and cowritten by John Cleese, of *Monty Python* fame. In every episode, one or more characters ends up spiraling further and further into absolute destruction and personal embarrassment, only to be rescued at the last second (barely). If you watch that series and most of the available episodes of *The Mary Tyler Moore Show*, you will learn 95 percent of everything you ever need to learn to write a sitcom.

It never hurts to bathe in genius.

The equation is simple: characterization + desire = goal, and goal + conflict = story.

Again, that equation applies equally well to dramatic series. Perhaps even more so, since you have to sustain that story over sixty minutes instead of thirty. You have to determine what your character wants, how far he will go to achieve it and how far someone else will go to try to stop him. What we as viewers tune in for is to see who blinks first.

Conflict, Conflict, Conflict

In television, as in any form of literature, you don't just tell a story; you *drive* a story. And nothing drives a story as well as conflict and emotion. An act is made up of individual scenes. So *make* them scenes. Give them a beginning, a middle and an end. Move them as fast as you can. Drive one scene into another. Give each scene *impact* so that by the time the act is over, your audience is exhausted and exhilarated by the roller-coaster ride they've just taken.

During my tenure as producer of *Murder, She Wrote*, the one thing that invariably killed a script or required a major rewrite was a conflict-poor structure. Jessica went from location A to location B, C and D, asking questions. Information was given. And she moved on to the next nearly identical scene. The resultant story was little more than a compilation of clues gained without much effort or color—exposition on parade.

Fixing those scenes required injections of conflict. Jessica goes to location A and asks for information. But it isn't forthcoming. The other character won't cooperate, says he doesn't remember (obviously lying) or is dead. So now our protagonist has to be smart, has to figure out some way to extract the information that the other person doesn't want to provide. It makes the process more interesting and dynamic.

But there has to be a balance.

If I may editorialize for a moment, the problem with a lot of contemporary dramatic scripts is that they concentrate exclusively on the C-word, *conflict*, and ignore the E-word, *emotion*. They go so far in the direction of conflict that their characters become annoying, shrill, unlikeable. I believe it's more satisfying to a viewer to see a mix of emotions rather than concentrating on anger and petulance. For example: You send your protagonist to a bar to find out information about the antagonist. The bartender wants nothing to do with the protagonist, who taunts the barkeep until finally he accidentally drops some vital piece of information just before your protagonist is thrown out into the street.

Conflict-driven action. All well and good. Now you move on to the next scene. You could very easily repeat that kind of structure if you so desired (question → refusal → conflict → revelation). But isn't it fundamentally more interesting, more varied and colorful if in the next scene, the protagonist goes to the home of the antagonist's mother, who hasn't heard from her son in years. She is vulnerable and concerned, and in her own way is trying just as hard to extract information about her son from your protagonist as he is trying to get information from her. She's no easier to pump for information than the barkeep, but her *reasons* for withholding information, and the means she uses, are diametrically different. She's a sympathetic character, and her situation moves us to compassion.

Straightforward, expository writing is fairly easy. Conflict is harder. And compassion, *real emotion*, is hardest of all. Which is why it's done least often, and least effectively. And, concurrently, why there is such a demand for those who can pull it off convincingly. A script about redemption as well as damnation is harder to write, rarer to find and considerably more valued than any other.

To briefly recap: The first way in which a script must be about something is that it must involve your characters in a story that is motivated by their emotions and desires. The second way in which a script must be about something has less to do with your characters than it does with what and who *you* are and what you bring to the writing process.

To illustrate the point . . .

The Quality of Passion

While I was story editing *The Twilight Zone*, we received a spec outline from a writer who had never previously sold to television. The story, entitled "The Hellgrammite Method," was the tale of an alcoholic who seeks a most unusual cure for his affliction. As I read the outline, which was an over-the-transom submission, unagented as far as I can remember, something significant struck me. To check my suspicion, we called in the writer to discuss the story.

Sure enough, there was a history of alcoholism in his family. He hadn't written this story just to try and sell to the series, he'd written it because *he was also trying to work something out inside himself.* You could see it in the way he spoke about it. He was burning.

Afterward, while debating whether to hand out an assignment to an untested writer, I lobbied strongly that we do so. Because I knew he burned, and that anger would drive him toward something truly extraordinary. *It was a story that mattered to him*, and thus I felt it should matter to us.

He got the assignment. Wrote the script. We produced the script. And that episode won a Scott Newman Award for its frank treatment of the problems of alcoholism.

Similarly, while I was on *Zone*, I wrote scripts about battered wives and lost childhoods, about the dilemma of growing old and the pain of losing loved ones, about the importance of memories and the fine line between self and patriotism. Stories, in short, that *mattered to me*. And before anyone points out how *Zone* is the exception to the rule, that has been the case on just about every script I've written. I always try to incorporate some aspect that means something to me personally—a character, a theme, a subtext that makes it more than just one more TV script in a business that eats up thousands of them every year without breaking a sweat. In addition, because I care about the subject area, it means that I'll work harder at making the story just right.

I honestly believe that that's one of the big reasons I and a few others tend to sell constantly. Enthusiasm counts for a lot, believe me. The flip side of this argument is the one presented by certain others—workshop teachers and authors of certain writing books, not to mention names or anything—who advocate adherence to a televison "formula," on the grounds that a formula script is most saleable. But no formula can possibly equal the fire and intensity of a script written out of conviction and passion. It's that fire that helped me succeed as a writer, and it's that fire that I look for in other writers when I story edit or produce a series. And I think that most story editors/producers would tell you the same thing.

So keep that in the back of your head as you write, not just in the beginning, but *permanently*. Don't lecture, don't be too on-the-nose about it, but find a story line that matters both to you and to your characters.

You'll be surprised at how much easier that makes the writing process.

STRUCTURE

Once you've developed the core of your story line, you now have to fit that story into the structural mold of a television episode, just as a poet shapes her inspiration to the rigors of a haiku or a sonnet.

And speaking of shaping your story to the show, let me take off my writer's hat for a moment and put on my producer's hat (the one that clamps off the blood vessels and lowers my IQ fifteen points). If there's any one problem that television producers have with freelance writers, it's the tendency of the writers to want to do stories about what they want to write about, as opposed to what's best for the show. As writer/producer, you create a number of characters and invest time and effort working out their backgrounds, histories, interests, relationships. All of this is given to the freelancer when she comes in for the initial meeting. You wait a week or two, then the writer comes in, and you expect to hear a great story about your characters. . . .

And what you get is a story about an outside character who comes in and has some adventures, a story in which your regular characters are either passive participants or downright irrelevant.

This sort of thing happens all the time in television. I've never worked on a series yet, or talked to anyone doing so, in which the producers haven't found themselves tearing their hair out after a while because they can't get anyone to write about their characters. So when you *do* develop your story, take this lesson to heart: If you can make your tale about the regular characters on the series, and not the guest star, and make it interesting and compelling, you will not only sell, you will work forever.

Details

In most cases, you'll want to begin act one (or the teaser) with a scene that introduces your main character(s). After all, a week has gone by since the program last aired, and it's always wise to take a few moments at the beginning of a script to get your audience comfortable and in sync with the characters. This is usually accomplished by a bit of dialogue or business between the characters that may or may not have anything to do with the plot, which emerges soon afterward. In one episode of *Murder, She Wrote*, for instance, I began act one with Jessica Fletcher on the phone to her publisher, giving corrections on the galleys of her new book. It's a brief and slightly humorous scene. She then checks her watch and ends the conversation hurriedly, mentioning that she has to hurry; today is her first day teaching class at Manhattan University. At that point, we smoothly cut to the university and segue into the story proper. Shows such as *The Trials of Rosie O'Neill* can adopt a more formal approach, in this case beginning each episode with Rosie talking to her therapist. The issues they discuss may or may not have anything to do with the story that follows, but without fail, they will give you a deeper insight into the character and thus make the story more interesting.

As well as making the audience comfortable, a quick scene with the characters at the top of your script gives *you* a chance to take a breath and play with the characters before plunging into the plot, giving you a feel for how they interact, which will be useful later.

Another way to handle the beginning of an episode is to move it *away* from your characters. For example: We see a trained assassin loading a high-powered rifle. On the table in front of him is a picture of a well-known political figure, marked with an X. We don't know who the assassin is or how he relates to the story, but the action holds our interest.

The story itself then begins when our protagonist (for our purposes a cop complaining about the potentially lethal coffee served in the cafeteria one floor below) is given the assignment of protecting a certain well-known politician during a campaign stop—the same one whose picture we saw moments earlier. These two images get the story moving and provide a certain amount of dramatic tension; we the audience know an assassin is stalking them, but will the detective realize that in time to stop the planned murder?

Having now established the basic premise of the episode, you begin to embroider. You start with character and history. Is the politician a pain in the butt? Have he and the detective been on opposing sides in the past? Does the politician not want protection? Or does he want protection better than the detective seems able to provide? Is the goal of the story to keep the politician alive, skewing the story toward action/suspense, or let him be killed in order to set up a murder mystery?

Always Ask the Next Question

Problems in story development almost always result from a lack of preparation and from not asking enough questions. Nine times out of ten a problem in act two isn't *really* a problem in act two; it's a problem in act *one*, where the proper foundations should have been established.

As you develop the story, remember that characters must have more than one side to make them compelling. Yes, the politician is a pain in the butt. But he's got a family, and he cares about them more than his career. If he and the detective have come into conflict, perhaps it's because they approach their work from different perspectives. Or you can reverse the equation and make the politician someone who seems quite dedicated, a crusader for the rights of the people—when in fact he's a real jerk. If you get to know your characters well enough, the story dictates itself.

Beating It Out

When it comes time to break down that story in more detail, you might want to try a little technique that works for me. I take a legal pad of yellow paper and draw an equilateral cross in the middle of one page, creating four quadrants on the sheet. I label the quadrants "Act One," "Act Two," "Act Three" and "Act Four." Then, in one-liners, I lay out the basic beats of each act. Here's one example from a *Murder* episode I wrote entitled "Incident in Lot 7."

Jessica Fletcher at the airport.

Arrival at the Studio.

Introduction to the producer who plans to adapt her novel.

Star argues with producer over role. Jessica encounters a real-life star (guest cameo).

We see a suspicious-looking fan sneak onto the studio lot.

Producer in car, on cellular phone, sets up tryst with mistress.

Jessica, taken on studio tour, ends at Psycho house (from the Psycho movies). From the shadows, someone is watching her. Who has broken into the Psycho house? And why?

Act out.

I've found that if I fill in all the lines in each quarter-page section, without going over or leaving lots of blank space, it times out exactly right when I get to outline and script. If I have to add stuff in marginalia or leave empty lines, the story inevitably comes in too long or too short, respectively. What's also good about this approach is that it lets you see the entire story at one glance and allows you to draw lines that move a beat from one act into another if you decide to alter the structure.

What you're looking for in any given script is about five or six major beats per act. (A *beat* is a pivotal dramatic action that propels the story forward.) The breakdown above includes not only the major beats, but the transitional beats as well. Some may amount to no more than a half-page of script (the call from the producer's car via cellular phone, for instance).

Here are some more suggestions to consider in constructing your story:

1. Keep your lead character active. Make good use of her. Avoid making your guest character the one who gets all the good lines and does all the work, leaving your main character to be passive or uninteresting. The main character should always be moving toward the resolution of the story, however convoluted the road.

2. Move the camera around. Don't spend too much time in any one location. If you go over two or at most three pages in the same scene, your characters are talking too much.

3. End each act on a dramatic high note, a complication that makes the viewer want to stick around after the commercial break. That can be a physical action, putting the lead character in jeopardy, or an emotional action, wherein some crucial and moving piece of information is revealed. In hour-dramatic structure, for instance, the act one curtain is often a threat against one of the guest characters or some terrible revelation about the character; at the bottom of act two, there's a murder; at the bottom of act three, you have the police arrest the wrong person, or you kill the character the audience is sure is actually the murderer, or you again reveal some terrible secret that changes the course of the story. And, of course, act four resolves all the questions and ends with the world being put right again. Until next week.

Please, don't take the foregoing too much to heart. It's not The Way Things Must Always Be Done; it's only one option of many. This is an example, not a formula or a requirement.

4. *Unless you have specific permission from the producer,* avoid injecting elements in your script that will affect the series after your episode is finished. In other words, don't kill the lead character's spouse, don't give her terminal cancer or change the venue (she quits her job permanently) without authorization.

5. Avoid convenience. Your characters must do things for a reason that makes sense to them, not just because you want them to. If, for instance, you need to get character A to the docks so that someone can murder him, don't send him out there on an evening constitutional. Have someone send him a message that lures him to that locale, a message he will heed because we've seen that he very much wants to meet that person.

6. Similarly, try to make every action and every scene do more than one thing at a time. For example: In a dinner scene, at which certain threats are made against character B, we also see that characters C and D are planting a gun in the room for use later. We see character A being slipped the note that will lure him to the docks that night, but we also should see him hide that note for some reason, and we should learn something about who he is and why he is the way he is. Exposition should always be counterbalanced by moments of characterization or action within the same scene. The note should play a vital role later as well as in this scene. Don't just drop something in for convenience, then promptly forget it, creating loose threads in your story line.

Write tightly and waste nothing. Remember, you've only got a comparatively short time in which to tell your story, so you've got to make the most of every possible moment.

7. Keep your characters different from one another. They must be distinct as individuals, no matter how similar they may be in background, social status or rank. Give them different voices, one character being formal and verbose, another who's full of colloquialisms, another who talks in short, sharply worded sentences. Make them react in different ways to the same situations. When a story editor is reading a script, sometimes names and characters blur. The more vibrant and distinct they are on the page, the easier the script is to read, and the more attractive it becomes.

8. Never cheat the audience. Elsewhere in this book is Chekov's rule of playwriting: If there is a gun on the wall in act one, scene one, you must fire that gun by act three, scene one. The inverse is also true: If you're going to fire the gun in act three, establish it in act one. The resolution

in any given story often depends on surprise, particularly in the crime or mystery genre. But that surprise should be hinted at earlier in the story so that the audience—should it so desire—could back up the videotape and see all of the clues that were obviously there from the beginning, had the viewer only known how to properly interpret those clues. But it's counterproductive to end your episode with the revelation "We knew Uncle Charlie had to be the killer because he was the only one in a yellow raincoat" if in fact we never see a yellow raincoat earlier in the story, however innocuous the context might be.

9. Make moments in your story. A *moment* is . . . well, it's hard to describe but easy to point to. Note the difference between these two situations: (1) A character is walking through a library at night, looking for a book, and turns a corner to encounter a threat. (2) A character is walking through the library, passing dark hallways. We see a shadow behind the character. Our character walks faster, hearing the sound of hurrying footsteps just behind and seeing a flash of movement out of the corner of her eye. A moment is something that involves the soul of your protagonist, an instant of profound revelation about who this character really is. If you can write a script that has two or three really solid, emotional moments for the lead character, you've got a substantially increased chance of making a sale. Create opportunities in your script for your lead character to give vent to some heartfelt emotion, where the character dances or laughs or cries or rages.

The best way to conceptualize a moment is to think of the Emmy Awards. You know those thirty-second clips they show on-screen when the nominees are read for Best Actress or Best Actor in a series? The clips chosen are invariably moments.

10. As you develop your story, you might find it easier to start with the end of the story and work forward, particularly in the case of mysteries. If you know ahead of time what happened, you can more easily layer in the clues needed earlier on.

11. Just as your character must get into trouble on her own, your character must get out of trouble the same way. Make your lead character resourceful and intelligent enough to escape whatever trap you've created.

12. Avoid false jeopardy. Let's be honest: Sometimes you come to a point in the story where the clock indicates you have to create an act break, but there doesn't seem to be any handy jeopardy around which to structure a break. Some writers just say "Screw it" and have somebody walk through the door with a gun, however illogical that action might be. Others stop, backtrack and try to find a thread in the story that can be either

moved up or moved back to provide an act curtain.

And some fudge it.

False jeopardy.

Not a good thing.

Reading vs. Speaking, and Other Suggestions

Let me close out this section by giving you two pieces of advice that will serve you in good stead:

First, until you develop an ear for dialogue, as you write your characters' lines, read them aloud. What you'll discover is that lines that work on the page don't always fit in the mouth. Loosen up your dialogue; don't fill it with formal language and stiff syntax. And avoid sibilance. Sometimes sibilance seems sensible; still, saying sentences staggered with *s*'s simply staggers some stars.

It's important to remember that even when you *have* been writing for a long time and you think you've got it licked, you can still screw up. In the pilot for *Babylon 5*, I wrote the following line: "Laurel, can you recalibrate the station's external sensors to scan for energy sources inside the station?" Stupidly, I didn't take the time to say that line aloud because if I had, I would have realized that I'd just handed the poor actor involved a mouthful. When performed, it sounds like a tongue twister. (As a small measure of compensation for the grief of that line, the costume designer and I awarded the actor a T-shirt with the words "I survived" above the line, reprinted verbatim.) I still cringe when I see that shot. Save yourself and your actors the kind of grief that shows up to haunt you years later on television.

Finally, and I know this is tough, but try it anyway: *Relax.* Have fun with the script. Play with the characters and situations. Make yourself laugh. Because if you enjoy the story, you increase the odds that someone else will feel the same way. There's tremendous pressure that comes with writing for television, and if you can't balance that out by having a good time with the writing process, it can become pretty dreary after a while. If you're not enjoying what you're doing, don't do it.

Chapter Three

The Craft of Telescripting

The *art* of scriptwriting has to do with the creative considerations that go into writing a television script; those things discussed in the previous chapter. The *craft* of scriptwriting deals with the physical details required to implement those creative decisions in a professional manner. Failing to perceive that there is a difference between art and craft is pernicious. It produces creative writers who can't sell, and selling scriptwriters who are bereft of the creative impetus to do great things. The craft of scriptwriting means knowing where to start, what to do and, almost as important, what *not* to do.

In a published interview, Garry Marshall, creator/producer of such series as *Happy Days* and *Laverne and Shirley*, once said, "[Scriptwriting] is a craft, not so much an art form. It takes a certain kind of head. You sit at a table and you sit there until you're finished. It sounds like a joke, but when you'd look for comedy writers, you'd look for people who had a terrible social life . . . they had no other life, and they'd stay there, night after night. It's a tough job. There is no looking around, saying, 'I think I'll go for a walk and look at the sky, and maybe I'll get a brilliant idea.' "

CORRECTING MYTHOLOGIES

It doesn't matter if writing is your full-time job, your part-time job, your avocation or your hobby, you must approach it in a professional manner. You must finish what you write. You must stay with it. Find an hour, a minute; write a page, a paragraph—however small the investment required to keep the dream alive. Or quit trying to convince us that you're serious about being a writer.

The only way to be taken seriously as a television writer is to write a script—not an outline, not a page with this really cool idea. Networks and producers and writers are deluged by amateurs who think they can sell their ideas to Hollywood. An idea, however wonderful it may sound to you, is meaningless on its own terms; give ten writers the same basic idea, and you'll get ten vastly different scripts. What the industry needs are *scripts* that they can take to a stage and shoot.

Unfortunately, the "sell an idea" mythology persists, which leaves writers vulnerable to being exploited. If I've sounded harsh here, it's to try to protect you from this exploitation.

For example: There are expensive books and high-priced seminars that claim they can teach you to sell your ideas. Some of these come from publishers who routinely publish softcover "books" comprised entirely of one-page ideas by unsold writers who buy space in the book hoping to sell that idea to Hollywood. Each page costs that writer a pretty hefty sum, hundreds of dollars that they can ill afford. I've seen these books, and they are less than useless. There is a dark cynicism behind some of these books, a subliminal evidence of people preying on the dreams of aspiring writers.

The one-page synopses published in these books are often on the order of, "I want to sell a story about how we should all appreciate each other more." They're sometimes painful to read. While from time to time you may run into a few decent ideas among the dross, that's all they are, formless ideas that get lost in the mountain of useless throwaways. I have never heard of a producer buying an idea from one of these publishers. In many cases, film and TV producers don't even want these books in their offices, won't look at them, because it opens them up to plagiarism suits. If a writer were to ask me about publishing his idea in one of these compendiums, I would advise him *not to*, in the strongest possible terms.

Here's another *don't*: If you're a newcomer, don't focus your energies on selling a new TV series that you've created. It doesn't matter how good your potential series might be—it won't sell. Just as producers want scripts, not ideas, networks and studios want series from people who have proven they can *run a show*, not just come up with a script or two. At each rung up the television ladder, the stakes get higher and the requirements get stiffer. Networks and studios are regularly pitched detective and hospital series and all of the other "franchises," some concepts not terribly different than the others. Which is picked? The one by a writer/producer who has shown that she can run the series. Because when a network commissions a series, it's investing as much as $33 million dollars for a full season, and that's just for production. It doesn't begin to include advertising fees, distribution fees or the hundreds of other hidden charges.

You think a network is going to hand over $33 million to somebody who hasn't sold even a script before? Or that a producer who *can* sell a series is going to want to give away half of his possible income by teaming up with a neophyte, who he'll have to front to the network, which will refuse to get involved anyway?

Won't happen. Just as you don't go from apprentice to master carpenter without doing the work. You have to go through the long process of career advancement in television before you can sell a pilot series.

You start off as a freelancer, become a staff writer, move up to story editor or executive story consultant. Then you're a coproducer on a series, then a producer. It's at this point that the networks and studios begin to notice you and listen to you, if grudgingly. And it's only at this level that you have even the vaguest chance of selling a series.

This may not be fair. This may not be the best way of improving television. But it is the way things are done. Television is a business, and if you ever let yourself forget that, even for a moment, you're doomed. Direct your energies where they will do the most good. In the case of television, that means writing spec scripts for and pitching to established series, not spending hours and weeks and months writing pilots.

Having now alienated or discouraged at least half the people likely to read this book by establishing what you shouldn't do, let's move on to what you *can* do to begin writing and selling to television.

STORY DEVELOPMENT

Once you come up with the basic idea for an episode of an established series, it next has to be developed. The first stage in that process is the synopsis. This is the essential nut of your idea, written in brief, narrative form. A synopsis can be as short as a paragraph (à la *TV Guide*) or as long as a page and a half to two pages. One page is best.

The synopsis is for use by you and by the producer if you choose to willingly provide it, say, at the end of a pitch meeting (more about that later). No producer can ask you for a synopsis or anything else in writing without giving you an assignment. To do so violates WGA rules. Mainly, the synopsis serves the writer as a sort of compass, keeping the heart of the story always before your eyes. By the time you get deep into the outline and script, it's sometimes easy to get lost. A synopsis reminds you of the point of your episode. And sometimes in the midst of writing the synopsis, you suddenly realize the story won't work, and it's better to discover that after writing one page than after fifty.

New writers frequently seem to have a hard time boiling their ideas down to one page. "It's too complex, too layered," goes the usual explanation. "If you're going to understand what my idea's about, it'll take a lot more than one page." That feeling is understandable; as the writer, you see the whole canvas of the story, with all its shadings and textures. But you have to find a way to summarize it anyway. One trick is to pretend that you just saw this story last night on television, and a friend who missed the broadcast wants to know what it was about. So you thumbnail it. This approach helps you distance yourself from the story a little.

Murdering a Synopsis

To best illustrate the process of development from synopsis to script, the previous version of this book went through an imaginary story for the M*A*S*H series. Since we covered the sitcom there, it makes sense to alternate in this book and cover a dramatic series. In addition, the process of developing a real story produced for a real series might prove to be more instructive. I've selected one of my episodes for *Murder, She Wrote*, entitled "The Committee."

A synopsis, like an outline, uses prose fiction margins, about an inch to an inch and a half on the left and right margins, an inch of white on the bottom and an inch or an inch and a half of white on top.

The synopsis for "The Committee" reads as follows:

Jessica Fletcher encounters an old friend who has done quite well for himself in recent years, earning millions of dollars and entering a new social world. Part of that new world is the Avernus Club, a Gentlemen's Club in the traditional sense. He asks her to be the first woman author to read her work at the club, and thus open the door for others to follow. She agrees.

What Jessica does *not* know is that her friend, Winston, is a member of the Committee, a frequently changing group of insiders who form a secret organization with the Avernus Club. Together, they vote to "sanction" one of their members, who has been acting outrageously. The vote to sanction is made via secret ballot, and just as secretly, one of them is selected to be the Enforcer. The Enforcer is chosen by each member of the Committee drawing a colored marble from a bag, and not showing it to the others. Whoever gets the gold marble is the Enforcer, and he may take whatever steps are necessary to sanction the disobedient member.

But when the member in question is murdered, it looks as if the Committee has commissioned a murder, and to complicate matters, none of them knows who the Enforcer was. It could have been any of them. Concerned that the police might consider this conspiracy to murder, concerned about the scandal, they vote to bring in Jessica to solve the murder . . . a most curious dilemma for Jessica, since she is being commissioned by a group that very likely includes the murderer.

The paranoia and cross-accusations mount rapidly, though we finally learn that it was the victim's own brother, and not a member of the Committee at all, who committed the murder, using an insider to rig the ballot, and make sure *none* of the Committee members got the gold marble, so that he alone would enforce the "sanction," knowing it would cause the rest to participate in the cover-up or be accused themselves.

All of the essentials are there: beginning, middle and end. It sets the basic story in motion, gives us some idea where the conflicts are, and what character relationships and dynamics are involved. What's missing are the details, the clues, the relationships, the specifics by which we get from A to B to C.

That's what the more detailed outlines are for.

Outlines

I hate outlines. Hate 'em, hate 'em, hate 'em. The point of the exercise is to tell a story, and once that's told in outline form, why write the script? The tension that propelled you to write the story has been exhausted. But even if the network or studios don't see them, producers require outlines before they'll commit to a script, so it's a necessary evil. An outline for a one-hour show can run anywhere from ten pages to thirty pages, depending on the show involved. An outline shows us where the act breaks are and the specific plot complications that propel us toward the resolution. In the case of "The Committee," that means learning who's sleeping with whom, who's sabotaging whose business deals, who has the most to gain from the murder in question, and the nature of the clues that our lead character gradually assembles.

An outline (also known as a treatment) should also contain moments of humor and moments in which our characters *relate* to one another in ways that may not necessarily advance the plot but that illustrate character and build sympathy for those involved in our story. What you're sketching out, really, is a *character arc*, a sense that our characters are learning something, growing or changing in some way as a result of our story.

Your outline should indicate how the series's regulars fit into the story, and it should use those characters in a meaningful fashion rather than shoehorning them in. Finally, your outline should be as readable as possible.

Write it as though you were writing a short story. A good prose style will carry you far in this business.

Be professional, and always be *specific*. Don't hype your outline *in* your outline ("In the exciting second act, we find our main character . . ."), and always show the details. If someone gets into trouble, don't just write "And then they rescue him and they ride off." How do they rescue him? What's involved? The more specific your outline, the better your story editor or producer will like it. In part, this is for your protection. If I know the specifics of a story, I can give the writer better advice and help you avoid pitfalls unique to our show. If I'm in the dark, I can't guide you properly—not that you'd get to leave the office in the dark anyway. If it wasn't clear in the outline, during the meeting I'll ask for clarifications, and it doesn't look good if you don't have that information. So you may as well do the work and figure it out while writing the outline.

You have to remember that the story editor or producer isn't there to give you a hard time. We're not the enemy or the competition; we're there to help the freelancer. Nothing makes me happier than receiving a script from a freelance writer that's absolutely spot-on. We just take it to the stage and shoot it.

You can include dialogue in your outline, or not, as you prefer; there's no hard-and-fast rule about this. And remember, always end each act on a hook in order to lure the audience back after the commercial break.

To demonstrate, here is act one of the outline for "The Committee."

MURDER, SHE WROTE
"The Committee"
J. Michael Straczynski

JESSICA is being feted at an autograph party at a leading New York bookstore when she looks up to see WINSTON DEVERMORE standing before her. In his sixties, with leonine white hair and a charismatic appeal, he is an old friend she has not seen in some time. He's spent the past year in France on business. He asks if she has any plans for after the party. Happily, she does not.

Later, at an exclusive uptown restaurant, they catch up on the news of their respective lives. Winston, we learn, is a stockbroker who was doing very well for himself when last she saw him, and is now doing *extremely* well for himself. He's too discreet to mention the degree of his success, but it's pretty clear that we're looking at easily a hundred million dollars or more. He seems utterly unaffected by it all, however. After a certain point, it's all just numbers on a ledger.

He's only allowed himself one indulgence: the Avernus Club, which he joined last year. Jessica has heard of the club . . . it's one of those elite gentlemen's clubs whose membership consists of the nation's movers and shakers . . . diplomats, former presidents, billionaires, secretaries of state . . . very heady company.

In the course of their discussion, he mentions that the club has a history of hosting readings and performances by some of the nation's finest writers, a list that includes Ernest Hemingway, Robert Frost and Carl Sandburg. "All men," Jessica notices. Winston explains that he hopes that she will help to change that, and become the first woman author to give a reading at the Avernus Club. Flattered, Jessica agrees.

The next morning finds us in the penthouse office of LAWRENCE CAYLE, late forties, who created an empire in real estate fortunes. He's worth about a billion dollars, owns casinos and hotels and goodly chunks of New York City. With him is his older brother, THEO, late fifties/early sixties, who acts as Lawrence's advisor and confidante. They are in the process of concluding a major deal when the arrival of GERALD LUCERNE is announced. A developer himself, Gerald is younger, more intense and impetuous.

Gerald has carved out an impressive fortune of his own. He's on the fast track. Which is why Lawrence called him here today. They had pooled their resources to finance the purchase of a major resort. Their deal was a fifty-fifty share in running the resort and sharing the profits. And the purchase has gone through.

But Gerald accuses Lawrence of changing the deal, of going through the back door with the stockbrokers to grab control of 70 percent of the resort. Gerald is outraged, demands equal say, equal money. Lawrence won't budge. He appreciates Gerald's position, but Gerald's a hothead, inexperienced at running an operation of this size. And Lawrence has heard that he's had some . . . problems lately that could complicate matters if he ran things. He should take the 30 percent and be happy with it. He won't have to do any work running the operation, can just sit back and reel in the profits. "I'm doing you a favor," Lawrence says.

But Gerald doesn't see it that way. He's angry, in part because Lawrence and he are "brothers" in the Avernus Club, and you're not supposed to do this to a brother member. Lawrence is unfazed. He's doing what's right for both of them.

Moments later, Lawrence's brother Theo is escorting Gerald down. Gerald is fuming . . . where does Lawrence get off? And what's all this about him having problems, being unable to run things . . . where does he hear stuff like that? Theo, ever the diplomat, says he really doesn't know, he doesn't have that much access to Lawrence's thoughts. Theo urges him to be patient. Others are having similar . . . difficulties with Lawrence right now, but he has every confidence that things will work out in the end.

Gerald gets into his limousine and as it drives away, he picks up the car phone. "Get Philip Dexter on the line," he tells his assistant. "Now."

Two nights later, Jessica is at the Avernus Club, reading a chapter from her latest novel. The members are present along with assorted wives, lady friends and hangers-on. She concludes the reading to rousing applause, and an after-reading party begins.

Jessica hooks up with her friend Winston, who in turn introduces her to PHILIP DEXTER, a much older man who has been a member of the club since dinosaurs ruled the earth, and EDWARD HELSINGER, a prominent banker in his forties.

They barely begin to talk, however, when Edward excuses himself and Philip is called away into a corner of the room by Gerald Lucerne, who Jessica notes appears rather annoyed.

Going for a refill of punch, Jessica witnesses a heated discussion between Edward Helsinger and Lawrence Cayle over some not-terribly-subtle moves Lawrence was putting on Edward's wife. Lawrence has had just a little too much to drink, and is less than polite about the whole thing. He implies that Edward's wife requested his company; she denies it, though with questionable sincerity. Theo enters in time to prevent things from getting messy, and leads Lawrence back into the rest of the party.

Shortly afterward, Jessica and her friend Winston are about to leave the club when a young employee presses an envelope into Winston's hand. Winston opens it to find a key, and a note with a single word: "Midnight."

Noting his troubled look, Jessica inquires about the note, but he shrugs it off as nothing important, and they head off.

Then:

Midnight, at the Avernus Club. Winston arrives and uses the key to gain access to a private room where five others are waiting for him: Edward Helsinger (the affronted husband), Philip Dexter, Gerald

Lucerne, and two other club members, HARCOURT FENTON and a younger member, MITCHELL RAY.

The Committee. The secret Star Chamber behind the leaded glass windows of the Avernus Club.

The meeting is chaired by Philip, who has seniority. The Committee has been called into session to discuss the matter of Lawrence Cayle. His behavior of late has been aberrant; his actions have been cause for some embarrassment and anger. They must decide whether or not to invoke a sanction from the Committee.

(As we will learn in more detail later, each member accepts the jurisdiction of the Committee, in part because however powerful any one of them may be, they don't exist in a vacuum; a banker needs a broker who needs a developer who needs the banker . . . they are interconnected and interreliant. To avoid any outside complications, the club polices itself via the Committee. And the makeup of the Committee changes regularly, assuring that no one holds a monopoly of power within the club.)

They debate whether or not Lawrence's behavior requires any sort of discipline, and finally it comes to a secret vote. At this moment, a young woman—LISA—is called into the room. She goes from one member of the Committee to another with a small pouch. (Note: She is not privy to the discussion, and at no time does she hear who is being discussed. She is there only to collect the votes.)

Each member of the Committee is given two ivory marbles, one black, one white. If they vote that Lawrence is innocent, and should not be penalized, they are to drop a white marble into the pouch. If they think action must be taken, they drop in a black marble. We don't see who drops what into the pouch.

Lisa finishes collecting the votes and empties the contents of the pouch into Philip Dexter's hands.

Four black marbles, one white.

The vote is to sanction Lawrence.

Now comes the second part: the selection of the Enforcer.

Before they even get that far, however, Harcourt Fenton rises. He's participated in more than his share of these "sanctions," and won't have any further part in it. If they want to select an enforcer, they'll do it without him. On that, he leaves the room.

The five men remaining in the room finish the task of selecting the enforcer.

Four red and one gold marble are put into the pouch, and again Lisa goes from one to the other. This time, though, each member *removes* one marble from the bag and, without anyone else looking at it, puts it in his pocket. Whoever gets the gold marble is selected to perform the sanction. No one else in the room will know who that person is. He will simply do what is necessary.

And the nature of that sanction is left entirely to the discretion of the chosen enforcer. It could be a massive fine, in the hundreds of thousands of dollars. It could be suspension from the club, or an actual attempt to inflict minor damage on a current project, in order to remind the errant member that they are all interdependent.

The possibilities are many, varied . . . and unpleasant.

The selection is finished. Everyone is sworn to secrecy over what took place in this room, and who cast what votes. Lisa leaves the room. We PAN the assembled five men. One among them is the enforcer, chosen to do some damage to Lawrence Cayle.

The question is . . . who is going to do the enforcing? And just how damaging will this turn out to be?

And on that note of mystery, we

End Act One

This excerpt from the outline incorporates all of the required elements: It introduces each of the guest characters who will appear in the episode, tells their ages and hints at their relationship to one another. It puts our lead character, Jessica Fletcher, at the center of the story. She is going to help break down the walls of a male-dominated society. She is the centerpiece of a prestigious event (two, actually, if you include the gathering where Winston finds her). It introduces the conflict and sets in motion the main plot: the selection of an enforcer, the reasons for that selection and the potential for this to go terribly wrong (which it proceeds to do).

In the case of clues and items that may require elaboration later on, it's OK to briefly jump out of the narrative flow for a parenthetical aside or two, as long as it doesn't get too convoluted.

Finally, the act break makes the viewer want to return to find out what's going to happen, who the enforcer is, and what the penalty is going to be. You create, in short, a *mystery* that lures the viewer back after the commercial break.

Back to the technical stuff . . .

The cover page of an outline features the name of the series and the title of your story in the center of the page, with *written by* six spaces below and your name two spaces below that. As a rule, if you're writing on assignment, you don't put your agent's name and address on the page.

An outline such as this also gives everyone a sense of the production values involved: sets, extras, locations and number of guest stars. This helps the producer determine right off what kind of script he's got. There are basically four kinds of scripts: good producible and bad producible, good unproducible and bad unproducible. You can write an absolutely dynamite script, but if it costs too much to produce, it'll never get made. It's at the outline stage that the producer determines which of those four categories applies to your story.

Second-Guessing

Once the outline is completed, and prior to turning it in, it's incumbent upon you to do a little second-guessing. Switch roles for a moment from writer to producer, and try to poke holes in your outline. Look at your work as dispassionately as possible, and find any weaknesses that might injure the outline and, later, the script itself. The best way to do this is to put the outline away for a couple of days, then come back to it wearing your "producer" hat.

If you *do* find any holes, discrepancies or weaknesses, you have several choices:

1. Ignore them—and you can bet good money that the first words out of the producer's mouth will be her concerns about those *exact* points.

2. Note them but don't change them if you can't figure out a way around the problems. The hope here is that a discussion with the producer will show you how to correct the problem.

3. Come up with a solution on your own, then go back and change whatever it is that doesn't work.

There are two reasons for including option number two. As stated, the producer or story editor wants a good story every bit as much as you want to deliver one—more so, since he has more riding on it. If there's something that isn't working, you shouldn't feel afraid to call the producer and discuss it. Don't be a pest, but be open and flexible to any support the producer can give you. In the long run, it'll save both of you a lot of time and grief.

Second, there are going to be times when That Which Does Not Work was included in your outline at the request of the producer or story editor. In other words, it ain't your fault. So there has to be a judgment call. If they absolutely want that stuff, then leave it in and let them see that it doesn't make sense, or raise your concerns about it when you turn it in. If, however, you sense flexibility on their part, then you can consider taking it out before turning the outline in and explaining at that time that "It just didn't work." At that point, the producer will either (1) ask you to explain why it didn't work; (2) tell you to "Make it work"; (3) let it slide; or (4) give you some other options.

When your outline is finally turned in, several things can happen. If the staff believes the story doesn't work and can't be made to work through anything short of a resurrection, you'll be cut off. And if they know, in their heart of hearts, that it wasn't your fault, they'll often try to develop a new outline with you. If it's problematic, and they're not sure of your ability to fix the problems, then the outline may be assigned to an in-house writer. If that happens, the revised outline may be given back to you for you to write the teleplay, or they may opt to also do the teleplay in-house. The best case scenario, of course, is that they will actually *recognize* genius when they see it and assign you to the next step in the process: the teleplay.

The Script

This is where your skills are put to their greatest test and where you have a chance to shine. A good script is as detailed and specific as a blueprint or a schematic. You must indicate clearly what your characters are saying, where they are going, what they are doing, how crucial shots are to be framed and any other information required for the director to understand your intent and for the viewer to understand the story.

While the outline hammered out the basic story line in broad strokes, now you must create the details that make your characters living, breathing people through mannerisms and attitudes and the subtleties of voice and inflection and movement. A good script must be written with a sensitivity to the sound and sense of words so they flow seamlessly across the page. The dialogue should sound natural and unforced. The script should be muscular, should drive from one scene right into the next so the reader is caught up in it.

For the balance of this chapter, and elsewhere in this book, I will give some hints and pointers in this area, but they are guideposts, nothing more. The only way to learn to write scripts is to write scripts.

But as stated, there are some lessons you can apply that will save you some trial and error in pursuing that goal.

1. Listen to people. No two people talk alike. Their word choices, the rhythms of their dialogue, their cadences and hesitations are all as unique as a fingerprint. Listen to them, and quietly pick apart how they are differ-

ent, what is emblematic of someone's speech pattern. The best test for this is to study the speech patterns of person A. Once you think you've got it down to a fine art, write a paragraph or two in that person's "voice." Then show it to person B, who also knows person A and several other mutual friends or relations. Ask that person to identify person A, using only the dialogue. If person B can figure it out, you've done your job.

2. Make your characters listen to one another. One of the worst things you can do in a script is to have your characters talking *at* one another rather than *to* one another. Have your characters respond to one another, react to what the other says. Give the sense of a real back-and-forth exchange. Let your characters get angry with one another, shocked or astonished by what the other person is doing. Don't just use them to advance the plot. Invest them with emotions and reactions, since those reactions will tell us a lot about who they are. For example, a stripper walks into a room. A matronly schoolteacher will react one way, a pool hustler another. That reaction informs us about the character.

3. Use parentheticals to take some of the burden off dialogue. You don't have to cover every aspect of dialogue *with* dialogue. Sometimes it's more powerful to let body language carry one part and only use dialogue for the important part. For instance, you can take a quick exchange and play it one of two ways:

HUSBAND

Do you have to go?

WIFE

Yes, I do. It's the only way.

Or:

HUSBAND

Do you have to go?

WIFE

(nods)

It's the only way.

The "Yes, I do" only gets in the way. What matters in the scene is the second sentence. If it's a simple response, a yes or a no, take it out of dialogue. You can also use parentheticals to imply things that the actor can use in the performance. For instance, there's nothing more to the following scene than it appears:

                        HUSBAND
        Is everything all right?

                          WIFE
        Everything's fine.

But now you add one little parenthetical:

                        HUSBAND
        Is everything all right?

                          WIFE
                      (she's lying)
        Everything's fine.

Suddenly the meaning, and the performance, totally changes. You can use this technique to add little nuances and be more subtle in your writing.

4. Begin each scene as late as possible, and end it as early as possible.

5. Be specific in your dialogue. God, as someone once noted, is in the details. Details are everything in dialogue and characterization. If a character likes fruit, don't just let him say, "I like fruit." Let him have specific preferences: He likes the black plums, not the red ones; he likes his vegetables steamed, not boiled. If he just finished his first flying lesson, specify what kind of plane it was. Like painting, the finer the brushstrokes, the more realistic the picture.

6. Flesh out your character beyond what's required in the story. Look in the people you know, and in your own background, for the little nuances of behavior that make a character come alive. Does she enjoy jazz? Is there an unfortunate stammer? Does she wear brown socks with black shoes? You may never even use some of this, but it'll always be there, in the back of your head, informing the characterization. If you should set a scene in the character's apartment, you'll already know whether or not she'll have Beethoven on the stereo or the Rams on the TV. Again, that choice tells us a lot about the character.

When writing "Dream Me a Life" for *The Twilight Zone*, I wanted a character to talk about his deceased wife and show how much he cared for her. Rather than just stating that flat out at the beginning, I wanted to sneak up on it a little by starting with the character talking about an argument. The emotions slide from pleasant nostalgia to a recollection of anger, through to loss and sadness. But what to pick to illustrate that?

Jam and jelly.

It's a personal thing: I call blueberry jam *jam* and my wife calls it *jelly*. It's trivial almost to the point of being laughable and thus was the perfect segue needed for this scene.

So in the episode, the character in question, Roger (played by Eddie Albert), is sitting with his friend Frank in the retirement home. Roger's just had a particularly bad night, and things are not going well for their friendship. Frank suspects it's due to Roger not yet coming to grips with his wife's death.

> FRANK
> Nothing's been the same, has it? Not since . . .
> (beat)
> Roger, it's been three years, it—
>
> ROGER
> No. It was yesterday.
> (beat)
> You know, I was thinking the other day about her. We could never get it straight between us, jam or jelly. I'd say, "Pass the jam, please," and she'd say, "Here's the jelly, dear." It was a game, I guess. Then one day I was in a bad mood, and we got in an argument about it, can you believe it? The stupid, petty little things people argue about—
> (beat, his eyes welling up)
> God, Frank, I miss her . . . so much.

Jam and jelly. There's no writing book, no school that can teach you about jam and jelly and all the other stupid things couples argue about. Except life. And it's when you're writing the script that we as an audience discover how well you've been paying attention to your own life and the lives of those around you.

7. Beware of speeches. Avoid long-winded speeches that run on for two or more pages. The thing about dialogue vs. action is that a page of action runs a lot faster when filmed and edited than a page of dialogue. A page of action can run half a minute; a page that is one solid block of dialogue can run a minute or more. Time expands when you talk. Break up large blocks of exposition with interjections from the other characters in the room.

Which is not to say you shouldn't have speeches at all; the monologue is a wonderful and very intense form. But you should use it sparingly and only where it will give you the greatest impact.

8. Avoid having characters talk to themselves. Or if you absolutely *must* do it (the door slams as character A exits in a huff, and character B, alone, shakes her head, muttering, "On the other hand, maybe you *don't* want to go out for dinner"), do it only when necessary, and only if you can get a good scene out of it.

9. Don't describe everything we're seeing. Case in point: While in the dialog mix stage of *Babylon 5*, I discovered that the sound editor had recorded some "extra lines" to cover some scenes where there was no dialogue. These were scenes that had been specifically written *without* dialogue, I hasten to add. Where one character was peering into a bright light, the editor had her say, "The light . . ." Where one character was trying to open an encounter suit (containing life-support mechanisms), he had the actor say, "There must be some mechanism . . ."

I cut them. Had they added some new dimension to the scene, for instance, in the bright light scene, had she said the light was hot or added some other aspect to what we were already seeing, then I would have let them stay. But do not use dialogue to narrate what we are already seeing. As Linda Ellerbee once pointed out, "If you can turn on the television, listen from another room and know everything that's happening, that's not television, it's radio."

10. When writing narrative passages, normally reserved for descriptions of place and action, avoid inserting explanations or clarifications of things that are not conveyed elsewhere in action or dialogue, with the assumption that you've therefore done your job. For example: "Alex pockets the cup because he is a collector of fine china." If that information is not given elsewhere, what's the point? If you have to explain it to the director because it's unclear elsewhere, how do you expect the viewer at home to figure it out?

11. Avoid padding, dialogue and scenes tossed in to fill up pages because your page count is short. If nothing is happening in the scene, cut it.

12. Make sure your script is properly and professionally typed. That means no hand-drawn lines indicating where bits of dialogue or scenes were supposed to go but were typed out of sequence. And no typos.

13. When setting a scene or describing an action, keep your descriptions short and to the point, letting the action continue smoothly. Nothing is served by getting bogged down in lengthy descriptions of the sun at twilight peeking through the elms. Similarly, as with dialogue, avoid long blocks of description; if it's a complex scene without dialogue to break up the narrative description, then find places in the narrative to double-space and break up the big block of text, making it easier to read.

Cameras and Bodies in Motion

The two elements of telescripting that inevitably trip up new writers are camera angles (moving the camera around) and blocking (moving the actors around onstage). The novice scriptwriter frequently feels it's necessary to spell out every single camera angle in order for the full meaning of his script to be understood. For writers who, in their quest for clarity, wander into this particular tar pit, I have one word of advice: Relax. You need not decide whether every shot is an up-angle or a downshot or a medium shot or a medium-close shot.

Once you indicate the location you're now in (such as EXT. WOODS - DAY), you write the scene in master shot, only changing when it's important to do so. If, for instance, it's necessary that your audience see a character sneaking a pistol out of his jacket pocket, then it's appropriate to make sure the action is highlighted. So you write

INSERT - JOHN'S HAND
   As it slips into his jacket pocket and removes a pistol.

BACK TO SCENE
   As they continue walking through the woods.

It's really as simple as that.

Beyond that, it's largely a matter of personal preference. You can use a lot of description, a lot of camera angles or a little; I've seen scripts with both. Mine tend to be a little more detailed, indicating when the CAMERA PANS THE ROOM or we PUSH IN ON a table where two characters are seated or we RACK FOCUS on something to emphasize its importance.

The point being, for dramatic scripts, this isn't something you *need* to worry about. Don't let yourself get caught up trying to figure out which angle to insert here. You can leave them all out, and it works just fine. Gradually, over time, as you learn more of your craft and learn how to frame shots, you may want to start inserting a few. But the emphasis of this book is on making that first sale, and as such, honest and truly, it ain't something you need to get all wrought up about.

After the first edition of this book was published, I received a number of frantic letters, and to this day continue to get them, in which writers are terribly worried that they've blown their chances of their script being taken seriously because they messed up the format by setting the narrative at 8 picas instead of 5. For heaven's sake, relax. This isn't a test. They're not going to fine you, kill you or put you in TeeVee prison if your script format is off by a pica or three. As long as it *looks* basically like a script, that's what matters. If the dialogue and narrative description are roughly in the proportion shown here in the samples, you're OK. Go to any script service, and order a random assortment of TV scripts. You'll notice that the margins vary all over the place. What's important is what's *inside* the margins, not the margins themselves. OK?

(You can come down off the roof now. Really. I wouldn't lie to you.)

Out on the Stage

There's one other important point related to how detailed your camera directions can get in an episodic drama. It's important not just to tell you *what* works, but *why* it works, so you understand the reasons behind it.

Watch a theatrical motion picture. Now go watch your average television drama. Compare the visual composition of the two. What you'll invariably notice is that the movie contains far more elaborate direction than the television episode. It's not terribly politic to say this, but most—not all, but most—television directing is not terribly imaginative. Often you're dealing with repeat sets, which are built to be shot the same way every time, so all you do is go in, throw on the lights that have been prerigged for the established look of that set and start shooting. An average movie shoots six to eight weeks (thirty to forty actual shooting days, since you don't tend to shoot on weekends) on an average 120-page script. That means you only have to shoot three to four pages per day, which gives you plenty of time to set up some pretty complex shots if you so desire.

Television directors generally shoot five to eight pages per day, and there just isn't the time for really elaborate stuff. You get your master shot (the whole room), a medium shot of the two people in the room, medium-close singles on each of the two, and maybe an extreme close-up on the star or other major character in the scene. It's as perfunctory and quick as you can get. And the sense of motion is very different in television: Characters enter a room, hit their marks and generally stay there. The more your actor moves, the more involved it becomes to get all your coverage.

Here's a trick for you. Watch a few episodic dramas. Now see how many times this happens: A and B enter a room. A hits his mark at the south side of the room; B hits his mark on the north side of the room. They stand and talk. Now they move, but in a very particular way: *They change places.* A is now standing *exactly* where B was standing, and now B is standing exactly where A was standing. Why? So you don't have to move the camera. You keep the camera on A. After a while, A exits frame. The camera keeps running as B enters frame, turns and now occupies the same position. Camera keeps running.

Once you become aware of that technique, you'll see it used endlessly on television. Such moves (called reverses) are also done in film but not in quite the same proportion. I hasten to add that this isn't due to a lack of talent on the part of most directors but simply to the exigencies of television production.

And as a consequence, if you've written a lot of complex camera angles for a television show, you can generally be sure they'll be ignored on the set. So it's best to write in master shots except for those elements that are absolutely *essential* to the story.

Here's another tip that'll save you endless grief and make your script more producible: Minimize your use of crowd scenes, such as parties, or scenes with more than three or four characters speaking at the same time. That may sound arbitrary, but it isn't. Go back a few paragraphs and read the list of shots when two people are in a room: master, two-shot and one or two singles per actor. If the scene lasts two pages, that particular scene will probably take about one-third of the day to shoot, with two actors.

Now, add two more actors. Now you have to get singles on each of the actors with any lines *and* reaction shots of those who don't have lines. In addition to the two-shots of A and B, you now have to get two-shots of C and D in various combinations with A and B to visually "lock" them into the scene. Also, any time you have an actor saying lines, you'll get x number of flubbed lines. Now multiply x times four actors instead of just two. You're rapidly edging into the rest of your shooting day. The scene now takes nearly twice as long to shoot.

If you're in a party or the scene takes place as part of a larger gathering of any kind, you've also got to get establishing shots of the other guests throughout the scene, make sure they're moving in and out correctly so if some leave the room at the top of the scene they're not suddenly back in the shot again when you turn the camera around. This means bringing in extras, maybe lots of them, and they have to be managed and directed. And if you need any of the partygoers to react to the ongoing discussion, you need day players, and *they* have to be covered.

Next thing you know, the director is running late, the show is falling behind schedule. You have to go overtime to make up the difference, which means you're now over budget on the episode, and the studio wants to know why, the network wants to know why, the cast is jittery, which leads to *more* retakes and *more* time being spent to get the shots finished . . . anyway, you get the idea.

The proper job of a television writer is to deliver a good story translated into a professional script that can be shot quickly and painlessly. The more you understand that going in and make your script adhere to the requirements of television production, the better the chance of not only selling one script, but of continuing to sell after that.

In sitcoms, incidentally, there are virtually no camera directions at all in the script. Since you're shooting video in an enclosed set, you don't generally get terribly fancy. It does no good to create a nifty shot if the audience there in the studio, which has to react with laughter, can't see it, since they're not in the director's booth. It's very much a stage play shot on tape. As a rule, all you have to worry about in a sitcom is indicating when characters enter and leave a room and what they might do of importance while they're there.

As it turns out, by the way, most situation comedies produced in front of a live audience are actually taped *twice*. No two audiences are ever the same, and a line that gets a small laugh during the first taping might get screams during the second. Later, the portions that were best received during either taping are edited together to form a cohesive (and funnier sounding) whole. If the staff and performers discover that a given scene or line is just not working at all—which you never really know for certain until you're in front of an audience—it's not at all unusual for the material in question to be quickly rewritten between the first and second taping.

While sitting in on the taping of one show, I saw the writer rewrite an entire act in the hour and a half between the first and second tapings. (If that doesn't tell you something about why television writers are paid so well, nothing will.)

Resources

As with every form of scriptwriting discussed in this book, the single best way to gain a working knowledge of scriptwriting is to read as many produced television scripts as possible, comparing what you see on the page with what appears on-screen. Surprisingly, it's not difficult at all to secure such scripts, either in original or bound form. Here are a few places you can go to find produced television scripts:

- Libraries. Public libraries frequently stock books that contain scripts from the Golden Age of Television; college or university libraries often have more recent material. One of the best collections of telescripts is *Great Television Plays*, published in two volumes by Dell Press. It contains such classics as Gerald DiPego's *I Heard the Owl Call My Name* and Rod Serling's *A Storm in Summer*.

• Magazines. Publications about the television industry can be valuable resources of information on finding television scripts. Foremost among these is *American Film*, the magazine of the American Film Institute. From time to time, some magazines have been known to publish scripts. Prior to its cancellation, *Twilight Zone Magazine* (which can still be found in some library archives) published a number of early *Twilight Zone* scripts by Rod Serling, Richard Matheson and others. *Isaac Asimov's Science Fiction Magazine* published Harlan Ellison's (unproduced) script for *I, Robot*. *Writer's Digest* magazine has frequently published excerpts of television scripts.

• Bookstores. Browse around the television and film sections of your local bookstore, and you'll find at least a few published television scripts, many of which include photographs from the productions. Somewhere on these dusty shelves, for instance, you can find published versions of *The Phantom of the Open Hearth*, Jean Shepherd's award-winning television movie produced by the Public Broadcasting System. Recently, many publishers have compiled retrospectives of such TV shows as *I Love Lucy* and *The Honeymooners*, complete with scripts. At least one or two new books containing TV scripts from current or classic shows are published yearly by major publishers (not including the occasional publication of books with scripts from well-known British TV series, such as *Fawlty Towers* or *Monty Python's Flying Circus* or *Blake's 7*.)

Depending on where you live, it is sometimes possible to find a bookstore that carries television scripts in original manuscript form, just the way they were typed by the writer. If you don't happen to live near a large city, you might want to contact the Hollywood Book and Poster Company at 6349 Hollywood Boulevard, Hollywood, California 90028, (213) 465-8764. It has one of the widest and most up-to-date selections of telescripts available. First drafts, final drafts, shooting scripts . . . and, yes, they handle mail-order requests. Other script mail-order services can be found in the back pages of the aforementioned *American Film Magazine* and other film- or television-oriented publications.

I have a long-standing love/hate relationship with these services. On the one hand, when I've needed to study a sample script from a given show and every other avenue has failed, I've generally found it at Hollywood Book and Poster. There's a story floating around town—possibly apocryphal, but this one might actually be true—about a major studio that lost the only file copy they had of the third draft of an important script. Unable to contact the author, who was out of the country, they sent a messenger down to HB&P, found a copy of the desired draft, and went on about their business.

On the other hand, it *is* a violation of copyright, and you feel it most profoundly when you start to find your *own* scripts in the pile along with everyone else's. One tends to feel, well, rather violated, and it certainly cuts into any opportunity you might have to make money down the road from selling copies of the script at local workshops or seminars. I've been in the dubious position of being asked to autograph a script obtained from one of these services—being asked, in other words, to endorse a process that, to whatever degree, may actually be hurting me. But on balance, I suppose the good that is served outweighs the bad.

For the diehard *Star Trek* fans among us, scripts from the various *Trek* motion pictures and series are available from Lincoln Enterprises.

• Studios. When in doubt, go straight to the source. Although it generally isn't publicized, scripts for television series currently in production can sometimes be obtained directly from the production company. I cannot stress enough, however, that this route should only be used as a last resort because if studios are flooded by such requests, they'll likely stop the practice altogether. As it is, you'll have to do a pretty good tap dance to get them to cough up a script or two. You'll have to emphasize that you're a major fan of this show, that you have your heart set on writing a spec script for it, but you've turned up empty-handed on all other sources, and you feel you cannot possibly do a decent job unless you can examine a produced script.

How do you find the entity producing a particular series? A partial list of studios can be found at the end of this book. In addition, the *Writer's Guild of America Journal* publishes a list monthly of shows currently in production; similar lists can be found in *Daily Variety*, *The Hollywood Reporter* and other industry magazines (check your library for the most up-to-date resources).

• To save you some time hunting, I've included with this edition of *The Complete Book of Scriptwriting* one complete produced television script.
• Finally, as a special service, I have made some of my own produced scripts available to anyone wishing a copy. These are copies of the original typed scripts, as used for television production. One copy is available for each of the following series: *Murder, She Wrote*; *The New Twilight Zone*; *Jake and the Fatman*; *Walker, Texas Ranger*; *Captain Power*; *Babylon 5*; *Showtime's*

Nightmare Classics Presents The Strange Case of Dr. Jekyll and Mr. Hyde (nominated for Writers Guild and Ace Awards); and the animated series *The Real Ghostbusters*. Cost is twenty dollars. Checks should be made out to Synthetic Worlds, Ltd. and sent to 14431 Ventura Boulevard, Suite 260, Sherman Oaks, California 91423. Specify which of the above series you'd prefer a script from.

Those are some of the ways you can acquire copies of actual produced telescripts. But if all you really want at this stage is to get the format down, simply read on.

FORMATS

There are different formats for television scripts, depending on which area you're working in. Knowing when to use the right one is like knowing the password into a speakeasy; it tells the people in charge that you know what you're doing. I've received manuscripts that were labeled "scripts" but bore no resemblance whatsoever to a real script. Generally they used a modified prose form, everything typed flush left, or simply used the wrong format (a sitcom format for a dramatic script, for instance).

With very few exceptions, there are four distinct television script formats currently in use. One script format is for programs shot on film, another is for situation comedies videotaped before a live audience, a third is for live variety shows or videotaped variety shows, with the final category being the two-column script (also called an audio-video script). Once quite popular, the two-column format is now primarily relegated for use in advertising copy for TV commercials.

Format #1: Film

One-hour dramatic series are always shot on film. This is because videotape looks and works best in the enclosed, controlled environment of a soundstage, without a lot of exterior shooting. Videotape also flattens the depth of field and isn't as good with subtle lighting and shadows and textures. Film gives you a richer, warmer texture and functions equally well in interior and exterior locations. A few television series are shot on 16 millimeter (mm), but the majority are filmed on 35mm, which provides greater image clarity and less graininess. Those that do film in 16mm do so knowing that on the small TV screen, the difference is not as noticeable as when projected on a movie screen.

It's possible that in the next ten to twenty years, videotape could supplant film, as video technology continues to leap forward. High-definition video, digital imaging and other new systems now coming on line show great promise, heralding a day when images are encoded onto laser discs during production, or are stored as they're created in digital computer systems integrated with the camera.

While sitcoms are almost always shot on videotape, there are exceptions. If the series has to venture outside, as was the case, for instance, with the M*A*S*H series, they use the film format instead.

Typographical dimensions. Although individual pages may vary in time when actually filmed, depending on how much action or dialogue is on the page, each film-format page averages out to about one minute.

Page one: Type series title in boldface at the top of the page (or type in all caps, for those not using word processors). Next line down is the episode title, in quotations. On the third line is the act designation (teaser, or act one), underlined. All three lines are centered:

MURDER, SHE WROTE

"Incident in Lot 7"

Act One

Each subsequent act begins on a separate page, with only the act designation (act two, act three) centered on the top line. Page numbers are usually located in the upper right-hand corner of the page.

You then drop down two lines and type FADE IN: at the left margin (about one and one-fourth inches from the left edge, or about 12 to 13 picas, with the right margin about one inch from the right edge of the page, about 65 picas). Drop down two more lines to your first slugline, either an exterior, EXT., or interior, INT., shot.

Regarding scene numbering, while this was once more commonly practiced at the early stages of a script, the good news is that you don't have to worry about scene numbering your scripts anymore. That is done at the last stage of story editing on the script, just before it goes into preproduction. So it's only something to worry about after you've sold the script, at which time the hassle is taken care of in-house by the production staff anyway.

Sluglines used to specify location and the body of the narrative descriptions are both typed flush left. The right margin is *not* justified. Narrative descriptions must contain whatever information is required to set the scene: location, time (day or night) and emphasis (a particular element of that location that we should notice). Narrative description is always single-spaced.

Transitions (FADE OUT, CUT TO, DISSOLVE TO) are flush right, equal with the right margin of the narrative description. The use of transitions, incidentally, has become more and more idiosyncratic over the last ten years. Many people (myself included) don't use them anymore except for visual impact on the page, and then only rarely. Other people use them consistently. Which approach is right? Neither. Choose whatever feels best for you. Unlike FADE INs, FADE OUTs are typed flush right, and they are only used at the end of each act.

Always double-space between blocks of narrative, between narrative and dialogue, between titles and FADE INs and between FADE INs and the slugline. There should be about an inch between the top of the page and your first line of text and between the bottom of the page and your last line of text. FADE INs are used only at the beginning of an act.

The result looks like this:

THE MURDER ZONE

FADE IN:

EXT. HOTEL - DAY

A luxury hotel somewhere in downtown New York. LIMOS pull up to the front entrance, GUESTS emerging and entering in BG. We PUSH IN on a window of the hotel and

CUT TO:

INT. HOTEL ROOM - CONTINUOUS ACTION

where a young woman is getting dressed. Call her SARAH. She looks in at the adjoining room, where WILLIAM BLAKEMORE, a United States Senator, is on the phone.

You'll notice a typographical gimmick in the preceding sample: The narrative descriptions and sluglines are written in such a way as to make them one sentence. The effect of this is to make the scenes flow more smoothly to the eye. It works best when the second scene is a subset of the one preceding, as the hotel room is a subset of the hotel proper. It's kind of a nifty device, but try not to overuse it because like anything else, it loses impact with repetition.

Whenever you introduce a character for the first time in your script, you must name that character, and that name will appear in all capital letters. Subsequent uses of the name are typed in regular upper- and lower-case letters.

Space in from the left-hand margin until you're 17 picas from your margin (*not* the edge of the page, 17 picas from the start of your narrative description). This is the left-hand margin for your dialogue. Parenthetical directions are typed at 22 picas from the main left margin (or 5 picas in from your dialogue margin). Parentheticals are any asides to the actor of a brief nature, not deserving of extended description in the narrative paragraphs. These include turning, nodding, a pause or beat, a hesitation or a notation of emotion that may not be clear in the dialogue or is intended as counterpoint to the dialogue. There are a hundred different ways someone can say, "Oh, hello . . . it's you again"—sexily, despairingly, annoyed. If you have a neutral sentence to which you wish to attach a particular spin, it's appropriate to add the correct parenthetical.

Character names go at 30 picas from the left-hand margin (or 12 picas in from the dialogue margin). The right-hand margin for dialogue is 50 to 53 picas from the main left margin and, as with narrative descriptions, is *not* justified. Script margins should never be justified because it throws off the timing; a producer assumes *x* pages translates out to *y* minutes of action. Justification puts large gaps between words, expanding dialogue and action and throwing off the timing. It also looks funky. Dialogue is also single-spaced. Put together, it looks like this:

> SENATOR
> (into phone)
> Look, I don't care *how* much it costs, I want those sup-
> plies delivered *on time*. Are we clear on this?
> (beat, listening)
> Good. I'll meet you at the Plaza at eight. And Jason . . .
> come alone.

He hangs up. Glances at Sarah, framed in the door.

> SARAH
> Pretty hard on him, weren't you?

Doesn't look so hard, now does it? So with that out of the way, let's now look at how one puts it all together in a script. Here are the first few pages from a produced *Murder, She Wrote* script, "The Committee," which we've developed from premise to outline and now taken to script.

MURDER, SHE WROTE
"The Committee"
<u>Act One</u>

FADE IN:

EXT. HOTEL - DAY

A prestigious hotel somewhere uptown.

INT. HOTEL - LOBBY

Start by a sign in the doorway that reads W.A.F.F.A. - WRITERS AND ARTISTS FOR THE FIRST AMENDMENT - FUND-RAISING PARTY 12-4 P.M. TUESDAY. FANS are lined up in front of several AUTHORS seated at a row of tables. We PAN ACROSS to the table where JESSICA FLETCHER sits as she finishes signing a book, then hands it to the FAN waiting in line. That fan moves aside to reveal another.

                    FAN
          Mrs. Fletcher, hi, I just wanted to say that I've been a
          big fan of yours ever since THE CORPSE DANCED AT
          MIDNIGHT.

                    JESSICA
          Well, thank you.

                    FAN
                    (re: the book)
          Could you make it out to Doris?

                    JESSICA
          Of course.

As Jessica signs, Jessica sees the organizer of the fund-raiser, MRS. PHIPPS, approaching.

                    JESSICA
                    (to Phipps)
          How are we doing?

                    PHIPPS
          Great, we've almost reached our goal. Mrs. Fletcher, I
          know it's getting late, but we've got people lined up all
          the way outside. If there's any way you could—

JESSICA

Certainly. Would another half hour be enough?

PHIPPS

That's perfect, thanks, you're a real lifesaver.

Phipps exits as Jessica hands the fan her book.

FAN

Thank you.

She moves on as Jessica pours a glass of water, not seeing the next person in line until:

WINSTON (os)

You always were willing to go the extra mile, Jessica.

She looks up to see WINSTON DEVERMORE standing before her. A handsome man in his late fifties or early sixties with a leonine head of hair and an elegant manner. Jessica is pleasantly astonished to see him. She rises, and they embrace, warmly, as good friends.

JESSICA

Winston?! Good heavens, where have you *been*? I haven't seen you in over a year!

WINSTON

I've been in France on business. Just got back. When I saw the notice in the paper about you being here today, I couldn't resist.

JESSICA

Well, I'm glad you didn't. It's been far too long.

WINSTON

My very thought. So after you're finished here, how about dinner?

JESSICA

Sounds wonderful.

WINSTON

Great. I know this quiet little place uptown . . . simple, rustic, nothing fancy.

And with a look that says she knows otherwise, we go to

EXT. RESTAURANT - THAT EVENING (STOCK)

Just as fancy as she'd expected: The trees outside are aglow with tiny white lights, valets stand at alert out front . . . a carefully restored brick-and-wood monument to good taste and refinement.

> WINSTON (vo)
> —so after Susann and I went our separate ways, I decided I could use a little adventure.

INT. RESTAURANT - CONTINUOUS

Jessica and Winston sit at a table covered in white cloth and topped by candles, flickering against the exterior night.

> WINSTON
> Then I heard about this little mining operation in Zimbabwe. They'd been trying to find diamonds for two years, without success. They were hard workers, good people . . . and they were running out of money fast. So I decided to take a chance. I invested nearly every cent I had, in exchange for a 50 percent ownership in the mine.

> JESSICA
> And? . . .

> WINSTON
> And . . . they hit the biggest lode anyone's found around there in twenty years.

> JESSICA
> That's wonderful, Winston. Congratulations. I'm not surprised, though. When we first met in Chicago, six years ago, I knew you were destined for great things.

> WINSTON
> Nonsense. . . .

> JESSICA
> It's true. To resign as CEO of a major corporation and start your whole life over again . . . that takes courage. And I think the universe rewards that kind of courage.

WINSTON
Well, thank you. I appreciate it.

The designation (vo) means voice-over, meaning that we hear the character talking over an establishing shot, say of a hotel or a restaurant or an office building, then cut inside to find the actor in action. The voice-over thus functions partly as a transitional device to smooth over a change in location. A similar direction is (os), which stands for off-screen, which means that the person doing the speaking is inside the same location but momentarily out of sight of the camera and/or the other character(s) in the room.

A notation of (beat) is used to establish a rhythm and cadence. Always be aware of the sound of your words and the way they look on the page. The more you can establish a rhythm and flow to your dialogue, the more you can make it sound natural, but at the same time crafted to say exactly what you want it to say, the better the finished product.

Format #2: Situation Comedies/Videotape

Because of the unique demands of television production on tape, a script format custom-designed to deal with these needs has emerged. The main reasons for the difference in format are (1) the frequent need for last-minute revision and (2) elaborate three-camera directions that are written alongside the script. The single-spaced film format doesn't need much room for changes handwritten in between the lines because there's usually enough time in the course of producing a dramatic series episode for changes in the script to be made, published and distributed to all parties prior to shooting. While dramas are shot over seven to nine days, situation comedies are taped more or less in real time. You have two opportunities, two tapings, usually on the same day, barely hours apart. Then it's over. As a result, last-minute rewrites are often penciled in on the original script.

Sitcoms are also shot using three cameras rather than one, edited more or less on the fly by the director, who sits in a control booth and calls out which camera is now primary. These camera and blocking directions are usually written along the margins of the script, creating a need for lots of blank space on the page. Consequently, each page equals about thirty to forty seconds, whereas film format works out to about a minute per page.

Typographical dimensions. Centered ten lines from the top of the page are the series title and two spaces below it the episode title. Drop down two more spaces, and type the act number. The series title and act number are always capitalized and underlined, while the episode title is written in upper- and lowercase letters, bracketed with quotation marks and under-lined. The two titles are omitted on the first pages of acts two and three, although the act number remains twelve spaces from the top.

In addition, each page must feature an act and scene number notation in the upper right-hand corner of the page. This is typed in full capitals on the first page of the act and typed in mixed upper- and lowercase and underlined on all subsequent pages of each act, for example, ACT I, SC. 1 and ACT 2, sc. 3. This makes it easier to locate a particular scene in the episode during rehearsal and production. (There are, incidentally, only about three scenes per act in the average situation comedy script.)

Cast names for the actors required to participate in any given scene are placed one line below the act and scene notation in the right-hand corner, single-spaced between 60 and 75 picas. Cast names are written in upper- and lowercase letters, separated by commas and bracketed by parentheses. They appear only at the beginning of each scene, with the page number appearing two spaces below (about seven lines from the top). Cast lists are omitted from subsequent pages of the same scene, with the page number rising to five spaces from the top.

Page numbers are placed at 75 picas and spaced from the top of the page according to the specifications spelled out in the preceding paragraph.

Dialogue is written in upper- and lowercase letters between 20 and 50 picas and double-spaced. You should refrain wherever possible from contin-uing a paragraph of dialogue from one page onto another. Because of the double-spacing, however, this can be difficult at times. So if a continuation becomes necessary, write the word MORE directly below the last line of dialogue on the first page. Type the abbreviation (CONT'D) beside the character's name on the following page, with the dialogue picking up where it left off, two spaces below, in the usual manner.

Names of characters are capitalized at 30 picas, and placed two spaces above the first line of dialogue.

Dialogue, scene, camera and blocking directions are all placed between 15 and 50 picas, capitalized, single-spaced and bracketed by parentheses.

Scene indications are capitalized and set within the same margins but are not accompanied by numbers directly beside them. The scene numbers at the top of the page are sufficient. All you need are the indications of INT. or EXT., the location and whether the action takes place at night or during the day.

Transitions and continuations are also handled simply. Each act begins with FADE IN: and ends with FADE OUT in capitals and underlined, placed at the far left margin (15 picas). Transitions are usually confined to simple blackouts, freeze-frames, and dissolves. They are placed at 65 picas and capitalized.

Each scene following a transition begins on a new page, with the scene indication beginning at ten spaces from the top of the page.

All this sounds a lot more complicated than it really is. The result is simply a television script that has a lot of "air" and is set largely on the left of the page, with constant little reminders about where we are on a scene-by-scene basis.

Format #3: Live Comedy/Variety Programs on Videotape

Just as situation comedy telescripts must be fashioned in a way that leaves them open for last-minute revision, so too must a television sketch or other live-broadcast material be open to changes—more so, in fact, because of the frenetic requirements of such programs.

The most immediately noticeable difference between the two formats is that the body of a television situation comedy script is placed on the left side of the page, while live or variety programs have the bulk of their material on the far right side of the page. This may seem rather arbitrary, but in the case of the live or variety telescript, there's a good reason for the distinction. It's not uncommon for these scripts to be changed, revised, polished, pulled and put into a program at the last minute to fill up time when the program runs short. This occurs to the understandable consternation of the cast members, who may find it difficult to memorize all the new lines without sufficient lead time. In order to help overcome this, the studio uses a teleprompter, a device that scans a sheet of paper and electronically displays the written copy on a screen directly above the television camera. And it just happens that teleprompters are built to scan the right side of the page.

By now you're probably wondering why situation comedy producers don't switch over to this format and thereby create some consistency and standardization. It's an obvious question, one I've asked of several other producers. In each case, I got the same response: a quizzical look, a shrug and "Because we've always done it this way, and always will." Go try and figure the world.

One other way the variety comedy script varies from the sitcom script is that the former is not generally divided into acts. Because they can be moved around within the course of an episode, each individual segment of the show (inclusive of comedy sketches, films and musical appearances by guest groups) is called an *item*. Each item is assigned its own number, according to its optimum sequence within the show, and begins on its own separate page. This way, should a producer decide at the last minute to replace one comedy sketch with another, she can do so without having to rewrite or retype the pages before and after it. Finally, there's less need to designate interior or exterior scenes, since as a rule, everything is shot inside the studio. (We'll deal with exceptions in a moment.)

The main physical requirement is to specify the kind of set the sketch takes place in, usually beginning with the words UP ON, which indicates that the camera dissolves to that set after taping the previous segment. For example: UP ON: A UNIVERSITY AUDITORIUM tells the director that the sketch takes place on a set built to resemble the interior of a large auditorium, with desks, a chalkboard and so on.

From time to time, comedy programs feature segments filmed or video-taped on location, outside the studio. In order to differentiate between the two, items written for production in-studio during live taping are accompanied by the notation (LIVE), while those that require exterior taping are indicated with the abbreviation (VTR). This means that the item is to be taped before the show, edited, cued up by the director during the studio taping and finally shown on studio monitors for the audience. Microphones recording audience response are left open so that applause and laughter can be recorded along with the tape for broadcast.

While the format for writing a pretaped sketch is the same as for a live sketch, the former is not included in the final overall script used during live production. Since the pretaped sketch has already been completed, there's no need to include that material in the production script. Instead, a single page is inserted into the production script as a place holder. This page contains the title of the sketch, the length in minutes and seconds, the opening shot that begins the sketch (which tells the director whether or not the tape has been cued up to the right point) and the outcue (the last word, sentence or scene in the sketch), which tells the director that the scene is concluding so he can get ready to segue into the next item.

To make sure that nothing gets out of sequence, the last line on the last page of each item gives the cue for the next item. For instance, on the bottom of the last page of an item immediately preceding a sketch about pirates would be the line (INTO: PIRATE SPOT).

Once again, this all sounds a lot more complicated than it really is. In reality, while the comedy itself is a difficult art form on the best of days, the sketch *format* is probably the easiest and simplest form of telescripting there is. They're totally self-contained, discreet and short. You don't have to worry about dividing the action into separate acts or maintaining an involved plot over a full thirty minutes. The sole task of a sketchwriter is to get in quickly, get the laughs, then run like hell so the next sketch can start.

Typographical dimensions. These standards apply to both live and videotaped items.

Page numbers are placed three spaces from the top of the page at 75 picas.

Item numbers are set at 33 picas, five lines from the top of the page, capitalized and underlined. On the first page of the individual item, the full item number is spelled out, for example, ITEM #4. On subsequent pages, only the Arabic number is used, bracketed by parentheses. In this case, (4).

Sketch titles appear at the fifth line from the top of each page at 53 picas. Titles are capitalized and underlined and should be a brief version of the full title, for example: PIRATE ATTACK ON THE U.S.S. HERMITAGE would be written simply as PIRATE ATTACK.

Live or videotaped notations appear directly after the title of the sketch, written in all caps and bracketed by parentheses. Hence, the above would read, in full, PIRATE ATTACK (LIVE) or PIRATE ATTACK (VTR).

Cast names for those actors required in the sketch are, as in the situation comedy format, written directly beneath the sketch title in upper- and lowercase letters, bracketed by parentheses.

Scene indications appear twelve lines from the top of the page, starting at 33 picas and ending at approximately 63 picas. As mentioned, scene indications always begin with the words UP ON, followed by the designation of the required set. They are written in capital letters and bracketed by parentheses and are single-spaced.

Scene descriptions and blocking directions are written in the same fashion as scene indications, occupying the same space on the page and using the same rules of capitalization.

Dialogue is double-spaced between 38 and 75 picas, written in upper- and lowercase letters.

Names of characters are typed in all capital letters at 53 picas. Double-space between the name of a character and her first line of dialogue. Note: When a sketch is first turned in by a writer, it may or may not use the actual cast names in place of characters. This usually happens when a sketch has been written specifically for one of the cast members. As a rule, however, producers prefer to receive a sketch using only the characters' names, allowing them to determine who will play any given role.

Transitional notations signaling the upcoming sketch are written on the last line of the sketch, centered, written in capital letters and bracketed by parentheses.

If you have written a sketch to be videotaped for later showing during the live production, you should include the one-page substitution sheet that will be used in the final production script. Here are the specifications for that accompanying page:

All the margins given earlier for item numbers, page numbers, sketch titles and cues for the following sketch still apply. Videotape recording notations are made directly after the title using the following: (VTR).

A VTR data box is made by putting a line of dashes from 33 picas to 75 picas at a point twelve spaces from the top of the page, and two spaces from the bottom of the last line of your outcue.

All the following are written in capitals, underlined, followed by a colon, double-spaced from one another and typed at 33 picas.

VTR #: The space for a number is left blank and inserted later. It designates the code number of the videotape containing your sketch. This lets the director place the tapes in the order in which they will be cued up.

TIME: This contains the approximate running time of your sketch in minutes and seconds.

OPENING SHOT: In as few words as possible, this describes what the director should be seeing on his monitor if the tape has been cued up properly to the beginning of the sketch.

OUTCUE: The signal for the director to prepare for the next scene, this is usually the last sentence or visual cue ending the sketch.

Once again, in order to get a better understanding of this script format, we'll illustrate the point with a few samples of the sketch and accompanying page formats written exclusively for this book. (See FIG. 1-6.)

Format #4: Two-Column Scripts

This particular format—the last we will examine in this chapter—was developed early on as an all-purpose kind of format, used for both film and videotape. In recent years, however, the rise of specialized formats has steadily eroded this intent. Today two-column scripts have been almost entirely relegated to television commercials.

This format can be distinguished from the rest by the fact that the script is neatly divided down the center, with visual directions on one side, dialogue on the other. The reason: Most television commercials consist mainly of narrations dubbed over a series of images of the product being hawked. It therefore becomes pointless after a while to keep writing

(VOICE-OVER) on every slice of dialogue on each page. In addition, dividing the text into two parts makes it easier to signal images in a montage without interrupting the flow of dialogue on the typewritten page.

It is important to note, however, that networks do not generally produce commercials. The exceptions are commercials or promotional spots made by the network to promote its own programs. All other TV commercials

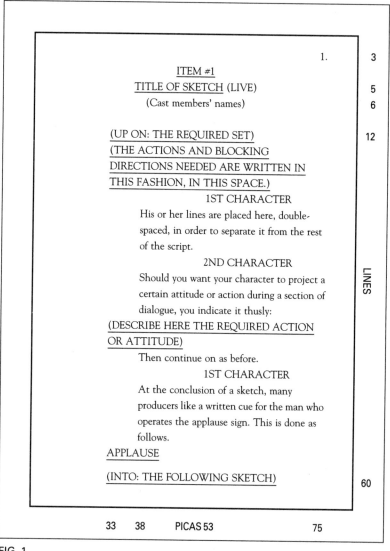

FIG. 1

are produced by high-priced advertising agencies working directly with sponsors. This format is only included because some TV writers do break in by working in this area. It's not a path I'd particularly recommend, but for some, it can be a useful opportunity to get firsthand experience with tape editing, mixing, camera work and so forth. So if you're the kind of person interested in writing television commercials, I recommend the following attack:

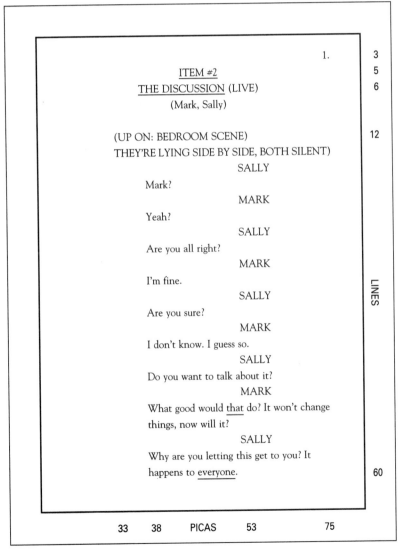

FIG. 2

1. Write anywhere from three to five one-minute commercial spots using the supplied format. Pick large, well-known sponsors.

2. Go through your telephone book and locate those advertising agencies in your community that produce commercials.

3. Write a letter of inquiry to the agency, stating your interest in writing television commercials for them on a freelance basis. Offer to send along a few samples of your work to give them a better idea of your skills.

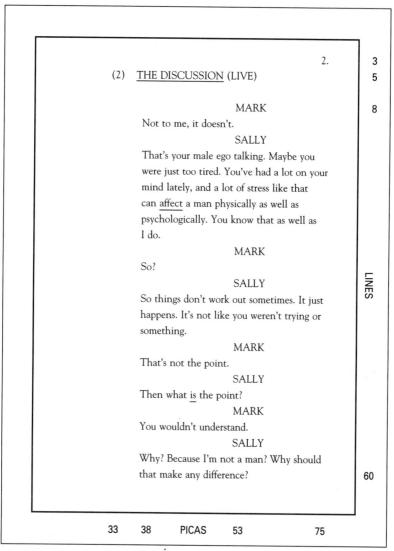

FIG. 3

4. Assuming a positive response to your inquiry, send off your packet of commercial scripts and follow up with a request for an interview after they have finished examining your material. If your scripts are good, there is a chance the agency will give you one or two trial assignments to see how you handle its clients. Should those turn out satisfactorily, the number of assignments will increase with time.

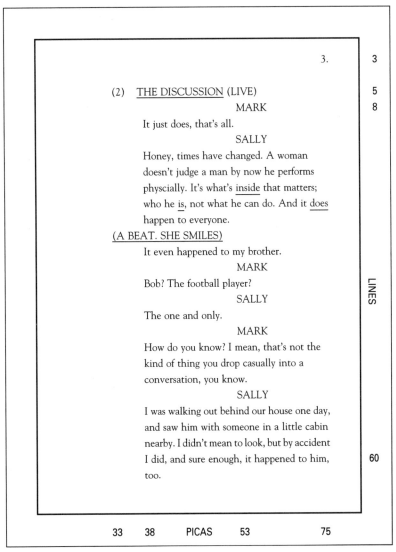

FIG. 4

It's usually better to approach a small agency first. Because of their less extensive staff, it's more likely they will be receptive to freelance material than a large agency that is fully staffed with a fair number of full-time copywriters.

Typographical dimensions. The name and address of the advertising agency appears at a point eight spaces from the top of the page and 8 picas from the left-hand edge of the page. Note: If you are operating as an independent or freelance copywriter, your name and address appear in this space.

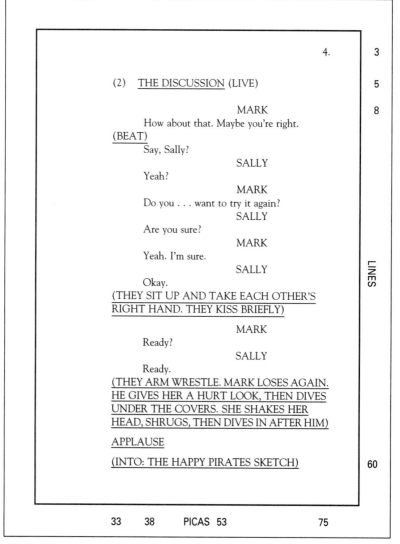

FIG. 5

Client information appears at 42 picas, eight spaces from the top of the page. One line apiece (flush left) goes to the name of the client, the product, the title of the commercial, the length of the spot and the production number (left blank until a number has been assigned by the advertising agency).

A line appears fourteen lines from the top, separating the information about the commercial from the actual body of the spot. The line extends

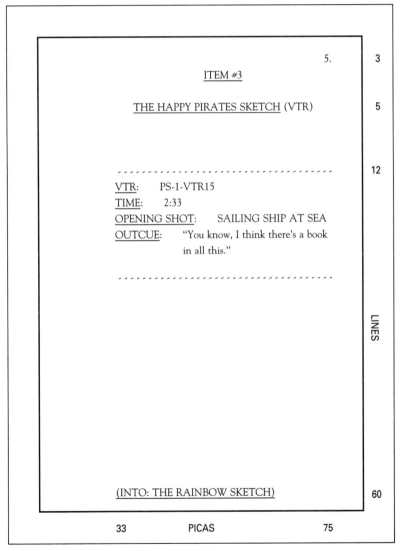

FIG. 6

from 8 picas to 75 picas.

Video and audio designations are set at, respectively, 8 and 42 picas. They are capitalized and underlined and appear at the sixteenth line from the top of the page.

Scene descriptions and directions always appear first, two spaces below the word *video*. When the scene has been adequately described, the dialogue begins on the same vertical line below the audio heading, immediately preceded by the identification of the speaker.

Chapter Four

Marketing the Television Script

L et's say you've just written a really terrific little script. The dialogue is sharp, the story is interesting, the characters ring true and there's all the drama or comedy (or both) a producer could ask for. It's been flawlessly typed, photocopied and bound with those annoying little brads that always catch and tear the corners of manila envelopes. Now what? You shouldn't just toss it in the closet; a script exists to be seen and produced. Writing for the trunk is unproductive. So what do you do, how do you do it and where do you go to do it?

WHO'S WHO, WHERE AND WHY

Part of knowing where to go is in knowing *who* to go to. If you look at the credits for just about any television series, you'll see a list of story editors, staff writers and all kinds of producers. Who *are* these people?

Creative Consultants

A creative consultant is usually a writer attached to a series because of some name value or contractual requirement.

A creative consultant has only tangential contact with the show on a day-to-day basis and is generally prohibited from rewriting scripts under WGA rules.

Usefulness in contacting the creative consultant if you want to sell a script: nil.

Staff Writer

The staff writer was previously a freelance writer who showed a facility for writing scripts for this particular series. She is contracted to write *x* number of episodes per season (usually no more than two are ever actually guaranteed per season, to avoid being locked into someone who ends up being difficult to work for). Sometimes a staff writer rewrites scripts, but that's generally frowned upon. She can take part in pitch sessions from freelancers but, again under WGA rules, doesn't usually speak during them. It is not her job, nor does she have the authority, to buy scripts. Freelancers are competitors at this level.

Usefulness in contacting: marginal.

Story Editor

As someone who has shown that he can not only write his own scripts, but can save otherwise unproducible scripts by other writers, he is a valued commodity. The story editor rewrites scripts, works out stories with freelancers, takes part in pitch meetings, but in general doesn't have final authority on buying stories. He can recommend, but the actual decision rests one or two rungs higher up. (There are some exceptions to this but not a lot.) His job is to find writers who can handle this series, as well as writing his own scripts. If he doesn't find writers, he's not doing his job properly, so that definitely helps make the story editor more open to outsiders.

Usefulness in contacting: good.

Executive Story Editor

This is either the story editor with seniority over the two to three other story writers, or the writer with the better agent.

Usefulness in contacting: good.

Coproducer

Now here you've got to be careful. A coproducer can be a writer/producer or someone in one of the technical areas used on the show. For instance, on my series *Babylon 5*, George Johnsen was listed as coproducer; George was in charge of postproduction, ran the editing department, handled sound mixing and so on. George doesn't write scripts or edit them.

A writer/coproducer is someone who's been promoted up the ranks from story editor or has been brought in from another show where her title was story editor or coproducer. (Generally, if you're at all good at what you do, you go up in rank one notch per season.)

In addition to writing scripts, editing freelance scripts, developing stories with freelancers and attending pitch meetings, a coproducer watches dailies, consults on the cut of her episode with the producer, attends casting when it's her episode and handles other chores not directly related to writing. (This is referred to as a "writer employed in additional capacities," under the WGA Television Minimum Basic Agreement.) A coproducer also doesn't usually have final say in buying a script but can function in that capacity if required, should the producer(s) be unavailable. A coproducer can sometimes rewrite the story editor.

How do you tell the two kinds of coproducers apart? Just watch the show. If you never see a writing credit by this person or see only one (meaning somebody got it written into her contract that she can take a shot at writing one episode even though that's not technically her area), pick somebody else.

Usefulness in contacting the right coproducer: very good.

Producer

At last, the Grail of the freelance TV writer: someone who is empowered to say yes and buy your story. A producer writes, rewrites others, including the staff writer, the story editor and the coproducer in some cases, and has all the responsibilities of the coproducer. In addition, the producer generally sits in on casting and works more directly with the actors and with the various technical departments (costuming, art direction and so on).

Once again, though, there are frequently producers who are in technical areas and not writers. Check to be sure whom you're approaching.

Usefulness in contacting: substantial.

Supervising Producer

This is sometimes an experienced writer/producer who hasn't quite reached show-runner status yet or a high-ranking nonwriting producer or a producer with a very good agent. He has the same level of responsibility as the producer, plus works in even greater detail with the various departments.

Usefulness in contacting: substantial.

Executive Producer

There is no higher position on a TV series than executive producer. The writing executive producer is usually referred to informally as the show-runner, to differentiate him from other possible executive producers or co-executive producers who don't write. Again, check writing credits to determine who's who.

A writing executive producer, or show-runner, sets the tone and direction for the series. Often she created the series or was brought in to run it when the series creator died, retired, moved on to other projects or was fired. The executive producer has authority of final cut on all episodes (not counting any notes that may come in from the studio or network). She has final say in buying stories. She approves costumes, set designs, directors and actors (except, again, where the studio or network intrudes); handles spotting (determining where sound and music cues go); functions as the direct liaison between the studio/network and the production team; writes scripts; and can rewrite anyone else in the writing/producing team.

If you can get the executive producer to back your work, you're golden. Actually *getting to her* is another and more difficult question, of course, because you'll discover that there is a platoon of people between you and your goal. Don't begrudge them that; it's their job.

Speaking personally for a moment, when I'm exec producing a series, I'm running madly between production meetings, editing, casting, the stage, tone meetings with directors and a thousand other things from early in the morning until eight or later in the evening. Then I come home and write until 3 A.M. Then the next day it starts all over again. I have little time and less patience for agents or spec material, in large measure because there's so much of it. A highly rated or high-visibility show can receive anywhere from two to four thousand unsolicited submissions per year, and that doesn't even include the agented scripts that come in.

That's why the executive producer has to rely on her story editor(s) and producer(s) to ferret out the likely prospects for assignments. My story editor reads sample scripts, for instance, and only brings me those that he feels represent good prospects for the show. These staffers function as gatekeepers—keeping some people out but letting others in. The key is to become one of those allowed inside. That's why it's important to understand who does what. If you dedicate yourself to getting to the exec right off the bat, you're probably going to get more frustrated than if you go for the story editor. Sometimes knowing who *not* to go through is almost as important as knowing who *to* go through.

Usefulness in contacting: extreme, *if* you can get in, but the odds are against it; better to start a notch or two farther down the ladder.

Those are the categories of people you'll be running into as you begin to market your script. Which brings us to an issue that has been debated as a recurring subject of controversy in the television industry, one that has often wracked the Writers Guild of America: the question of staff writer/producers vs. freelancers.

STAFF VS. FREELANCE ISSUES

Let's say you've just been hired as a producer on a TV series for a major network. You have twenty-two episodes to produce, meaning you need to get twenty-two scripts in shape to shoot. Your reputation, your livelihood and millions of dollars are on the line.

You put the word on the grapevine that you're looking for writers. They come to you, and you add some whom you've worked with before or know by reputation and want to work with now. The scripts begin to come in. Most are OK, requiring minor rewriting. Some are absolutely horrible, requiring massive rewriting and the occasional resurrection. And some are brilliant. You just take them to the stage and shoot them. Now, the writer of the brilliant script is going to move on to the next show—unless you decide to lock up the writer with a long-term contract as a staff writer, story editor or writer/producer. And this is exactly what happens on many television series. It's nothing more or less than the producer taking steps to guarantee that there will be solid, quality scripts throughout the season. Over the years, with more and more on the line, larger budgets, shorter initial series orders, this has led to the development of large writing staffs as a staple of television. Each staffer generally has a guarantee of x number of scripts, anywhere from two to six scripts per season, depending on the writer's clout and how badly the network/studio wants her.

Over the last fifteen years or so, the split in the WGA between freelancers and staffers has grown more pronounced, vocal and angry. The staffers feel that the freelancers don't understand the pressures they're under and the steps they've had to take not only to protect their jobs, but to serve their employers. The freelancers feel they've been locked out, disenfranchised and otherwise cut off at the knees.

Which side is right? Both of them.

Yes, this does make it more difficult to sell a script, in that there are often fewer slots available in any given series for freelancers. But I've never yet met a producer who wouldn't kill to get a great script out of the blue sky one morning. In the final analysis, the only thing that matters is the quality of the writing. Period. Quality always wins out. And if the script is good enough, there's the possibility of being asked to come on staff yourself, as has happened to me and many others.

So having established the obstacles confronting every new television writer, how do you overcome them?

To expand upon what was explained about who does what within a production company, the answer to that question lies in part in defining what you should *not* do with a script for an episodic television series. Do not send your telescripts to a network—ever. Along with sending your script wrapped in used butcher's paper, this is probably the single worst thing you can do in marketing your script. People at networks don't want to see scripts, don't want to hear about how you spent the last five years putting one together, have no one available to read your script even if they were interested and would frankly prefer that you dropped into a convenient chuckhole somewhere. Why? Because the networks do not generally produce the programs they broadcast. Networks underwrite the production of programming. There's a very important and subtle distinction between the two; understanding that difference is vital to selling your scripts.

NETWORK AND STUDIO RELATIONSHIPS

An established producer of television programs—someone the networks trust and know to be capable of delivering what he promises—approaches a network with an idea for a television series. Depending on how reputable the producer is, he may have to present several scripts, a series bible or treatment and thoughts on casting—or he may need just the basic premise. (Norman Lear is reported to have sold several different series with just a one-paragraph synopsis and an improvised scene from the pilot episode.) He may also provide a written estimate of what the shows will cost, individually and in groups of six, twelve and twenty-two. Should the network find the concept interesting, it options the project, puts it into development (writing scripts and shooting a pilot) and then decides whether to actually finance the series.

Most leading producers are affiliated with a major studio, so the network works through that studio, which subcontracts with the producer's company to produce the series. The network's contribution is what's called a *license fee*, often between $850,000 and $1 million per hour, depending on the show. In most cases, the cost of actually producing the series runs much higher than the license fee; the overbudget can be anywhere from $100,000 to $200,000 per hour. The studio then eats this cost, called *deficit financing*, figuring it can make it back when the show hits syndication. Now you understand why producers link up with major studios; for any single producer to deficit finance a whole series means a potential investment—and potential loss—of as much as $4 to $5 million, and I can't think of many producers who can handle that kind of risk.

At one time, each network financed a new series for an entire season. In recent years, however, as ratings have become even more critical and the patience of network executives has grown shorter, that period of support has decreased severely. Networks now underwrite the production of six episodes and the scripting of six more. Should the series bomb, the network ceases its underwriting, writes the additional scripts off as a loss, and the series dies. If, on the other hand, the ratings show that the series has potential but hasn't found its audience yet, the network will approve the production of six or twelve more shows, depending on how late in the season the series debuts and how confident the network is of the series's eventual success. It is at this point that we see why the networks commission six full episodes and six scripts to begin with. The OK for additional episodes often comes at the last possible minute, and without scripts on hand, it would be impossible to keep production on schedule.

Thus is a television series born. As the seasons pass, it will continue to be financed by the networks as long as it pulls in the ratings—which leads to an interesting conundrum. It is actually possible for producers and studios to lose money with a successful series and make money on a series that has been canceled.

Don't look at me like that. I know it sounds like the plot for the film *The Producers*, but it makes sense. Since the networks only underwrite the actual cost of production, the production company responsible for the series isn't making a profit. Deficit financing, remember? Expenses are being covered, everyone's getting a salary, but for the most part, the producer is treading water—the financing goes out as fast as it comes in—and the studio is losing $4 to $5 million per season. Meanwhile expenses that are non-production-related (distribution, advertising, duplication, satellite fees) also grow with time, steadily whittling away at the company's finances. The networks, meanwhile, continue to make a profit by charging extraordinary amounts of money for commercial airtime during the series.

The only time a producer and her studio/company make a profit is when the show hits syndication. In the past, reruns on independent stations and network affiliates started only after the series was canceled. But that has changed. One of the first shows to break the mold was *The Mary Tyler Moore Show*, which (according to one MTM representative) was losing money even though it was a top-rated program. As a consequence, the producers demanded and received permission to syndicate the series even though it was still being aired in prime time. The networks initially were unhappy with the idea, naturally afraid that this move might hurt the new shows. Just how much Mary Tyler Moore could viewers sustain? As it turned out, the syndication didn't hurt the network's ratings and, in many instances, actually seemed to help by making the show available in the afternoon to people who might not otherwise have seen it. As a consequence, it is now much easier for other series to receive similar permission, with the resultant money going into the development of new series.

Since the purpose of this book is to help prepare you for the exigencies of television, here's an aside on how all this directly affects writers. (If this angers you, that's fine.) In addition to syndication outlets for network series, a number of basic cable operations have sprung up, like the USA Network and TNT and others, that buy the rights to network reruns. The WGA minimum basic agreement for syndication is based on the number of reruns: a major percentage of the original script fee for the first rerun, slightly less for the next few, on and on. The very first residual for an hour drama can be as much as $8,000 or more. The formula for cable residuals is different, wherein the writer fees are based on a percentage of what the cable network pays for the show.

Universal Television, for instance, owns *Murder, She Wrote*. Universal is also part owner of the USA Network. At first, Universal sold reruns to USA based on traditional high rates. Then one day, somebody in accounting woke up and realized that they were selling these shows to *themselves*—and charging big bucks—so why not sell the show to themselves for a lot less, meaning more initial profit. And given that the writer's rerun fees are a percentage of *that* fee . . .

Long story made short: The residuals check for my first rerun on the USA Network came to approximately twenty-four dollars.

(Are you *really* sure you want to get into this business?)

If you're still determined to give this a try, we'll now turn our attention to the step-by-step process by which you can get your script into the hands of a television producer. This will be primarily a "do-it-yourself" procedure. We'll examine the role of agents and how to secure one in the chapter titled "The Art of Getting and Keeping an Agent."

SELLING THE EPISODIC SCRIPT

Step One: Locate the Producer

There are several ways of going about this, depending upon how much time and money you want to invest and the kind of information you want.

Start by watching the credits as they roll by at the conclusion of the program you want to write for. You'll find there the name of the production company. You can find the name of the producer or story editor in either the opening or closing credits. Next, dial Directory Assistance for the metropolitan area in which the show is produced (usually either New York or Los Angeles), and ask for the phone number and, if the operator will provide it, the address of the production company. Although this frequently results in the mailing information you need, it does not always work; a given production company may be only an informal division of a much larger company and, therefore, may not have a separate listing.

One of the most comprehensive listings of television and film production companies is the *Pacific Coast Studio Directory*, P.O. Box V, Frazier Park, California 93222. It's published quarterly and also provides a list of unions, agents, artists representatives, publicity organizations and television stations. As well as covering Los Angeles, it also contains listings for Arizona, Colorado, Hawaii, Utah and British Columbia, among others. They do not provide the names of television series, however, so there's no way of knowing who does what unless you've noted the name of the company in the show's credits.

One publication that will consistently make your life simpler is the *Newsletter of the Writers Guild of America, West*, published by the WGA, 8955 Beverly Boulevard, Los Angeles, California 90048. You don't need to be a WGA member to subscribe, and the monthly newsletter contains a double-page spread listing every series currently in production, and whether it's booked or still open, whether it requires agents or will accept release forms. This section also supplies you with the name of the person responsible for freelance writers and the phone number of the production company.

In addition, both *Daily Variety* and *The Hollywood Reporter* (available at most large libraries) regularly publish television production charts, providing much the same information, minus the parts about agents and whether they're still open to outside scripts—information that can be gained through a quick phone call.

From time to time, other periodicals appear, such as the *Hollywood Creative Directory*, but you should consider these prior publications your primary sources of information.

Step Two: Contact the Producer

Once you've located the right producer, draft a polite letter of inquiry. I stress *polite* because all too often a letter will cross my desk from a neophyte writer who states, "I've been watching your show for months now, and I think the writing really sucks. I know how to help make it better and save your show for you." Suffice to say this does not endear you to the producer in question. The letter should state the following:

1. Your familiarity with the show and its characters and your enthusiasm for that show.

2. The fact that you have studied the show to get a feeling for what it's trying to accomplish and the kinds of stories it tends to present.

3. That after studying the series, you have developed a spec script and several additional stories consistent with the series. Don't overhype your work; be cool and professional.

4. That you would like to submit the script or treatment on a spec basis for consideration by the producer/story editor.

5. That in the absence of an agent (should that be the case) you will be happy to enclose a standard release form with the material or use the release form preferred by the production company.

While their number has never been large, there continue to be series that are happy to accept unagented submissions with a release form. The various *Star Trek* series, in fact, provided a telephone hot line allowing the studio to send prospective writers a "pitch kit" consisting of sample material, guidelines on story construction and a release form.

6. Any writing credits or background information that you feel will help or that will demonstrate some unique qualification you have for writing this show. For example: If you're a retired police officer who worked homicide for twenty-five years, that would go far toward getting your script in the door of a cop series. If your credentials are minimal or nonexistent, it's better to say nothing at all. Curiously, if a producer receives a well-written, thoughtful query letter without a list of credentials, he will often assume you have more background than you really do. I have yet to figure out why this is so.

7. Reaffirmation of your appreciation for the series and your conviction that the material you have developed is suitable for the series. State that you hope to hear from the producer/story editor in the near future. These remarks are appropriate in the closing paragraph of your letter.

If you'll look back at points two through four, you'll notice a certain careful phrasing. On the one hand, it's important to communicate to the producer that you have developed a certain idea, but on the other hand, you should *not* describe that story in any detail in your query letter. You should never send anything—script, treatment, story, synopsis—to a producer unannounced or unsolicited. If you send in a script, it will be returned in a larger envelope, unopened (although there will often be a tiny tear in one of the corners of the original envelope, made by a secretary to verify that it contained a script). If you even include a brief synopsis in your query letter in a regular #10 envelope, it will be returned, opened (since they had no way of knowing what it was), with a curt note asking that you not bother them any more.

It is unprofessional, it is rude and it will effectively kill any chance you have of selling to this company. There are rules, and you must play by them. This and only this distinguishes you from the loonies of the world who would send in a notion and sue three weeks later. One individual I encountered had written a spec *Terminator 3* script, hoping to either send it to producer James Cameron and later sue Cameron because this person was sure this would be the next story or tempt Cameron to sue him, which would force Cameron to read the script, after which he would be so thoroughly blinded by the script's brilliance that he'd buy it instantly. (No, I'm not making this up.)

Unsolicited manuscripts are the constant nightmare of every producer. Let's say that, based upon your market analysis of a series, you have developed a script that you believe is perfect for the show, and you send it off to the unsuspecting producer. Upon its arrival, let's assume that one of the secretaries accidentally opens the envelope containing your script. Within seconds, she repackages your script and sends it back with a note explaining that they don't accept unsolicited manuscripts. You finally receive the returned script, assume because it was removed from its original envelope that they at least looked at it and accept the rejection quietly.

But now things start to get tricky because if your market analysis was accurate, there's a better than even chance that the series will eventually feature an episode along the lines of your script. It may even be that they had a similar one already in development. When that episode finally airs, you could accuse the producer of plagiarism and take him to court. You could also very possibly win the case, since plagiarism suits hinge on the question of access, and when the secretary opened the envelope containing your script, the company gained access to your idea. It then becomes incumbent upon the company to prove it did not take advantage of this accessibility, which is very hard.

Writers for the series M*A*S*H stated on several occasions that the one story they could never do was one in which Hawkeye had to perform an operation on Trapper John, for the simple reason that that story had been written in literally hundreds of spec scripts and that they knew at least one of these people would claim plagiarism, even though it's the obvious story for a series like that.

A considerate, well-written query letter and a release form are the only protection a producer has against plagiarism suits. (A model standard release form is included in the appendixes.) By dealing forthrightly with these concerns, you increase the odds that the producer will look at your manuscript, which is, after all, the point of the exercise. Remember, producers are always on the lookout for new material and new writers. They *want* to find them. But in the initial phases of contact, the only criterion they have to go by is whether the writer follows all the correct procedures.

Step Three: Follow-Up

Assuming your query letter receives a positive response from the producer, your next step is to prepare your manuscript for immediate mailing. You should make a clean and clear photocopy of the script or treatment, on three-hole 20-pound paper. You should also type a cover page for your manuscript, as well as one sheet for your casting and set requirements. (See pages 89 and 90.)

Though certainly not required, you may want to consider copying your cover onto heavy (40-pound or so) colored stock and providing a backing sheet of the same stock. This keeps the script from bending too much in the mail and makes for a neater presentation. Don't choose too flashy a color, just primary colors and subtle shades, like sky blue, rust or gray.

Finally, bind your script with brass paper fasteners. Don't use elephant clips or folders or staples. Enclose a letter with it confirming your receipt of the producer's go-ahead to submit the script, your enthusiasm for the series and your conviction that the script may prove suitable for the series. Close your letter on the usual amenities. The package should also contain a self-addressed, stamped return envelope and your signed release form. Somewhere on the exterior of the mailing envelope should be written, in large, friendly letters, the following: RELEASE FORM ENCLOSED, AS REQUESTED. If you don't, it might get bounced back to you, since these words are the only clue a secretary has that you've cleared this submission with the producer, which she will verify by checking the enclosed letter and asking the producer. Sometimes they'll have your name on a list, but don't bank on that.

Which script to spec. There's some debate, by the way, about which show to send your spec script; some producers don't want to see a spec for their own series because they're too close to them and can't step back enough to forgive any points where the script isn't 100 percent dead-on. They prefer to see scripts written for other shows, where they can be more objective. Other producers and story editors only want to see specs for their specific series. But logically speaking, you can't go around writing a dozen spec scripts for every show.

I recommend a middle road. Pick a current show in the genre that interests you, one that's doing well enough in the ratings that it'll conceivably be around for a year or two more, which will give your spec greater longevity. I'd recommend *against* picking a megahit series because everyone on the planet will be speccing out a script for the megahit, and yours will just get lost in the pile. I judged the Writer's Digest Script Competition at a time when *Magnum PI* was still on the air and killing everything in sight. I cannot tell you the sheer number of *Magnum* scripts I waded through. It became a welcome relief to get something, anything, written

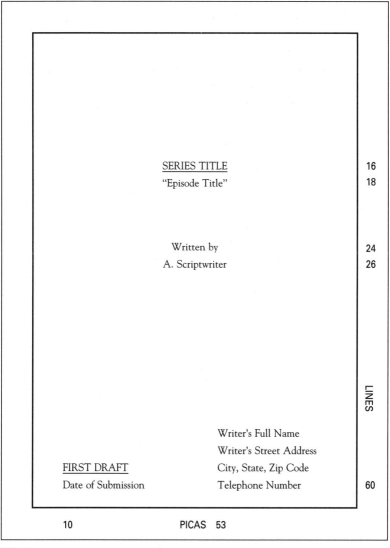

FIG. 7

for another show.

Make this your sample for most shows in that genre. If there's one series in particular that you're dying to write for, then check (in your query letter) to find out if the producer would prefer a general script or one for that show. If the latter, then under those conditions, you may want to spec one out specifically for that series.

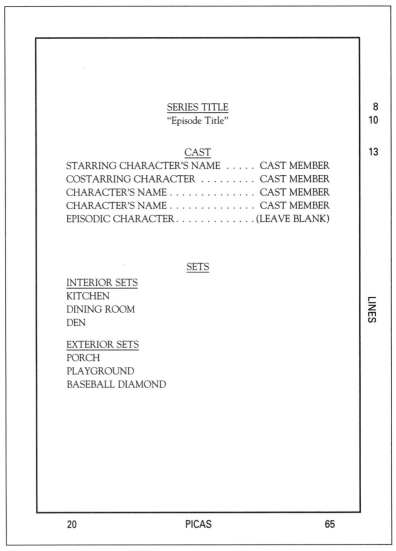

SERIES TITLE   8
"Episode Title"   10

CAST   13
STARRING CHARACTER'S NAME . . . . . CAST MEMBER
COSTARRING CHARACTER . . . . CAST MEMBER
CHARACTER'S NAME . . . . CAST MEMBER
CHARACTER'S NAME . . . . CAST MEMBER
EPISODIC CHARACTER . . . . (LEAVE BLANK)

SETS

INTERIOR SETS
KITCHEN
DINING ROOM
DEN

EXTERIOR SETS
PORCH
PLAYGROUND
BASEBALL DIAMOND

LINES

20   PICAS   65

FIG. 8

After preparing your manuscript and dropping it into the corner mailbox comes the hardest part of all: waiting and silently wondering, *What are they doing with my child?*

Step Four: Dealing With the Response

When you finally hear back from the producer, which generally takes from two to four weeks after you've sent in your material, the reply will come in one of three forms: rejection of the script, acceptance of the script or rejection of the script but not of you as a writer.

Let's take these one at a time, starting with the worst possible scenario.

Flat-out rejection. The note accompanying your returned script thanks you for giving them the opportunity to examine your manuscript, but it does not meet their current needs, or they already have a story like this in the works, or a black cat crossed in front of the producer while he was reading your script—whatever. Anyway, the answer is *no*. Your immediate visceral reaction to this news is entirely up to you. If it makes you feel better to punch a wall, jump up and down on the letter, cast aspersions on the producer's sexual proclivities, malign his lineage, make faces, yell at the cat, stick pins in a doll marked "Producer," fine, do it. Get it out of your system. You can't be expected to hit a home run the first time you come up to the plate; that doesn't mean you have to swear never to go back there again or burn any bridges.

Once you've calmed down (and reassured the cat), it behooves you to sit down and write a polite note to the producer to thank him for taking the time to review your material, indicate that your enthusiasm for the show hasn't diminished and state your hope that you can submit additional material in the future. If you're going to do this, if you're really serious about doing this—and if not why are you reading this?—then you've got to be persistent and show that persistence but not be obnoxious about it. Remember that the person at the other end of your letter got there because he was persistent, and we tend to admire in others those qualities we perceive within ourselves as virtues. (I'm not endorsing the stance, simply commenting on the underlying psychology.)

Keep the door open, and you may have the opportunity to pass through it later—maybe on the same show or when the producer/story editor moves on to another show.

Acceptance of the script. This is what we all hope for, and by way of the perverse operation of the universe, this is the rarest eventuality of all. It's like hitting the lottery, beating a traffic ticket and falling in love all on the same day. It can happen, but we're not talking about a common event.

Go out, buy your loved one dinner, call your relatives and celebrate. Then come up with another story as soon as possible, and try it again.

Script rejected, you're accepted. It's very common that the script you've written won't work for the show for any number of reasons—budget, the fact that they've just written an episode with that premise, other complications—so they can't or won't buy that particular script. It happens. What's important is that it's proven to the producers that you can write for this show, tell their stories about their characters the way they want them told. The real point of the exercise, far more than selling the one script, is to sell yourself as a writer. If you can do this, the script has served its purpose.

Should this happen, you will be invited in for a pitch meeting. At this meeting, you will be asked to verbally describe some stories you'd like to write for the series, in the hope of selling one of them. No producer can ask you to write premises or stories on spec and submit them; that is a clear and flagrant violation of Writers Guild working rules. That's why pitch meetings are verbal; if you're going to write, you should get paid for it. The operative word in the sentence, of course, is *ask*. Let's face it. Not all of us are seasoned performers. Telling a story is tough; and on top of all that, you often have to rely on the story editor or producer to relay your story accurately to the exec producer, and we've all played telephone enough times as children to know how that process works. As a result, some writers who don't feel comfortable pitching either write up premises on their own and send them along in lieu of a pitch meeting or come in for the meeting, do the pitch, and leave behind some pages, ostensibly to help jog the producer's memory but mainly to insure that your story is presented accurately.

Pitching

If the entire idea of pitching scares the bejesus out of you, don't feel bad; you're not alone. I'm in the same boat. I hate pitching. I don't think it really has much to do with what makes a good television episode. Writer A comes in with a slick, superficial story, full of holes, but she gives a great pitch, tap-dances around the illogics, charms the room, gets the assignment. And the episode is mediocre. Writer B comes in with a fully worked-out story, but he doesn't present it as well as he might, stumbles over himself and walks out the door without an assignment, even though on the scale of Platonic ideals, his would probably have been the better episode. Is it fair? Absolutely not. Is it the way the business runs? Absolutely. Are you going to have to get used to it if you want to sell to television (and film, for that matter)? You betcha.

There are several things you can do, however, to minimize the trauma and increase the odds of selling your story.

1. Don't get too bogged down in details. Come up with the broad strokes of your story, beginning, middle and end, so we can follow where the story's going, who it affects and how and the means by which we resolve it. If you get too detailed, you run the risk of forgetting stuff or losing the attention of your audience.

2. Don't go for too many stories. Four to six stories are more than sufficient. This forces you to pick only the best instead of scattergunning, and, frankly, we who sit on the other side of the desk begin to zone out after about six or seven pitches. It's terrible to admit that, but we do, particularly when you bear in mind that each pitch can take ten to fifteen minutes. So six pitches means sitting and listening to one voice for anywhere from an hour to ninety minutes.

3. Bring an assortment of pitches, three to four fully worked-out ideas, as described before, and a couple of two-line quickies. Strangely enough, I've made many sales at the end of the pitch session that have been of the two-line quickie version. I suspect that the reason for this is that at that level, without everything worked out, there's a lot of room for the producers to fill in the gaps on how the story might go, and that makes it appealing to them.

4. Don't try to read your pitches from a page; *tell* the story, the way you would around a campfire. What I usually do is allocate one page per pitch; write in big bold legible letters a few words for each important beat (KILLER ARRIVES, MYSTERIOUS MAN RENTS BEACH HOUSE, etc.). This way I can keep the pages in my lap and be able to glance down and easily know where I am without having to fumble. The one-liners serve as memory ticklers to keep me on track. The rest you fill as you go, and you can adjust just how much you fill in by how much time is remaining in the meeting; if you're stuck to a written script, it's harder to be flexible, and you're flipping pages trying to find your place.

5. Public opinion surveys have consistently shown that the greatest common fear is the mortal dread of speaking in public or having to give a speech. Consequently, pitching can cause tremendous stress and panic, particularly when one considers that a good pitch can spell the difference between perceived failure and that first break into television writing. (I say perceived because there's always the next time; it's just hard for us to see that when we fall on our faces.) Nor is this problem only something

neophytes experience; many leading TV writers continue to suffer great angst when pitching. So for starters, if you feel this way, don't be worried by it or ashamed of it. Just try to do what you can to work around it.

Public speaking classes at junior colleges, universities or adult schools can help. Taking an assertive position and speaking at your local clubs, churches, watering holes and social events can also be beneficial. Take any opportunity you can to speak publicly to prepare you for pitching.

Once you've finished your pitches, you'll know very soon if any of them have hit home. Sometimes you'll know immediately, but usually someone with the show will get back to you within a few days. If the answer is no, try and find out what you did right, what you did wrong, where you came close and where you were totally off the mark. You can use this information when you come back again (should they allow this) and later on other shows. If the answer is yes, then you're clear to begin writing your outline, as described earlier in this chapter. You'll get about two weeks to write the outline. Then, after you turn it in, comes a second trial by fire: the story conference.

The Story Conference: Revisions

Begin with a harried producer, a nervous freelance writer, a story editor (whose task it is to keep the series' continuity going from episode to episode), several staff writers (who have their own ideas about your story and how it might be improved), one or two producers and sometimes an assistant who takes notes. Stuff them all into the same room, add several pots of coffee and some Chinese food from around the corner. Start the cooking process by debating the propriety of each line of the story, baste liberally with some nicely developed egos and lock the door. The goal and the eternal hope of story conferencing is that the resultant explosion will eventually lead to a solid script.

A story conference can be one of the hardest things for a new television writer to handle. It's the first definite indication that your words are not sacrosanct. There's a terrible feeling that arises from the pit of your stomach when the producer or the story editor says, "I think act two, scene three is a little too slow, so let's just drop it," and there's sufficient agreement for the scene to be dropped. It doesn't particularly matter if you spent three whole days working out act two, scene three or that it's your favorite scene of the whole story. It's out.

Should you find yourself in this position, try to follow this rule of thumb: Only fight for something if you feel it is vital to your story. Don't fight every single line change simply because you want it to stay exactly as you originally wrote it. But don't crumble either. If you think it's important, fight for it—politely. Let your creative integrity be your guide.

Always bring a tape recorder with you to catch all of the notes because invariably you'll miss something otherwise. If a producer is good at what she does, when she tells you to revise a part of your story, she'll tell you why, where the problem is and possible solutions to the problem. If there are lots of other people in the room, things can get pretty freewheeling, and that's when a recorder can be very useful. It also can come in handy as evidence should the producer later decide he hates something that he specifically requested you insert in the next draft but now denies. Always try to get the producer or story editor to be as specific as possible; sometimes we/they speak in shorthand that may not be immediately apparent to anyone on the outside. When I wrote my first *Twilight Zone* script for CBS, the producer looked at the first draft and his primary note was "Reverse the polarity of the story." I had no idea what he was talking about. But then, as I discovered later, neither did anyone else in the room. I still don't. But whatever I did must've been right since it went into production not long thereafter. As a story editor or producer, my task is to help my writers get a feeling for and an understanding of the process of writing for my show. If I cannot communicate clearly enough to you my notes and concerns, in a constructive and specific fashion, then I'm not doing my job.

Once you've gotten your notes, you go away and revise the outline. When that's done, you turn in the second draft outline, and should it pass muster, you're approved to script, sometimes with more notes to be implemented at that stage. And, of course, when you turn in your first draft script, what do you likely have to look forward to? Yep. Another story conference. If the show is up against the wall and needs the script to go into production immediately, it may be taken in after the first draft for revision by staffers. Other times, when there isn't a crunch on, you get your notes, you go home, you do your revised draft and you turn it in. Often that's more than sufficient. Just as often, the producers may take it in-house and make additional changes, sometimes for story reasons, other times for production purposes.

Being Rewritten

This is one of the biggest problems for freelance writers in television, certainly one of the key flashpoints in any dicussion of TV writing between staffers and freelancers. The key point to remember is to not take in-house rewriting personally. Very often freelancers look at the finished script or episode after revisions in-house and complain that changes were made without apparent reason: moving a scene from a pool hall to a living room, for instance, which takes away the great pool-hustler scene. What the freelancer doesn't know is that at the last minute the pool hall the studio had contracted to use for the location shoot had an accident in which the sprinkler system went off, ruining the furniture and making it impossible to shoot there. Or suddenly the actor signed to play a character's father falls sick, and the role has to be changed to a mother because you happened to have a good female actor on hand auditioning for another role. Stuff happens.

Finally, sometimes, the deeper the producers get into the script, the more small problems become visible, requiring repair. This isn't to say that changes are always made with good reason; networks, studios, and yes, even producers sometimes do dumb things for even dumber reasons. Case in point: While I was working as coproducer on *Jake and the Fatman*, I wrote a script that involved a cop's cat-and-mouse pursuit of a criminal, one that lasted several years. At one point, the two have a scene together. The criminal says, "I should be flattered; not everyone has his own personal Ahab." Now, all modesty aside, I thought this was a pretty cool line. So you can imagine my chagrin when the network called, asking for the line to be deleted. What on Earth could've offended them? I checked back. The network liaison said, "It's inconsistent. We hear about this Ahab guy, but we never see him. Who is he and what's his connection to the story?"

After ten seconds of silence as vast as space: "Uhm, y'see, Ahab is a character in a book called *Moby Dick*. It's a literary reference. No one named Ahab is actually *in* this episode of *Jake and the Fatman*."

"Well, I've got an MBA, and I've never heard of Ahab, and if I've never heard of him, nobody else has either, so take it out."

And so it went.

(A few weeks later, I went to my local comic book store and purchased a Classics Illustrated version of *Moby Dick* and mailed it to him.)

The occasional dumb note notwithstanding, most rewriting is done in an honest effort by the staff to make the script as good and as producible as humanly possible. The only other time one encounters gray areas is when staffers take the next step of adding their names to freelance scripts. Yes, that's right; you can write a script for television, turn it in, switch on the TV and find someone else's name right there alongside your own—or above your own or there as sole writer—with only *story by* credit next to your name. You see it all the time on TV shows as a viewer, and it's something that freelancers must understand before going into the business.

Credit Sharing and Arbitration

Under WGA guidelines, if a story editor or producer rewrites your script and contributes roughly 50 percent or more to the finished script, he can attach his name to your script as cowriter. If it's a page-one rewrite, so that the totality of the script is profoundly altered, the staffer can claim sole script credit and relegate your credit to only *story by*. But this is not the end of the process; the script and all prior versions are required to automatically be sent for WGA arbitration as soon as a staffer alters the writing credit. The various drafts are then examined by objective outsiders (your name is not present on the script) to determine the amount of new material added by the staffer. The WGA then makes the final determination about credits.

This is a very sensitive issue within the WGA because the moment a staffer adds her name to your script, that staffer then shares in your residuals *in perpetuity*. The more staffers who share in your credit, the less you get. And more than a few shows produce scripts with three, four or, in some cases, even six credits. Consequently, many freelancers feel that staffers rewrite unnecessarily simply in order to jump their credits. Staffers, in turn, complain that if they have to take time away from their scripts to totally rewrite an otherwise unproducible script, killing their weekends and nights with work the freelancer should've done right in the first place, they deserve some compensation.

Where in this is the truth? Somewhere in between, I suspect. I don't think many producers indulge in credit jumping. Some do, but they're the minority. And freelancers are wrong in that they see conspiracy and cupidity where in fact the problem is an attitudinal one. Arbitration is too often done simply as a matter of course, indiscriminately. Producers have grown too casual about it; arbitrations must be considered individually and invoked sparingly. Staffers are already earning a salary; the only income the freelancer has is from the residuals. Why cut into that so casually? I've worked on nearly four hundred scripts on various television series over the last decade; given the amount of rewriting I tend to do, I could've put my name on one-third to one-half of that figure. Instead, I've added my name to only about half a dozen, and even then only under unusual or extreme circumstances. On many shows I've worked on, like *Murder, She Wrote* (under the tenure of me and exec producer David Moessinger) and

Babylon 5, we imposed a strict nonarbitration policy favoring freelancers. Because if you're gonna talk the talk, you better walk the walk.

Post-Revisionist Scripting

Once a script is completed (having sometimes been revised to within an inch of its life), the script enters the production stage. It is broken down by locations and sets, since standard practice is to lump all of the scenes that take place in one set together and shoot them out of sequence before moving on to the next set. Costume designers and other production staff get into the act. In the case of sitcoms and a few dramatic series, the script is read by the cast gathered around a big table, at which time some additional line tweaking can take place.

If the writing staff has done its job correctly, the cast and director receive their final production scripts a week or two prior to shooting. If not, sometimes scripts can end up being revised during shooting, which is a nightmare no freelancer ever wants to experience. Some shows have had to slow down production while they wait for new pages to slow-dance out of the producer's office.

Some shows have a funny attitude toward their writers, in that they're happy to have them around when the script is actually being written, but once it's turned in, they'd much prefer it if you vanished altogether. The reason for this, I'm told, is that sometimes the presence of a writer on the set can so thoroughly unman the director that he falls apart (a notion much in conflict with the proffered image of the director as the one unflappable captain at the wheel). Other shows welcome their freelance and staff writers and encourage them to be present on the set to assist with any changes that might be required. Anyone reading this book can probably guess which approach seems the more sensible. A writer on-set or later in the production process is a valuable resource too often discarded.

When I adapted *The Strange Case of Dr. Jekyll and Mr. Hyde* for Showtime, I indicated that I'd like to be present at the final audio mix. There was much resistance, particularly from the director, but eventually they relented, and I attended and sat quietly throughout the mixing process—until the end. As I watched, the character of Mr. Hyde drew close, walking through the shadows, the light casting great shadows on his face, the music swelling, the camera moving—and no dialogue came from his mouth. Now, I knew there were supposed to be lines at that point— *important* lines, because they explained much of what had gone before.

I looked around to see if anyone else had noticed the glitch, but each person there—the director, the sound effects designer, the editor, the composer—was focused on his or her area of specialization. There was, in short, no one looking out for the script. At the end of the session, just as they prepared to lock down the show and ship it, I held up my hand and said, "I think we've got a problem." From their expressions, I knew what they were thinking: another troublesome freelance writer. Very patiently, I explained what I'd seen: missing lines.

Under protest, they rolled back the film, convinced that there *were* no lines in that part. Then they looked at the film more closely and saw that his lips were moving. Words were supposed to be there. They checked the audio logs and discovered that the actor had skipped the lines because of sound problems on the stage, and the editor had forgotten to lay the lines back in again. A few minutes later, they found the missing lines and, rather sheepishly, put them back in again.

If a writer hadn't been there, at that exact moment, the problem would either have gone undetected until broadcast, at which time there would've been hell to pay, or it would've cost a great deal of money to go back into the audio studio to remix the episode just to drop in three or four lines of dialogue. So to the directors and producers out there who think that a writer on premises is more trouble than it's worth, you're wrong. As executive producer for *Babylon 5*, I instituted standard policy that the freelance writers were not only welcome, but encouraged to come to the set, to modify lines or answer questions from the cast or director in the eventuality that I might not be available. It's simply common sense.

Once shooting is completed, the script is locked down, but even that can change in editing. (I recommend all fledgling television writers find some way to get into an editing room and watch the process of putting a show together; you will learn more about structure in those few hours than nearly anywhere else.) In editing, you discover that whole scenes can be moved around without damaging the structure of the drama and, in some cases, may even make the show better. A structure that looks good on paper sometimes changes when the script has been filmed. Once you actually see the finished scene in editing, sometimes you discover that a story point isn't sufficiently clear, and the actors are brought in to loop dialogue, either replacing original dialogue (done by cutting to another person, over whose face we hear the new lines) or adding whole new passages (using the same technique or showing the back of the head of the person doing the talking—and believe me, I've seen more than my share of follicles in my time). On other occasions, you'll find that the episode is too long or too short. The producer then starts cutting a few lines here and there and those long, lingering pans and establishing shots that directors love so much. Often major amounts of story material have to be cut from or added to the episode. (When that happens, the first thing invariably cut is humor, then characterization, then action, then plot.) I've even shunted whole scenes (usually character-oriented scenes that are capable of standing alone) *between episodes* when one came in short and the other long.

Once editing is completed, the episode is spotted (the producer indicates where music and sound effects go within the episode), color-corrected, special effects are inserted into the final cut, and at last, the show is audio-mixed and delivered to the network or studio. It's now that the freelance writer gets a finished copy of his work, sometimes up to three months after turning it in. At that point, the only important thing is that you have your first produced television episode in your hands, and that can open a lot of doors. The broadcast earns you exposure; the episode becomes a calling card and initiates you into the sometimes rather loopy fraternity of TeeVee writers. So go home, call all your family and friends (and the few who said you'd never make it) and throw a big party the night it airs. You've earned it.

But that's not the end of the story, not if you're serious about television writing. If this is something other than a test to see if you can do it, you have to press on; try to sell another script to the same show or another show in the same genre. If your initial query letter to agents and producers netted you few replies, the ability to now add to your letter "and I just had my latest script produced by *Star Trek: Space Monkeys on Patrol*" will result in a greater proportion of positive responses.

Over time, you'll discover that you're developing a track record, a reputation. Producers come to know what they can expect from you in terms of style, plot and your ability to meet deadlines. When this happens, producers start calling you and asking if you'd like to take a shot at writing for their new shows. Like anyone else, producers are often most comfortable when they're dealing with a known quantity. That's why some writers make it a point to develop specific reputations. Some are good rewriters, "body and fender men," to use a common, though sexist, term; some are "firemen," producer/writers who are brought in to save a struggling show; others are good at plotting, while others find their forte is scripting dialogue (with the two often working together, which is why you frequently see two names on a scriptwriting credit); others specialize by genre. Networks come to know you by name and ask for you. Studios want to put you under contract in-house to produce or create your own series.

A Show of Your Own

Once again, this isn't something a new writer should even attempt. This can happen only after you've gone through all the stages of acceptance described above. I tell this to new writers over and over, but invariably most of them don't listen and thus waste valuable time better spent establishing themselves with current shows. "Oh, but I've got a friend who has an in with a producer," they tell me at conventions and seminars, "who's got a deal with the network, and it's a sure thing. They just need the finished treatment to make the deal."

"And have they paid you for this yet?"

"No, but it's a sure thing. They just can't pay me until it's approved by the network."

If you hear this from someone who wants you to write a series for her, you're being exploited. I take pains to describe this exactly because this is the sort of line that's used repeatedly on young writers who don't know any better by fledgling or phony producers who *should* know better. Don't fall for it.

And even if you are an established writer, the odds of selling a series aren't great. Perry Lafferty, a prime-time programming executive at CBS responsible for shepherding such programs as *Rawhide*, *The Twilight Zone*, *All in the Family*, *Maude* and *The Mary Tyler Moore Show*, succinctly described the plight of selling original programs: "Each network gets in the vicinity of three thousand bona fide submissions a year. Most of them are quickly discarded because they're bad. It usually comes down to ordering up about one hundred scripts out of those three thousand ideas. Out of those hundred scripts, you make about twenty-five pilots, and out of those twenty-five pilots, you may get about four on the air. And out of the four, maybe one will last and continue into a second season. These are the worst odds I've ever heard, but everybody in town is trying to sell the networks programs."

As a footnote to the preceding, the remaining twenty-one pilots are almost always aired sooner or later, though not necessarily in prime time. The networks have to at least try and recoup the losses incurred in production, so they usually end up broadcasting the programs late at night, when they hope no one important is watching, and charge advertisers just to balance out the cost of production.

There are basically two ways of selling a series.

1. As mentioned, a studio makes an overall development deal with you. You generally move into an office on the studio lot and write for some of

the current shows as well as develop series concepts. The studio takes you to meetings with the networks, where the idea is pitched. If the network likes it, it pays to develop the idea further, through series bible, outline and script. (A *series bible* contains all of the data needed to know where the show is going: characters, basic story line, sample episode synopses, probable budget and other items.) Sometimes, if a studio is very excited about a project or it wants greater ownership of the property, it'll pay to develop the property in-house, then take it to the networks when it's more complete.

2. The writer develops the material on his own time and then takes the finished material around to studios, in the hope they will back it at a network, or the writer takes the property to a network, which if it likes the project assigns it to a studio or production company.

THE TELEVISION MOVIE (MOW)

Over the years, movies made for television have grown in prominence and quantity, particularly since it can often cost almost as much to license a theatrical film for first-run broadcast as it does to actually produce an entire television movie. In addition, the audience for first-run motion picture showings on television has decreased because of the pay cable industry. Why should a viewer watch a sanitized version of a popular motion picture on commercial television when he can watch an unedited version of the movie on cable, six months or a year sooner, without commercial interruption?

Which is also why you can see a nifty motion picture in a theater one week, and not long thereafter, find a movie-for-television that deals with a similar topic, but slanted enough to make it different. The philosophy here is that the appetite of the audience has been whetted by the film, thereby guaranteeing a hefty rating for a television movie along similar lines.

Most TV movies are topical in nature, often based on the latest head-lines before the newsprint has had the chance to dry completely. Whenever a spectacular court case takes place, network executives and producers are quickly on the scene, trying to purchase the principal's rights to the story, racing to be the first network to air a TV movie based on the case. In the case of the 1993 Waco, Texas, shootout between police and members of a cult organization, producers were shooting a television movie during the standoff, changing events in the script to reflect new twists in the real story happening outside.

Because network demographics have indicated that the primary audience for TV movies are women, most such projects are skewed toward women's interests, or more generalized "illness of the week" stories.

But a good TV movie need not be based on real events to be good drama. And it's here that the division between the broadcsat and cable networks becomes most clear. Networks, which have the capacity to move more quickly, and have large amounts of money to throw around, tend to favor the docudrama format. Cable networks such as USA or TNT generally can't move as quickly, and have fewer resources, and thus tend to favor fictional stories, which are more "evergreen" in nature, not necessarily tied into any current news story. Broadcast network revenues are pinned to first-run, whereas cable revenues accumulate over time and through reruns. Knowing this will help you determine where to pitch your TV movie project.

One ancillary benefit to a successful fictional TV movie is that it has the potential of being turned into a regular prime-time series. This is known in the business as "a backdoor series." This is probably the one means by which a new writer can even nominally circumvent the gatekeeping process by which networks determine who can sell them series. Here, again, you're going to have to write the full script on spec, using the film format provided here, and in the screenwriting section. If you think the movie could serve as a backdoor pilot, then it's in your vested interest to write a brief (10-20 page) treatment expanding on the movie, and how it could be made to function as a weekly series. This treatment should provide further information about the characters, how they relate over time, what makes the show different from others currently on the air (or what makes it similar to a successful series on another network), and what kinds of stories could be presented in such a series. Whatever your idea might be, it must have the potential for new plots to develop spontaneously. If the only way to bring in characters and new stories is to force the issue, the series will stagnate and quickly run out of ideas. (This is one of the key factors that producers use in determining backdoor pilots . . . will all the stories be the same, and if not, how do the characters get into these other stories?)

In order to sell such a program, it is almost mandatory to have some kind of representation, usually an agent. But if you've got a dynamite television movie script on your hands, you won't have too much trouble getting an agent to represent it. And if the concept is that good, the odds are fair you'll at least get the networks to look at it.

Chapter Five

A Look at the Future

For most of television's history, the three networks had a seemingly unbreakable grip on programming. Viewers had to take whatever was offered because, with the exception of syndicated reruns and movies on independent local stations, there simply wasn't much else to look at. Then came cable television, video stores, videocassette recorders, laser discs, direct broadcast satellite services, computers, CD-ROM, CD-I and the lure of interactive TV and virtual reality just over the horizon. In short, we have a wider selection of means of distracting ourselves.

The impact made by these technological breakthroughs has already been significant. Network and independent studies have shown that in the two-year span between November 1978 and November 1980, competing program sources such as those noted above eroded the networks' share of the total national viewing audience from 93.3 percent to 88.5 percent.

In addition, the broadcast marketplace has begun to alter in significant ways. As of 1995, recent regulatory changes by the FCC will allow the networks to own and produce their own programs, instead of having to contract out to major studios for the majority of their programs. This is one of the major reasons for the recent development of studio-based networks, such as the Universal Action-Pack, the Warner Bros. Network, the Prime-Time Entertainment Network, and the United Paramount Network, all of which went on-line by 1995. The studios now realize they don't have a death grip on network programming, which will probably be shifted to in-house network operations. If the networks stop buying their shows, they feel they have no choice but to create their *own* networks.

This situation will have long-term effects on the marketplace for the next five to ten years, as stations shift alliances and the longevity of these fledgling networks is decided in the court of public opinion. In 1994 alone, a large number of CBS stations went over to Fox in a move that shocked industry watchers, causing CBS to grab for independent stations, which in turn are being wooed by the new networks.

While this may be less than reassuring for the networks, the rise of competing networks and program sources would seem to herald a boom of immense proportions for television writers. The more program providers there are, the more programs they'll need to provide, meaning that much more potential work for TV writers.

BASIC CABLE

The cable industry started primarily as a means of routing television signals to locations too distant or obscured by natural obstacles to receive their local stations clearly. But the technology of cablecasting makes it capable of carrying an immense number of signals, far more than the few local stations availing themselves of this technology. This has led to the development of new local cable-only stations, which costs considerably less than opening up a broadcast station. This has led to a substantive increase in locally and minority-oriented programs. Where none existed before, there are now Spanish- and Japanese-language television stations, religious stations, public service and information stations, all requiring written material. Stations such as these provide an excellent educational tool and an outlet for local television writers who lack the experience to approach the networks. It is expected that independent cablecasting will continue to grow at a rapid rate, providing an ever-increasing stream of opportunities for fledgling telescripters.

Along with the small independent cablecasters, the last few years have seen the rise of massive cable networks, starting with Ted Turner's Cable News Networks (CNN) and the Entertainment and Sports Programming Network (ESPN), each carried without additional charge by the subscribing cable company. Now we have the Sci-Fi Channel, E! Entertainment, Comedy Central, MTV, VH1, superstations WOR and WGN, Court TV, Nickelodeon, Arts & Entertainment Network, the Discovery Channel, Bravo, a plethora of shopping channels, The Learning Channel and, the soon-to-come Romance Channel and other special interest cable networks.

Each of these new operations promises expanded opportunities for television writers in the area of basic cable—opportunities that show no sign of decreasing in the near future. (In the next few years, incidentally, insiders expect MTV to initiate greater amounts of youth-oriented dramatic- and comedy-series programming, possibly keying into some local broadcast stations to expand their viewership.) Most of the growth will be in the area of TV movies, though some, such as Comedy Central and the Sci-Fi Channel, are already moving into producing original series. The

USA Network has, until now, been primarily a venue for original movies but is also beginning to expand into series production.

PAY CABLE

Along with the rise of basic cable, for which viewers pay a monthly service fee, came the idea of pay cable, which also was warmly received. For an additional monthly fee, the viewer is given access to any of a number of pay cable services, which provide a wide selection of movies and variety specials piped in along the same cable. By 1981, there were already three major pay cable programmers: Home Box Office (HBO), owned by Time, Inc.; Showtime, owned by Teleprompter and Viacom; and The Movie Channel, owned by Warner Communications and American Express. By that same year, each of these programmers was earning, respectively, $432 million, $96 million and $48 million in yearly revenues. By 1985, estimates for total revenue by pay cable operations came to nearly $6 billion.

At first, it seemed as if the only impact this new service would have on scriptwriters would be a modest increase in revenues earned through residuals on motion pictures. But pay cable programmers discovered early on that their systems had a high rate of disconnects. Although the movies shown on their systems were cablecast before the networks were able to do so, it seemed that customers just weren't content to wait through three days of rerun features to see something new. It quickly became obvious that they would need to (1) buy as many features as possible to limit the number of reruns, and (2) expand the nature of their service to include original programming.

As a consequence, the pay cable industries have begun producing their own serials, weekly series, miniseries, documentary specials and biographical specials keyed to recent news events. HBO in particular has led the vanguard of original programming, producing comedy specials, series such as *Tales From the Crypt*, *Dream On*, *The Larry Sanders Show* and highly rated original movies such as *Fatherland* and *Barbarians at the Gate*. In 1995, a new *Outer Limits* series began on Showtime, which also produced *Shelley Duvall's Nightmare Classics* (which gave me the wonderful opportunity to work with Shelley on several projects).

One of the benefits of pay cable—aside from the expanded opportunities—is the fact that language and mature content restrictions are considerably looser than on either the broadcast or basic cable operations. If you feel the need to avail yourself of the more colorful portions of the language, you can do so. Also, there are no commercial interruptions to break up the flow of the story.

One addendum, though: Increasingly in the last few years, and into the foreseeable future, the pay cable services are forming alliances with broadcast operations to help defray the costs of production. Shows that run on pay cable are promised to one or another broadcast venue in return for up-front licensing fees. As a result, original programs made for pay cable are often filmed two ways, with and without nudity or harsh language. And while the cablecast may not have any commercial breaks, the later rebroadcast on regular stations will have them, so it still behooves television writers to think in fairly standard structure when writing their programs for pay cable.

PAY-PER-VIEW CABLE

At the present time, this isn't offering substantial benefits to writers, since most pay-per-view (PPV) programs tend to be sports programs or otherwise built around events or spectacles. The remaining PPV programs are usually recent movies that haven't yet been released to pay cable and can be purchased one viewing at a time from cable systems that offer interactive remotes. Some cable systems are also using this system to offer adult fare and even X-rated shopping services.

In the next few years, however, industry analysts feel that PPV may include original programming, mainly in the form of movies and miniseries, as well as music and comedy specials. It seems very doubtful at this point that weekly series will ever be offered through PPV.

DIRECT BROADCAST SATELLITES

At this juncture, despite its high-tech nature, Direct Broadcast Satellites (DBS) remain primarily a delivery system as opposed to a programming system. Through eighteen-inch satellite receivers (small enough to be mounted unobtrusively outside the house), viewers have access to all basic and pay cable systems, PPV and other services, delivered in digital audio and video for maximum clarity. The system is having a hard time getting off the ground, as it were, due to the fact that local stations can't be carried by DBS. Meaning that even with all the fancy bells and whistles, you still need either a standard antenna or basic cable system to pull in your local network affiliates. There is as yet no clear indication as to whether there will ever be a need for original programming produced specifically for DBS.

VIDEOCASSETTES AND VIDEODISCS

With the vast proliferation of videotape decks and laser disc players, this market has exploded, pulling in as much as $5 billion annually or more.

At first considered of use mainly to professionals in the field, the home videocassette recorder (VCR) has had a profound impact on the networks. In addition to providing alternate programming, they wreaked havoc with the ratings system because while the television might be turned to one station, the VCR could very well be tuned to another network altogether, recording the program for later viewing. Fittingly, the networks are largely responsible for the increasing popularity of VCRs. It all started with the idea of counterprogramming: If ABC was running a blockbuster program at 9:00 P.M., CBS and NBC countered by running equally monumental programs at the same time. As a result, everyone lost. The viewer had to choose between three equally attractive options, and each of the networks only received half or a third of the possible ratings they might have won if they'd run their programs without such stiff competition. VCRs negated that dilemma once and for all.

But the role of VCRs has expanded beyond merely recording counter-programmed television broadcasts. Theatrical films no sooner leave the local theater than they show up on cassette, usually before being sold to cable, in order to maximize income from viewers who simply *have* to own a particular film. One of the newer growth industries in Los Angeles and other major cities is the construction of entire home theaters for viewing such movies in maximum comfort. This has been further encouraged by the development of laser discs, which provide far greater video and audio quality and come very close to approximating the experience of watching a film in your local theater.

Starting about 1989, as well as selling theatrical films into cassette markets, studios began playing with the notion of producing original movies for cassette, a market that soon came to be known as "direct to video." Paramount was one of the first to jump on this new market, creating several in-house entities specifically to produce low-budget (usually in the $3 million range) movies for release on cassette. For the most part, such movies tend to be thrillers, often with a slightly mature, exploitational or erotic theme, to make them more enticing to adults looking for something to watch on a Friday night.

Such low-budget features have proven to be a good means of breaking in for new writers. There is every indication that the direct-to-video market will continue to grow and need scripts, and to further expand into other areas, such as children's programs. In fact, the entire Barney the Dinosaur megamillion dollar empire was built upon a small operation creating and selling direct-to-video children's programs.

DESKTOP TELEVISION

Here's a term you will begin hearing more and more as we creep toward the turn of the century. Call it the democratization of television.

By the mid-1990s, the line between home computers and home television systems had begun to blur, and within the next five to ten years that line may very well vanish altogether. The system I'm using to revise this book comes with a sound and video system capable of playing and, in limited ways, recording both video and audio signals. For an additional five-hundred-dollar hookup, I can attach video cameras and create short programs that are digitally encoded and saved as files on the hard drive. Right now, it's only the size of the drive and the system's memory capacity that limit the size of the program. Already you can download clips from various TV shows from national computer networks like CompuServe, GEnie and America OnLine to play on your home system; in a very short time, you'll be able to download entire movies into your computer for playback on either your system's monitor or the home TV.

Babylon 5 is perhaps the first series produced entirely as a slightly more advanced form of desktop television. Once the episode is filmed, the film is transferred to videotape. The videotape is then run through an Avid computer so that every take of every scene is available in digitized form on the hard drive. (The Avid, though on the expensive side, is not that much larger than many contemporary home systems.) The episode is then edited on the Avid, and when finally edited down to size, the data from the Avid is transferred to another disk and shipped to the postproduction house, The film is assembled overnight by a supercomputer. The cost is substantially less than standard editing.

The Emmy-winning effects on *Babylon 5* are also desktop in nature: The computer-generated images (CGI) are produced on a series of Amiga and IBM computers not much different from the one I'm using as a word processor. Rotoscope effects (gun blasts and other opticals) are done on a souped-up Macintosh home computer. Our matte paintings for composite shots are done in northern California on our designer's home system and modemed or shipped down to us on disk. *Babylon 5* has also pioneered the use of virtual sets, using computers to digitally create a room or a starship or the surface of a planet and compositing the actor directly into the computer-generated background. Though often indistinguishable from a real set, there is in reality only an actor and a blue screen.

Within the next few years, what once cost up to a million dollars to produce for television, affordable only by networks, will be able to be done (nonunion) at a cost of maybe $30,000 to $40,000 or less, well within the budget of someone really determined to get her vision out where other people can see it. What desktop publishing did to revolutionize the magazine and book industry, it will also do to the television industry.

By the turn of the century, you could have a scenario in which you go to a local desktop television facility (assuming you don't already own one), create a one-hour or two-hour program for about what it costs to create a self-published novel and make it available via download from a computer network or sell it on cassette, CD-ROM, or videodisc.

But more than anything else, there is one important way in which this will affect the television industry over the next ten years. This will not only have a direct impact on how TV writers make their living, but the form of the markets themselves, and in a way ties back to the history of television.

Ever since television came along, the production of TV series and movies has been almost exclusively the province of the major studios. As mentioned, if you sell a concept to a network on your own, you are assigned to a studio, assuming you haven't already come in with one. (Each major studio has literally dozens of subcompanies and independent production companies working on its lot, but they're all still under the aegis of the major studio, and none of them can currently decide on its own to produce a series without the cooperation of the studio.) This is because of the traditionally high cost of television production. Generally, a network pays the studio a license fee to produce the show, roughly $800,000 per hour. But most series cost considerably more than that, from $1 million to $1.9 million per hour. No independent producer in Hollywood could conceivably cover that much extra cost (deficit financing). Only a studio could handle it, knowing that if the series goes on a few years, the studio can recoup its investment in long-term syndication.

But we're rapidly approaching a point where the cost of making a TV series is dropping and can drop further if handled properly. *Babylon 5* was just such an effort, produced off the studio lot for a fixed fee from the network. Using the full resources of desktop television, *Babylon 5* became the first science fiction series ever produced to come in under budget; the pilot, the first season and the second season to date have all cost slightly less than the allocated license fee.

What this means is that, just as with desktop publishing, desktop television will lead to the ability of independent producers to come to the plate and produce entire series for the license fee, without having to go to a studio for deficit financing. So instead of having a handful of monolithic studios, you may very well end up with dozens of boutique production companies capable of buying, selling and producing TV series. The more buyers, the better the chance of selling your property and the greater the competition for material.

This will be further complicated by the fact that the studios are still applying their original approach from the 1950s in their attempts to create networks in the 1990s (showing, again, why knowing the history of the medium can come in handy). During their first attempt at network birthing, the motivation was to use a new network to employ actors, directors, writers and crews already under contract. Similarly, the studios today are hoping to use their new networks mainly to employ their own people, i.e., Paramount would like all the shows on its network to be produced in-house by Paramount, Warner Bros. would prefer that it produce the shows to air on the Warners Network, but the stations committed to these networks are already concerned about letting any studio have a monopoly on producing their series. They believe (wisely) that competition from outside producers will result in a better selection of material. If over the long haul any of the new networks lock out all other producers except for its own people, it runs the risk of eventually being nailed legally, just as Paramount was forced to divest its theater chain because of the monopoly involved.

Since the notion of one studio selling to the network owned by another studio is going to be awkward, given the competition sure to arise between them, this will further necessitate the rise of smaller, independent companies capable of producing series off the lot. And once again, the more buyers, the better your chances of selling to one of them.

NETWORKS

Will this form of alternative programming pose another threat to network programming? No, not really. The networks have always thrived on two things: spectacle and star performers, neither of which will be in the hands of average folks. And to be sure, much of the desktop television will be on a par with much of desktop publishing—eccentric, specialized and often not very good. But as a venue, it's coming, it's already real and it's going to need scripts like everything else.

The death of the networks has been announced many times over the last dozen years, and each time they have come back from the grave and show every sign of continuing to survive into the twenty-first century. Part of this is due simply to the comfort factor; they're *there*, they often do very good work, we've grown up with them, we're comfortable with them. . . .

Let me be absolutely clear on what follows: This is not the voice of the author speaking. This is what I was told by one high-ranking executive with one of the networks when I wondered aloud about the future of the networks. (I don't make the news, I just report it, in this case without comment.) "The networks aren't going anywhere. You know why? Because the stone cold fact is that not everybody out there can afford to buy a VCR or a computer or a laser disc player. Hell, there are folks out there who can barely afford a black-and-white TV, but they've got to have their TV. We provide that. Now, what that means is that as time goes on and consumers with disposable income—the more educated viewers, for the most part—move on to discs and tape and satellites, we'll end up with less-educated, somewhat lower-income viewers. But even viewers in these demographics have to eat, brush their teeth, buy new tires and clothes for their kids. Sure, to some extent we may have to adjust our programming slightly to appeal more to that audience, but one way or another, the networks are here to stay."

Anything I would have to say after that would only be redundant.

In the next five years or so, expect one of the major film studios to purchase one of the networks, consolidating both the means of production and the means of distribution of television product.

TECHNOLOGICAL ADVANCES

The emerging technologies may have ancillary and unexpected benefits for television writers. While it is still necessary to live in Los Angeles in order to break into TV writing, it is no longer entirely necessary (though still helpful) for you to live there once you've broken in.

Most of the TV production houses utilize standardized software for scripts, usually Movie Master or Scriptor. So if you're working in one of these formats, the need to present a hard copy (paper) version of your script is reduced; you can just send it in via phone lines direct from your home computer to the system at the office. In just the last two seasons of *Babylon 5*, freelance writers modemed me their scripts from northern California and as far east as Long Island. A writer on another series currently living in Italy does the same.

Modems can also help new writers by allowing them to plug into the many national computer systems where other writers, story editors and producers hang out, sometimes informally, other times to promote specific programs. I'm regularly on several different computer networks, as are many other writer/producers, including Chris Carter, executive producer of *The X-Files*. There are whole sections of these networks set aside for new writers where they can ask questions of professional TV writers and make valuable contacts. Some, such as GEnie or CompuServe, even provide on-line scriptwriting workshops for television writers. When I'm on the Internet (my address is straczynski@geis.com), I respond directly to questions from hundreds of people across the country who might never otherwise have the opportunity to speak with someone in this position.

Just one more aspect of the democratization of television.

CONCLUSIONS

Trying to predict the future is a mug's game on the best of days, and if the history of television teaches us anything, it's that the beast has more twists and turns and surprises than a carny roller coaster without a safety permit. But there is one trait of television that will continue to be emblematic of the medium for the foreseeable decades: It will continue to expand and provide more and varied opportunities for new and established television writers.

Whether you become a part of that expansion depends on your answers to some basic questions: How badly do you want it, and how far are you prepared to go in pursuing it? Do you actually want a career in television writing, or do you simply want the Pointy Hat that says "I Did It"?

Assuming for the moment that you're one of the majority of people who don't live in Los Angeles, are you prepared to uproot your life, move to Los Angeles, and spend a minimum of three years (the average time required to sell a first script) knocking on doors and pounding the pavement? Because that's what it takes.

Someone once said, "Many people mistake a love of reading for a passion to write." Similarly, many people mistake a love of television—our friend through childhood, companion on cold nights, provider of status and royalty checks—with the desire to tell a story within the confines of that medium. Be *honest* with yourself: What do you want, and why? Many of us admire the skill of a physician, but do you want to spend the years required for medical training, or is what you really want simply the experience of participating in a heart transplant to see what it's like?

I cannot overemphasize this point: If you want to come and play in the big leagues—network television, TV movies, cable, syndication—you're going to have to learn your craft, same as a doctor or a lawyer. I'm a *writer*. This is my chosen profession. I work at it every day, trying to get better. The field is deluged with dilettantes and tourists and wanna-bes. They're not storytellers; they just want the money and the status.

If it seems I'm being harsh, more so than in the other chapters of this book, you're correct. But I do so out of concern. Because of this book, my work for Writer's Digest and having labored in this particular field for so long, I've had occasion to see many, many people come here without being sufficiently prepared or disciplined or determined, and more than any other medium, television is a cruel mistress when she rejects you. I've seen people lured here and spend their hard-won savings on bogus workshops and groups and "agents" who charge inappropriate fees, nickeling-and-diming them to death . . . I've seen people's dreams destroyed before their very eyes.

The lucky ones finally go home, devastated but intact, and apply their acquired skills to other venues. The unlucky ones linger on, sometimes for years. They're never any closer to the brass ring that dangles tantalizingly close to their eyes every day, dying by inches when each new "sure thing" falls apart, growing resentful and angry over the unfairness of it all.

Understand: This is a town where hope can kill you.

But it is also a town where dreams are rewarded for those who can fashion them with skill and grace.

If you have a story to tell and the talent to tell it well, television provides the rare and wonderful opportunity to transmit your stories to millions of homes, touching the hearts and minds of a nation. For those with the required levels of determination, talent, persistence and luck, the financial rewards can be immense.

Within the next five to ten years, industry analysts predict as many as five hundred competing channels, offering dramas, sitcoms, movies, miniseries and a host of other programs. That hunger must be fed. And if it is indeed your desire to be a part of that, a decision made with eyes open and aware, then you are welcome to the community of writers. Because television benefits from a multiplicity of voices, from perspectives gained in parts of the country other than the Valley and Beverly Hills. The more of *you* there are working *here*, the more *here* will gradually become more representative of all of you out *there*.

And that can only be a good thing for both sides.

Good luck.

PART II

Motion Pictures

You have to remember that as soon as you hand in a finished script, the producer says to you, "This is a great script!" Then they hire two guys to rewrite you.
—Mario Puzo

It's easy to sit at your desk and write in the script, "The desert. Dawn." But five months later, you're waking up at 3 A.M. in a motel outside Flagstaff, wondering what the hell you're doing there.
—Marshall Brickman

Chapter Six

A Brief History of Motion Pictures

The age of motion pictures is generally conceded to have begun at the end of the nineteenth century with the invention and subsequent patenting of a device called a *Kinetoscope*, developed by Thomas Edison. This device allowed a series of transparencies to be recorded sequentially onto a single strip of negative film. When developed, printed and replayed at the original recording speed, it created a moving picture. Prior to this time, most so-called "moving pictures" known to the general public were available only in penny arcades and consisted of machines that would flip a series of still photographs one atop the other at a rate sufficient to create the illusion of motion.

As soon as the process of making motion pictures became relatively bug proof, the entrepreneurs moved in. In short order, arcades offering *nickelodeons*—machines similar to their still-photograph predecessors but using Edison's newly developed technology—began popping up across the country. To avoid paying the going rate for Edison's newly patented device, many of these entrepreneurs built variations on the camera equipment he pioneered, pilfering his work and his techniques without paying either royalties or the least attention to the patent laws. In the interests of accuracy and fairness, it should be mentioned, however, that not all producers of early films adapted the technology of Edison's cameras; only about a third of those in the business built and adapted the technology.

Another third purchased the equipment legally and in strict adherence to U.S. patent laws. The remaining third just said the heck with it, went out and stole the equipment. Such is the nature of progress.

Edison took everyone who violated his patent to court and invariably won. He was appropriately ruthless in the defense of his patent, and as a result, many early filmmakers decided to rethink their positions. It made no sense for these filmmakers, all based on the East Coast within spitting distance of Edison's lawyers, to steal from him. Logic and morality told them that at that kind of proximity they would only be caught and fined.

So they did the smart thing.

They left town.

Groups of filmmakers fled the East Coast and headed west to avoid inspection by Edison's agents or government officials. Since California was pretty much as far west as they could travel without getting their equipment wet, that's where many of these filmmakers decided to set up permanent camp. In time, legitimate filmmakers also ventured westward, lured not by escape but by the tantalizing prospect of making films all year long, thanks to California's sunny climate (useful for the slow film and poor lighting conditions) and mild winters.

This confluence of events led to a flood of silent movies being shipped out of California. Given that vast portions of California were still undeveloped, it made sense that most of these films were westerns. Western filmmakers didn't need to construct elaborate sets; the only requirements were a horse, a star, a wide-eyed palpitating heroine and a few hills. In fact, many filmmakers simply purchased vacant lots, propped up a few rudimentary sets, which they recycled from movie to movie with minimal redressing, and called the result a studio. (Hence the reason motion picture studios are called "lots" to this day.) The first four-walled studio that really deserved that appellation was constructed by director Francis Boggs in 1909. His efforts were so well received that he was promptly shot and killed by a nearby Japanese gardener who took exception to the racket caused by Boggs's filmmaking.

By 1910, actors were being paid the hefty sum of five dollars per day and generally worked without on-screen credit. Many were professional stage actors who couldn't find work elsewhere and were ashamed of appearing in what were often referred to as "galloping tintypes." As a result, they were as much surprised as anyone else when a huge market developed for these one- or two-reel westerns. As the number of films being produced escalated, with some filmmakers turning out as many as a film each week, the number of studios proper (or improper) also swelled. Anyone who could afford to buy a camera and enlist the support of a few good performers headed west in hopes of starting his own cinematic empire.

The second gold rush was on.

A good number of the silent films ground out during this period were, of necessity, pretty awful. But enough good ones made it through that even die-hard skeptics had to sit up and take notice. These films were the work of such men as Cecil B. DeMille; William Fox, the creator of what is now Twentieth Century Fox; and Adolph Zukor, founder of Paramount

Pictures. As the form became more respectable and more profitable, the films became more ambitious. In short order, the nation was flooded with epic westerns, love stories, comedies and Egyptian sagas, which were very much in vogue then. These were the banner years that gave us Chaplin and Lloyd and Fairbanks and Clara Bow and Theda Bara and many others.

Interestingly enough, while silent-film actors and directors became widely known and respected, writers were almost invisible, in large measure because they often didn't exist. The director decided what he wanted in a scene, performers knew how to stage a fight or fall down a flight of stairs upon demand . . . what else was needed? The only real writing that went into these early silent films was the continuity cards inserted at critical moments to advance the plot, and these were usually written slapdash by the director or a company flunky. One director of the time termed writers "more or less useless" and doubted if the written word would ever play a substantial role in filmmaking beyond simply setting up the general idea and the rough progression of events.

Which is of course very different from the way films are made today. Today, they only *think* they can get by without writers.

CHANGES, SOCIAL AND OTHERWISE

To fully understand the early film years and the great changes that have taken place, it's necessary to reinforce just how different the filmgoing experience was during those early years. The majority of theaters boasted what were called traveling tabloid performances, or simply "tab shows." In addition to the feature presentation, audiences were treated to two or more live orchestral pieces, a musical dance number, an occasional recital, a newsreel, a short subject and whatever else the theater owner could think of to throw into the batch. It was a whole day's outing, a community event where you'd say hello to friends or leave the kids for the afternoon, returning for the later showings to enjoy the work of vaudevillians whose regular venues were being driven out of business by the movies.

To go to a movie house then was an event.

The first really significant change that rocked the film industry for studios and patrons alike was the advent of sound movies. Over the course of three successive years, Warners Bros. made movie history by introducing the first picture with a synchronized musical score, *Don Juan*, in 1926; the first film with spoken dialogue, Al Jolson's *The Jazz Singer*, in 1927; and then, in 1928, the first all-talkie, *The Lights of New York*, with Brian Foy.

Many producers of the day, fearful for their positions, wrote off these breakthroughs as nothing more than gimmicks that would never catch on.

But whether they recognized it or not, a new era was upon them, and it quickly won the appreciation of audiences, for whom the silent films suddenly weren't enough anymore.

The development of sound movies was crucial to the position of writers because sound meant words and words meant dialogue, something with which filmmakers hadn't previously had to contend.

To fill that suddenly obvious gap, the studios went out and began actively soliciting writers, with varying degrees of success. Many established writers of the period looked at motion pictures with disdain and generally opted to have little to do with them. That at least was their official position, though quite a few were willing to contribute material under the table if the price was right and no one mentioned their names.

Among other places the studios turned to, one of the most fruitful sources turned out to be vaudeville. Movie studio agents haunted vaudeville clubs and theaters in much the same way that agents for variety television shows now hang out at comedy clubs and nightclubs, seeking someone whose talent will translate into a different medium. Thus it was that such vaudevillians as W.C. Fields, George Burns, Bob Hope and the Marx Brothers fell into the film business.

But all was not happy endings and golden opportunities. For every career launched by the arrival of talkies, another was destroyed. Many silent-film performers simply couldn't adapt to the change, despite voice and diction lessons. Silent-film actors were hired for their looks, not their voices, and in the case of one actress, she had a voice that sounded "like an audible hangover," according to one director. As actors hung onto their positions long after common sense dictated a discreet exit, audiences found considerable humor in the fact that the Egyptian queen or French maiden had an accent distinctly Bronx in origin. While individuals suffered or prospered, the studios grew more megalithic, powerful . . . and profitable. During the 1930s, the studios wielded an influence unlike anything today. They owned chains of theaters across the country, often dictating what films each of these theaters would show, regardless of actual box office potential. This was done by pairing a grade B film with a slightly better production and forcing both down the throats of theater managers as a take-it-or-leave-it double bill, a process known as "block booking." They placed substantial numbers of writers, performers, directors and crew members under long-term contracts, sometimes loaning performers to other studios the way you might loan someone a car. And just as putting a performer under contract could make you a star, it could destroy you just as easily. Provoke a studio exec to anger, and he might well decide to keep you out of any further movies for the duration of your contract. They might pay you, but your face would disappear from movie screens for one or two years or longer, effectively killing your career.

The contract system also left much to be desired as far as writers were concerned; they lacked creative control, were little respected, were paid modest salaries and were allowed no back talk. But to be fair, there were some benefits as well. The contract system provided opportunities for novice scriptwriters, who were taken under the studio's wing and taught the techniques of moviewriting. In addition, writers were given the opportunity to work on many different types of films, whether they wanted to or not, acquiring useful experience writing mysteries, love stories, musicals, adventures and gangster movies—an uncommon situation today, when writers tend to specialize in one or at most two genres. (When was the last time you saw a science fiction film by Neil Simon? Or a musical comedy by Oliver Stone?) Many writers refer to those years as the "good-old/bad-old days." More films were made during each of those years than at any time since. The studios developed concepts they felt would do well in the motion picture marketplace, selected a cast from among their biggest contract players and then assigned one of their staff writers to actually write the film. (Sometimes, however, a staff writer would develop an idea of her own and follow the project through to completion.) Thanks to block booking, the studios could rest assured that none of their films would fail to bring in at least a modest return.

Overall, it wasn't a bad deal.

Until 1948.

THE END OF THE STUDIO SYSTEM

Following a Supreme Court antitrust decision, the federal government issued *consent decrees* requiring the studios to divest themselves of their theater chains, a crushing blow that led to the elimination of the contract system. As if this wasn't bad enough, the film industry also had to deal with something it'd hoped would simply go away if ignored long enough: television. Once considered only a toy within the industry with limited audience potential, by the 1950s, television was steadily eroding the box office, the very foundation of the film business. In a way, it was a repeat of the error many studio executives made concerning talkies: They were fearful of a new technology and the changes it might mean, so they simply closed their eyes and continued doing what they were doing, unmindful of the pendulum swinging ever nearer their throats.

Ironically, the television industry succeeded at undermining the power of movies by doing just what filmmakers had done in the early motion picture business: It invested heavily in genres. Westerns, crime dramas, comedy and variety shows peopled by performers stolen from radio—these and other genre shows were daily television fare. Why, audiences wondered, should they pay money to see a western at a movie house when they could see the same thing in the ease and privacy of their own homes? And there was the novelty factor: Television was a bright and shiny new toy, and like any toy, its early years saw a lot of use by its purchasers. The American public was fascinated by the one-eyed newcomer to their home and spent as much time as possible playing with it.

The impact of the antitrust decision on the studios, coming as it did alongside the growth of television, was devastating. Between 1948 and 1955, movie attendance dropped from 90 million per week to 46 million per week. The studios, no longer sure of a return on their productions, responded by making fewer films. They studied television carefully and set out to make films that could provide things the small tube could not, given the limitations of the day: exotic locations, expensive sets, long and involved plots, popular stars, sweeping epics and high-paced adventure. Some studios, unable to adapt to the new demands of the world around them, went into bankruptcy and oblivion.

In the midst of all this confusion, the studios had to contend with the growing influence of unions and the gradual disintegration of the contract system in favor of the star system. Actors, writers and directors formed collective bargaining organizations (writers organized the Screen Writers Guild, which later became the Writers Guild of America) that applied pressure for higher salaries and increased creative input. Stars left the shelter of the studios to become free agents, roaming wherever the money was best, rejecting projects they would have been forced to accept previously, reversing the previous studio hierarchy—a condition that persists to this day. If you can guarantee Dustin Hoffman, Al Pacino and Tom Cruise for a film project, that film *will* be made.

But there are no bankable studio executives. And, as William Goldman has pointed out, no bankable writers.

Taken together, these sometimes overwhelming changes led many studio executives to wonder if there were any open windows still available on Wall Street. But they persevered by

1. further reducing the number of films produced
2. gearing films to a specific audience

3. featuring big-name stars with box office draw

4. working where possible only with established writers, producers and directors

5. offering audiences additional incentives to leave the house, premiums that ranged from door prizes and flatware to a 1957 sweepstakes trip to the Academy Awards ceremony.

Although audiences continued to decline, reaching an all-time low of 36.6 million in 1958, the studios were surviving.

Just when things seemed to be leveling out for the studios, however, yet another player was preparing to step onto the stage and grab the spotlight: the independent producer, whose rise proved to be a boon to novice screenwriters.

Some producers grew tired of a studio system that was slow to respond to changes in society and cultural tastes and of waiting endlessly for projects to get the green light by the ever-more-cautious studio bureaucracy. These producers dropped out of the system and decided to produce their own films. It was, in a sense, a return to the early days of filmmaking, with skeleton crews and a guerrilla mentality: Get in fast, make the movie and get out. Instead of filing for permits to shoot on location, they would wait until a Sunday when nobody was around, run in, set up the equipment as fast as possible, nail the footage and get out before the cops showed up.

They had neither the resources, the talent pool, the stages nor the money of the major studios, but what they did have was zeal, a vested personal interest in the subjects they were exploring and speed. They were the mice to the studio system's elephant. Because independent production companies were small entities that lived literally from film to film, they didn't need as high a return on each production as the studios, so they didn't need to produce megahits. Even a modestly successful film would be enough to keep them solvent for a year or two. The independent producers were also forced to listen to the audience. And what the audience missed were the days of double bills, which ended when the studios lowered their output. So the independent producers (called "indies") decided to fill that gap by churning out a phenomenal number of quick, low-budget pictures for drive-ins and small theaters across the country. Because their organizational structure was less monolithic, they were able to respond quickly to changing audience demands, particularly the demands of teenagers, who frequented drive-ins for reasons that were not always honorable. Thus were born youth-in-rebellion movies, five-dollar-budget science fiction movies, and other cinematic creations of the "I Married a Teenage Biker From

Outer Space During Beach Blanket Bingo" genre.

Because of their minimal production budgets, the independent produc-ers were unable to afford established writers, directors and performers. As a result, they turned to the vast pool of unproven writers who had been pounding against the studio gates, unable to get in. They were quick, young, eager to learn and, most important, they were willing to work cheap.

One big result of this development was the creation of a whole new audience: the so-called "teen market," those seventeen to twenty year olds who couldn't relate to films aimed at an older audience, whose needs were not *their* needs and who wouldn't be caught dead at a Disney film. Prior to this time, there had never really been such a thing as a teenager or a teenage market. There were kids, and there were adults, and at some point, usually when you graduated high school, you stopped being a kid and you became an adult. If you look at documentary films from the 1950s, you see kids in high school, wearing short-sleeved shirts and jeans . . . and the very next thing you know, as soon as they get out of college, they started in on jackets and white shirts and they were adults in miniature, and in fashion, if not in fact.

Internally, however, they were desperately in search of an identity.

And for good or bad, the youth movies of the 1950s helped to provide that identity.

They didn't much care that the budgets were slim or that you could see the boom mikes in some of the shots or that the music was canned (and some of the acting should have been canned) . . . they cared only that for the first time, they saw kids their own age—*teenagers*—dealing with the problems that affected them on a daily basis: peer pressure, girls, cars, girls, parents, girls, music, girls, school and . . . oh yeah . . . girls. The films not only provided them with role models but, just as important, an excuse to get out of the house. As with the tab shows of an earlier decade, which became social events, the Saturday night matinee or drive-in became a place to gather with their peers and share films that dealt with topics avoided by the major studios, directed specifically toward their tastes and attitudes. They perceived these films as being made by rebels, people who had dropped out of the studio system, which though correct on one level was vastly erroneous on another. Often these independent "rebels" were every bit as conservative as their studio counterparts; with some exceptions, they cared little for the issues they were promoting and often spoke of the audience with all the soulful interest of a certified public accountant. In that respect, the only real difference between the indies and the studios was that the indies were able to exploit the youth market more efficiently.

That is, I grant you, a very cynical appraisal. But as Henry Kissinger has remarked from time to time, "It has the added benefit of being true."

Nonetheless, these films held power and helped define the growing youth consciousness in the 1950s and early 1960s, even helping to sow some of the seeds of disaffection that led to the generation gap of the middle 1960s. It was only one factor, to be sure, among others that were infinitely more powerful—the draft, the senseless slaughter of presidents and candidates and ministers and an unfortunate interlude in southeast Asia—but the youth rebel films of those years certainly had their influence as well.

Theater owners found these films a godsend. They could once again boast double bills, and drive-ins sprouted like weeds across the country.

Novice writers and performers were finally able to see the fruits of their labors up on the screen, and as they continued to amass credits, they were soon able to graduate to more established studios. This constant turnover resulted in a steady flow of opportunities for newer talent eager to get into the industry. And the independents were eager to give them this chance, since every star or writer who went on to recognition lent more credibility to the producer's efforts and meant more money at the box office with each re-release of the early film. Oh . . . and the newcomers worked cheap.

As for the major studios . . . well, they fussed and fumed and crabbed and muttered and generally carried on crankily whenever a reporter brought up the subject. Their public stance was that the independents were pandering to the lowest common denominator, stealing their audience and lowering the cinematic art form to previously undreamed of depths. But deep inside their cash-register hearts, the studios were not as displeased with the indies as they made out. For one thing, they were producing the sorts of films that the majors either didn't make any longer—grade B cheapies—or wouldn't touch with a ten-foot boom mike. For another, the studios benefited greatly as the writers, actors and directors who had cut their teeth in independent films arrived at the studios already knowing their professions and with some small name value. But most importantly, they recognized that the independents were renewing the moviegoing habit in a whole new generation of potential audience members.

In short, movie attendance was on its way up again.

THE RETURN OF THE STUDIOS

By the mid-1960s and 1970s, the movie industry was regaining its financial legs. More films were being produced, although the number would never again reach the pre-1948 level. The independents continued to cater to specific audiences with their quick-buck films, while the major studios went on making films with big-name stars and steadily growing budgets. In time, the two sides formed a workable, if sometimes uneasy, alliance. For instance, an independent filmmaker might produce a film on a negative pickup basis. This meant that the producer would raise the money himself and make the film on his own, after which he would bring the completed project to a major studio and sell it. The studio would then repay anywhere from 50 to 100 percent of the film's cost, depending upon what percentage of the profits the producer wanted, in exchange for ownership and distribution rights. This way, the studios always knew what they were purchasing, never had to worry about the project suddenly going over budget and had a finished product that was ready to distribute under their banners at minimal risk.

These two practices—bigger-budget films and negative pickup deals—became more common during the 1970s and the first part of the 1980s. Confident that audiences could be induced to leave their homes only if a bigger-than-life epic awaited them at the theater, budgets for studio films continued to skyrocket. Where a film could once be made for $1 million to $3 million, the budgets of individual films now soared to $6 million to $30 million. This also meant greater risks, however. The higher the budget, the more the film had to recoup at the box office in order to show a profit. A film with a $25 million budget couldn't be just successful; to break even it had to be a blockbuster . . . and if it wasn't, the studio people who had approved the project were often asked to retire. This made studio executives understandably twitchy, and even more than before, they approached the question of financing a film by asking "How commercial is it?" rather than "How good is it?"

This continued the downward trend of producing fewer films because the money that could have been used to make four or five medium-budget films went into one big-budget extravaganza. By the early 1980s, the studios had been burned by big-budget flops in sufficient number that the trend began to reverse itself. With some exceptions, such as *Total Recall*, *Terminator 2*, *Waterworld* and just about any Spielberg film, the emphasis is coming back around to securing medium-budget properties.

There has also developed a symbiotic relationship between the studios and cable television networks, many of which are owned in part or in full by . . . that's right . . . the studios. Universal Studios, for instance, will finance a low-budget film, shoot it on the Universal-owned California or Florida lot, give it a run at the theaters, then forever after broadcast the film on USA Network, owned in large measure by Universal.

Paramount has similar arrangements, even going so far as to initiate a program of seeking out screenplays for $1 million to $2 million movies that are released straight to the videocassette market, usually thrillers or romances or other genres that don't require massive special effects or locations.

The result?

The studios have won. There are still plenty of independent producers out there, but on balance, they now work hand-in-glove with the studios. They have offices on the studio lots. They are given three-picture deals, which are contingent upon studio approval. The studios have, in essence, tamed the animal and brought it back safely into the film community. It's simply become too expensive for most independent filmmakers to continue churning out middle-list films now that "middle-list" usually means about $20 million to $40 million. And the studios continue to distinguish themselves from the indies by insisting that audiences don't want middle-list films: They want known actors and quality effects and a genuine filmgoing *experience*.

Not that the independents are completely gone, mind you; there are still some out there, but the majority seem to have moved even farther toward the fringe. Remember: The goal of the independent producer, the renegade, the rogue, is to produce whatever it is the studios won't or can't produce themselves, particularly if that can be aimed at a youth market. As a result, a lot of the quickie films that get made today (leaving out documentaries such as *Roger and Me* for the moment) are films like *Henry: Portrait of a Serial Killer* and *Ozone Attack of the Redneck Zombies* and *The Dead Next Door*.

An entire subgenre of super-8 movies has developed over the last few years, as the technology of low-end moviemaking has become increasingly available to consumers. Ragged, rough-hewn sixty-minute movies are coming out from all parts of the country, with the biggest center for such projects being New York City. The majority of these are renegade, hard-edged, often violent or socially dysfunctional, but in amidst the gravel are gemstones, lacking polish but showing great dramatic potential.

And, of course, you'll find the usual surefire quick-buck films relying on violence, drugs, girls, rock 'n' roll and zombies.

And girls.

Some things never change.

As well as integrating smoothly today with cable and videocassette sales, an alliance has also been made with what was once the dreaded enemy of moviemaking: broadcast television. Studios are now able to recoup at least some of their production costs by preselling films to television, often making the sale before the movie is released to the theaters. This development presents a double-edged danger: If the film is a surprise success, the payment the studio receives will probably be less than could have been secured after the film's release. On the other hand, if the film is expected to do well, gets a sizable purchase from a network, then bombs at the box office, the studio will have gotten far more than the picture was probably worth.

Some studios, particularly those that own both television and film divisions, have recently developed a standing policy on their films: If the film has screen quality and looks like it will do well at the box office, it will be released as a feature. On the other hand, if they review the finished film and decide its appeal is limited, it will be released as a television movie. In rarer cases, if a studio's television division comes up with a surprisingly good television movie, the company may release the project here or overseas as a feature film. This was how the nuclear-war-themed telefilm *Testament* ended up in movie theaters.

GLOBALIZATION

Finally, the 1990s brought a new wrinkle to the business of filmmaking: globalization. The buzzword in modern Hollywood is "foreign money." In the past, the usual process for making a film was to shoot it here, then you dub it and sell it overseas. Now, however, as the studios have become more cautious, they have begun to ask why the overseas partners get off easy, paying only after the project is finished. More and more, studios are saying that they will provide part of the financing for a movie, telling the producer to try getting foreign money before, as a last resort, releasing the funds themselves. Sometimes these overseas contributions can take the form of direct participation in the financing of the film itself, in return for a piece of the profits, or it can come by way of prepayment on videocassette options and advances on overseas theatrical bookings.

And make no mistake: Overseas partners are more than willing to try their hands at moviemaking. The Japanese have already purchased two major studios—Warner Bros. and Universal—and are eying others, with Australian and German entrepreneurs among others quickly getting into the act. There are film offices from dozens of countries in Hollywood and brokers who work with those offices, passing along likely projects to their backers from any of a dozen different countries.

One drawback to this development for writers is that the foreign investors sometimes can bring influence to bear on the screenwriting process, which can cause a film to wander. Audiences in different countries often have different perceptions or priorities when it comes to what constitutes good drama or comedy.

On the other hand, it could lead to a film community that is less provincial in its tastes.

Which option is more likely?

Both of them.

What it does, ultimately, is create an additional layer of complication in an already astonishingly complicated industry.

That also means that there are now more routes to production than ever before. Where the fate of a script once rested with a handful of people, now there are a variety of resources available to the scriptwriter hoping for a sale and production.

Having set down some of the history and ground rules by which the industry works and how it got here, we now proceed to the obvious question: Why would anyone in her right mind want to work in the film business in the first place?

Chapter Seven

The Benefits and Drawbacks of Screenwriting

I f you ask around, it's tough to find anyone who wouldn't like to be part of the movie business in one way or another. People from all walks of life easily become hypnotized by the buzzwords and catchphrases of H*O*L*L*Y*W*O*O*D: Package deals. The cinema. Cannes. Westerns, adventures, romances, horror and science fiction. Grade As and grade Bs; PGs, Rs, Gs, Xs and NC-17s—the whole alphabet soup of morality in filmmaking. Flicks and photoplays. Movies and moguls. The silver screen. Hey, baby, loved your last flick, have your secretary call my secretary and we'll do lunch some time. Filmic catchphrases voiced with the kind of fervent reverence normally reserved for Hindu mantras, recipes for aphrodisiacs and the Pledge of Allegiance at a VFW convention.

It's a cinematic lexicon that boils down to one thing: big bucks in Tinseltown.

Hollywood. It's a word that has become associated around the world with images of a fast-lane-only galaxy of high finance, nonstop excitement, fame, fortune and mind-wrenching glamour.

And the surprising thing is that about half of what you read and believe about Hollywood is true. Because even that half is a lot; it offers the lure of fame and money and success beyond the dreams of avarice.

The other half, however, involves heartbreak and frustration and years of thankless toil. If you're coming here for the money or the glamour or the high life, don't bother. Stay home. The stakes are too terribly high for any motivation other than the single-minded need to tell stories.

THE BENEFITS

The first benefit of screenwriting is probably the one most obvious: the financial rewards. Depending on the film's budget and the writer's reputation, a screenplay can bring in anywhere from $16,000 for a new writer working on a low-budget film to $500,000 or more. In the last year or two, prices as high as $1 million to $3 million have been paid for screenplays. And that's only the initial fee. On top of that, there's a bonus should the film actually go into production, the negotiation for net points (a percentage of the net profit of a property after the studio has recouped all of its expenses), a small cut of the merchandising should any of the characters or objects in the film end up in toy stores, the possibility of sequels and, of course, the standard residuals structure established under WGA rules that guarantees a modest annuity in perpetuity once the movie hits the small screen.

If you're new to the business, not every deal will include all of those benefits or tap the upper regions of payment (though one recent first-time screenplay sold for $1 million). Even so, the fees paid are still far beyond what most writers could expect to receive in any other medium, unless, of course, you happen to be a James Michener or a John Irving and can churn out one best-seller after another. The money looks better yet when you look at the amount of actual work involved.

A motion picture screenplay runs anywhere from 100 to 130 pages. Upon purchase, the very least a writer can expect to make right off the top is guild scale, which as of the first part of 1995 was $68,753, assuming the film's overall production budget is over $1 million (and films coming in under that figure are pretty rare these days). Most any agent worth his salt can at least negotiate what's called a "scale-plus-ten" deal: An agent takes a 10 percent commission, and in many cases, the agent can convince the studio to pay an additional 10 percent to cover that fee.

On top of that, if the film goes before the cameras, there's a production bonus of usually one-third to one-half of the initial fee. In this case, that's another $15,000 to $20,000. So leaving out the points and ancillary rights, the minimum you can probably expect to get from a screenplay sale and production is about $83,000.

(A *point* is a percentage of the film's profits. 1 point = 1 percent. The key is the difference between *net* profit and *gross* profit. Net points are generally called "monkey points" because you'll never see a dime off them; the studios make it a point to juggle the income on the film to make sure it never shows a profit on paper. Sadly, it's extremely difficult if not impossible for the majority of writers to get gross points on a feature film, even though they may often be offered as inducement for certain directors or performers.)

By way of comparison, a book publisher pays an average advance of anywhere from $3,000 to $15,000 for a first novel, which can run 300 to 600 pages. Royalties of 10 to 15 percent of the net price for each book purchased can bring in a fair hunk of change, but it takes a lot of years, and you don't see any of that money until after the publisher recoups the advance.

In screenwriting, payment is not made against the film's eventual profits. You get a fee, free and clear, and residuals; despite the monkey points, it's still a better deal page for page than any first novel.

Selling a screenplay makes you an attractive prospect to producers who figure you must know what you're doing; you need only sell one screenplay every year or two to live comfortably. Your output needn't be as great or as hurried as a novelist or journalist, so you can take your time and try to do a good job.

A strange Hollywood paradox makes it wholly possible to make almost as much money by being a failure as by being a success. On one hand, we have many writers who churn out a disquietingly large number of spec screenplays annually. These are knowledgeable writers producing scripts they believe in, and/or scripts that are highly commercial, i.e., topical. These scripts are then marketed and optioned on by one of the major studios. An *option*, as we'll discuss in more detail in "Marketing the Screenplay," is a fee, usually around $5,000 or so, paid by a studio in return for movie rights to the script for a year or sometimes two. The studio hasn't bought the script but is holding on to the property until a decision is made or until the script becomes commercial. At the end of the option period, the studio may either renew the contract under similar terms or fail to do so, which means the writer can take the script to another studio and do the whole thing all over again. In this way, even though her scripts may never get produced, she is making a living by screenwriting.

And, of course, there are the many screenplays written on direct commission, based on either a pitch by a reliable scriptwriter or on a request for a screenwriter to adapt another's work. A studio may purchase movie rights to a popular book, but it doesn't want the author to do the script. So the studio gives the assignment to a scriptwriter who can give an idea of what the book will look like as a screenplay. Either way, the studio may eventually decide the book just doesn't work as a movie and give up on the project. But the screenwriter got paid and has another credit to his resume, even though his work was never produced!

Like I said . . . it's a screwy business.

Another benefit of screenwriting is less tangible but important nonetheless. It has to do with prestige, both inside the industry and among the general public. It is a simple reality that screenwriters' names are more easily recognizable than the names of television or radio writers. In these latter media, the writer's name rolls by or is mentioned once, and that's about it. But motion picture credits are listed in newspaper advertisements, on television and radio ads, in reviews, on theater programs and, of course, on the screen itself. Not a small part of this is the result of the Writers Guild insisting that writers' credits get equal space in advertisements.

There is another less tangible benefit of screenwriting: The characters who populate your script are entirely of your own invention. You don't usually have to worry about tailoring the characters to fit someone else's preconceptions, as you must with television series and certain radio programs that use continuing characters. For as long as the script is in your typewriter, the only person you have to please is yourself. (What happens after the script leaves your typewriter we'll discuss shortly.)

(The foregoing applies primarily to spec screenplays, as opposed to screenplays written during development, where you can have lots and lots of people giving you input—wanted or not.)

Finally, a good screenplay or, more realistically, several good screenplays can be your route to producing or directing your own films. A substantial number of film producers and directors started as screenwriters, and most now direct or produce their own scripts. Steven Spielberg, Francis Ford Coppola, George Lucas, John Carpenter, George Romero, Woody Allen . . . these are only a few of the better-known writers who have gone on to produce and direct as well as write films. An old film industry adage is that if you've written an exceptionally hot property, you can name your price and, in a fair number of cases, expect to get what you asked for.

No one, for example, wanted Sylvester Stallone to star in *Rocky*, which he'd written specifically with an eye toward portraying the main character. The studios argued. They pleaded, thundered, grumbled and complained. Stallone wasn't a box-office name, and they felt that without the presence of a name star, the film wouldn't do well financially. But Stallone stood firm. He dug his heels into the dirt, crossed his arms and faced into the wind, knowing that he had something they wanted and that sooner or later, if they wanted it badly enough, they'd cave in.

They did, and the rest is history.

THE DRAWBACKS

All of these things, then, are the nicenesses that inhabit the world of a screenwriter. But be advised that this is not the whole story: There is a flip side to the film business, and if you ignore the darksome aspects of screenwriting in deference to the tinsel-and-cute-little-bunny-rabbits image the industry tries to project, you will be inviting grief into your home.

Yes, the financial rewards of screenwriting are considerable. As a consequence, after seeing the latest weekly box-office receipts listed in *Daily Variety*, new screenwriters can sometimes be convinced to take a smaller fee up front in return for a few percentage points of the film's net profits. If you ever receive such an offer, then I and every other writer who's ever been involved in the film business can offer only one piece of advice: Don't take it.

To elaborate on the point raised earlier . . . never forget that motion picture studios are in the illusion business, and their creativity does not always stop at the door to the bookkeeping office. By tacking on little costs here and there, both during and after production, these necromancers can make even the most successful film look like a failure. Vaguely worded distribution fees, overhead charges, film duplication costs and other ancillary fees can ratchet up the "cost" of a film to stratospheric and utterly unbelievable levels. The film, as far as they're concerned, will always be in the red, which means that anyone waiting for a percentage of the profits will have a long wait ahead of her.

This is nothing new. It's been going on for decades. Neither is it entirely illegal, since it involves cross-dealings between different branches of the same production organization, each arm billing the other arm for its services. But there is hope this practice may change during the next decade. As of this writing, nearly a dozen cases are in litigation as writers and directors and performers try to get a percentage of what is rightfully theirs and to open the studio's books to an examination by their attorneys.

So always be wary of anyone who tries to sell you on taking a smaller fee in return for a few points unless you're dealing with a respected figure whose credibility cannot be challenged. George Lucas is such a person, and traditionally anyone who works at Lucasfilms, including the guy who sweeps the floor, is offered, and receives, a percentage of the profits. In most other cases, the producers or studios know they can juggle the figures so the film appears to be a loser, or they know it will never make enough money (after they take out their own fees) for there to be enough to worry about anyway.

When it comes to dealing with independent producers, the waters are filled with sharks. For someone to claim that he is a *television* producer, the individual in question must be under contract to a network or studio and will have worked on any number of television series. There will be a paper and screen trail of credits. But anyone can, with a few bucks, rent an office on Sunset Boulevard, come up with a snazzy name for the template, and announce that he is an independent producer. If challenged by anyone wanting to know what he's done in the past, he can simply shrug and say he has had several deals "in development" with major stars and directors, that he helped put this deal or that deal together but just didn't get credit. Statements like that are nearly impossible to refute, since just about everybody in Hollywood has something in development, and the other principals he claims to have been involved with are usually next to impossible to locate for verification.

These are the people to beware of. They are the fast-talkers, the ones who answer questions in generalities, who know almost nothing about the film business and are therefore bound to fail, usually taking someone else down with them. Hollywood is filled with horror stories about unwitting writers and performers who got involved with shady operators and are still recovering from it.

Here's one of those stories: A friend of mine was contacted by an independent production company I shall refer to as the DoubleCross Corporation. He had a few produced plays under his belt and was thrilled at the prospect of being in the Movie Biz. So he agreed to and signed a contract for one percentage point of the profits, what was then Guild minimum for a screenplay. But the payments were to be made on a deferred basis, the terms of which are given here verbatim: "Producer agrees to pay Employee the sum of $14,000, which shall be distributed in the following manner: Ten percent on the date whereon the budget for the motion picture is allocated to the Producer; forty percent on the date of the Employer's commencement of principal photography of a motion picture based on said property; and fifty percent to be paid on the last day of actual photography. In addition to this fee, Producer agrees to pay to Employee one percent of the net profit from the motion picture. Producer agrees to use its reasonable efforts to effect production of a motion picture based upon said property. In the event, however, that Producer is unable to begin or complete production of the Photoplay, Producer shall provide to the Employee the compensatory sum of $1,000." (This kind of arrangement, by the way, is patently forbidden by the Writers Guild.)

"It was," my friend has said on many occasions, "the biggest mistake I ever made in my entire life." Here's what happened: The DoubleCross Corporation was never able to receive financial backing for the project, since the alleged producer had never worked in the industry before and was recognized as a less-than-reliable character. That took care of the $14,000. So the writer tried to get his $1,000 kill fee. But the producer had an out, a loophole: The contract specified that the kill fee only went into effect after all reasonable efforts to secure production of the script had been made. So whenever my friend tried to get his money, all the producer had to say, truthfully or otherwise, was that he had shuttled the script to yet another studio and that they were looking at it. This constituted reasonable effort. Translation: It would be impossible for the writer to *ever* collect his kill fee, since the producer could claim indefinitely that reasonable efforts were being made to produce the screenplay. And since no time limit was attached, the reasonable efforts could go on forever.

The result of all this? The writer wrote a very good script, for which he never received a single penny and probably never will. He cannot market the screenplay as is because even though he was never paid for his work, it contractually belongs to DoubleCross. Now, he could almost certainly break the contract in court, given the circumstances, but at first, the cost was prohibitive. Finally the producer, along with the DoubleCross Corporation, simply vanished. Telephone disconnected, no forwarding address and a solid year of work down the drain.

The writer, of course, has said that he harbors no grudges. "But if I ever find that guy," he added in a recent conversation, "I'm gonna chew on his eyes."

Moral: Whenever dealing with an independent production company, check it out with the Writers Guild and the Better Business Bureau, unless, of course, it has some kind of track record or is known personally by you. Do not sign any contracts until you have talked to an attorney. A little caution can save you years of heartbreak.

Sharks aside, other potential drawbacks lie in wait for the dedicated screenwriter.

Once you've turned your script over to a director, a producer and a cast, your words can be changed in a thousand different ways. For most original screenplays (as opposed to an adaptation of someone else's work), you are given the right to do the first rewrite and to be on hand for revisions, but other changes can still be made. After you've done the first full rewrite, the studio has the right to bring in another writer to totally rewrite your material. A director can opt to change lines and will almost certainly change your camera directions. Cast members will grouse that they can't say the lines as written or that the lines don't mesh with the character (who they, of course, know better than the writer, who created the characters in the first place). If the cast members have enough clout, they can change the lines.

Even if your lines are preserved pretty much as-is during production, they're still not safe. Writers have seen the entire thrust of a script turned inside out as the film is edited. Lines can be juggled, dubbed, looped or cut altogether, thereby subtly changing the nature of the film. Often, a writer's contract will specify that she is allowed a say in the editing process and can view the finished version, or "final cut," as it's usually known. But the right to actually do the final cut rests with the director or sometimes the producer.

If the film succeeds, everyone involved in the other aspects of production will claim it was successful in spite of the script; if not, they will explain that it failed because of the script. As stated before, it's a mug's game.

Those, then, are the essential benefits and drawbacks to screenwriting. Although some of the information might belong in the section on marketing, I believe you should know up front exactly what kind of world you'll be dealing with as a screenwriter. In the interest of objectivity, I should also state that although many screenwriters tell endless horror stories about their misadventures, there are also those who manage to avoid the pitfalls, who always get paid on time, whose words are not significantly changed and who have never been on the wrong end of a bad contract.

The interesting thing about all this is that despite the hazards, the attraction of screenwriting lives on. Even the most battle-scarred screenwriter is willing to give it another try, given the choice. Why? Why do salmon swim upstream? Why do lemmings rush off cliffs into the sea and drown? Why?

Because even with its attendant sharks, warts, pitfalls, fast waters and six-foot-tall man-eating rabbits, even with all that, it's still a chance to be part of the Movies, to see, for a brief moment, your name flickering across the silver screen of cinematic immortality.

And maybe Ethel Merman was right: Maybe there really is no business like show business. And as long as there's an actor waiting for the words that will give life to a character who will fire the imagination of moviegoers around the world, who will enliven them with the realization that they have just seen a little of The Truth in their local cinema, then there will always be people willing to write those special words, no matter what the risk might be.

Chapter Eight

The Art of the Screenplay

Putting together a screenplay differs in many ways from writing a tele-script. Probably the most obvious difference is the length involved. A screenplay can run anywhere from 101 pages for the ninety-minute movie, such as *The Producers*, to 160 pages, which was the length of the original shooting scripts for *Network* and *The Empire Strikes Back*. (The only forms of telescripting that come near to this length are, of course, the television movie and miniseries.)

Because of this length, a screenplay is a complex creature that requires considerable forethought and planning and a large chunk of time devoted to the actual writing process. Never undertake the writing of a screenplay without a complete belief in its importance. Otherwise, very quickly you'll lose interest, your enthusiasm will wane, the amount of time involved in writing something this long will suddenly become overwhelming and you'll get bogged down halfway through. A screenplay written under such circum-stances will rarely be completed, which makes it that much harder to start the next one.

Writing a screenplay requires a certain degree of craftworthiness. You've got to have a genuine feel for the development of a script, the pacing, the proper length of a scene, transitional devices, realistic-sounding dialogue and so forth. Anyone who expects to sit down at his desk and, as his first venture into scriptwriting, produce a perfectly polished screenplay is just asking for an ulcer. Not that it's impossible to complete *a* screenplay under such conditions, to just fill out the required number of pages with words in some kind of logical and grammatical order. Just that it takes time to learn how to do it *well*. Usually you won't fully understand what it is you're really trying to accomplish, what techniques are useful to you, until you're about two-thirds of the way through, after which you then have to go back to page one and start revising.

We learn by doing. But there are some shortcuts you can take to better prepare yourself for the undertaking.

IMMERSE YOURSELF

First, the cardinal rule of all scriptwriting: Read as many examples of the particular genre as you can find. Happily, it's considerably easier to locate published film scripts than it is to secure television or radio scripts. Major studios sometimes release screenplays through a publishing company, usually accompanied by stills from the movie. So keep a sharp eye on the movie section of your local bookstore for these releases.

I feel the best recent publications of screenplays have come through Ballantine Books. I refer specifically to their publication of *The Art of Star Wars*, *The Empire Strikes Back Notebook* and *Raiders of the Lost Ark: The Illustrated Screenplay*. These large editions contain not only the complete produced scripts, but other production information as well, including a hefty number of production drawings and storyboard sketches that illustrate the action that occurs around the written word. I cannot recommend them highly enough to the writer trying to figure out what a screenplay involves. (I am confident that as the other six episodes of Lucas's *Star Wars* triple-triptych are released, more of these editions will be published.)

If you're interested in studying movie screenplays of the past, a number of publishers are actively engaged in publishing such scripts. Among the most prominent of these is the Wisconsin/Warner Bros. Screenplay Series, published by the University of Wisconsin Press. These clothbound editions are available through most bookstores and contain the scripts for *The Jazz Singer*, *Treasure of the Sierra Madre*, *To Have and Have Not*, *White Heat*, *The Corn Is Green*, *The Big Sleep*, *Arsenic and Old Lace* and others.

Another invaluable source is the MGM Library of Film Scripts, published by Viking Compass Books. Available through this publisher are *North by Northwest*, *Ninotchka*, *Adam's Rib*, *Singin' in the Rain*, *A Night at the Opera* and *A Day at the Races*. What's nifty about this series is that in some cases, specifically the last two scripts mentioned, the book contains both the original script and the script as it finally ended up on the screen. This provides a remarkable insight into what changes a "finished" screenplay can undergo after it leaves the writer's hands, and it's often amusing to sit back and imagine the process that led to some of the more bizarre changes.

More recently, you can find the screenplays for most of Oliver Stone's movies, as well as other major motion picture hits, in any bookstore with a good-size film section. Where once published screenplays were few and far between, presumed to be of interest only to other writers and academics, over the last few years, they have become more commonplace.

If you own or have access to a laser disc player, you have additional resources at your disposal. Many higher-priced laser discs come with ancillary material, ranging from interviews to trailers, publicity stills . . . and the entire screenplay. The Criterion editions often have this supplementary material, in some cases actually showing how a scene looks on the page, then comparing it with the filmed version. This can be a highly effective means of seeing how a script goes from paper to film.

As a subset of this cardinal rule, it's imperative you see as many movies as your finances can support. Watch current films for an understanding of where the medium is now and what's currently considered marketable, as well as all the old films you can, preferably uncut, either on tape or laser disc or at whatever theaters in your area showcase film classics. Make it a point to see the good films, the films that garner the Oscars and the best reviews, as well as the real stinkers. A well-crafted film will stay in your mind as an example of the best the medium can accomplish, and though you may not be able to pinpoint exactly what it was that made it a winner, somewhere in the back of your mind the various components of the film will be categorized and filed away for future use. Upon seeing a really bad film, it's easy to pick out where it failed and where you, as a writer, could have made it better by changing this character or heightening that plot element. In some ways, you can almost learn more about good writing by seeing a really bad film than by seeing a good one.

There is a price attached to this, of course. Once you've decided to become a screenwriter, you can never again go out and enjoy a movie. Give it up, you're finished. Because a really good movie can leave you depressed, confident that you'll never be able to turn out something that good. On the other hand, if you see a bad film, you make yourself crazy thinking, *How come that piece of garbage got produced, when my stuff is still sitting in a trunk in Toledo?* It can make you crazy either way.

In further preparing to write a screenplay, it's a good idea to write one or more one-hour dramatic television scripts, or at least two or three half-hour scripts in film format. This gives you a feeling for dramatic structure, dialogue and all the other elements we mentioned earlier. Once you've written a complete story that's thirty or fifty pages long, the prospect of writing one hundred plus pages of film script becomes less intimidating. As a second benefit, the finished scripts are samples of your writing, should you ever approach an agent or a producer who first wants to see some of your work.

FEATURE FILM VS. TELEVISION

In considering some of the other creative aspects of screenwriting, it's worth remembering that there are distinct, if subtle, differences between the topics covered in a movie and those examined in a television series or telefilm.

The average television series is either character oriented, as in most situation comedies and a few family-oriented dramatic series, or it is action directed, as exemplified by police dramas, rescue programs, detective series and the like. In the former, the premise of each episode is built upon the interrelationships of the characters. In the latter, the characters sometimes take second position to the plot or the action, with characterization more leavening than point.

A motion picture, on the other hand, must balance both aspects if it is to be worth anything. You can't rely on the audience coming to know your characters over the course of a season. You've got roughly two hours to make your audience feel they know your characters well enough to care what happens to them. At the same time, while you're sketching out your characters, something must be happening on screen. That something needn't be bombs exploding or machine guns barking; it can be the tension that grows steadily within a family on the verge of disintegration or a character teetering on the edge of madness. But if there isn't something going on to hold your audience's attention, you've got a problem.

Television movies also tend to combine characterization and action, but they are usually issue or headline oriented, to wit: A network, studio executive, producer or writer sees an issue, a news headline or a topic of considerable controversy. She then goes out and either finds the real person at the center of the story and options the rights to the story or creates a fictional character and builds a similar story around that person. Some network executives have staff members who do almost nothing but go through stacks of newspapers, sifting through the passions of the day for stories that might lend themselves to a telefilm format.

Motion pictures intended for general release can also be issue oriented, but the percentage is considerably smaller than is the case with telefilms. There are two reasons for this. First, films that deal predominantly with issues can be risky at the box office. If the film's point of view runs counter to public attitudes, values or norms, the studio runs the chance of taking a financial bath; as a result, studios are understandably leery of such endeavors and require certain box-office guarantees. The award-winning film *Philadelphia* probably would never have been made without the box office security the studios had in the presence of such name performers as Tom

Hanks and Denzel Washington. Similarly, *To Wong Fu, Thanks for Everything, Julie Newmar*, a film about cross-dressers, probably would never have been made without the presence of bankable action stars as the lead characters.

The second reason is related to the constantly changing current of popular opinion. Since it takes anywhere from one to three years for a film to be made, from the first treatment to the distributed movie, if a studio produces a film that capitalizes on a popular issue or media trend, it is very likely that the issue will be passé, no longer hot by the time the film is finally released. What was once a hot property is suddenly no more interesting than a celluloid-wrapped dead fish. This was precisely what happened to a film by Marble Arch Productions entitled *Can't Stop the Music*, which featured Valerie Perrine and The Village People in their first starring role. The film was an attempt to exploit the disco craze then sweeping the country. But when the movie was finally released, disco had not only become passé, a vociferous backlash had developed against it. Disco records were publicly burned at stadiums and arenas, and the film, released to much ballyhooing by the studio press office, died a swift and terrible death.

(At a subsequent public seminar held in Hollywood, Marble Arch Vice-President Howard Alston asked the two hundred plus people in the gallery, "How many of you would have predicted that *Can't Stop the Music* would have died at the box office?" Almost everyone's hand went up, proving again that maybe the public better understands what makes a good film, and what will and won't sell, than do the executives at the major centers of film production.)

On the other hand, television lives and dies on controversy and issues of the day. Networks can get TV movies and miniseries going in far less time than is required for a motion picture.

Probably the single greatest distinction between writing for a television series and a movie is that a movie is more of a real *story* than a television program.

Consider it. If you were to sit down after watching your favorite sitcom or an hour-long dramatic series and attempt to rewrite the program as a short story, you probably wouldn't have much of a story. Individual episodes of a television series are like separate scenes in a short story or novel. The characters generally don't change much in the process of one episode; the story is mainly oriented around a specific incident or a personal crisis. It's only by watching the continuity of the series over time that you, as a viewer, really get a strong feeling for the characters and their situations. A single episode of *Dr. Quinn, Medicine Woman* might give you a glimpse into one particular facet of a character or how he deals with one particular situation (the young boy is afraid of ghosts and comes to deal with his fear in a constructive fashion), but you probably won't get a sense of the totality of the character in lots of other ways, and the story itself is structurally very simple: one obstacle or problem that must be dealt with, in this case a soft problem.

But if you follow the series week after week, year after year, you come to know the characters and can pick up on small changes in those characters over time as the result of the events portrayed in different episodes.

A motion picture, on the other hand, must be wholly self-contained. Like a short story, it has a clearly defined beginning, middle and end, and your characters must come to life within those strict borders. You can't tack on an epilogue in which you explain why your characters did such and such, or what this event over here really means and what it will lead to. The audience can't come back next week to find out more about the situation, and in most cases, they can't come to the movie with any previous knowledge of your characters upon which to build a whole portrait—unless you're dealing with an established name, such as in the James Bond or Batman movies. You've got to tell your story, reveal your characters and get out cleanly because once it's released, there's no going back.

The final aspect that differentiates a motion picture screenplay from a telescript is not essentially creative in nature, but it does have an impact on the creative process. In nearly every instance, a motion picture will have a bigger budget than a television movie: Bigger budgets give screenwriters greater latitude in determining what action will take place and where. If your script calls for the protagonist to scale the Eiffel Tower, the overseas jaunt will be figured into the overall production cost.

The danger is in letting this more substantive budget get in the way of creativity. You should never throw in an extravagant scene just because it might be kind of fun. Any action or locale used in your script must be necessary to the story. So if your action is to be set in some exotic locale, there'd better be a damned good reason why it's taking place there instead of, say, Cleveland. And the only acceptable reason is that it's happening *here* because it couldn't happen the same way anywhere else. The same applies to action. As someone who spent over seven years reviewing films in print and on the air, as well as being an audience member myself, I have seen quite enough purely gratuitous car crashes, thank you very much. If there's no need for cars careening into one another at high speed or for any other such non-plot-related action, drop it. Omit it. Bury it and lose your map. A really good script is as spare as you can make it. Don't let the quality of your script get lost beneath a mass of unnecessary and distracting action.

Which brings me to an important point I want to get out of the way right now: In every writing class, seminar or lecture I've encountered, I've heard such phrases as "the obligatory chase scene," "the obligatory sex scene" and "the obligatory throat-cutting-in-graphic-detail scene." To be totally blunt with you, that is a load of absolute, unmitigated ka-ka.

Nothing is ever obligatory! An attitude of "Well, this scene is expected, and everyone *else* is doing it" can cripple what might otherwise be a fine film. The only thing you as a screenwriter are obliged to do is tell your story. Period. You don't have to follow the standard formula used in *x* number of other films because if you do, then it isn't your script anymore; it's a formula script, and it will never be anything more than that. If you put in one single, solitary, crummy little scene not because you think it belongs there, but because you think it's expected, then forget it. You've just sold out.

There's nothing wrong with a chase scene *if* that scene is an essential part of your story that grows naturally out of the events that precede it. But to do it because it's "obligatory" is just plain dumb. Worse than dumb, in fact, because it's the first step down the road toward losing your integrity as an artist.

And for those who feel that every instant of bloodshed must be splashed in Technicolor Type O across the screen, I refer you to the work done by Alfred Hitchcock and Val Lewton, who managed to create a more vivid sense of horror through subtlety and indirection than could ever be realistically recreated and photographed. Let your audience's imagination do most of your work for you.

End of sermon.

To recap, these are the steps involved in the creation of a screenplay: You must come up with a story you feel very strongly about. It must have a self-contained beginning, middle and end. It should not be trendy, unless you can be absolutely sure that the trend will be going on when the film is finally released, and preferably long thereafter. It should have strongly defined characters at the center of the story, but something must be *happening* as well. The action, on the other hand, should not get in the way of your characterizations. The characters should undergo some change over the course of the story, and the plot should be fully resolved by the script's conclusion; the audience should feel they know the characters. The action should take place in an orderly, logical fashion. You should be familiar with the techniques of dialogue, pacing and description, either from studying films or writing practice television scripts or both. The script should be as spare as you can make it, eliminating any unnecessary or "obligatory" action.

Thus armed with the tools of your craft and ready to begin transplanting ideas from your imagination to a blank sheet of paper, you can now move on to the actual mechanics of putting together a script, from start to finish.

Chapter Nine

The Craft of Screenwriting

A screenplay starts out with an idea that, using the criteria established earlier and in previous chapters, you can develop into an interesting story you would like to tell and that you as an audience member would like to watch. "Wouldn't it be cool if . . ." is a perfectly legitimate place at which to begin your development process. Don't second-guess yourself too much; find what interests you, and you'll rarely stray too far from an interesting story.

Your next step is to develop that story through all the stages mentioned previously in "The Craft of Telescripting." You must transform the idea first into a brief synopsis, so you can see the core of the story in one lump, then an outline (a treatment), and, finally, the script itself. Because some of these terms have slightly different applications than we've seen up until now and all of them are equally essential if you intend to produce a marketable screenplay, we'll stop to look at them more carefully.

THE SYNOPSIS

You must be able to sum up your idea as briefly as possible, usually a paragraph or two. A lot of writers find this very difficult, since they are so intimately connected with their characters and their story. As mentioned earlier, the process is really no different from when a friend asks you about the movie you saw last night and you sum up the whole two-hour story in a couple of sentences.

The synopsis serves two purposes.

1. Once you get into the process of actually writing or outlining the script, it can be quite easy to stray from the core of what you wanted to write when you began the process. The synopsis keeps you aimed toward your target.

2. The synopis becomes incredibly important when it comes time to pitch your story. As we read in "Marketing the Television Script," the fine art of pitching is an inescapable evil. We'll get into pitching a little more later in this chapter, but for now, suffice it to say you may be asked to simply describe your story before you're allowed to submit it. Other times, if you're trying to work out a development deal to write a screenplay, it's absolutely necessary in all cases to be able to pitch the story effectively and clearly and entertainingly, in as brief a space as possible. The synopsis can help with that process later.

Believe it or not, deals for screenplays, even whole films are made solely on the basis of a synopsis of no more than a few sentences. The science fiction film *Outland* was one of these. The deal for that movie was made on the basis of one sentence. Writer/director Peter Hyams went to Warner Bros. and simply told them, "It's High Noon in outer space." Thus was born a motion picture. A deal was arranged on the spot, and preproduction was initiated not long thereafter.

Should you ever give producers or studio execs a copy of the synopsis, with or without an accompanying screenplay? No; always avoid this if you can. Because they'll ask. They'll ask because certain execs believe they're too busy to actually read the whole screenplay; they'll want to read something shorter. In most cases, this is coverage provided by a studio reader. They can make their decision to pass on the project not based on its merits, but on how well it's been encapsulated on paper. So why give them one more potential barrier to put between you and your goal?

The synopsis is for your use, nobody else's.

THE OUTLINE (PERSONAL VS. DEVELOPMENT)

An outline serves different purposes depending on the players involved. It serves the writer primarily in a spec writing situation; this is where you break down your story and write it out in somewhat abbreviated form so you can see the whole of it at once and work out any plot holes or problems before finally committing to the full-length screenplay. (If you have a huge, gaping logic problem in your script, better to find it out in a 20-page outline than in the last part of a 120-page script, requiring massive rewriting.)

But an outline is virtually never submitted to producers or agents or studio execs as a spec submission. They only have contact with outlines in the development stage (more on that later). Here the outline serves them by making sure they know which way the writer is going with the story before they let her wander off and do the full script.

Motion picture outlines can be peculiar little critters. No two writers do them quite the same way. Although there is general agreement on the length of an outline (anywhere from ten to forty-five pages), there is some disagreement about its complexity. A number of writers (I will take my life in my hands and hazard to say a majority of them) prefer the narrative prose format associated with the television treatment (see "The Craft of Telescripting for samples). No camera angles, just the story, presented almost *as* a short story or novelette, though not quite as detailed in description as a fiction piece.

Some writers' style is very prosaic, while others try to use the tools of fiction writing to give the outlines energy and style and excitement. Jim Cameron's style of outline writing, for such films as *Aliens*, is almost poetic—short, fast images, one line at a time, not even paragraphs—more like haiku or blank verse, designed to create flashes of imagery.

A primarily narrative style of outline would read as follows:

"Dawn. The desert. Cold night air whips the open door of an abandoned house back and forth. A semi-truck appears suddenly and grinds to a stop out front, and a MAN emerges, wearing studded boots, denim jeans and shirt. Call him RUSS."

Other screenwriters get very technical in their outlines, filling them with specific camera directions, transitional devices, blocking directions and so forth. The theory there is to create a first-level blueprint for the film *as* a film, conveying the screenplay as much through the techniques used as the story itself.

So a more technical outline of the same sequence would read something like this:

"EXT. DESERT. Dawn. Nothing moving except
A DOOR slamming open and shut in the wind. We PULL BACK to reveal the abandoned house it belongs to, as we hear a SOUND, the sound of
A SEMI-TRUCK that rumbles toward us and grinds to a halt. The driver's side door pops open as
ANGLE - A PAIR OF BOOTS steps down from the front cab, and we meet RUSS."

From personal experience and conversations with other writers, producers and directors, I recommend the simpler narrative prose format. It's almost always shorter, and since many studio execs don't like to read and can be daunted by massive outlines, brevity is a good thing. Don't worry about camera angles and the like until you get into your treatment and script; concern yourself primarily with telling your story in as cogent and undistracted a fashion as possible.

If you're writing the outline mostly for your own use, you can be as sloppy or haphazard in how it looks and is structured as you want; nobody has to understand it but you. I will confess that when I do a spec screenplay, mainly because I've done this for a long time now, I don't outline every detail. And it isn't all precisely written down in clear typed form. It consists of a quick series of notes in one computer file, placed in order, sometimes just a word or two to remind me about where a particular story beat goes . . . with other story elements scattered around on pieces of paper—Post-its, the backs of magazine subscription cards, anything that isn't nailed down or on fire. That's only possible because I've been doing this a long time, and I've learned my own shorthand. Don't try this technique—if I can call it that—until you've gone through the more formal stages of outline development, as I did. Then you can get . . . well, eccentric.

If you're writing an outline for someone else to read, you're going to have to be clearer and more objectively detailed. Which gets us back into the script development process, which I promised a moment ago to explore in more detail. And this is important because as vital as what's in your outline might be, who and what it's *intended for* is every bit as important.

Spec screenplays aside, this is how most motion pictures get made and written.

Having written a series of sample (spec) scripts, or done other work in areas of interest to producers, and having secured an agent, a producer with an independent movie company or major studio reads your stuff. He likes it. He calls your agent and asks if you have any ideas for other projects. Your agent says yes, even if that's absolutely not true, because you can always come up with something. (And a good writer always does.) So you spend the next several days putting together some ideas for a pitch meeting.

(Go back and read "Pitching" in chapter four, which is as relevant here as there. We'll wait for you to catch up. Go on. I *know* it's television, not films, but the same rules apply, trust me.)

Having pitched your four or five ideas, either the producer thanks you and sends you away, or one of your ideas catches his fancy. The producer may consult with other producers in the same company, or a superior. You may have to pitch it again. Note: There is a limit to how many times a producer can ask you to pitch an idea; if he exceeds that number, usually two or three such meetings, he is required to pay you for it. If all goes well, the producer makes you a development deal.

Meaning . . . you go away, think about the story some more, jot down some notes, come back and talk about it once or twice more. Then you go away again (writers go away a lot because that's where most execs like us . . . somewhere *away* . . . usually from them) to write the outline. Because most development deals are for story with an option for script, you can see now why it's vital to make the outline as interesting and dynamic as possible. Otherwise your story may die at the outline stage, "cut off in development," as we say around town.

Outline for Development

The studio development process can be extremely long; I've worked on projects for major studios that between pitch, outline and finished script consumed as much as a year of my time or more. It's valuable to many writers to get a development deal rather than write the script on spec, mainly because you're being paid while you're doing it. An outline grosses between $11,000 and $27,000 for a scale deal (depending on the projected budget), before taxes. This is not insubstantial.

The development process at the outline stage can also be extremely frustrating, because in most situations you're going to have to answer to a lot of people, all of whom have input into the story—executives, assistants to executives, coexecutives, rafts of producers, the director (if he's involved at this early stage), the studio money boys—and the outline can go through many permutations during this process, ending up as something potentially very different than what you began with.

By contrast, if you write the outline, the core of your story, on your own, there's nobody to interfere in the process except those you might choose to discuss it with—a friend, a loved one, a cat.

Before getting involved in a development deal, find out as much as possible about who's running the show and how many people are going to have input into the story in the development process, and check around to see if anyone else has had experience with them. If you're going to lock yourself in a small room with two to seven people for six months to a year of your life, you'd better be sure you can work with them.

Personally, having worked both ways—and this is just one man's opinion—I much prefer to write a script on spec than through a development deal. If I'm going to invest that much time and effort into writing a 120-page story, I'd rather it be *my* story rather than a committee's. Once it's finished, if others get into the process and notes come, that's fine. What matters is that at least once I got the story written exactly as I wanted it to be written.

The last two development deals I was involved with are both indicative of what's best and worst in the process. One was a project for Ivan Reitman, producer of *Twins* and *Ghostbusters*, for Columbia Pictures. I worked with producers Michael Gross and Joe Medjuck over the process of about a year, maybe a smidge more. I discussed a project with them, they liked it and we went into development. For months, there was a great give and take, and we had a great deal of fun. It was hard work, but in the end, we got through the outline and had a finished script in hand that would've made a terrific movie. It never got made, however, mainly because the effects and stunt work pushed it past the realm of fiscal reality, and the nature of the concept as it was finally realized precluded compromising the material. In other words, if we radically changed or cut the elements that were expensive, there would be nothing left worth producing.

So there was a year spent well, for which I was paid well, but which ultimately went nowhere.

Then there was another development deal for an independent company attached to Paramount. (I won't list any names because I don't want to embarrass them; what happened was not intrinsically their fault.) The people were good to work with, but there were too many involved. We went through endless rewrites, meetings, changes, sudden shifts in the story that meant going back and changing everything up to that point. Each version of the outline was more radically different than the one before it, and from my perspective, just as radically less interesting.

The outline development itself took almost a full year, including time for multiple drafts, periods of waiting, scheduling conflicts, people leaving town . . . so that by the end of the outline process, the only thing I wanted was out. I'd turn in a revision and dread getting a call for another meeting to "discuss some of the details" one more time. I couldn't feel the core of the story anymore. It had all become a process of accommodating notes instead of telling a story, and if I'd had to write the screenplay, I probably would've blown my brains out to avoid doing it. You can really learn to hate a story after you've redone it six times over twelve months. By this time, though, the studio's emphasis had moved on to other kinds of projects, and it never got to that stage.

Development can make you crazy. It can also make studio execs twitchy after a while because while they may sense, on a cellular level, what they don't like or what they want in a story, because they're not writers, they often don't have the language or vocabulary to successfully communicate their desires. I've received notes as vague as "DB" on a scene (meaning Do Better), without any sense of what that person would consider better or what was wrong with the scene in the first place.

This is probably one reason—if a small one—why studio development deals have slowly decreased over the last ten years. The larger cause, and the other reason I recommend the spec script approach, has to deal with a major event in the screenwriting business that is still having its effect seven years after the fact.

In 1988, the Writers Guild of America went on strike for six long months, a period of time that nearly destroyed the careers of many writers. Many writers seized on this opportunity to go ahead and write, on spec, and on their own schedule, the screenplay they'd always wanted to write or to have something in hand to send around the second the strike ended.

Which is exactly what happened. Twenty-four hours after the strike ended, the industry was flooded by spec screenplays. The money usually allocated for script development was cut back because there was an entire ocean of fresh, new screenplays on the market. Many of these were snatched up at competitive prices, which encouraged more people to write specs. Long story made short, each new successive wave of spec scripts has led to more waves, with the result that most studios tend to use their development funds for their A-list writers (with some exceptions) and look to the spec script market far more than ever before. It enables them to skip months of meetings and hassle and stubborn writers. The thing is *done*; all they have to do is buy it.

Lest you think writing a spec script is only of benefit to the studios, it also serves the interests of writers. Creatively, as noted before, you get to write it your way. Financially, if a hot script goes to market, it can be auctioned for substantial amounts of money, far more than would probably have been paid if the script had been developed in-house.

OUTLINE MECHANICS

Assuming you're going to write the outline to show it to other people, whether as part of a development deal or to get input from other writers or on the off chance you can find someone, somewhere, who'll read it at this stage, there are a number of requisites to bear in mind.

The outline should include each scene that will appear in your screenplay.

One good way to organize your outline is to start by briefly describing each scene on individual 3″ × 5″ index cards. Each card contains the location of the scene in terms of exterior or interior settings, an encapsulization of the action that takes place and a few snippets of dialogue to jog your memory when it comes time to actually script the scene. Each card should be numbered, roughly in the sequence in which it will appear in your script. Write each number in pencil in the upper left-hand corner of each card, since it may develop that after looking over the finished order, you'll want to shuffle the sequence of events.

TRANSITIONS, CAMERA ANGLES (if necessary), EFFECTS, note-worthy VISUAL EVENTS and CHARACTER INTRODUCTIONS are capitalized throughout. (After first introducing a character, you can cease capitalizing the entire name.)

The title appears in all capital letters, centered on the page eight vertical lines from the top. Two spaces below this is your name, followed two lines later by the date the treatment is being written. Drop down four to six more lines, then begin your first line of the treatment.

The treatment continues in this fashion until the entire story has been told. Since you're not necessarily breaking the script up into discrete acts (though you can do that if you so desire), it's helpful in reading and organiz-ing to put in breaks of four blank lines between "movements" in a script, to give a sense of transition and pacing. You don't have to include dialogue, but if you do so, include only your strongest and best-crafted pieces of dialogue, thereby giving the reader a feeling for your writing at its best.

Usually a "just the facts" attitude is best when writing an outline. An outline should be uncluttered, using short story techniques. Avoid asides, long-winded explanations or lingering descriptions of scenes. Just tell your story. If it's an interesting idea, you won't need artificial adornments. If it isn't, then all the asides and marvelous prose descriptions in the world won't help you.

Keep your paragraphs short, about as long as the one immediately pre-ceding this one, and punchy. If it isn't interesting to read, you're in trouble. So you may want to drop in rhythmic devices to break up the monotony of one paragraph after another.

Just quickies.

Like this.

Which just makes for a better presentation, and done properly doesn't get in the way of continuing the outline proper. It shouldn't be a diversion from the outline as much as a kind of stylistic punctuation.

Herewith is a sample of the first six pages of an outline for a screenplay I wrote in 1994 as a development deal for Wilshire Court Productions, a prominent and well-established production company based in Los Angeles. It's a suspense drama set in cyberspace entitled *The Virtual Highway*. (The outline was very long, and due to the complex details involved, including the use of extensive computer graphics, ended up at forty-four pages.)

For my purposes, I blended the two narrative styles to create a sense of rhythm, while at the same time communicating the detailed camera and production elements required.

A SAMPLE OUTLINE

THE VIRTUAL HIGHWAY
J. Michael Straczynski
August 3, 1994
Outline

Begin with NEWS COVERAGE of the gala opening of the new Los Angeles-based CyberNet center. (Handheld videotape camera POV.) VOICE-OVER establishes a REPORTER who comments that this center is "the largest one yet for CyberNet, which in 2011 went public and instantly became one of the hottest items on the New York Stock Exchange. In the two years since then, the virtual reality corporation has gone international, with stunning success."

The reporter gives us a quick taste of background: the rise of virtual reality as a national obsession/craze. CyberNet is the biggest company of its kind, with hundreds of walk-in centers and thousands of high-priced home systems. In the course of the report, we meet several of the people responsible for either maintaining or working on CyberNet, including psychologist DR. PAMELA MORRIS, 30s, attractive, sometimes a little too serious and intense. She forces a smile for the cameras and enters the gala reception.

END report with the rumor that the reclusive head of CyberNet, Devon Sanders, may actually make an appearance at this reception. An older, reclusive, Howard Hughes-like figure, this would be Devon's first public appearance in nearly a year.

CUT TO a CGI CYBERSPACE shot, where a computer-generated MAN (stylized, metallic) is desperately fleeing someone else . . .

CUT BACK TO the party, where some of the celebrants privately express concern about the new system that's about to go on-line. It's hundreds of times more complex than anything they've used before, and that worries Dr. Morris; the more complex the system, the more likely it is to break down. Chaos theory in action.

Others disagree. The system *has* to be this complex in order to compete with other companies in creating the most elaborate virtual reality worlds available. This new system is almost as fast and elaborate as the human mind itself. No one knows how Devon was able to create a system this amazing. He's an unmitigated genius. No one else comes close.

CUT BACK TO the CGI environment, where the two-man chase is continuing. It ends when the computer-generated figure of the escaping man hits a wall, and shatters. The remaining CGI figure smiles, content with the security of the blocks he's set up throughout CyberNet's neural pathways. This is our introduction to DEVON SANDERS, genius behind CyberNet. As the last of the hacker's computer-generated extension disintegrates, Devon remarks that no hacker has ever made it into the CyberNet system, and never will, and suggests that whoever just tried convey that information to his associates. CyberNet is *solid*.

Devon floats upward, a CGI figure in negative space, through a universe of doors and relays. His computer form slides down a neural transit point and comes out on the beach. It's a very computer-looking beach at first, a CGI/film composite, back-framed into the CGI. Then the scene slides into realistic film, and a "real" Devon stands on a "real" beach, enjoying the view. We see that he is dynamic and youthful.

There on the beach beside him is LAURA, a virtual-reality woman (again, this is regular real-film, not CGI at this point) in a breathtakingly small bikini. She approaches him, chides him for being away so long. He starts to move toward her, touching her . . . as a VOICE echoes through the landscape: his secretary, telling him to come out. Reluctantly, he lets Laura go, promising to return as soon as possible.

With that, the scene transforms through to CGI/composite, and he rises back through the neural channels, until we're in his ornate office. He removes the skinsuit interface that links him into CyberNet, and we DISCOVER that Devon is much older than the dashing young man he seems to be in the CyberNet. He is in his sixties, thin but rail-straight. On his desk is a photo of Devon as a young man . . . and this is the image of him that we have just seen in the CyberNet, the way he still sees himself.

From offscreen, his secretary tells him that his doctor called—again—to remind him to come in for some more tests, and reminds him that he was supposed to be downstairs an hour ago for the ongoing party to celebrate the new center. He should leave hacker-tracking to the security people, that's what he pays them for. Devon shrugs, smiles; he likes to keep in practice.

As the secretary enters frame, we see that it's the same woman from the virtual-reality beach, only a far more prim and proper version of that woman. She asks what on earth he finds so fascinating in his own little virtual world. He smiles, shrugs off the question, and pulls on his jacket, dressing to join the festivities.

As he stands, he leans forward slightly on the desk, catching his breath. He opens and closes his left hand in some discomfort, then pushes through it and exits.

BRIEF MONTAGE of scenes that reveal Devon Sanders as a man more comfortable with machines than people. Finally, with much applause, he throws the switch that sets the new system online.

Go to a CGI sequence, inside CyberNet itself, as the new center plugs into the neural relays that link centers across the country, ribboning patterns that flow and connect and intersect. Then a strange darkness slowly filters out into the system. . . .

CUT TO the next day, and a meeting in the corporate offices of CyberNet. Dr. Morris chairs a status report meeting, at which she raises her concerns about the system. Ever since the new relays went on-line, she's noticed glitches in the software for which she can find no explanation. Clients have reported unplanned events in their programmed virtual-reality vacations: a couple who booked a virtual reality tour of ancient Egypt reported seeing what looked like someone in a black corvette riding in King Tutankhamen's royal parade . . . another purchased a virtual sunny vacation only to find it raining all the time. The control staff couldn't turn the rain off, and finally had to reboot the system in order to stop the virtual rain.

Not unsympathetic, Devon counters that he's examined her data, and can't find anything physical in the system that could be doing this. He reminds her that the system creates virtual worlds in tune with the desires and thoughts of their users, so the "glitch" may be with the users, not the system. All of the information is subjective and anecdotal.

Others weigh in, noting that some random events are bound to crop up in some programs, given how extensive the system has become. They'll work out the bugs in time. It seems like a "let's gang up on Pamela and impress the boss" moment, which Devon notes.

He indicates that he is sensitive to her concerns, and he brought her on board to speak her mind. She has done so, and should continue to investigate this. Meanwhile, if any of their clients have less than satisfactory experiences, CyberNet will happily refund their fees and investigate their complaints.

CUT TO the Los Angeles CyberNet center, where clients continue to arrive, eager to experience a dream or a reality all their own. Feature three of them as they check in:

GLORIA PEARL, an elderly woman who has saved her money for the last several years for one big, long CyberNet ride, a virtual dream in which she corrects a mistake made many years before, when she chose to marry the wrong man. She was invited to a dance by a man who loved her profoundly. She chose not to go, and missed seeing him on his last night in town before leaving to pursue a life outside the small town they lived in. In a snit, angry that he would go—despite promises to return—she went to another man, and by the time he did come back, she was married.

She has always regretted not going to that dance and wants the chance to relive that night, and what might have been . . . to be that young girl once again, and spend that one night with the man who loved her. To see what *might* have happened.

HORACE FILBEE, a quiet, mousy little man who asks if he can enter his virtual world preferences into the CyberNet console *privately*. He's told by a female counselor that each design has to be supervised in order to prevent misuse of the system by creating disturbing or inappropriate virtual worlds. With considerable chagrin, he shows her a description of the world he wants to explore. She smiles. He's not at all alone in what he wants to do. It's a very commonplace fantasy.

Finally there is CLIFF WATERMAN, formerly a soldier who lost many of his team in a firefight overseas . . . a firefight he missed because he was wounded the week before and was in evac when it happened. He has carried the guilt over not being there when his team needed him ever since; has always believed that he could have saved them. He feels that by recreating that battle, and by being there this time with his team, he can resolve this once and for all. He brings photos of his team members, and asks if they can be scanned and used for the journey. They can. He will see his fellow soldiers one more time . . . and perhaps finally be able to get on with his life once more.

INTERCUT

INT. DEVON'S OFFICE as Devon returns from lunch. He checks his computer e-mail, and finds a disturbing message. Just the same words, flashing on his screen over and over: HELLO, DEVON. GOODBYE, DEVON. HELLO, DEVON. GOODBYE, DEVON. The message can't be tracked, has no source code, no "fingerprints," nothing to trace how it got into the system. It's as though the message somehow came from *inside* the system itself. . . .

INT. THE CENTER as one by one, the three newest visitors to CyberNet are hooked into the system. A display monitoring CyberNet reveals that there are just over ten thousand people worldwide hooked into CyberNet at this moment. The relays are hooked in, they're slipped into the skinsuits that assure complete sensory input from CyberNet . . . all seems well.

INT. DEVON'S OFFICE . . . as the monitor on his screen that also monitors CyberNet flashes GOODBYE, DEVON one last time, and suddenly goes black. All the monitors tied into CyberNet go down. "Oh, my god," Devon mutters.

INT. THE CENTER, at that exact moment, as ALARMS sound. Technicians race to their stations, system displays redline, sparks flash. Something's wrong with CyberNet.

All outside control over the Net is gone. Consoles no longer monitor the thousands of virtual worlds their clients are experiencing. They can't shut it down, can't control it.

A technician orders the clients unplugged. One technician goes to a bed on which one of the clients (not one of our three) is resting. Starts to pull the plug . . . and a neural feedback erupts . . . the client screams in pain . . . then falls to the floor.

Dead.

OUTLINE INTO SCRIPT

The outline for *The Virtual Highway* went through about four or five drafts before everyone decided they liked all the parts and pieces. That's about average for a development deal; the number of drafts can go much higher.

Upon finishing a spec outline, you may want to give it to someone you know and solicit criticism. If so, make sure it's someone who will tell you what she really thinks of your work. Do not go to your mother or your father. Your sister or brother, maybe; siblings are notoriously ruthless. A few friends or other writers. Be careful to tell the difference between actual story problems they might find and the other person's inevitable tendency to criticize something on the grounds that this isn't how *they* would write it. You have to do this your way; let 'em go write their own movie.

But if they point out obvious holes in the plot, objectively stiff dialogue or problems in structure, consider the advice carefully and, if you agree, make the changes in your treatment. Once you've gone through all this, and completed the outline, there's a temptation to stop and say, "Well, that's it, the story's done, now who wants to buy it?" If you're an established writer, with lots of credits, you can possibly shop around something at this stage. If you're a new writer, without credits, you'll find it tough going. So I strongly recommend that you do go ahead and write the finished screenplay before you begin marketing your story.

"But what if I write this whole long script and nobody buys it?" I hear someone ask from the back of the room. Then nobody buys it. *Today.* Tomorrow, it may have a better chance. A screenplay is an evergreen; studio executives are always moving in and out, trends come and go and what doesn't sell today can be a hot property six months down the road.

Meanwhile, you write another one. Because this book assumes you're here because you want a *career* as a scriptwriter, that you're not just a tourist who wants immediate gratification. A career takes work, usually in the form of trial and error. A painter isn't likely to sell his very first canvas. Why should writing be any different? Answer: It isn't.

And bear in mind that your first completed script may not, in fact, be altogether terrific. I'm not saying that it's guaranteed to be less than wonderful, only that the odds are stacked against it being golden the first time at bat. But just in finishing the script, you're instantly light-years ahead of the majority of would-be screenwriters who talk a good game, who tap out a page or two here and there but have never been able to finish a complete screenplay. Which will make your second screenplay just that much easier to write.

No time spent behind the typewriter is ever wasted. Not only has the writing made you better at your craft, but even an unsold, unproduced screenplay can be given to an agent as a sample of your work, thereby securing representation, which is invaluable at this point in your career. It can also be shown to a producer with the goal of getting you an assignment on some other project. Studios and producers often option the rights to various projects—novels, comic books, true stories—or have ideas of their own they'd like to see developed. If your sample shows you can handle that particular kind of story, it may land you a development deal in a related genre, taking someone's raw material and turning it into a finished screenplay.

Chapter Ten

The Screenplay

ome writers, having followed their stories through the developmental stages detailed thus far, find the task of writing the screenplays a bit anticlimactic. Which is why many spec screenplays die on the vine at the outline stage; the notion of tackling the same story one more time can be terribly daunting. This is perfectly understandable. One of the primary forces that makes a writer write is an internal pressure, an inner drive that won't rest until the tale has been told. Once this has been done, one's interest wanes.

It's at this point that a screenwriter must develop a highly tuned sense of discipline, a willingness to write and rewrite the same story as often as necessary, to polish it until it is as hard and bright as a diamond. You have to have an almost infinite capacity to look at your own words and the objectivity to restructure and rewrite as necessary, without holding onto something just because it's what you wrote that first day.

If it helps, remember that in truth, the whole story has *not* been told. The outline has conveyed the events, names and places that make up the high points of your story, but only in abbreviated form. The characters remain largely unexplored. Oh, there have been glimpses here and there, certainly. But it's only within the body of the screenplay that you have the opportunity to really develop your characters.

Your outline should function as a road map through the maze of your story, rather than an iron lock on your story. It will keep you on the right track as you move from one place and one event to another. But like anyone visiting a foreign country, never pay so much attention to the road map that you miss all the scenery. Your characters are the scenery in this case, and as long as you know where you are in your story and what should come next, never be afraid to poke around a few back roads or linger for a moment here and there, if in the end it gives you and your audience the chance to better understand who these extraordinary people really are.

To be perfectly honest . . . in almost two decades of writing, I have never followed an outline 100 percent faithfully from start to finish. As someone once said about war plans, "no outline has ever survived contact with the enemy," in this case, the script. Scripts live and die by how well they can surprise you as an audience member; and if you can leave room to be surprised by the turn of events in your story, you'll do better in the long run.

SCREENPLAY TIPS

Here are some other hints that may prove useful in writing your screenplay.

Avoid long, potentially tedious monologues. An unbroken speech that runs as a page or more can slow the pace of your screenplay to a torturous crawl. Handled well and carefully crafted, a brief speech can be a stirring, moving moment in your story. Handled improperly, long monologues can be deadly to an otherwise sterling script. If it's essential that a lot of information be conveyed during a single scene, try to break it up with occasional reactions from the other person or persons in the room. Even if the remarks only amount to observations of shock or astonishment, use them anyway. And be honest; how often in real life are any of us allowed to speak at length without someone or something—a ringing telephone, a solicitor at the front door—interrupting the flow of things? We rarely sit still while someone declaims for five minutes; let your characters react just the way you might in similar circumstances.

Now, on some occasions, you might actually want to write a long-winded monologue, to say something about the character involved. If the speaker is long-winded himself, or pompous, you can use the monologue as a device to reinforce this detail. If you desire, you can heighten this effect by having other characters try to get a word in edgewise, and fail. A long monologue can also be used in the context of a sermon or a broadcaster's delivery of the day's news. Paddy Chayefsky's screenplay for the motion picture *Network* is filled with such speeches, each brilliantly crafted to tell us about the characters involved. Thus, monologues function on two levels: They convey information overtly through the spoken word, while covertly telling us something about the person doing the talking.

A long monologue can serve other purposes as well; the character may be trying to avoid a topic and keeps going on about something quite irrelevant because it's far too frightening to talk about what *is* relevant. This can be a powerful tool for showing character.

(Here's a homework assignment: Write a speech in which someone talks about a given subject and the character never uses the word *I*, but ends up telling us more about the character than the subject at hand. After the first few tries, you'll find this a very useful tool.)

If you do decide to use the device of the long monologue, use it sparingly. There's a classic scene in *The Great Muppet Caper* wherein actress Diana Rigg delivers a long, involved monologue filled with more information than anyone could possibly care to hear. After the speech, Miss Piggy (manned—or perhaps pigged—by Frank Oz) asks, "Why are you telling me all this?" Rigg simply shrugs and says, "It's exposition. It has to go *somewhere*."

In addition, it's always a good idea to break up any scenes that, viewed in sequence, give the script a static feel. If you've got several scenes in a row where your characters are sitting around a room talking, you might want to throw a more active scene into the middle, get them out of the room, even if it's only the character driving toward the place where the next scene is set. Try to avoid using the same set too many times in a row, and try to layer your exterior and interior scenes as evenly as possible.

Calling the Shots

You should write primarily in master shots. Tell us where the scene is taking place (INT. BOB'S HOUSE - DINING ROOM), tell us when it is taking place, describe it briefly in narrative, then let it go. Use camera angles and secondary-shot descriptions when necessary to your story and to emphasize visual elements. And do so in clear terms; don't get too bogged down in technical language, for example, CLOSE - ON MARCUS, instead of ECU-MARCUS, with the latter standing for extreme close-up. If a non-technically inclined reader has to stop and translate as she reads, consequently falling out of the story, you're in trouble. Prevailing wisdom tells us that detailed camera directions will inevitably be ignored by the director. This is often true. One director I know makes it a point to take a felt-tip pen and black out all but the most essential directions on any script he directs. "What writers must remember," he explained, "is that they are responsible for the story, yes. But the director is responsible for the look of the film. There are a dozen ways that any shot can be filmed, and it is the director's responsibility, using his experience and training, to look at the finished set, the dynamics of the performers and a thousand other factors and decide which would be the best shot. To do less than that is to abnegate one's obligations as a filmmaker."

There is, however, a certain arrogance implicit in that statement. Yes, it is the director's job to translate the script to film. But it is the writer's obligation to *explain* that story and that vision to the director and others in the production food chain as clearly as humanly possible so there is no chance of misunderstanding the writer's intent in the story. So to that end, I always include camera angles and other specific information when I feel it is appropriate and necessary to fully understanding how a given scene is to be played out and what it fundamentally means.

If the director wants to black out the directions, that's his prerogative, but at least *once* it got written the way I felt was correct. And if he's got nothing better to do than play with felt-tip black pens, well, then I'm happy to have provided a moment's inspiration.

On the question of CUT TO in scripts . . . once these were commonly used as a transition device between scenes. It looked like this:

". . . and Bob exits the bedroom, casting a glance back as he goes. Sarah wonders what she's going to do next.

CUT TO:

INT. RACQUETBALL COURT

Bob's hitting the ball pretty hard."

No more. A few writers here and there drop them into a script for effect, but for the most part, the use of CUT TO has fallen by the wayside. Most times, when it's used at all, it's incorporated into the narrative descriptions rather than being isolated on a separate line.

". . . and Bob exits the bedroom, casting a glance back as he goes. As Sarah wonders what to do next, we go to

INT. RACQUETBALL COURT

where Bob's hitting the ball pretty hard."

The effect of this is to give the scenes a sense of narrative flow, moving naturally one into another and carrying the reader along smoothly rather than bumping into the cuts.

Similarly, only call for such transitions as a dissolve if it is your intention to indicate an interlude in time; or use a *wipe* (the introduction of the new scene by having it "wipe" across the screen from side to side, or from one corner to the other) if it is your intention to convey the feeling of an old movie, since this device was used frequently in the late silent-film era, and for such serials as *Buck Rogers*.

Plots and Pacing

One of the most common errors new screenwriters make is to start out too slowly, with characters walking into a room, saying hi, engaging in chitchat, and slowly getting around to the events of the story. Now, if you're David Mamet, this can be a wonderful device. But if you're starting out and just learning your craft, you may want to strengthen your position and start your screenplay on a strong point, a hook that will get the audience immediately interested in your story. Remember, you're fighting for the attention of an audience that just paid five or seven dollars per ticket and wants to get its money's worth from the moment the lights go down and the projector grinds to life. Naturally, your script continues to build toward a strong resolution with a series of smaller crests along the way, similar to hooks in television and radio writing, to help sustain the audience's interest. You don't have commercials to worry about here, but you still need those bumps in the story line to nudge the audience from time to time and reestablish interest.

Until you are secure with the techniques of screenwriting, it's often best to stick with a linear plot. Unless handled properly, jumping all over the place in time and space and the excessive use of flashbacks can confuse and even irritate an audience. Woody Allen's *Annie Hall* is a good example of a nonlinear plot properly handled, as are his *Stardust Memories* and *Interiors*. Vonnegut's *Slaughterhouse Five* (adapted by Stephen Geller, directed by George Roy Hill) is another prime example of how this device can be used well. *The Usual Suspects*, which won the Oscar for best screenplay in 1996, also used a nonlinear structure.

At risk of repeating information stated elsewhere, the single most important advice I can give you is to always, always remember that a script is made up of scenes that must stand on their own as well as serving to advance the larger story line. Each individual scene in your script has a beginning, a middle and an end; it has its own rhythm and logic, and each must be compelling in its own right. If an audience walks out of a theater having seen three or four really solid, dramatic, moving or action-packed scenes, they'll often feel the investment has been worth it, even if the plot per se was nothing to write home about.

Finally, when it comes time to resolve your story, be sure the resolution comes naturally. It should be organic, growing out of what went before. Dropping in a sudden, unexpected solution—the poverty-stricken mother of eight suddenly wins the Irish Sweepstakes, the real murderer confesses out of compassion at the very last moment—can get a hostile response from an audience that feels it's been cheated of a solid, well-crafted story.

The deus ex machina school of thought may have worked for the ancient Greeks, but in contemporary society, it's bound to have your audiences demanding their money back. It's best if your characters are *personally* responsible for the film's resolution. You don't send a hot shot New York cop to track down a murderer only to have the case solved by a street cop we've only seen for five minutes. If we care about the characters, we want to see them succeed. Let your main characters work their own way out of whatever dilemma you've put them in.

Or, as someone once said, "The practice of drama is to get your character stuck up a tree and then throw rocks at him." It's no fun to have someone else come along and take the rocks away. Your character has to save himself on his own.

SCREENPLAY FORM

Beyond these basic requirements, the form taken by your screenplay is largely determined by your own interests and attitudes and the kind of story you've chosen to tell.

The only other requirement to consider is the typographical format used in motion picture scripts.

The screenplay format is virtually identical to the format for television movies and for other programs produced on film.

All dialogue and scene descriptions are single-spaced and written in upper- and lowercase letters.

Double-space between two different sections of dialogue and between scene descriptions and dialogue.

When used in direct conjunction with dialogue, the NAMES of characters are capitalized and typed at 40 picas.

Dialogue directions and indications for inflection appear at 35 picas.

Dialogue itself appears between 30 and 60 picas, and its right margin is not justified.

The page number appears at 75 picas, usually four spaces from the top of the page.

The first page of your screenplay begins with the title, all in capital letters and underlined, centered on the page at seven lines from the top of the page. Five spaces below that, at twelve lines, the words FADE IN: appear, with the first scene appearing two lines farther down, at fourteen lines.

Each subsequent page begins with the page number in the upper right-hand corner at 75 picas, three lines, and the first continuing scene indicated seven lines from the top of the page.

Your title page is simple. The title of the script is typed in all capital letters and underlined at twenty-two lines from the top of the page, centered. Four spaces below that, at twenty-six lines, appear the words *An Original Screenplay* followed two lines later with *By [Your Name]*. Your name and address appear in the lower right-hand corner, single-spaced, written in upper- and lowercase letters. If you have an agent, his or her name is placed here instead, preceded by the note *Literary Representation:*. If it is a first draft, this is noted in the lower left-hand corner in all capital letters and underlined. (This is the case for whatever draft it might be.) Single-spaced below this is the date upon which the particular draft was completed.

This title page format is the same used for television or radio. The difference, of course, is that the series title is capitalized, followed two lines later by the individual episode title, written in upper- and lowercase and bracketed by quotation marks. The rest is the same.

The preceding typographical requirements are far less daunting than they used to be, thanks to computerized word processing programs designed especially for scriptwriters, such as Movie Master and Scriptor, among others. These programs make the process of hitting all the margins and tabs transparent so you can concentrate on the story, the dialogue and the characters.

When completed, your script will look something like the one shown here from *The Strange Case of Christine Collins*. I've selected the opening sequence from a spec screenplay I wrote that has been optioned repeatedly by studios and independent producers, including Shelly Duvall's Think Entertainment, and is currently under option to another company. I picked this excerpt because it uses a number of different techniques—voice-over, varying locales, transitions and other devices, superimpositions, period drama, camera directions, montage—best explained by example than anything else.

THE STRANGE CASE OF CHRISTINE COLLINS

FADE IN:

BLACK SCREEN

where we HOLD for just a BEAT, under the SOUND of phone lines buzzing, a flurry of women's voices answering phones and routing calls, and a strange noise . . . the sound of metal wheels rolling on a hardwood floor.

> OPERATORS
> (vo)
> Yes, sir, I'll route that call . . . I'm afraid no one
> answers . . . Crestwood 6-900, yes, just a moment . . .
> that will be station-to-station, ma'am. . . .

Then suddenly we're in

INT. PHONE COMPANY - SWITCHING ROOM - <u>1928</u>

LOW ANGLE passing banks of phone equipment where women sit hitting switches and plugging lines from one maze of sockets into another. This is practically the dawn of the telephone age, and everything is oversized . . . a collection of wires and headphones and large headsets.

CAMERA MOVES SMOOTHLY along the floor, turning a corner and going around the other side to yet another bank of operator stations. The NOISE generated by the calls, the buzzers and the operators is amazing. And over it all the low sound of metal wheels on hardwood continues. <u>SUPERIMPOSE: LOS ANGELES, MARCH 9, 1928.</u>

> OPERATORS
> I'm sorry, we can't give out that kind of information . . .
> Yes, ma'am, I'm still trying . . . my supervisor? Just one
> moment. (calling) Christine!

ON CHRISTINE COLLINS

Middle thirties, attractive, and no-nonsense . . . despite the fact that she's wearing roller skates and has been skating down the rows of phone banks. (At that time the phone banks were so large you had to wear skates to keep moving from one to the other quickly.) That is the sound we've been hearing.

Christine glances up as her name is called, and skates to one of the operator booths. The operator is MARGARET MASTERS, about the same age, and very attractive. She holds up her headset.

> MARGARET
> Says he wants to talk to my supervisor.

She hands the heavy headset to Christine, who puts it on.

> CHRISTINE
> Yes?

> MAN
>> (vo)

I want to talk to the supervisor.

> CHRISTINE

Speaking.

> MAN
>> (vo)

What're you trying to pull? I wasn't born yesterday. Now
let me talk to the guy in charge.

> CHRISTINE

Speaking.

> MAN

Okay, fine, you want to be that way, swell . . . I'll call
back later and when I get hold of the supervisor, you'll
hear about it big time!

He hangs up with a loud CLICK. She hands the headset back to Margaret,
who's smiling.

> MARGARET

Works every time. You know, if you were a guy, I'd have
a lot more complaints on my record.

> CHRISTINE

Not for long. I've seen you—

> MARGARET

Now, let's not get personal. That was only once, and it
was a long time ago. I'm a married woman now.
Besides . . . he was cute.

> CHRISTINE

Margaret . . . did you ever meet a guy you *didn't* think
was cute?

> MARGARET

I forget.

Christine smiles, looks up . . . and notices the wall clock. Three o'clock.

> CHRISTINE

I'd better get moving or I'll miss the Big Red!

She skates away. Margaret calls after her.

> MARGARET
> What about dinner tomorrow night? It's Frank's card
> night. Bring Walter.

> CHRISTINE
> (calling back)
> Done! See you then!

And she's gone. Margaret goes back to the phone bank.

EXT. PHONE COMPANY - DAY

Having put on regular shoes, Christine emerges from the front of the office
and to her chagrin sees

A STREETCAR

loading the last of its passengers. (The Los Angeles streetcar line was then
called the Big Red.)

CHRISTINE

races toward it as the last passenger gets in and it starts to close its doors.

> CHRISTINE
> Wait! Wait!

It does. The doors open and she climbs inside. The streetcar pulls away
and heads off into the distance. This leads us into

MONTAGE

showing a little of Los Angeles, circa 1928. Kids on the street selling newspapers. Apple vendors. Classic model cars lining the street. The scenes are
slow, lyrical, establishing place and time . . . less hectic than today, but
industrious. Vibrant.

EXT. SCHOOL - DAY

The streetcar stops, and Christine emerges. She puts her purse down on
the bench, straightens her hair a little, then moves toward

EXT. PLAYGROUND - WIDE SHOT

where we SEE several groups of children getting out of school, and HEAR the end-of-day bell RINGING in background. She is at some distance from us as she moves through the crowd of parents and children until finally we HEAR:

> WALTER
> (os)
>
> Mom!

She kneels as WALTER COLLINS, age nine, rushes into her arms, which envelop him. We're far enough away that we can't see the details of his face, just enough to see his size, and to know from her expression that this is her son, and that she loves him very much.

> CHRISTINE
>
> Hi, champ. How was your day?

She takes his hand and leads him out of the playground.

> WALTER
>
> It was okay. Billy Waters tried to take my Lone Ranger ring, then he punched me.

> CHRISTINE
>
> Did you punch him back?

> WALTER
>
> Yes.

> CHRISTINE
>
> Good. There's nothing wrong with standing up for yourself, Walter. Never start a fight . . . but always finish it.

> WALTER
>
> Can we see a movie tomorrow?

> CHRISTINE
>
> Well, let's see: Tomorrow's Saturday. I've got the whole day off . . . how about we see *two* movies? There's a new Chaplin movie at the Chinese theater, and a new Buster Keaton . . . and Margaret was telling me they're going to show a brand new kind of movie on Saturday. A talking movie. How's that sound?

> WALTER

Great!

> CHRISTINE

Then it's a deal.

And they head around a corner, disappearing from view.

EXT. COLLINS HOUSE - NIGHT

210 North Avenue 23. A small, pleasant house in a small, pleasant neighborhood. Trees line the streets, and we can see the occasional couple walking hand in hand down the street.

A few lights are burning downstairs in the Collins house. From one window, we can just make out the SOUND of a radio broadcast . . . the *Lone Ranger*.

INT. COLLINS HOUSE - KITCHEN - CONTINUOUS

Christine is drying dishes and putting them into a cabinet. In the background, we continue to hear the sound of the *Lone Ranger* radio show. She puts the last dish away, closes the cabinet and glances at her watch.

> CHRISTINE

Walter? Time for bed, champ.

She takes off the apron and enters

LIVING ROOM - CONTINUOUS

where Walter is curled up on the floor in front of the radio, fast asleep. She gently picks him up. It's not as easy as it used to be; he's getting big. She carries him upstairs to

INT. BEDROOM - MOMENTS LATER

she's gotten him changed and into bed. He stirs, only vaguely visible in the night, as she tucks him in.

> WALTER

I didn't hear how it ended. . . .

> CHRISTINE

The Lone Ranger got the bad guy.

> WALTER

You sure?

> CHRISTINE

He always does.

> WALTER

Can I wear my Lone Ranger ring to bed?

> CHRISTINE

No . . . it's not good to wear it at night, it's too tight, it'll cut off the circulation. Here . . .

She takes the ring, and places it on the bedstand.

> CHRISTINE

Now go on to sleep, we've got a busy day ahead of us tomorrow. We'll have lots of fun. But for now . . . sleep.

> WALTER

Okay . . . g'night.

> CHRISTINE

Good night.

She gives him a kiss. He rolls over and is asleep instantly. She sits on the edge of the bed, just looking at him for a long moment. Her eyes have that look that only parents understand when they look at something marvelous and miraculous . . . a new life, full of potential.

Finally, she stands, goes to the door and closes it most of the way, open just an inch for the light to spill in.
As he falls asleep, we PAN ACROSS to

THE LONE RANGER RING

on the bedstand, PUSHING IN until it FILLS FRAME, glittering in the moonlight. HOLD on it for a BEAT. It's important that we be able to recognize it.

INT. LIVING ROOM - CLOSE ON THE RADIO

The *Lone Ranger* drama concludes as Christine reaches INTO FRAME and switches off the radio. As the light behind the radio dial slowly fades, we

DISSOLVE TO:

EXT. COLLINS HOUSE - MORNING

An occasional car passing by, children playing in the neighboring yards. A beautiful March day.

INT. CHRISTINE'S BEDROOM - CONTINUOUS

She's finishing getting dressed as we see the blur that is Walter rush past her door.

> CHRISTINE
>
> Are you ready to go, Walter?

> WALTER
>
> Almost.

> CHRISTINE
>
> Well, you'd better hurry if you want to get to the movies on time.

> WALTER
>
> Okay.

She takes one last look in the mirror, and starts out when the phone rings. She hesitates, glancing at her watch . . . can she take the time for whatever this is? Finally, she picks up the phone.

> CHRISTINE
>
> Hello?

> MARGARET
> (vo)
>
> Hi, Chris. It's Margaret. I'm at the office.

INT. PHONE COMPANY - PHONE BANKS

We INTERCUT with Christine at home. Margaret looks harried.

> CHRISTINE
>
> What're you doing at the office on a Saturday?

> MARGARET
>
> The same thing you're about to be doing: working your fingers off. I got the call about an hour ago. Half the girls

are out with the flu that's going around. We're running out of hands. We could sure use yours.

> CHRISTINE
>
> But I can't—I was just about to —

> MARGARET
>
> I know it's short notice, Chris, but the place is a mad-house. We really need you. They're paying time and a half—

> CHRISTINE
>
> It's not that, it's just . . . I promised Walter I'd take him to the movies. I had to cancel our plans last weekend, and I'd hate to disappoint him twice.

> MARGARET
>
> You can take him tomorrow. It's only for a few hours, from now until . . . say . . . three or four o'clock. Please say yes, Chris. We need you.

Christine agonizes over it, then finally nods.

> CHRISTINE
>
> All right. But only until four. I'll be there as soon as I can.

> MARGARET
>
> Thanks, Chris! You're a lifesaver!

INT. CHRISTINE'S BEDROOM - CONTINUOUS

As she hangs up the phone and glances to the door. She's not looking forward to this. She straightens, and heads out.

INT. KITCHEN - MOMENTS LATER

Christine is making a sandwich and putting it on a plate, the phone cradled to her ear.

> CHRISTINE
>
> —so I was wondering if you could send Jamie over to watch Walter for me. It's just for a few hours, until about four. I see. Well, if she *does* call in, could you send her over? Thanks, Jean.

She hangs up, puts the plate and sandwich into the icebox, and steps out into

INT. LIVING ROOM

where Walter is playing listlessly with his Lone Ranger Decoder Ring as she pulls on her coat. He's not happy with the delay. She senses it, but there's nothing she can do.

> CHRISTINE
> I called Mrs. Riley, and she'll send Jamie over as soon as she gets in.

> WALTER
> I don't need a baby-sitter. I'm in fourth grade.

> CHRISTINE
> I know. And you've looked after yourself before. You're a big boy. But it never hurts to have an extra pair of eyes.
> (beat)
> I'll just be gone a few hours, champ. Four o'clock, latest. We'll go to the movies tomorrow, I promise. Maybe we can even find a *Lone Ranger* serial. Deal?

Walter nods glumly. She ruffles his hair, stands, moves away.

INT. PHONE COMPANY - PHONE BANKS

And if the place was noisy and hectic before, now it's even worse. Lines buzzing, voices chattering, two or three other operators at Christine's elbow, following her around with papers and requests.

> OPERATORS
> We've got lines jammed all the way from here to Ohio . . .
> Christine, he *insists* on talking to someone in charge . . .
> I've tried everything and the console's just dead . . . I need your signature here for a supply requisition. . . .

Christine keeps track of the requests as best she can, glancing up at

THE CLOCK

which now reads 4:12. She's already late getting home.

CHRISTINE

has to do what she has to do . . . and takes charge.

> CHRISTINE
> All right, get me the Omaha switcher system, see if we
> can route the calls through their facilities . . . and let's
> get that console running. . . .

She hurries off to take care of it all, the others following.

EXT. LOS ANGELES - ESTABLISHING - EARLY EVENING

The shadows are lengthening into twilight.

EXT. STREET - EVENING

as an exhausted Christine Collins gets off the streetcar. She glances at the clock on a gas station there at the corner. It's 6:15. She shakes her head, bone weary, and turns the corner to begin the long walk up the street toward home.

NOTE: as she turns the corner, half a block down the street, we SEE a pickup moving down the street, away from her position. We don't feature it, it's just there for a moment, and then gone. It should be a distinctive truck. We'll see it again.

TRACK WITH CHRISTINE

as she passes the other houses on the pleasant, green street, each with its lights on. We can HEAR conversations coming from inside, parents telling their kids to come in for dinner, radios playing music or dramas . . . Christine smiles at it, if only barely. It's her neighorhood. Home. She looks to

EXT. COLLINS HOUSE

dark, closed up. No lights on inside, no music or dramas on the radio. Dead silent.

CHRISTINE

stops. Noting the silence. The darkness. She picks up her pace, just a little. No need to panic, he could be upstairs asleep, could be in the back of the house, where the lights wouldn't show.

But she moves a little faster still as she crosses the lawn. She gets to the door. It's unlocked. She opens it and enters

INT. LIVING ROOM

dark, silent. Puts her purse down. Looks around.

                    CHRISTINE
          Walter?

Nothing. She goes into

INT. KITCHEN

switching on lights as she goes. Nothing. She opens the door to the refrigerator. The sandwich is still there. She closes it and heads out.

                    CHRISTINE
          Walter? . . .

INT. WALTER'S ROOM

She opens the door to his room. Toys are scattered on the floor, clothes on the bed. But no Walter. She goes back out again.

EXT. COLLINS HOUSE

She walks out onto the porch. Looks up and down the street. Pulls her sweater closer around her.

                    CHRISTINE
          Walter? Honey? Time to come in.

No response. No Walter. She steps down off the porch onto the lawn. Toward the sidewalk. Looking this way and that. A little GIRL on a tricycle rolls past.

                    CHRISTINE
          Susie . . . Susie, honey, have you seen Walter?
                    GIRL
          Uh, uh.

The girl continues on her way. Christine still hasn't hit the panic button yet; this happens all the time with kids. She crosses the street to

EXT. RILEY HOUSE

where she knocks on the door. Waits. A light comes on, and the door opens. MRS. RILEY, forties, stands in the doorway.

> CHRISTINE
> Mrs. Riley, I'm sorry to bother you at dinnertime, but I was wondering if Walter was here.

> MRS. RILEY
> No, no I'm afraid not.

> CHRISTINE
> Do you know if Jamie was able to look in on him?

> MRS. RILEY
> Well, I mentioned it to her, but she was going to a party with some of her friends and they were running late . . . you know how teenagers are, I don't think she had a chance. Is something wrong?

> CHRISTINE
> I don't know. I hope not. Thank you, Mrs. Riley.

Christine heads back down the porch, going back the way she came. The door closes behind her.

EXT. STREET

Christine stops at the sidewalk. Again looks up and down, up and down the street. Arms folded against the growing chill.

> CHRISTINE
> Walter? . . . Walter!

She starts walking again. Faster now. We STAY WITH HER. Looking around trees and porches, anywhere a nine-year-old boy might hide. Looks at the houses, from which the now-taunting sound of laughter and conversation continues, houses where everything is all right, where they don't have to worry about where their children are.

She hears the sound of children playing. Laughing. She picks up her pace, homing in on the sound. He's there. He must be there. He just got busy, forgot the time. . . .

She turns the corner. Three children are playing. None of them are Walter. She stops there, looks down each of the intersecting streets. Not a sign of anyone, let alone Walter.

And now, the worry growing, she heads back the way she came. Faster now. Heels clicking quickly on the hard sidewalk. She rushes back into

INT. COLLINS HOUSE - LIVING ROOM

where she bursts in, leaving the door open, looking frantically in the hope he might have come back.

> CHRISTINE
>
> *Walter?* . . .

But the room, and the house, is empty. And now she *is* getting worried. And scared. She crosses to the phone. Hesitates for the barest moment, then picks up the receiver.

> CHRISTINE
>
> Yes, Operator, give me the police, please.

You'll note that the sluglines are used, as noted earlier, for both location information and to give us a sense of narrative flow; you go from the larger location to emphasizing Christine in the shot, then move around the locale further. It's a way of writing ANGLE - CLOSE ON CHRISTINE without having to write all that out. The key, again, is to make the story flow in the page. Feel free to be visual in your writing style, to include elements that don't directly involve dialogue but that help to set the scene.

In the previous version of this book, I indicated that you should number your scenes. This has been all but eliminated at every stage until the script finally enters preproduction. This isn't anything you need to worry about any longer. When prep starts on a script, it's either scanned in (if typewritten) or an ASCII version of the script (assuming it was written on a computer but not with one of the available script-format programs) is inserted into a script-breakdown program, and a scene-numbered script is turned out by the script coordinator.

This is a good thing; omitting scene numbers in early drafts saves a great deal of hassle in the revision process because you're not constantly having to change scene numbers throughout the entire script to accommodate an omitted or juxtaposed scene.

Bottom line on screenwriting: Write the movie that you would like to see, a movie you'd gladly spend seven dollars to see; try to visualize it as clearly as you can, and describe that in as much detail as is required for someone outside your head to see what you're seeing. If you follow those simple rules, even if you're off format a little here and there, you'll be fine.

Once you've finished your first draft, there are several questions you must ask yourself.

Is it too long or too short? (Reading the script aloud will help you determine this.) If the former, then eliminate any scenes that are not truly necessary, that don't advance the plot or characters. If the latter, then go back into your scenes and see if they're too dry, too perfunctory. If so, fill out those scenes with more characterization or more action.

In analyzing your script to decide if it's too short or too long, remember that some scenes that might take only a paragraph to describe last several minutes on film. Likewise, a scene that takes a complete page of careful description might require only a few seconds on film. Try and compensate for this in your reading.

Does the script say what you wanted it to say? If your script, and the resultant movie, is intended to be more than just a shoot-em-up, if it is supposed to *say* something about an issue that matters to you, has that been conveyed clearly without bashing the viewer over the head with it? I quote Mark Twain: "If you would have your work last forever, and by forever I mean fifty years, it must neither overtly preach nor overtly teach; but it must *covertly* preach and *covertly* teach."

Is it dull? Too obscure? Too dry? Does enough *happen* in the story to hold the attention of your audience?

Ask yourself honestly if the script would do better as a television movie or a feature film. If you finally decide it might not have the special magic that would qualify it as a feature film, that it might not be *big* enough or promotable enough, try marketing it as a television movie.

Although cover art is no longer in vogue, some writers do from time to time consider artwork in the interior of the script, between pages. Be cautious about this. Don't do it just to do it, just to be showy. If there's some visual concept in your script that could use elaboration, that's fine; otherwise, err in the direction of exclusion. If you *do* include any kind of storyboard or visual breakdown or illustration inside the script, be sure it's done professionally and looks great, otherwise you're dead because you *know* that the first thing the studio exec is going to do is flip to the picture, and if it isn't dynamite, if it reflects poorly on you, he'll be prejudiced instantly, regardless of the quality of the writing.

Once your script is finished, check it one more time for typographical errors or glitches made in your final edits. Remember, professionalism counts for a lot. Then take the script to your nearest copy store and have copies run off on standard three-hole paper. Clean, crisp white paper, not pastels or colored fancy papers or parchments. The copies should be sharp, easily read and unwrinkled.

Never send your original copy to a producer; you can be sure he'll lose it or spill coffee on it. Keep it in a safe place, and use it only for making more copies. If a copy starts looking ragged or dog-eared, toss it out; if it looks like it's been shopped a lot, that can work against you psychologically.

Your cover sheet can be either standard three-hole paper, or copied onto a heavier stock of three-hole paper, with the option there of using colored paper. Sixty-pound bond is usually preferred. If you do use color, try gray, deep blue or cream-colored stock. Make sure the backing sheet is the same stock. Then bind the whole thing together with brass paper fasteners.

Finally, hold the script in your hands and heft it a few times. Go ahead every writer does it. A finished, bound, snazzy-looking script is a joy to behold. You shouldn't feel the least bit sheepish if you stand there, a silly grin on your face, hefting the script, glancing through it, holding it at a distance for a better look and generally carrying on. Why not? You've put in an awful lot of work, and a little aesthetic appreciation is small enough reward.

Besides, now comes the hard part. It's time to go back to work.

Chapter Eleven

Marketing the Screenplay

A t long last, you've got a finished screenplay for a feature film in your hands, ready to go. Now what?

First, you start off by accepting the sobering fact that yours is now one of 50,000 to 100,000 unsold scripts floating around Hollywood. Not long ago, the heads of some of the largest agencies in town got together and determined that the odds of a new writer selling his first screenplay were 140,000 to 1. Many studios read as many as 5,000 screenplays each year or more, looking to find the 12 scripts they will eventually produce.

So assuming that that cold reality isn't enough to stop you, your next step is to proceed logically to make your script stand out from the rest of the pack. Accept that you have an advantage going in because the majority of those other scripts are either poorly written or poorly marketed by people who don't understand the nature of the business and thus are crippled right from the start.

Stop now. Go back and read that last sentence again. And again, until you really get it, because what I'm about to say is probably not politic or kind or friendly, but it happens to be the truth. There's a reason so many unsold scripts are floating around Hollywood: The majority of them, as much as 70 percent or more, generally those by first-timers, are just plain awful. They're by people who thought they could write a script as good as anybody else without learning the techniques or the craft of writing.

While working as story editor or producer on series, and in my capacity judging the Writer's Digest Scripts Competition for five years running, I've seen a *lot* of neophyte scripts. They're usually written with the best of intentions, and God love 'em they try really hard, but what are the odds of real, genuine quality in the novels section of your local bookstore? The majority are OK, many are marginal, a very few are genuinely terrific. And that's among those good enough to be published. Now consider what *didn't* make it into published form.

Same rule applies to scripts by those just now trying to break into the business.

Which is why I've hammered at you about learning the rules and structuring your story and making it as good as you humanly can. That can only help to elevate it and draw attention to it. A good script glows in the dark against the general competition.

GETTING AN AGENT

Now, back to the question: Once you have a finished script, what do you do with it?

The first and foremost goal is to use it to help secure an agent to represent you to the studios, networks and producers. This process is discussed in detail in "The Art of Getting and Keeping an Agent." To sum up: Using the list of agencies provided in the Writers Guild Signatory Agency List, you begin sending out query letters offering the script, collecting responses, sending the script to those who respond positively to your inquiry, then setting up meetings.

Although the rest of this chapter will examine how to try to sell your script on your own, the importance of an agent—a known person in the Hollywood community who knows your work, respects it and can front it to the rest of our sometimes dysfunctional industry—cannot be overstated. It can save you hideous amounts of time and legwork in selling your script.

A good agent knows what stars have development deals at the studios and can direct a script that's perfect for a given star to that person. A good agent knows what studios have recently acquired the rights to books or stories that might suit your abilities. An agent at this stage of your career can be invaluable in getting you in the door for get-acquainted meetings with execs. You shouldn't always aim for the big agencies either; you can get lost there. And the title of a major agency isn't always the surest indicator of quality. One producer I know is always willing to read scripts by new writers represented by a certain smaller, boutique agency because he knows it's picky about its writer-clients and that whatever comes across his desk from that agency is going to be interesting reading.

SELLING IT YOURSELF

Can you sell your script without an agent? Yes, it's possible. Difficult, but possible. It simply requires patience, persistence and an adherence to the rough guidelines that follow.

The first thing you'll want to decide is to whom to send your screenplay. Part of this decision is estimating, in your own mind, the approximate budget for the screenplay should it get produced. Nothing specific, mind you; you don't have to say it'll be around $6 million or $7.5 million. Just realistically decide, as closely as you can, whether it will be a big-budget film or a small-budget film. If it calls for a lot of exotic locations, special effects or very extensive sets, you can reasonably assume it's a big-budget film. If it needs only a small cast, simple locations and minimal effects, you could safely classify it as a low-budget film. Within the filmmaking community, a low budget is anything under about $5 million to $6 million, although for its own purposes in deciding what a writer should be paid, the Writers Guild defines a low-budget film as anything below about $1 million.

This determination will narrow down the process of selecting a likely producer. Most independent producers probably can't handle the overwhelming costs of a huge film. By the same token, you'd have a better chance placing a low-budget film with an independent producer than with a major studio, at least as of this writing. The studios currently have the notion that to be successful, the film has to be a *spectacle*, offering something huge, something you can't get on TV. But considering the success of smaller films like *The Bridges of Madison County* and such recent big-budget disasters as *Waterworld*, it's likely this trend will reverse itself a little in coming years, and the major studios will soon begin looking for more low-budget films to produce and distribute.

So a low- or medium-budget film gives you greater flexibility, allowing you the choice of approaching either a major studio or an independent producer. Don't cheat your script of what's necessary to tell the story, but don't overly burden your script with unnecessary or excessive production values. It's also easier for a screenwriter who hasn't previously sold a script to sell a low-budget script than a high-budget screenplay, simply because the producer won't risk as much should the film fail to become a big hit. Remember, the more you can minimize the risks of production, the greater the chances of your script being both sold *and* produced.

Your next step is to narrow down the possible alternatives to specific production companies.

You can use a number of resources to get a list of current film producers who might be interested in your particular script. There are many publications that provide extensive lists of film producers. All of these can be found at either well-stocked newsstands or libraries.

Boxoffice, a monthly trade magazine aimed at movie distributors, provides a good deal of information about what kinds of films the studios are currently producing. This is particularly true of its annual *Buyer's Guide Directory*, which is published in August.

Pacific Coast Studio Directory, a quarterly directory that has been called the "bible of the entertainment industry" is a slim volume that contains the names, addresses and phone numbers of virtually every production company in Los Angeles, San Francisco, Arizona, Hawaii and ten other states. In addition, it includes the same information on talent agencies, publications, industry craftspeople, the different unions, advertisers and film/television bureaus in each state listed. If you want to contact a major studio or a small, independent producer, you'll probably find either of them listed here somewhere. Of course, you have to know the name of the company before you can look it up. *Pacific Coast Studio Directory* may be a bit difficult to find outside Los Angeles, so you may want to call Directory Assistance for Los Angeles to obtain the current address.

The Hollywood Reporter Bluebook is an annual volume that contains hundreds of listings of different production companies and their needs. It's particularly useful for a scriptwriter, and it makes a good companion volume to the *Pacific Coast Studio Directory*.

Daily Variety and *The Hollywood Reporter* are both excellent sources of information on current trends in filmmaking and are published on a daily basis. The former publication publishes regular film and television production charts, complete with telephone numbers.

Probably the single most useful directory, the *Hollywood Creative Directory* is also the most expensive (the latest edition at this writing, volume 24, cost a hefty forty-five dollars) and is nearly impossible to find outside Los Angeles. Currently published out of the HCD offices in Santa Monica, California, the directory has detailed staff listings for every major studio and production company, is nicely cross-referenced and has a list of studios that currently have development deals with actors who may be best suited to your story.

Previous editions of this book have contained listings of current film production companies. However, more and more production has gone to independent producers who often form a corporation just to do one or two projects and whose addresses often change. Incorporating those addresses into the current edition becomes problematic at best and may end up providing inaccurate data. As a result, that feature has been omitted.

Choosing a Market

Using these resources, pick out a handful of production companies you believe might be appropriate for your screenplay. Rank them in order, from the largest to the smallest company. You must also decide whether you want to approach all these producers simultaneously or if you would prefer to market your script to one producer at a time. A case can be made for and against both these routes. Marketing your script to one producer at a time can be very time-consuming. But many producers like to think that they, or at most one or two others, are the only ones who have seen the script. So sending your script all over Hollywood in a massive assault may alienate some producers and can be an expensive proposition. However, if you manage to get two studios interested in your script, you can have them bid on the property, thereby raising the ceiling on what you'll get up front. Auctions have become fairly common in Los Angeles, but primarily through agents.

Do *not*, as I've seen done on occasion, send out mass copies of your script and tell producers they've got a deadline or that you're holding an auction of your own. Only the top agents are qualified to do this, and this will only get laughs at the other end as your script is either roundfiled or sent back.

My personal feeling is that you should market your script on an individual basis or, at most, to two producers simultaneously. Any more than that and you're risking trouble.

Having selected the first producer you intend to approach, you must then invest a little more money in a telephone call. Call the specific production company you're interested in and ask for the story department. It's not at all uncommon for as many as a dozen production companies to be situated on the same lot, using the same switchboard, so be absolutely certain that the switchboard operator knows which production company you want. If the production company has its own direct outside line, then this isn't a problem. Note: The *Hollywood Creative Directory* routinely includes this information as part of its listings.

Once you've been transferred to the story department, ask for the name of the story editor. Don't ask to speak with the person, just get the name, thank the answerer for her time and hang up. Note: Some studios refer to their story editor types as "creative executives." This is yet another piece of what may seem to be a conspiracy designed to confuse you.

To understand why this bit of information is important, it is necessary to first explain a little about how a production company works.

In some respects, a production company is not unlike a book publishing company. Each is literally flooded by a steady flow of manuscripts, solicited and otherwise. Consequently, production companies employ one or more story editors to deal with this; in turn, beneath the story editors are large numbers of professional readers charged with the responsibility of wading through the dreck and finding the occasional jewels. There are several ways studio readers differ from the readers at a book publishing company. First, they are all members of a union, specifically the Story Analysts division of the International Alliance of Theatrical Stage Employees (I.A.T.S.E.), Local 854. Second, many of these readers are retained on a part-time basis and may work for several different studios. Finally, not a few of these readers—who often prefer to be called story analysts—are, themselves, writers. Some of them are Writers Guild members, but most of them are beginning writers who want to learn something about script-writing firsthand or want to slip in a script or two of their own along the way. If you are a resident of the Hollywood/Los Angeles area and would like to try this route, you should contact I.A.T.S.E. and find out the procedures.

One way in which studio readers are like publishing readers is that unless you specifically address your manuscript to someone there, you're likely to have a more difficult time getting anyone's attention. Putting someone's name on the letter of inquiry instead of simply addressing it to the story department makes that person at least partly responsible for your manuscript. It also gives the reader the feeling that if you know whom to approach, you must know what you're doing . . . and, again, that impression is always important in the screenwriting business.

Even though you have the story editor's name, and even though the story editor may read your letter of inquiry and may even respond personally, if you're an unknown commodity your script will almost always be read first by a reader, who will then decide if it's worth the story editor's time. Yeah, it's profoundly unfair. But it's the nature of the beast.

Most readers are either in college or fresh out of college, still trying to figure out for themselves what makes a good story. Their journey being far from over, that may not put them in the best position to evaluate a script written by, say, a five-time Oscar winner. Understanding story takes time and effort and experience and a few years to *really* understand what makes a story work. If the story editor is being paid big bucks to read scripts, he ought to read them instead of fobbing them off on readers. Once a curious journalist submitted a retyped copy of the script for *The Maltese Falcon* to dozens of studio readers. The readers not only didn't *recognize* the script, but they actually *rejected* that script on the basis that they didn't think it would make a good movie.

The Query Letter

Once you have the story editor's name, write a query letter because an unsolicited script arriving without prior warning is anathema to film producers just as it is for television and radio producers.

Your query letter, like your script, should be spare and to the point. You should state that you are familiar with the films they produce; that you have developed a feature film screenplay that is consistent with their trends in production; that you have followed this development through the synopsis, outline and final screenplay stages; and that the script is currently available for examination. You should also point out that you own all the rights to the screenplay, that it is an original work (or, if it's based on a true story, that you own all the pertinent rights to that story) and that since it's consistent with popular trends, it will likely be a very commercial property. If you have any special qualifications—a degree in an area touched upon by the script, for instance, or direct access to someone involved in the story on which the script is based—mention them as well. You can indicate in general terms the type of screenplay you have—"It's a mystery thriller with an erotic underpinning that ties into the big controversy about capital punishment and dog training"—but do not include specific, detailed information about the story. This will protect both you and the studio from complications concerning plagiarism.

Conclude by stating that if the story editor would be interested in reading the completed screenplay, you would be pleased to send it along for his examination. Also state that you are happy to enclose a release form (available in the appendix) with your submission, but that if there is a specifically worded release form the company prefers, ask that it be forwarded so you can include it with your submission.

As a rule, your finished query letter should run about a page long, and certainly no more than a page and a half. It should be as tightly and well written as possible. I say this because I've seen a lot of writers who can turn out fantastic scripts but who slapdash off some of the crummiest queries I've ever seen. If you've just spent half a year of your life working on a screenplay, it only makes sense to put a little effort and forethought into your query. You should also be sure to keep a copy of the query for reference in writing future letters to the story editor and so that you can just retype (or print out) another should you need to approach another studio.

For further assistance in writing a query letter, a sample letter is printed here. Needless to say, it should not be copied verbatim. It would cause much concern if story editors here in Los Angeles were to suddenly begin getting a series of identical query letters.

Mr. William Young
Creative Executive
Warner Bros. Pictures
4000 Warner Boulevard
Burbank, California 91522

Dear Mr. Young,

I have recently completed an original screenplay that I believe is consistent with the quality and type of film produced by Warner Bros.

Entitled *The Nightshade Equation*, the screenplay includes many of the elements of supernaturalism that have become popular in recent years, while taking an entirely different approach that has not been previously explored: the relationship between the supernatural and the Internal Revenue Service.

While not a member of the Writers Guild, I have been a freelance writer in other media for several years, and *The Nightshade Equation* is partly based on actual research that I carried out in the area of the occult and which formed the basis for several articles and short stories that I have published on this area in leading regional magazines. (I still retain all rights to the idea, however.)

I would appreciate the opportunity to submit this screenplay for evaluation by the Warner Bros. Story Department on a purely speculative basis. I will be happy to enclose a standard release form with the submission or if there is an in-house release preferred by Warners, I will sign and enclose that one instead.

Hoping that I shall hear from you soon in this regard, I remain

Most sincerely yours,
A. Nother Writer

Follow-Up

Surprising as it may seem, you probably won't have to wait long for a reply. You'll sometimes get word back from the studio within a few weeks, or maybe as much as a month, after you sent off your query. During this period, you can realistically look forward to one of two responses. The first is that they simply cannot look at any script unless it's submitted by an agent. But don't let this discourage you because there are many other producers that *don't* require an agent. They're not as numerous, but they are there; it just may take you a while to find them. (Remember what we said earlier about not trying this business if you're not dedicated to it? This is where the crunch comes.)

The second possibility is the sought-after permission to submit your screenplay for review. In this latter case, they may tell you to use your own release form, or they will send one along.

Before sending anything off, however, you should take one more step, largely for your own protection. Register the script with the Writers Guild of America, west. It's unlikely anyone will plagiarize your script, but it's never a bad idea to cover all your bets. The steps for registering a script are simple; just send a copy and the appropriate fee to the WGAw office in Los Angeles. The WGAw is located at 7000 West Third Street, Los Angeles, California 90048-4329. The main telephone number is (213) 782-4520. Information about script registration can be obtained by calling (213) 782-4540.

The registration fee is fairly small compared to the huge expenses in establishing the date of origin of a concept or a script long after the fact; the usual registration fee is around fifteen to twenty dollars for nonmembers. With this done, you have the option of including the line *Registered, WGAw* on the title page of your screenplay, directly under the date in the lower left-hand corner, along with the serial number the Guild will have assigned your script. Including this information isn't really necessary; as long as you know it's there, that's what matters most . . . and some producers may even look upon this with a jaundiced eye, taking this as a sign that you think they might try to steal your material. Suffice to say this will not endear you to them.

With your material finally collected and your release form filled in, you can then send the material to the person who responded to your letter. Be sure to refer back to your earlier letter and to having received her responding letter so the secretary who opens all the mail will know your property is not coming in unexpected. You should also write the words *Release Form Enclosed: As Requested* on the outside of your mailing envelope.

Then . . . well, then you wait.

Alternate Strategies

While you're waiting for a reaction to this direct approach, let's consider some of the other, less direct means of selling your screenplay.

If you have decided to write a screenplay with a specific actor in mind—one currently under contract to a studio for a set number of motion pictures—you should state this in your query letter to that studio. (For all other studios, don't mention the casting element, since the actor may not be available to them anyway.) This can further help to move your property along since the performers who enter such deals frequently put pressure on the story department to come up with the perfect vehicle for their talents, and if such a script comes in over the transom, so much the better. Again, trade magazines are a valuable means for determining which actor has a multipicture deal with the various studios, as is the *Hollywood Creative Directory*. (Example: According to the current *HCD*, Dustin Hoffman's Punch Entertainment has such a deal with Columbia Pictures.)

Should you have a specific performer in mind who may not be under contract for a certain number of movies but who is just perfect for the starring role, you have the option of approaching the performer directly. This can be difficult. Once upon a time, the Screen Actors Guild routinely forwarded letters to their members. No more. One option is to contact SAG, ask for the agent of a given performer and attempt to write the actor in care of that agent.

More and more actors are forming their own independent production companies, and that information can be gleaned from the industry trades and the other publications mentioned here. Actor Shelley Duvall, for instance, has her own independent company, Think Entertainment, based in Studio City.

In your query letter to a performer, you should include all the information included in your query to a producer, adding your conviction that the role is consistent with the performer's other roles but also allows the actor to expand beyond what has been offered in the past. (Many actors yearn for the opportunity to show they can do more than one kind of role but rarely get the scripts that allow them to do this. Comic actor Jim Carey is dying to do a serious dramatic role.) If you sincerely believe it, or can convince yourself of same, you could even state that you wrote the script *specifically* with that performer in mind.

If the performer likes the script, he can option your screenplay directly, individually or through the performer's production or loan-out company, or can approach a studio with the desire to do your screenplay. This technique is a long shot but has worked from time to time. In fact, it was precisely through this method that Frank Sinatra read, liked and agreed to star in *Von Ryan's Express*.

So it *can* be done. The question is, *should* you do it? If you fail to get any kind of representation, that narrows your marketing options to individual effort. But always go the way of the agent first. Writing a script is a difficult task at best; marketing it adds a second layer of difficulty that will in the end cut into the time you can spend behind the keyboard writing new scripts. And the odds are good that if your script really is good enough, it will eventually find someone willing to represent it.

Which brings us to a sidelight to agenting that is primarily related to the movie business: the *packager*.

In recent years, a growing number of agencies have begun following the example set by such monolithic corporations as ICM (International Creative Management), CAA (Creative Artists Agency, led until recently by the mega-agent Michael Ovitz) and the William Morris Agency and have become more active participants in the filmmaking business. They have done so through the clout provided by representing writers, actors and directors. If a packager agrees to represent a new writer's script, she can then call a studio and offer not only the script, but an established performer and a director, both picked from the agent's stable. In essence, packagers hand a studio a film ready to be shot, with all the major players in position. This is what's known in the business as a "package deal."

A package deal can occur for many reasons. It could be that the agent has a good script that he knows is going to require a big budget, but it's by an unproven writer. By throwing in an established name performer and director, he maximizes the studio's chances of breaking even, sells the new writer's script and gets his other two clients some work. In the past, if an agent spotted a coming trend, she could call a studio and promise the studio a certain number of name performers and a director, with the script to be written at a later date that capitalizes upon that trend. But as time has passed, one element has made rationalizations for package deals consistently less necessary: money. An agent who puts together a package for a movie using his own clients not only gets the agenting fee for the services of those clients, but can also negotiate, and usually get, a separate *packaging* fee, either as a flat fee or a percentage of the film's profits. And the packaging fee on a successful major motion picture can be *substantial*.

The Process Continues

To return to the mechanics of the submission process . . . once your script actually arrives at the studio, if you're not a known commodity (and sometimes even if you *are*), the script is turned over to one of the readers (aka story analysts), who reads the entire screenplay for the first time. If it is, in his estimate, unproducible, uninteresting or similar to something the studio is already doing . . . or, simply, if the reader just doesn't like it . . . the script will be shunted back to you (or your agent) with a brief note indicating that it's not their type of film, or they were unable to generate enough interest in it to pursue it further or suchlike.

If, on the other hand, it is producible, interesting and looks like a property that might fit in well with the studio's other projects, the reader will write three things: a synopsis of the script in a page or two of narrative; an appraisal of the script, its strengths, weaknesses, its potential audience; and, on occasion, a recommendation of a specific producer. This done, he then kicks the screenplay back to the story editor with the written commentaries.

The story editor is the next person to read your script. Upon doing so, she may choose to reject the script and return it, or she may bump the script on to the next person in the chain of command, adding her own comments to the reader's.

It's when the script leaves the story editor's office that things really start to get confusing. Based upon my experiences and those of other writers, and after having spoken with representatives of a dozen major studios and independent production companies, it seems safe to say that there is no clear-cut chain of command. "Every script is different," explained a story editor at Paramount Pictures. "I've never yet seen two scripts take the same route on the way to a possible production. There are often group creative meetings, someone may come in from inside the company and personally take over or a director might come to us specifically asking to do that particular script. But there's no one person anywhere along the line who can decide that the company's going to do a particular screenplay, with the exception of the president of the company, who has the final word on all projects submitted for our examination."

Here, however, are some examples of what can happen and what frequently does happen: The script may go from the story editor to an individual producer within the company whom the editor believes might be interested in the project. If so, the producer approaches the president directly and, after a long negotiation process, gets the go-ahead to proceed with the film. This is the quickest route.

If the story editor can't come up with an interested producer, the script goes to any one of the many vice-presidents in charge of production. More people read the script. More appraisals are written, initialed and shuttled on. More meetings are held. Copies of the script may be sent to outside (independent) producers and directors to solicit their support for the property. If enough interest is developed, the entire project is laid at the feet of the president, who makes the final decision.

The script may find its way into the hands of an inside producer who likes it even though others want to pass on it. In such a situation, he may option the script personally, promising to work with the scriptwriter until the property is appropriate for production. At that time, he will secure producer status for the property.

The script may also be sent on to an executive producer within the company. The executive producer, who carries a hefty amount of weight with the company, may get permission from the president to pursue a development deal. With this, she will assign a producer to the property and attempt to find a director.

If you've submitted your script to an independent production company, a producer within that company may choose to approach a major studio with which the company may (or may not) be affiliated for a set number of movies.

Possible Responses

There are other possibilities beyond those listed here, and even if it gets very high up in the chain, it's still possible that someone may opt to pass on the script anywhere along the line. But if not, here are the potential responses you will get. (The response time, by the way, can range anywhere from a few weeks to several months.)

Again, there's always the possibility of flat-out rejection.

The studio may decide to option the script for one or two years while deciding whether or not to purchase it outright. An *option* means that the studio will agree to pay you a certain fee, usually anywhere from $5,000 to $10,000, to hold onto your script during that time while it tries to set it up. You, in turn, promise not to market the script anywhere else until the option period has expired. During the period covered by the option, you may be asked to rewrite the screenplay for additional money. The studio will use this time to make up its mind once and for all whether to go ahead with the film or not. Once so decided, the studio puts together a deal and gets the film moving into preproduction.

Finally, the studio may opt to purchase the script outright and move directly into preproduction. If this is the case, you will be offered a flat fee, the possibility of a percentage and possibly a salary for further revisions. We'll take a closer look at the dollars and cents involved, but for the moment it's important to emphasize two points:

First, even though your script may be optioned or even purchased, this does not guarantee production. Many more scripts are purchased each year than are ever produced, and nearly three times as many scripts are optioned annually than are purchased and produced. But having one script optioned or purchased is a vital first step. You may receive an assignment to write another film for the same studio, and your next original treatment will be given even greater consideration.

Second, either of these two occurrences will allow you to join the Writers Guild and to get an agent. I strongly urge anyone who receives any kind of offer whatsoever from a studio to immediately contact an agent. Explain that a deal is already in progress, sign a representation contract and have the agent step in and negotiate the sometimes awesome legal machinations that arise whenever one deals with the film industry.

Two final caveats: Once your script has landed at a major studio and the reader has turned in his or her written analysis (referred to as "coverage"), that coverage almost always remains at the studio indefinitely. What does that mean for you? It means that if the script is deemed poorly written or unproducible, it is effectively dead at that studio for the foreseeable future. This is the other reason I dislike the concept of studio readers. If you happen to get a reader who just doesn't like romantic movies, a perfectly good script in that genre, which another reader, story editor or producer might love, is essentially blackballed, a stain that persists long after the individual(s) responsible has moved on.

This is compounded by the fact that there are not that many major studios capable of financing big films, even though a smaller production company can sometimes finance its own lower-budget films. This becomes a problem for writers when the independent producer asks for a "free option." A free option means . . . well, it's free—to the producer, anyway—so you give him the right to take your script to the major studios and try to get money for a development deal.

Many beginning writers fall for this ploy. It sounds so reasonable. "Listen, I think it's a great script, we have a director who's dying to do it, I think we can get Stallone, but we need to get a major studio on board for a movie like this. So what I'd like to do is just send it, discreetly, to a couple of people I know at Paramount and Universal. I've already talked to them about it off the record, and they're interested. So what I'd like is a free option for just ninety days while I try to get them onboard. If we wait to do an option here, it'll tie things up for weeks, and the property is hot. Besides, as much as I like it, you're a new writer, and I think the boss'll be more inclined to green light the project if we can get a major to sign on."

And you know what happens then? If you say yes, the script goes to the two major studios, and if for whatever reason they reject it—and sometimes that rejection can have more to do with the indie producer than with your words—the coverage stays at the studio, and you've just lost two of the major venues to get your script produced. If you go to another independent producer, that producer then can't go back to Paramount or Universal because it's dead there. You've let someone kill off two of the major opportunities for your work to be produced without even paying you for it.

This, not to put too fine a point on it, is not a good thing.

Insist on an option for money before letting an independent producer take your script to a studio. I don't care how much she wheedles, begs, connives, convinces, persuades, threatens or carries on cranky. I've been down this road, and so have many other writers. It's a dead end. If you fall for it now, it's your own fault.

The second real concern you have to be aware of going in is that once a studio purchases your script, nine times out of ten it will turn around and assign it to another writer to rewrite. That writer may even get more money to rewrite your script than you got to write it. You may end up sharing your writing credit with two, four or even six other writers. And the final product may be *nothing* like what you'd originally written. It's unfortunate, and self-destructive on the part of the studios, and in the long term diffuses the voice of the original writer . . . but it's now so firmly entrenched as studio policy that you have to expect it going in. There are whole lists of writers who do nothing but rewrite other writers. Many of the trades, such as *Daily Variety*, have now begun announcing the name of the rewriter in the same article in which they announce the name of the script purchased and the original writer.

It stinks.

But it's the business.

There are, on the other hand, some producers who will stay with the original writer, a commendable practice. And you can build in some protection, but you have to be ready to walk if it doesn't work. For starters, the Writers Guild generally insists that the original writer be given the right to do the first rewrite of an original property. Producers will sometimes get around this by asking if you'll just defer or going ahead and paying you for the rewrite, even letting you proceed with the rewrite while they give the script to someone else to rewrite behind you. Are they required by the WGA to tell you when they do this? Of course. Do they? Rarely. But always insist on your right to do the first rewrite. After that, it's up to you as to how far you want to push it.

WGA 1995 Theatrical and Television Basic Agreement
Theatrical Compensation

	Effective 5/2/95-5/1/96		Effective 5/2/96-5/1/97				Effective 5/2/97-5/1/98					
	LOW	HIGH	LOW	LOW	HIGH	HIGH	LOW	LOW	LOW	HIGH	HIGH	HIGH
Screenplay With Treatment	$34,528	$64,207	$35,564	$35,736	$66,133	$66,454	$36,809	$36,987	$37,165	$68,448	$68,779	$69,112
Screenplay Without Treatment	21,575	44,399	22,222	22,330	45,731	45,953	23,000	23,112	23,223	47,332	47,560	47,791
Story or Treatment	12,946	19,736	13,334	13,399	20,328	20,427	13,801	13,868	13,935	21,039	21,142	21,244
Original Treatment	17,877	29,603	18,413	18,503	30,491	30,639	19,057	19,150	19,243	31,558	31,711	31,865
Screenplay Rewrite	12,946	19,736	13,334	13,399	20,328	20,427	13,801	13,868	13,935	21,039	21,142	21,244
Screenplay Polish	6,476	9,867	6,670	6,703	10,163	10,212	6,903	6,938	6,971	10,519	10,570	10,620

LOW BUDGET-Photoplay costing less than $2.5 million

HIGH BUDGET-Photoplay costing $2.5 million or more

But remember, only do this if you're really and totally sincere and willing to walk away if it doesn't go your way. And much as it pains me to say it, when you're at the beginning of your career, as many reading this probably are, you may want to just bite down and bear with it rather than risk blowing your first deal. Save this for later.

RATES OF PAY

Any legitimate studio, upon deciding to option or purchase your script, will pay you according to Writers Guild minimums. After your first couple of sales to WGA signatories, you're required to join the WGA if you wish to continue writing for WGA signatory studios. If you're writing for non-WGA signatory companies, you're not bound to do this. Remember, the Guild exists to protect the interests of scriptwriters, and it is in your best interest to join as soon as you are qualified.

The chart at left shows the prescribed minimum fees for a motion picture screenplay purchased by a studio or independent producer. Obviously the amount paid can go up from these figures.

When the studio decides to purchase your screenplay, assuming this hasn't been written on assignment where the contract is already in place, you will then be asked to sign a contract with the production company. If you're not working through an agent, you may want to get one now or bring the contract to an entertainment attorney for examination to be sure you know what rights are being purchased, and what you will receive in return.

Happily, most legitimate studios use a standard contract whenever concluding such an arrangement. A sample contract is provided here. If the contract you receive is substantially different from this one, you should contact the studio and find out why there is a discrepancy, contact the WGA or ask your attorney what it means and how it will affect your rights.

Writer's Flat Deal Contract

EMPLOYMENT AGREEMENT between _____ (hereinafter sometimes referred to as "Company") and _____ (hereinafter sometimes referred to as "Writer"), dated this _____ day of _____ , 19 ____ .

1. The Company employs the Writer to write a complete and finished screenplay, presently entitled or designated _____, including the following:

Treatment
Original Treatment
Story
First Draft Screenplay
Final Draft Screenplay
Rewrite of Screenplay
(Draw a line through portions not applicable)

2. (a) The Writer represents that (s)he is a member in good standing of the Writers Guild of America, West, Inc., and warrants that he will maintain his membership in Writers Guild of America, West, Inc. in good standing during the term of this employment.

   (b) The Company warrants that it is a party to the Writers Guild of America Theatrical and Television Film Basic Agreement of 1981 (which agreement is herein designated "MBA").

   (c) Should any of the terms hereof be less advantageous to the Writer than the minimums provided in said MBA, then the terms of the MBA shall supersede such terms hereof.

   Without limiting the generality of the foregoing, it is agreed that screen credits for authorship shall be determined pursuant to the provisions of Schedule A of the MBA in accordance with its terms at the time of determination.

3. The Company will pay to the Writer as full compensation for his services hereunder the sum of _____ DOLLARS ($_____), payable as follows:

   (a) Not less than EIGHT HUNDRED EIGHTY DOLLARS ($880.00) shall be paid not later than the first regular weekly pay day of the Company following the expiration of the first week of the Writer's employment.

   (b) _____ DOLLARS ($_____) shall be paid within forty-eight (48) hours after delivery of the TREATMENT, ORIGINAL TREATMENT, or STORY, whichever is appropriate, to the Company.

   (c) _____ DOLLARS ($_____) shall be paid within forty-eight (48) hours after delivery of the FIRST DRAFT SCREENPLAY to the Company; and

   (d) _____ DOLLARS ($_____) shall be paid within forty-eight (48) hours after delivery of the FINAL DRAFT SCREENPLAY.

   (e) _____ DOLLARS ($_____) shall be paid within forty-eight (48) hours after delivery of the REWRITE.

4. The Writer will immediately on the execution hereof diligently proceed to render services hereunder and will so continue until such services are completed.

5. On delivery of a treatment to the Company, the Company may call for changes within three (3) days thereafter; if the Company fails in writing to call for any such changes, the treatment shall be deemed approved, and the Writer shall proceed with the first draft screenplay based on such treatment or adaptation.

   On delivery of a first draft screenplay to the Company, the Company may call for changes within three (3) days thereafter; if the Company fails in writing to call for any such changes, the first draft screenplay shall be deemed approved, and the Writer shall proceed with the final draft screenplay.

   On delivery of the final draft screenplay to the Company, the Company may call for changes within three (3) days thereafter; if the Company fails in writing to call for any such changes, the final draft screenplay shall be deemed approved.

6. This contract is entire, that is, the services contemplated hereunder include all of the writing necessary to complete the final screenplay above described, and this Agreement contemplates payment of the entire agreed compensation.

(Company)   (Writer)

By _____   Address _____

Title _____   _____

Address _____   _____

_____

_____

A few words of explanation about the preceding contract sample: If this is your first sale, you need not be a member of the Writers Guild, as specified by paragraph 2(a), provided that you do join immediately after you sign the contract and maintain your membership in good standing.

Section 3(a) is made operative in the case of those writers who are specifically hired to write a screenplay and treatment on assignment.

Section 3(b) becomes operative if you have written a treatment, and the Company agrees to purchase it, or the writer on assignment turns in the first treatment. If you are selling your screenplay sans a treatment, then obviously this payment is not activated.

Section 3(c) is the actual sum paid for your original screenplay should the Company agree to purchase it. This is also the amount paid to the writer on assignment when, having secured approval on the treatment, she turns in the first screenplay.

Sections 3(d), 3(e) and 5 have to do with rewriting. The studio may purchase your screenplay but, upon purchasing it, stipulate that certain changes must be made. (And for the record, changes are almost always made, to varying degrees.)

Frequently, this contract is filled out after the screenplay has been submitted, in the case of an outside submission such as the type described here. In those cases, the contract is retroactive as far as the original, first draft screenplay is concerned, and the application to the rewrites remains the same.

The thing to remember here is that the preceding contract is intended to be an all-purpose agreement and, as indicated in the first part, where it states that those portions not applicable are to be crossed out, may not apply in all ways to your own work. But the gist of it always holds.

It is, of course, fully within the rights of both parties to attach a rider to the contract specifying an agreed-upon salary and a percentage of the film's net profits.

Beyond the task of attending to whatever revisions may be called for, the extent of your further responsibilities as a writer will depend on the circumstances of your employment and the wishes of the producers. You may be asked to be on-set to make any last-minute changes, in which case you may be given a salary and per diem expenses. (Some producers and a lot of directors, however, don't want writers lingering on the set.) You may be asked to contribute to the final cutting and editing of the film. (Odds: slim.) You may be asked to stay home and stay out from underfoot. But upon becoming a member of the Writers Guild, you do have two rights: the right to view the final cut and the first revision.

SNEAKING IN THE BACK WAY

The bulk of this chapter has been dedicated to the techniques of selling an actual, typewritten screenplay for production as a feature film for general distribution. But there is one more way into the film business. It is, in fact, a route being taken by more writers now than ever before. Many of them find it quite successful.

Do what William Peter Blatty did with *The Exorcist*: Write it as a book, and get the thing published. If the book sells reasonably well and has an applicability to a screenplay format, the studios will come to you. They will offer to purchase the screen rights, and you can then hold them up for the right to do the first draft screenplay.

Some writers have even taken the step of writing both the screenplay and the novelization at the same time. You're probably better off finishing the novel first and getting it out to some book publishers while you're finishing the screenplay.

If your story is worth some studio's spending several million dollars in producing, then it's got to be worth a publisher's investing several thousands of dollars to publish. And what's more, since the film and book publishing businesses are becoming more entwined every day, publishers are actively looking for novels that have movie potential since they get a cut of the screen rights. So if they know you are also working on a screen version, they will probably be even more disposed toward publishing the book.

You can either wait until the book is published and out on the market before doing anything or play both ends of the street simultaneously. By that, I mean that you can send the book off to publishers stating that a screenplay is being written and/or currently marketed and write to the studios explaining that your book, upon which the screenplay is based, is either being considered by a publisher or is definitely being published by someone. This way, if the book sells first, you can expect more for the screenplay. If, on the other hand, the screenplay sells first, you can demand more for the book rights.

Because producers are not always willing to take chances on untested properties, a story that has either been proven in the book marketplace or that has been accepted by a major publisher removes a lot of that fear. As a consequence, it's happening more and more each year. In fact, the movie rights for *Ordinary People* were purchased by Robert Redford while the book was still in its rough typeset (galley) stage, and that, I remind one and all, was Judith Guest's first novel.

So when all else fails or might take too long, you can always go in through the back door when nobody's watching.

THE FUTURE OF CINEMA

The filmmaking industry, like any other business, creative and otherwise, has its fair share of doomsayers. When television made its debut, everyone predicted it would mean the end of the motion picture business, and while it did have a temporary adverse effect, movies continued to be made. There are fewer films being made in the 1990s than in decades previous, but that's still a lot of product, and the number of films seems to be on the rise again.

In 1995, according to the Motion Picture Association of America, 426 "legitimate" films were produced vs. 390 in 1994, with total 1995 box-office receipts slightly in excess of $5.2 billion. In addition, the growth in independent films as the technology of filmmaking has grown less expensive promises more alternatives to beginning writers.

Where there was once just a single venue for motion picture scripts, the growth of cable and direct-to-video sales has also opened up new opportunities for screenwriters. If you can't find a buyer for your screenplay at TriStar or Columbia or Universal, you now have Showtime and HBO and the Family Channel and Lifetime and other opportunities to tell that story.

The biggest problem studios face in the 1990s is the recent hideous escalation in production budgets, as high as $160 million just for Kevin Costner's *Waterworld*. The more big-budget films you make, the fewer medium-budget films get made, and the overall number of films decreases. In addition, the possibility of a flop $100 million film can kill a studio; it's all or nothing.

In a funny way, this ties back to the early history of filmmaking. Audiences at the dawn of the movie business went into small theaters to see train wrecks and horse chases and rockets crashing into the eye of the moon . . . it was about spectacle. After a flirtation with serious drama, it seems that movies are now spiraling back in the direction of spectacles, in large measure to counteract the influence of television, providing what you could never hope to get on a small screen.

But there has to be a diminishment of returns, and as the film economy tightens and more independent films are made and show a modest profit, it will likely become harder for the studios to justify the huge-budget blockbusters.

People go to the movies because they want to experience something, to live someone else's life for two hours, to go somewhere and do something they've never done before, to be *moved*—and you don't need $100 million to do that. It's an opportunity to block out the real world with cushioned seats and red curtains and live out the film, something that cannot really be done at home, surrounded by reminders of daily life, the bills that have to be paid lying on the coffee table, the dog that wants to be walked and so forth.

Movies are a group experience. They are a chance for a family or a group of friends to get out of the house for a little while. In this respect, films will always be a large part of the social life of teenagers, who want to get away from the house to engage in the traditional courtship behavior of youth.

It is, therefore, reasonable to expect that in one form or another, the motion picture business will continue to be with us for many years to come.

There will, however, be some changes in the scriptwriting marketplace. The studios may begin soliciting safer material that is more likely to turn a profit. Commerciality may become an even greater factor in the decision to produce a film than it is today. My hope is that that prediction may prove too pessimistic. We'll just have to wait and see.

In terms of the opportunities for screenwriters, though, it can be stated with some accuracy that the marketplace will increase during the next decade.

The aforementioned growth of cable movies and direct-to-video sales alone has prompted nearly 70 percent of the major studios to add divisions to their corporate structure that deal directly with the cable and video corporations. This trend toward making movies for video and cable led to one of the most hotly contested demands of the 1981 Writers Guild strike. The writers, the producers and the studios all knew that production for the video industry would, within the next two decades, become a potent arm of the entertainment industry overall, and the writers wanted to make sure that a part of the action was given to those who write the words.

(The studios won that one, by the way; writers get so little from the sales of videocassettes that the figures almost aren't worth computing. Cable sales and residuals are only a fraction of what they are elsewhere. This debacle so divided the WGA that it led directly into the Great Strike of 1988, which lasted for six months . . . and again didn't achieve much, except to propel these questions again to the forefront, where with luck they will be eventually dealt with.)

Finally, the growth of the personal computer industry has led to a dramatic new wealth of possibilities; interactive or somewhat more passive movies are now being produced directly for CD-ROM, ranging from the highly elaborate *Wing Commander* projects to more mainstream mysteries like *Voyeur* and *Phantasmagoria*. They are even calling upon the talents of leading actors, such as Malcolm McDowell, Mark Hamill and others. This is an area that is as wide open today as the original film industry was in the 1920s; the technology is still being worked out, the shape of this new beast is still being determined by new writers who are given undreamt-of tools. If there is any single industry that promises to seriously threaten to supplant conventional means of making movies and TV, this is it.

The next ten years, according to most industry watchers, will see more independent movies, more original movies produced for the burgeoning cable and direct-to-video marketplace, more CD-ROM movies, and, of course, the studios will continue to turn out spectacles and dramas of various sizes. All of which will mean a host of continued opportunities for new screenwriters. As the need for feature-length productions increases, so will the demand for scripts, and that means that more scriptwriters than ever before will have the opportunity to make their first big break into showbiz tinsel, troubles, splendor, aggravation and all.

See you at the movies.

PART III

Animation

The business of writing cartoons has always been tough; it's a bunny-eat-bunny world out there.

—Anonymous

Chapter Twelve

Animation: Past, Present and Future

The birth of animation came with two devices: the *flip-book*, and the first *nickelodeons*. The former consisted of a book upon whose pages a sequence of actions had been drawn, one under the other. When the pages were riffled, the figures seemed to move. The same basic principle applied to the nickelodeons, machines with narrow viewing slots that looked into a continuous wheel-shaped strip of paper, or a series of flip-cards, on which the drawings had been made. By turning the wheel, or flipping the cards, the pictures came to life.

It was a form that lent itself admirably to film, which is after all only a rapid-fire sequence of images, each overlapping the other and creating the illusion of motion through the phenomenon known as persistence of vision. The only difference is that one uses actors and the other uses two-dimensional figures. Germany and France leapt to the forefront in pioneering some of the more experimental elements of animation, including three-dimensional stop-motion photography, a trial-and-error period that produced some wonderfully surreal material. Flat and three-dimensional animation accompanied classical compositions and were used in a sometimes stream of consciousness fashion to create dreamlike landscapes.

On the other side of the Atlantic, the United States took a little longer to get into the more exotic uses of film, leaning toward more conservative (and therefore more accessible) imagery. This restraint was balanced by a slight technological edge that made early American animated films easier to produce and slightly less expensive.

Silent animated shorts quickly began to take their place on movie screens alongside the live-action silent films of the period. Many of those early efforts were crude, little more than line drawings against a stark white background, but they showed considerable promise. By the middle 1920s, there was some brilliant work coming from many sectors, including the silent Koko cartoons by Max Fleischer, who mixed live-action footage with animation and invented the *rotoscope* (tracing animated characters over filmed images of real people) to give his characters fluidity of movement. Max's brother, Dave, was in fact the model for Koko, even going so far as to hand-make a clown costume used during rotoscoping.

One of the problems inherent in animation, which persists to this day, is that it's easier to make an animated animal or inanimate object look intelligent and give it character than to make a drawing of a human being look realistic enough for an audience to accept it as such. Consequently, the subject matter of animated films has generally favored talking mice, dogs, ducks, pigs, cars, clocks, chickens and wolves by the sackful.

One important distinction must be drawn between animation of this early period—including the later color and talking cartoons—and what's available today. The animated shorts from Disney, Warner Bros., MGM and the Fleischer brothers' Inkwell Studios, among others, were made for theatrical release. They were usually written on two levels: with lots of physical gags for the younger members of the audience and with political or contemporary social references for the enjoyment of adults. The best of these shorts could be viewed and appreciated equally from either perspective.

There was often, therefore, more than a little sexuality implicit even in many of these early mainstream cartoons, ranging from Wolfie and Red Hot Riding Hood of the Tex Avery cartoons to Bugs Bunny's penchant for cross-dressing and the obvious sensuality of Betty Boop—at least until the censors got hold of her.

What's particularly significant for writers about this period in film history is that on average, there really weren't such creatures as animation writers. Much of what ended up on the screen was cobbled together by storyboard artists, gag men and directors, based loosely around a story provided by a third party. Various people would contribute different bits that would be incorporated into the finished film. It was only decades later that full-length scripts were used for animated programs and features, often over the considerable objections of old-guard animators. Disney held to this tradition as late as 1985, with the *Black Cauldron*, the last such film made the old-fashioned way, without a script. It should be taken as compelling evidence of the importance of the writer that it was after this, with feature films written by animation writers like Linda Woolverton, that the Disney animated films reentered the rarefied world of box-office success.

Early animators often took months to turn out a single cartoon, investing considerable time and effort and money into making the film look as good as possible. Gradually, however, the expenses involved in laboriously producing six to ten minutes of high-quality animation began to make the enterprise impractical. In the 1930s, you could turn out a decent cartoon for about $25,000. By the early 1940s, the initial cost of the seventeen *Superman* cartoons turned out by Max and Dave Fleischer was a staggering $90,000 per short, which subsequently capped off at $100,000 apiece. These rising costs forced the quality down, led to the increased use of stock footage and finally made it impossible to keep producing the shorts with the degree of quality so vital to the Fleischers.

When you could produce a one- or two-reel live-action movie for nearly what it cost to produce a six- or ten-minute animated short, the latter began to fall by the wayside. Disney's solution was to make longer animated movies, thus amortizing the costs, a move that at first drew considerable skepticism. Many critics thought that no one would sit still for ninety minutes of animation.

True to form, the critics were wrong.

From the 1950s up through the early 1960s, only the major studios, such as Disney, Warners and MGM, could afford to continue working in animation, turning out a diminishing number of shorts and classic films. The smaller studios, unable to compete, went out of business.

TELEVISION'S INFLUENCE

It was the coming of television that gave animation its first real rebirth. Symbolically enough, one of the first images broadcast via television was that of Felix the Cat, selected because he had strong black-and-white resolution and clean lines and because he was willing to sit still for a very long time without eating or calling his agent.

Because early television budgets were breathtakingly small, the animation that began to appear on TV was often as crude as the earliest animated shorts, noted for their grainy black-and-white images, crude drawings, limited range of movement and simplest possible backgrounds. Producers of some shows, including *Crusader Rabbit*, arguably the first regular animated series produced for television, worked hard to produce quality animation, but they were very much the exception. This was due in part to the fact that in the early days of television, there was much more of an emphasis on locally originated programming. You didn't have national sponsors, you had local commercials, which further cut into your budget. As a result, many shows made during this time were virtually unheard-of outside of the few states in the area where the show was made.

I remember clearly watching a series called *Planet Patrol* on WPIX in the 1950s. In later years, living on the West Coast, no one had ever heard of it and refused to believe such a show existed. It took me five years to find anyone else who had ever seen it . . . and naturally it was a relocated New Yorker.

Another such series, *Colonel Bleep*, was almost unknown outside of the East Coast. It was a one-man operation based in a garage in Florida. The animation, though of archival interest, is . . . well, pretty awful. About the only thing cheaper than such crude animation was puppetry, which also made inroads into television, ranging from *Howdy Doody* and *Kookla, Fran and Ollie* to the aforementioned *Planet Patrol*. Then, of course, there were the franchised shows, like *Bozo* and *Romper Room*, that used different hosts in different cities—but were all tied to the same format.

FOR KIDS ONLY

It was at this point that the tone of animation, and thus the way in which people perceived it, began to change. The animated series being produced for television were meant almost exclusively for kids, an approach buttressed by the inclusion of short introductory sections with live actors playing host—usually in costume—to rows of vaguely interested kids. The *Colonel Bleep* host, for instance, generally occupied a seat behind a cardboard cutout of a rocket ship, and tried to convince his audience that the tricked-out adding machine in front of him was really a space-a-phone.

The popular attitude toward animation as an art form meant exclusively for kids is recent but by no means universal. Other countries, such as France, Germany, Italy and Japan—*especially* Japan—take their animation far more seriously than Americans do. In terms of adult story lines and sophistication, Japanese *anime* is considered on a par with most prime-time American series. Back here in the States, television animation improved slightly in the 1960s, though it continued to be strictly limited animation, not the classic, full animation so prominent in the theatrical shorts. *Limited animation* gets its name not only from the fewer elements that go into it, but the fact that fewer actual frames of animation are produced per second, repeating the same frames every third or fourth frame to reduce the cost. *Classic animation* generally doesn't repeat frames; every subsequent frame is one move away from the one before it. Even though computer animation has begun to ease the process a little, television budgets can't yet accommodate the amount of time or money required for that level of high-quality animation. In the late 1960s and early 1970s, Hanna-Barbera, Ruby Spears and Filmation were the major players in the area of limited animation. *Space Ghost*, *Tom and Jerry*, *Huckleberry Hound*, *The Flintstones* (produced for prime time), the return of Felix and the introduction of *Rocky and*

Bullwinkle . . . these comprise some of the best offerings from this period.

This situation changed little even as late as the early 1980s, with television animation being produced exclusively for the networks. Then in 1984, there appeared the animated series *He-Man and the Masters of the Universe*, produced by Filmation. I'll have more to say about that particular series later in this chapter, but for now, suffice it to say that this show, based upon a popular toy line, was the first animated series to become a major hit in syndication, outside the network system. It was the first to weigh in at sixty-five produced original episodes per season, instead of the usual thirteen to twenty-two episodes per season. It also launched the notion of *stripping original shows*, i.e., broadcasting first-run episodes on a daily basis, Monday through Friday, which helped it overwhelm a programming schedule glutted with repeats.

PRODUCT-ORIENTED ANIMATION

Close upon the heels of *He-Man* and its sister series *She-Ra, Princess of Power*, there came a sudden flurry of imitators, knockoffs and a few good efforts as well, almost all of them based on "pre-existing properties," either a movie or a product tie-in, such as a toy. Toy company sponsors were willing to pay huge chunks of money to finance animated series based on their product line because in the long run, a successful series would result in increased sales revenue. The *He-Man* line brought in such huge revenues that the cost of the series was minimal in comparison. On the other hand, despite what producers wanted toy companies to believe, being on TV did not necessarily guarantee sales. But by the time this was known, the studio or producer in question had generated a minimum of sixty-five episodes and made a bit of a killing at the same time.

In retrospect, it's sad that many of the producers who entered the field at this time did not do so out of any particular affection for the form, but rather because they saw a quick buck—correction, a *lot* of quick bucks— to be made by convincing toy companies to finance animated television series based on their products. This had a profound downside: the further diminishment of the value of animation in the public's eye. Toy-based series were viewed by critics as little more than half-hour commercials. This criticism was valid in some circumstances, less so in others. A few producers were willing to stand up to the toy companies and prevent them from gaining story control. The majority were not quite so strenuous in their objections. As a rule of thumb, if the toy company had any sort of story control, the series was doomed.

Producers of product-oriented series quickly glutted the marketplace with inferior products made solely for merchandising purposes. They strip-mined the field, squeezing out every last dollar without compassion and usually without comprehending the inevitable and terrible consequences of their own greed.

THE CARTOON CRASH OF 1989

This crassly commercial attitude led to the Great Animation Glut of 1989. If you remember anything about population growth among fruit flies from your Biology 101 class, you don't need me to explain that a closed system can only support so much life before it dies out for lack of sustenance. This was the case with television animation. There were too many series and not enough available time slots, a problem that was compounded by the bad rap many of these series had earned through their toy tie-ins. The sponsors finally saw what was happening and started to pull out. Series that were on the drawing boards fell off the drawing boards. The large influx of writers who had moved into animation during the glut suddenly found themselves fighting for the few remaining jobs, which suddenly paid far less than they had paid before. Those few remaining product-oriented series that managed to find a berth in the crowded marketplace were usually shuttled into the 5 A.M. graveyard, where they ran out their commitment largely unseen.

When the sponsors fled, many of the producers cashed in their chips and left the business or left the country. To give you some idea of the money involved, animation producer Jean Chalopin, in business less than eight years, took out his share of profit, sold out his ownership in his company and literally bought not just a castle, but an entire *village* in France.

Some studios disappeared entirely, while others hung on by their finger-nails, lurching from check to check, from one small-order network show to the next.

By the early 1990s, with few exceptions, the independent studios had all but collapsed, leaving the majority of syndicated shows to be produced by the major studios, who were able to afford the investment. These include Warner Bros.' *Tiny Toons*, *Animaniacs* and animated *Batman* cartoons, and Disney's slate of animated series. The majority of television animation ended up right back where it was ten years ago: in the hands of the networks, airing once a week. As some indication of how bad things got, some shows wound up on the networks' schedules not because they were good, but because the networks knew that if Studio X *didn't* get a show on the air this season, it'd have to close down, which would eliminate one more source of programming. With the number of animation studios steadily eroding, this is something the networks could ill afford.

CARTOONING ON THE CUSP

As I write this, the animation industry is on a cusp. Conventional animation techniques, farmed out to Japan and other countries to save money, are becoming too expensive even to be done that way. But new technologies are emerging that will allow animated series to be visualized entirely by computer-generated imagery, something that has already been tried on a limited basis on some series. It will shortly become cheaper to produce shows via computer than through the painstaking process of individually hand-painting animation cels. When that happens, the price will come down substantially, the techniques of animation will become easily accessible to anyone with a computer (the term *desktop production* is bandied about more and more each day) and we will see another surge in television animation.

But regardless of the actual physical means used to produce the animation, the need for writers will still be there. Even Disney's learned that lesson. The field isn't as populous as it was before the Cartoon Crash of 1989, when all those syndicated series evaporated, but there's still an awful lot of work being done, and there is more on the way. Finding good writers who can handle the form is difficult. There are very few who work in animation with any regularity, despite the fact that each new season requires upward of three hundred half-hour episodes of animation that need to be written.

So there's still plenty of gold in them thar Toons, if you know how to mine it. Which is something we'll discuss after a couple of final notes, just to finish bringing us up to date on the current state of animation.

Prime-time animation has begun a comeback with such series as *The Simpsons*, *The Critic*, *Capitol Critters*, *Fish Police* and *Family Dog*, among others. Animation has also begun to show up in alternative venues, such as MTV (*Beavis and Butthead*, *Aeon Flux*) and cable channels such as Nickelodeon (*Ren and Stimpy*, *Rugrats*). In many cases, as with Spumco's *Ren and Stimpy*, these shows are the product of very small, personalized operations. What's encouraging about these series is that they hearken back to the roots of animation, with elements that appeal both to adults and to kids. At present, every network (cable or broadcast) has at least one new prime-time animated series in development. Although they can't all get on the air, enough of them *will* go on to make a difference.

Finally, insofar as films are concerned, as of this writing, Disney continues its dominant position in the marketplace, though a few independently produced animated features still get made, ranging from such adult fare as *Heavy Metal* and *Cool World* to more innocuous offerings such as *An American Tail*, *The Land Before Time* and *All Dogs Go to Heaven*. As the aforementioned computer technology becomes more readily available, there will doubtless be more animated films made. *Beauty and the Beast* made considerable use of computer designed and produced animation; *Toy Story* made even greater use of it; *The Mask* took live action, inserted cartoon-style animation and blended it with computer technology, taking the form to a new level. But as with all such projects, they will continue to need writers.

THE FUTURE OF ANIMATION

At present, Disney Animation is in its second golden age, raking in huge profits at the box office. With the success of Disney's animated films, more and more studios are cranking up animation divisions that have been dormant for years; Warner Bros. is already on the move, and Universal has recently revived its long-dead animation interests with a whole division committed to feature and television animation. Inside information says that Paramount and other studios aren't far behind.

Prime-time animation has been shown to be successful with *The Simpsons*, but thus far, no other series has cracked the evening hours with any real success, so it may take a few more years before we see more than one or two shows a season occupying those time slots.

On the other hand, it has been demonstrated through such sophisticated or adult-oriented series as the aforementioned *Simpsons*, *Ren and Stimpy*, *Duckman*, *Aeon Flux* and Fox Television's *X-Men* that the audience for animation is broader than the prepubescent crowd. This bodes well for the creation of more sophisticated series in the foreseeable future with more complex characters and interesting stories.

New Technologies

As the tools for animation continue to drop in price, through the use of computers and other techniques, you will see more and more products being produced by independent contractors for cable, network and syndication.

The physical production of animation has begun to move back into the United States in limited ways and will continue to do so as the means of producing animation continues to simplify with growing technology. What initially fueled the explosion of animation on TV was that it was considerably cheaper to finance. A half-hour cartoon might cost $175,000 to $200,000 around 1984 or 1985, well below the cost of a live-action half hour, which would come in often at $350,000 to $400,000 or more. Right around the time of the Cartoon Crash of 1989, with rising costs overseas for producing animation and with fewer such houses available to handle a growing amount of work, the cost of an animated half hour came to almost the same level as a live-action half-hour.

With the cost dropping again because of the new technologies, you can reasonably expect to see more animation creeping its way back into television over the next five years and beyond. The *Daily Variety* of September 22, 1994, lists the firm commitments for animated series for the fall of 1995, detailing no less than seventy-nine first-run animated series on the air: twenty-two on the broadcast networks, sixteen in original first-run cable (MTV, USA, Nickelodeon and the like), and forty-one in first-run syndication. As more cable networks come on-line, and as the cable networks already present expand their operations, you can expect this to expand even further. This will counter the expected slight decrease in syndicated shows that will come as the result of new and old broadcast networks chewing up the few remaining independent TV stations nationwide.

There's also a new player coming onto the field: CD-ROM technology. In the last few years, there has been a subtle but growing blend between standard computer games and animation. Until recently, the animation has consisted in the main only of ships in battle sequences; lately, as with games such as *Rise of the Dragon* and *Wing Commander*, there are real stories, featuring animated characters speaking dialogue you hear on your computer speakers.

New Opportunities for Writers

As a result, the programmers who have created computer games in the past have found themselves overwhelmed by the need to create animated stories. And who have they turned to? Yep, animation writers such as Christy Marx and Ellen Guon and Katherine Lawrence and many others. As computer imaging continues to improve, making it easier to render more realistic looking characters and situations, I wouldn't be surprised to see the CD-ROM industry actually grow larger in its use of animation and animation writers than the networks and studios combined.

This information signals a growing need per se for animation writers (though the incline will, I think, be fairly slow for the next one to two years, picking up thereafter), and this ties into the history portion of this chapter. Prior to the 1984 gold rush of animation, there weren't many writers working in animation. When the crash hit in 1989, many of them defected into other areas, such as live action, feature films or children's books. Many others just plain got out of the business, having only entered it because there was a need and it paid well, not out of any real desire to write. The overall number of writers ended up slashed by nearly two-thirds. In other words, we're looking at a bell curve. We are now at the skinny part of the curve; the pool of available animation writers today simply isn't as large as it was and certainly isn't large enough to sustain the coming growth. Just about all the animation writers I know who have any credits at all are under contract with Warner Bros. or Universal or Spumco or Matt Groening; there aren't many freelancers left. So who's going to end up writing these forthcoming animated CD-ROM and new animated series? (Yes, you may consider that a rhetorical question.)

Chapter 13

The Art and Craft of the Animation Script

From a writer's perspective, there are many advantages to writing an animated script over a live-action script for television or film. There are also some disadvantages, most having to do with the business aspects. But we'll get to that later.

The first creative advantage to animation is that of scope. If you want to blow up a building . . . or a city . . . or a planet . . . or an entire galaxy, you can do it. It doesn't cost that much more to draw an exploding planet than it does to draw an exploding car. To look at it in less destructive terms, it doesn't cost you anything more to draw an alien world or a city out of the European past or an underwater environment or a lunar colony than it costs to draw a conventional present-day city. Many of the limitations of live-action scripts just don't apply.

In animation, anything can be alive, can be a character. A person, a poodle, a doorknob, a crow, a painting . . . the entire world is available to you in terms of characterization. With that flexibility comes questions, challenges and character opportunities impossible elsewhere. What does the last unicorn think about its status? What does a door knocker think about the people who come banging its face every day, day after day after day? If cats could talk, what would they say, and would any of us *really* want to hear it?

The potential for exploring new perspectives through animated characters is highly appealing. When done correctly, it ends up telling us a little more about what it is to be human, by showing us the effect our actions have on the world around us.

Also rewarding is the fact that in an animated script, the writer is in many ways the director. As we'll see in the craft section of this chapter, the animation writer's job is to describe exactly what will be seen, shot by shot. Once the script is locked down, the structure of each shot, as written in the script, can't be changed. How that shot is visualized is as individual as the director or the storyboard artist or the animator, but insofar as dialogue, action and point of view are concerned, it's all done just as the writer stipulated.

Which doesn't mean there aren't mistakes, particularly when sending American scripts overseas for translation and animation. From time to time, cultural and language barriers create unique problems, particularly when colloquialisms are used. In one case I know of, the script described a character seated in a starship as being "belted in." That phrase was translated into Korean as "tied down with ropes," which was what was drawn and sent back. Similarly, another script described a character as "hauling ass" across the room. What came back from Tokyo was a shot of the character with both his hands on his posterior as he ran across the room.

Since every shot will be filmed as written, it's incumbent upon the writer to become the camera. Where a live-action script is written mainly in master shots, with the director deciding when to reverse the camera or change angles, in animation that is the writer's obligation. It requires that you develop a heightened sense of timing and visualization. You have to intuitively know when one particular angle or shot is running long and when to cut it or how long you should stay on one character in a dialogue before reversing the shot to show the other character's reaction.

Do you stay on one character during a long speech and push in, or intercut with reaction shots? Do you pan from the speaker to an establishing shot of the location, turning the dialogue into a voice-over? Or do you not show the speaker at all and only stay on the reactions of those hearing it? What happens onscreen, and what happens offscreen?

You also have the flexibility of playing with a veritable toy chest of visual and sound effects. Characters show speed trails to indicate velocity; they splat against walls, or do Tex Avery "takes," eyes bulging out to triple normal size. To move between one scene and another, you might use a *zip-pan* (flashes of color and a sense of movement too blurry to be seen), a *diagonal wipe* (the new picture appears at the upper left corner, moving across to the lower right corner), a *vertical wipe* or a plain old cut.

These are a few of your tools, and every time you finish writing a scene, you get to choose which ones you will use. We'll cover the more practical uses for these tools a bit later and how they can be used to give your animation a particular feel, very much unlike live action.

That "feel" is important in other ways. One of the most interesting comments I ever received on a script was, "The good news is, this could be a live-action script. The bad news is, this could be a live-action script." If it can be shot either way, you've missed something in the writing. You're not fully taking advantage of what makes animation *different*. If something can be shot, as written, in live action, then why do it in animation? If the story is fairly conventional from a production standpoint, then write it as a live-action script and reserve animation for something truly extraordinary. But the decision shouldn't just involve the decision about whether it would be too expensive to shoot live action. There should be a reason for the *animation* per se . . . a point of view that would be impossible to express with live actors or visuals far beyond anything that can be constructed in a three-dimensional world no matter how much money you had . . . something that says, "This script can only be done properly in the animated format."

In many ways, the art of the animated script is not much different from the art of the live-action television script. There are, however, some specific elements that need to be emphasized.

1. Make use of the form. Be a little reckless visually; take advantage of the opportunities inherent in animation.

2. Try this experiment as you work. Prior to writing your scene, close your eyes and try and see it the way you would in a movie theater or on TV. Play the scene out, over and over, until you can see it clearly . . . every angle, every close-up. Don't try to just vary your shots randomly or because you think you have to because you've been in one shot too long. *Feel* the scene as it flows, and then, *only* then, "rewind" the film and write down what you see, shot by shot.

3. Where possible, keep your dialogue brief, much briefer than in live action. No matter how good the animation, a lengthy monologue that would work wonderfully in a live-action movie or TV show will simply kill you in animation. Partly because the longer you look at someone talking, the more you realize that you're looking at a cartoon, which breaks the illusion, but mostly because there has never been a piece of painted plastic that can act as well as, say, Marlon Brando.

4. Never assume that the animation will always carry a scene; you should generally underline an action with dialogue. In live action, you could get away with the stage direction, "She looks at him without understanding." Now try to animate that. Half the time it will work, sort of, and the other half it'll look like she's got gas. While it's simultaneously dopey and regrettable, until the visuals of animation reach the same complexity as the human face, you're probably going to have to underscore that kind of scene with the character saying, "I don't understand."

5. In terms of animated television, remember that even though the recurring characters are little more than moving cels, on one level they're *people* and have their own unique background, personalities and characteristics. If you're trying to write for an established show, you should be every bit as rigorous with your characters here as with a live-action series.

6. On a related note, if you genuinely want your script to stand out from the rest and get noticed, your single best bet is to hook it into the characters. The most common kind of script, and the least effective, is the McGuffin script. A McGuffin script is one that is centered on finding something. "Gee, Professor, we have to find the Magic Crystal Powerstone before Nightfire does or the world is doomed!" Stories like that are a dime a dozen, and frankly they're snoozers. But it seems like nine out of ten spec animation scripts I've ever read have had something like that at their core. If you can take one of my characters from my show and sell him or her to me as a *person*, whose attributes, unique to my show, are what propels him into the story, you've got a sale.

7. Verbal humor is fine in animation, but once again, due to the limitations of the form, it can be less than 100 percent effective. Consequently, you should try to learn to think more in terms of visual humor here than you would in live action. Probably the best executed animated series ever done in terms of visual humor is the prime-time series *The Simpsons*. Watch and study this show. There are episodes where characters go almost a full minute without dialogue of any kind, relying only on visual humor. Those moments constitute the purest forms of animation.

Beyond that, as stated, the art of live-action scripts and that of animated scripts are very similar (despite the financial and professional inequities between forms).

STRUCTURE

An animated half-hour television episode usually breaks down into one of the following categories: two acts, two acts and a teaser or a tag or, in rare cases, three acts. This is equally true whether the show is for a network or first-run syndication.

The first act can begin by delving immediately into the main story or prior to getting down to business, it can take a few moments to set up a subplot or a dramatic aside. Each act ends on a cliff-hanger or story revelation, as is traditional. One difference between live action and animation is that whereas a cliff-hanger in a live-action program can be an emotional confrontation or a personal revelation, this is less often the case in animation, where the cliff-hangers tend to be more physical in nature, e.g., your character is on a sinking ship surrounded by sharks. This doesn't preclude other, less physical act-outs, but because of the limitations on characterization imposed by most television animation, they're difficult to pull off convincingly.

In a typical half-hour episode, you actually have only twenty-two to twenty-four minutes for your story, depending on whether the show is for syndication or network, respectively. You're always desperately pressed for time—time to introduce your story and the guest characters that go with it, time to move your regular characters into the thick of things, time for a few character bits and the resolution of the story. Consequently, you'll find that there isn't much opportunity to develop a subplot or B-story in your script. Which is not to say that it's impossible, only that if you want a decent B-story, you may have to simplify your A-story considerably.

THE PREMISE

A written *premise* is the first step in the TV animation writing process. It's written in prose form, two to five pages in length and spells out the basic story line without getting into too much detail. In many cases, the premise will also indicate the act breaks, though this is not always a requirement. What you want is to spell out the conflict, the resolution and how they affect the characters. Dialogue is optional. Though dialogue helps demonstrate that you can handle the characters, it's perfectly acceptable just to tell the story in narrative.

I must make clear a distinction between live action and animation in terms of what's initially expected of the writer. Under the rules of the Writers Guild of America, you—whether a WGA member or not—cannot be asked by any WGA signatory producer to write anything on speculation for free. Not a script, not a treatment, not a premise, not a syllable or a comma. It is strictly *verboten*. The WGA contract covers television, movies, radio, news programs. . . .

But it does not cover animation.

I've fought this in meetings with network brass and producers, in magazine articles and interviews and in sworn testimony in hearings before the NLRB (National Labor Relations Board). So far, zilch, but this may change. Those of us who have taken on the fight against this are as determined as the opposition. But I suppose I should get to the point and tell you how this directly affects animation writers.

Unlike live action, the producer or story editor of an animated television series can ask you for work—premises as long as five or more pages—without ever paying you a dime and without incurring any obligations whatsoever toward you. I'll get more into the details of this when we turn our attention to marketing an animated television script, but for now all you have to know is that the job of a series producer/story editor in animation is to solicit written premises from freelancers, then sift through them, select the best of the batch and forward them on to the network and the studio for final approval.

No approval, no money.

It's not uncommon for freelancers to come up with four or five premises at a shot. Potentially, that's ten to twenty-five pages of writing that may not net you a dime. Some shows have received as many as one hundred written premises for as few as twenty available assignments. There are ways a story editor can mitigate the situation a little in the freelancer's favor. One way is by discussing story areas over the phone rather than waiting for the material to arrive already written, but even so . . . it stinks.

The Real Ghostbusters: A Sample Premise

For purposes of illustration, the following is one of the premises I wrote for ABC's *The Real Ghostbusters*. I've picked this one because those who don't know the series have a good chance of having seen the movie upon which it's based and because this series is still fairly popular and can be found on many cable networks (including USA Network) in morning hours. Although I served as story editor and wrote roughly twenty-five produced episodes for that series, I've deliberately selected a premise that was *not* produced. Why? Because I like this one enormously, and since it was never produced, I wanted it to see light somewhere.

THE REAL GHOSTBUSTERS
"Midnight on the *Lady M.*"
Premise
J. Michael Straczynski

The place: New Orleans. The present.

Carnival. The last day before the end of Mardi Gras.

Streets full of partygoers. Floats being readied on side streets and alleys. Masques and sequins and satins and banners and laughter littering the night like broken glass.

Carnival!

Hysteria on the half shell, cakewalks down the middle of Bourbon Street, hustlers and singers and jugglers and mimes and three-card Monte on the corner. A kaleidoscope of colors and blissful anonymity.

It is Carnival, and anything goes.

And it is in this fantastic scene that we find our five visitors among a tidal wave of masked faces: Peter, eyes wide with anticipation, ready for anything; Ray, his face boyish and aglow with excitement; Winston, who finds it all very comfortable and very right; and Egon, as relaxed as a cat in a room full of heavily armed mice.

"AWFULLY LOUD OUT HERE, ISN'T IT?" Egon says.

Peter looks over at him with benign interest. "What did you say?"

"I SAID IT'S —" He stops. "You're toying with me again, aren't you, Peter?"

"Moi?" Peter asks innocently, blowing a party favor that stretches out nearly five feet to tickle the ear of a female partygoer, who is phenomenally gorgeous. She laughs, winks at him flirtatiously. "You I'm simply annoying. *Her* I'm toying with."

She comes over, takes Peter by the arm. "Later, Egon," Peter says, tossing Egon the party favor as they go off arm in arm. Egon examines the party favor as though it were an alien life-form. Then he notices another very attractive woman giving him a come-hither look. Egon smiles as best he can and blows the party favor. It gets about a foot before sagging. The woman giggles, moves off. Winston puts a consoling hand on his shoulder. "Happens to the best of us, m'man."

On that the remaining three set off to find their hotel. They've come for the Twenty-Third Annual Symposium On The Fantastic, which only Egon is interested in. The rest are there strictly for Mardi Gras, having missed it the last time they were in the area.

Those attending the Symposium are just about as oddball as those outside in the streets of New Orleans . . . difference is, they're like this *all the time.* Swamis, gurus, healers, psychics, channelers, you name it, you'll find it. The Ghostbusters are scheduled to give a talk on scientific means of dealing with the supernatural, which doesn't go down well with this crowd.

They find particular annoyance with the turbaned Swami Kishnu Wannaberichrich, who sniffs with great disdain at their equipment. He is an eccentric's eccentric. He keeps switching on Egon's proton pack while Egon tries to check them in.

"Don't touch," Egon says.

Kishnu does it again, this time also backing into Ray and knocking his PKE meter to the floor.

"Dangerous stuff!" Egon warns.

"Pfah! Tinkertoys!" Kishnu snorts. "Bright lights! Pretty sounds! But what does it do!?"

Egon turns on him. Nose to nose. "I could use it to part your hair."

"And what is so special about that?"

"I could do it from across the room. Through your hat."

Winston intervenes to calm things a little. "After all, we're all here for the same reason, right?"

Kishnu stalks off, utterly uncooperative.

"Let me just take a little off the top," Egon says quietly, hand on the proton pack. "I'll even leave one eye open."

Winston convinces him to go back to registering as Peter enters, covered in confetti, a big grin on his face, a woman on his arm. She is, it should be noted, *not* the same woman he had on his arm a few moments ago. He looks utterly mussed.

Ray goes to him. "Peter?"

"Mmm?"

"You okay?"

"Mmmm."

"What happened to you?"

Peter leans toward him, eyes wide. "*Carnival!*" He gives Ray his bags and heads back out into the night, where he disappears in a flurry of movement and color and music.

Ray watches him go, and allows a smile. "Carnival," he whispers. And the smile gets bigger.

Later, the team set off for their separate evenings. Winston and Ray leave to check out New Orleans, while Egon is in heated debate with, well, just about everyone within range.

Not long after they get swept up by the flowing crowd, Winston and Ray get separated. Ray doesn't much mind, he's having too good a time.

After a bit, Ray steps out into a side street to catch his breath. He looks down the street and sees a woman standing alone, watching the parade go by. She is stunningly attractive, but in a very refined, gentle fashion. Her dress is distinctly late 1800s in design. There is something almost wistful about the way she watches the partygoers dancing past.

Summoning up his courage, Ray approaches her and tries to find his voice. "Hi," he finally manages to squeak out.

She looks at him, and the moon and stars and everything in between are there in her eyes. "Hello."

He rocks on his heels, smile frozen on his face in utter terror. He's not very good at this. "Come here often?" he says, wincing at his own use of that pickup line.

She nods. "Every year. Lovely, isn't it?"

He looks out at the street. "Yes, it is."

They talk briefly, a tentative conversation full of feints and false starts. Then she begins to move off. "I have to go home," she explains. "I have to get ready. We're all leaving tomorrow night after Mardi Gras."

"I—could walk you there," Ray offers. Silence. "At least part of the way."

She accedes.

Their walk, mostly in silence, sometimes with a few words, tells us very quickly that Ray is smitten by her. Her name, he discovers, is Elizabeth Metairie. Their quiet is in sharp contrast to the streets around them, which echo with the sounds of carnival. They come to a small rise, on one side of which she stops and thanks him for the walk home. "I'm sailing tomorrow night on the *Lady* M.," she says. Her voice is wistful, sad.

"Don't you want to go?"

"I must go," she says, without further explanation. "But perhaps I will see you again, before then."

Ray says that that would be very nice. With a smile, she turns and heads over the rise in the hill, disappearing down the other side. Ray starts back the way he came when he suddenly stops, realizes that he didn't get her address. He turns and hurries after her, cresting the top of the hill, and calling to her—

Only to stop dead in his tracks as he looks down on what is on the other side of the hill.

The Greenwood Cemetery.

Rows and rows of mausoleums and tombs and marble vaults, spires climbing against the night sky like bone-white fingers.

And there is no trace of Elizabeth Metairie . . . except for a tombstone bearing her name.

Act Out

In Act Two, we follow the three threads of our story: Mardi Gras itself, with Peter bouncing from one oddball confrontation to another, poker games, parties, everything; the Symposium, and Egon dealing with the eccentrics there; and Ray tracking down the facts about Elizabeth Metairie.

He finds that Elizabeth Metairie died the last night of Mardi Gras in 1853 when the boiler on the steamship *Lady M.* exploded, sinking the grand paddle wheeler and killing all aboard. It's rumored that every year at midnight, at the end of Mardis Gras, the spectral ship rises from the bottom of the Mississippi, and in that moment, all is as it was before: the fine dresses, the roulette wheel doing business on the main deck, costumes and laughter and the glittering madness of Mardi Gras.

The steamship is trying to navigate its way past the fate that struck it last time.

It is trying to reach . . . the other side.

And year after year, it fails.

We follow the love-struck Ray as he unearths the truth and decides that they must try and help. Kishnu, overhearing part of this, decides to intervene *his* way and nearly botches everything. Peter, lost to the city's pleasures, at first declines, only to return when he is most needed, ready to put his life on the line to free the spirits of those trying to reach the other side.

And it *is* a dangerous proposition . . . because the only way to safeguard the *Lady* M. is to stand on the bow of the ship, proton guns at the ready, blasting at obstructions. Sounding the river, keeping the ship safe.

And there are other, dark forces that do not wish to see the ship reach its special safe harbor. Creatures of darkness that surround the ship, plucking at its defenders, trying to pull them off.

As if matters weren't bad enough, even if the Ghostbusters somehow succeed, if they don't get off the ship in time, they'll be caught up and taken to the other side along with the rest of the ghostly passengers.

With barely a minute to spare, they achieve the task. The way to the other side opens up. Winston, Peter and Egon pile off, with only Ray lingering briefly to say a difficult goodbye to Elizabeth, to whom he confesses his love. For a moment, it looks as though he might not make it off the ship in time, that he might willingly accompany her to the other side. But at her urging, at the last moment, he dives off the ship and into the river, watching as it melts into the sky, disappearing.

Soaked, they make it back to town just in time for the last few hours of Mardi Gras. They go into a club, and raise a toast: to the memory of the *Lady* M.

THE OUTLINE

Once the premise is approved, it becomes the basis for the outline, which usually runs from ten to fifteen pages, written in the same prose style as a live-action outline. The main difference between a premise and an outline is that in the latter, each plot turn is spelled out clearly. For example, instead of saying, "Ray discovers the truth about Elizabeth Metairie," we indicate that he searches the local newspaper for the date and means of her death; that he goes to a nearby museum that has photos of the *Lady* M. in which we can see Elizabeth Metairie and so on.

Invariably, the producer, the story editor and the network (or any combination thereof) will have notes on the premise, which are incorporated at the first-draft outline stage. If there's something you don't agree with, feel free to fight it, but at some point, the story editor has to close out the argument if you haven't managed to convince him of the rightness of your views. Be firm, but don't kick over the table.

Unlike a premise, an outline is an actual assignment, for which you must be compensated, usually at the rate of 30 to 50 percent of the total price of the script. The first-draft outline is due on average one to two weeks after approval of the premise and may lead to a second (or possibly third) draft of the outline.

THE SCRIPT

Once the outline is approved, you'll have two to three weeks in which to turn in the first-draft script. It's at the script stage that the difference between live-action writing and animation writing becomes most pronounced.

In live-action writing, you generally write in master shots, calling out individual angles only when it's necessary to emphasize something important to the story line. As noted earlier, in animation every individual angle or shot must be called out in detail, and no single shot tends to run more than about half or one-third of a page.

So the animation writer not only has to tell the story, he also has to consider, Who needs to be in this shot? Should this be a wide shot, a two-shot (just two characters in frame) or a close shot? Should the dialogue be over this scene, or should we actually see who's talking?

This is necessary not only in action scenes, in order to make clear who's doing what to whom, but even in quieter scenes. Take, for instance, a dinner conversation. The following is excerpted from "The Haunting of Heck House," a tribute to the work of Shirley Jackson and Richard Matheson that I wrote for *The Real Ghostbusters*. In this scene, the characters have taken on a million-dollar bet that they can cleanse a chronically haunted house of its ghosts *without* the use of their proton packs. (The Slimer referred to is the little green ectoplasmic spud from the first movie who hangs around with the guys these days.)

As we join the story in progress, it is now nearly midnight, and they have gone through far more trauma than they had expected. Ray and Winston have had an encounter with something that's shaken them to their core, and it's slowly dawning on them that they are in serious trouble.

INT. DINING ROOM—NIGHT—WIDE

Dark wood paneling, shadows and paintings and candles and a long table set for dinner, where we FIND Peter, Ray and Winston. In front of each of them is a plate, a cup of coffee, and an unwrapped sandwich. But only Peter is eating. Ray and Winston look frazzled, eyes glazed, fixed at a nowhere spot in front of them. They look like they've just come out of a war.

RAY
(softly, numb)

—and it, it tried to grab me . . .

TWO-SHOT—RAY AND WINSTON

As Winston shakes his head. His voice is low.

WINSTON

I don't want to remember. Eat your dinner.

RAY

Yeah. I'll eat my dinner. Good idea.
(he doesn't)

It was green, Winston.

WINSTON
(sighs)

WIDEN TO INCLUDE WHOLE ROOM

As Egon enters, carrying an armful of books. He heads toward Peter, at the end of the table, who looks up at him glumly.

> PETER
>
> There you are. Say, Egon, you've got some medical training, don't you?

TIGHTEN—EGON AND PETER

Egon sets the books down at the corner of the table beside Peter.

> EGON
>
> A little, mostly in first-aid. Why?

> PETER
>
> I need something removed.

Peter puts his left foot up on the table. And we find Slimer wrapped around his ankles, shivering, frightened, holding on so tight it'd take a crowbar to peel him off. Egon shakes his head.

> EGON
>
> Not qualified.

> PETER
>
> I'm hip.

PULL BACK

Peter lets his foot fall back down to the floor with a THUMP and a SQUISH.

> SLIMER
> (os)
>
> Owww . . .

> PETER
>
> Sorry, spud.
> (to Egon)
> So where've you been all this time?

> EGON
>
> In the library. I've found some things that—
> (noting Ray, Winston)
> What's wrong with them?

ON RAY AND WINSTON

Who haven't so much as budged, eyes fixed on something only they can see.

> PETER
> (os)
> I don't know. I think they saw something upstairs.

> RAY
> And it—it had two hundred eyes. I know. I counted.

ANGLE—FAVORING EGON

As Egon opens up one of the books and turns to selected pages.

> EGON
> Listen, everyone, I've found something that could help us survive the night. This book contains the history of Heck House, everyone who's ever lived here—or tried to.

ANGLE—ON THE BOOK

As Egon flips pages, we SEE handwritten entries, drawings, old photos of people in circular holes, on and on.

> EGON
> (os)
> They recorded what they saw. With a little work I was able to cross-reference the data and come up with a figure.

ON EGON

Pushing back his glasses, looking rather proud of himself.

> EGON
> Based on that, I have a rough idea of how many ghosts are in this house.

DRAMATIC ANGLES:

ON PETER

> EGON
> (os)
> By way of comparison, the Whatley house in Arkham had 13.

ON WINSTON

EGON
(os)
The Vincent mansion had 10.

ON RAY

Still numb, listening.

EGON
(os)
And the most haunted house on record, the Crowley house in London had 25.

ON SLIMER

Poking his head and eyes about the tabletop, staring across at Egon.

PETER
(os)
Okay, Egon. Don't hold us in suspense. How many ghosts are in *this* house?

ON EGON

Who closes the book with a THUMP.

EGON
Two thousand, four hundred and thirty seven.

SLIMER
(os)
YEEOOOWWW!

And there's the SOUND of a CRASH.

ANGLE—ON WALL

Where we find a Slimer-shaped hole in the wall.

MEDIUM SHOT—PETER AND EGON

Peter raises his foot again, revealing Slimer gone. He nods to Egon.

PETER
Good job.

EGON
Wait till you get my bill.

To explain why some things were done in that section . . .

If you're going to have a goodly sized chunk of exposition, it's a good idea to use the visuals to break up the exposition with either camera angles or movement. In other words, we start with a character explaining something, cut to someone else listening to what's being said as the dialogue continues offscreen (os), then go back again at the end. The longer the exposition or the more people in the room, the greater your opportunity to break things up a little, rather than leaving the camera on one character for a prolonged chunk of exposition.

Offscreen dialogue can also be used as a transition between shots, as when Egon asks what's with Ray and Winston, and we have Peter's reply under the shot of those two characters. His reply becomes the transition. Ray's line at the beginning of the scene acts as a transition from the previous scene.

Studios and animators also like offscreen dialogue because that means they can get away with not animating the mouth. Watch almost any animated program, particularly low-budget programs, and you'll see that they cut away from the mouth as often as possible. You'll see somebody else listening or the back of the person's head or just their eyes or a long shot of them walking, whatever it takes to get away from the mouth. That's because getting the lips to correctly sync with the English language is one of the toughest steps in animation, particularly when the episode is being animated overseas. You not only have to get the shape of the mouth right to form the correct sounds, you have to pause at all the right inflections. So whenever they can get away with not doing this, animators tend to do so.

One of the things many contemporary animation writers never seem to appreciate is the use of offscreen dialogue or movement to convey action in lieu of showing everything. As was done most effectively in the Warner Bros. cartoons, sometimes what you *don't* see is funnier or more dramatic than what you *do* see. Hence, we don't actually see Slimer being stepped on or going through the wall. We *hear* the first instance and see the *result* of the second (the hole in the wall).

The more elaborate the scene, the more action, the more you have to keep things moving. The images must connect, and the description must be explicit. You can't just write, for instance, "And the battle is joined. The Gray Army gains the advantage at first but is then pushed back to the sea." The secret of animation writing is in the details. This is a strictly subjective opinion, your mileage may vary, but I feel strongly that animation writing is fundamentally more difficult than live-action writing because of the need to direct the episode on paper. I've seen a lot of animation writers make the transition to live action, but very few seem able to move in the opposite direction.

The length of your script can vary widely and is determined by a number of factors, including the studio's set policy, the timing on the voice track and the storyboarder. I've written and story edited half-hour scripts that have been as short as thirty pages and as long as sixty pages. Since much of this is determined in the production stage, it now behooves us to examine that aspect.

PRODUCTION

One reason that half-hour animation scripts vary widely in length is that some studios tend to animate their programs fast, while others prefer to animate slow. Shows like *Tiny Toons* or *Animaniacs*, for instance, are animated with tremendous speed, at times too much so. *He-Man and the Masters of the Universe*, on the other hand, contained some of the slowest animation and longest pans in the history of modern television. The slower the animation, the fewer cels are required; the fewer the cels, the cheaper the final product.

In addition, after being involved with a given series for a while, the story editor usually has some idea of how the voice actors pace themselves when they act out a script. Between that and knowing the *dry-time* of the show (how many minutes it actually runs, before the addition of commercials), she should be able to give the freelancer a good idea of the preferred script length.

Once you've written the script to the correct length as stipulated by the studio, the script then goes to a storyboard artist, who sketches out every scene in the script.

This is the first step in actually bringing a script to life. The storyboard artist roughs out the action on sheets of paper with six or eight panels per sheet, indicating who's in the frame, how the action is handled and which characters are leaving the shot, entering the shot, already in the shot or out of the shot (all based on the script). He also indicates the kinds of transitions to be used (wipes vs. dissolves vs. cuts) and the time in seconds that each shot should last in finished animation. Through the storyboard, the network for the first time gets a real feel for how the episode is going to look when completed.

It's also at the storyboard point that wars start.

Most animated series can be lumped into one of two categories: Is it a writer's show or a director's show? The storyboard is the point of demarcation between the two. That's the moment when the story editor gets back the storyboard from the art department and discovers whether the material she (or her writer) wrote is still there . . . or if the director has decided to toss everything out the window and fill the show with his own ideas/gags/ asides.

The storyboard also contains key elements, such as props or locations specifically designed by the episode, and key facial or body expressions. This is important because the storyboards, once approved, are usually sent overseas. The foreign animation studios don't tend to design elements; they take what's provided to them and animate it to the best of their ability. So if it isn't right in the storyboard, you can be reasonably sure that it won't get any better once you get back film footage. (This should not be taken as xenophobic; I've also seen locally produced animation messed up when things weren't made absolutely crystal clear in the storyboard.)

At roughly the same time that the storyboard is sent out, the actors are convened for a voice session. This is done prior to receiving the finished film so that the animated film can match the voices, rather than trying to make the voices match the picture. In some rare cases, actors are isolated from one another and read separately, but in general, the actors are all put into the same room, where they can develop a chemistry and react to one another's performances.

Either the writer or the story editor will try to be present for the voice session to indicate what a given character should sound like—deep voice, high voice, gravelly voice—and to explain the characters further to the actors. This is because the actors generally don't have full scripts in front of them, only the actual dialogue, which is excerpted from the original script to make live reading simpler. In some cases, artwork of the characters in question will be provided so that the actors can get a feel for their attitudes.

This, for me, has always been the most exciting part of the whole process. It all comes alive when you hear the voices.

Once the voice track is completed, it too is shipped overseas to be tied in with the developing animation. It's often as much as six weeks later that you finally start to receive film of the animated sequences, which are then edited together and scored.

At the conclusion of this long process, you have a half hour of animated television. Then all you have to do is do it again. And again and again and again. Given that syndicated series run sixty-five episodes per year (I once story edited seventy-eight in one season—a record), you get some idea of the monstrous amount of work involved.

I've dealt here mainly with television animation because that's where 95 percent of all the work is done these days, and because from a technical standpoint, there's no significant difference in format between a script for a big-budget animated motion picture costing $35 million and a half-hour cartoon costing $350,000.

Chapter Fourteen

Marketing the Animated Script

A
s with the discussion of premises, there are a few things you need to
understand about the animation marketplace that are less than
utterly terrific.

As stated in the previous chapter, the WGA does not regulate
animation, though it has recently established an animation caucus to help
develop links in that area. This doesn't just affect the animation writer in
terms of free premises; it affects you at every level.

With very few, extremely rare situations, *there are no residuals in television
animation.* A live-action script, once sold and produced, can bring in some
money, however small, for the rest of your life. But in animation, you get
the script money, and that's all. No residuals, no royalties, no percentage
of cassette sales.

This lack of residuals is one of the terrible inequities of animation writing. Another involves credit. You're lucky if your name stays on the show
at *all.* There have been many cases of animation producers taking the
names off shows written by Americans or replacing them with the right-
sounding foreign names in order to sell them into markets outside the
United States. You can write a full script, turn it in, get lightly rewritten
and lose complete script credit on the episode, getting only a "story by"
credit, if that. You can be asked to do endless rewrites without further
compensation. As of the date this book goes to press, and for the foreseeable
future, there are no rules regulating animation writing, no safeguards to
protect you from story editors or producers. You are entirely at the mercy
of the person you're dealing with.

You *have* to know that going in. This situation may change someday,
but for now, you need to be braced with that knowledge so you won't be
hurt by what you encounter.

Script fees are also nowhere near the level of live-action television, and
again, due to the lack of regulation, there are no set fees. You are paid

whatever the market will bear and whatever the producer thinks he can get away with. Half-hour cartoons can go from $3,500 to $12,000, depending on who you are and if your name lends any value to the show. Networks generally pay near the higher end, $8,000-$10,000, syndication much lower. One of the more insidious trends recently in television animation is the deal between an animation house and a story editor. The story editor is given x number of dollars to generate sixty-five scripts for one season. Her story editing fees come out of that bulk amount. So it now behooves her to lower the fees paid to the writers as much as possible. This arrangement corrupts the story editor/freelance writer relationship and encourages writers to turn against their fellow writers in order to shave off a few dollars here and there. If the freelance writers complain that the studio is deliberately trying to drive down fees, the studio can shrug and say it's got nothing to do with it, the fees are entirely at the discretion of its subcontractor, the story editor. Naturally, the original per-script fee allocated by the studio is a tightly kept secret.

Now, to the average person, $8,000 for a script (choosing a median figure) is hardly chicken feed. You can write a thirty- or sixty-page short story or novella and receive a lot less than $8,000—more like maybe $500-$1,000 if you're very lucky and hit a big market. So all this stuff about residuals may seem like whining to the average person. If you sell just five scripts per year, that's $40,000, and compared to other professions, that ain't bad at all. It's just when compared to what the producers make on the episode that the real inequity becomes apparent.

So the question before us now is a very simple one, and it's one you should consider and answer before venturing into animation: Given the problems, the inequities, the general garden variety weirdness of animation writing, why do it?

When you come down to it, there are only two valid reasons:

1. Experienced live-action writers tend not to do animation; consequently, the animation field is good for neophytes who want to break in, get some experience and then move on.
2. You're silly enough to *enjoy* animation and want to be part of it.

SELLING

Once you've made that decision, the process of selling a script to an animation studio is slightly different than with live action. The one commonality, however, is the spec script. That is your key through the front door no matter which form you pursue. In this case, you begin by writing script based on a reasonably current animation series. Get it as good as you can, and begin sending it around. Animation writing still isn't as heavily agented a field as live action, so many writers still tend to represent themselves in the early stages. In many cases, you won't even need a release form.

To get more specific for a moment . . .

1. Determine which animated series are currently being produced. Not which ones are on, which are being *made*. There's a quantum difference. Sometimes a show can hit the air with the producers knowing it won't get picked up for a second season, and they move on. *Daily Variety*, available at most libraries, does a roundup of animation each year and carries general animation news sporadically throughout the year. (Its animation coverage is slightly better than *The Hollywood Reporter's*.)

2. Write your spec for one of these shows or a recent one.

3. Through Directory Assistance, get the phone number for the studio producing the series. This isn't hard. There are only three area codes in the greater Los Angeles area to worry about—818, 213 and 310—and it's bound to be in one of those three. Call the studio and ask for the name of the story editor on the series. Ask for the story editor's assistant. Explain that you are a writer and you would like to either spec out a script for that series or send in a general-use spec. Ask if the show is still being produced and if there are any assignments still open. Assuming the answer is yes, you then ask if they can send you a writer's bible and/or sample scripts. You will be surprised at how many times you will be sent this material.

4. Study the material and, if your spec is for this show, try to adjust your script if it's off in some areas. Also, the bible or writer's guidelines will often indicate what kinds of stories they really don't want to see.

5. If they don't or can't send the material, send the spec script with a cover letter to the story editor, explaining your interest in the show and your availability to write for it.

As you can see from points 1-5 above, it really is a more straightforward process than live-action television, resembling more the world of magazine articles and short stories. And very often, if the script is good, or better than good, you may get a shot.

Case in point: my first animation sale. I will cop to having actually watched, and rather enjoyed, the animated series *He-Man and the Masters of the Universe*. It was dopey but fun, and I liked some of the mythos behind the series, enjoyed some of the characters and generally thought it was a hoot. So one day I decided to spec out a script. I found a sample script at a local bookshop, which gave me some sense of the typographical format, wrote the spec and sent it, cold, to the producer of the series.

About a week later, the phone rang. It was the producer, who had received, read and liked the script, although it was too close to something they were already doing for him to purchase it. I was, however, welcome to come in and pitch some stories. I readily agreed and went in the following week.

I pitched four stories. He liked one of the four and commissioned an outline. The outline was written and approved, and I went to script. I wrote two or three more after that. Then one day, after I'd finished my pitch, the producer noted that he was running out of money for freelance script assignments, but would I mind coming on staff? (This was at a time when it was commonplace in many studios to incorporate script fees as part of your salary. This is still practiced in a few places, but generally, script fees are over and above your weekly salary.) I considered it and agreed and came on as staff writer at Filmation Studios, quickly progressing to story editor.

It sounds easy, and I suppose on one level it was. Good animation writing is hard to come by, and if you can deliver it, you'll find a berth here, particularly if you can bring a real enthusiasm for the form to your writing.

There is, of course, one caveat. There's *always* at least one caveat, and it's the same one that applies if you intend to try to write live-action television: Your chances of making a sale increase with your proximity to Los Angeles. With the influx of computer technology and modems and faxes, there's been a generalized spread, with writers working farther and farther afield from the Los Angeles environs, but for newcomers, it's still a factor to be considered.

Because after you've read the bible and sent in your script, you're most likely still going to have to pitch some ideas for stories. The story editor may let you do this over the phone or may require a meeting. (Check the chapter on "Marketing the Telescript" for information on pitching.)

Based upon your pitch, you either will or won't get an assignment. If not, move on. Keep trying. If they do give you an assignment, it is certainly in your best interests to try to find an agent with ties to animation who can use this sale to start leveraging other pitch meetings around town. (You can pretty much forget trying to get an animation agent without at least one sale; there aren't many of them, and they're very fussy about who they represent. It may even take you two to three sales before you can attract a reasonably good agent.)

You'll note that I did not give suggestions or guidelines for selling an animated feature film. That's because in nearly every case that I'm familiar with, animated feature films come out of long in-house development at the studios. The odds of selling an original animated feature are, frankly, slim and none.

PART IV

Radio

It is not enough to pay attention to words only when you face the task of writing. That is like playing the violin only on the night of the concert. You must attend the words when you read, when you speak, when others speak. Words must become ever present in your waking life, an incessant concern, like color and design if the graphic arts matter to you, or pitch and rhythm if it is music, or speed and form if it is athletics. Words, in short, must be there, not unseen and unheard, as they probably are and have been up to now. It is proper for the ordinary reader to absorb the meaning of a story or description as if the words were a transparent sheet of glass. But he can do so only because the writer has taken pains to choose and adjust them with care. They were not glass to him, but mere lumps of potential meaning. He had to weigh them and fuse them before his purposed meaning could shine through.

—Jacques Barzun

Chapter Fifteen

Radiodrama Scripting:
Past, Present and Future

R adio has its earliest roots in the work of Scottish physicist James Clark Maxwell, who in 1864 theorized the existence of certain frequency waves whose modulation could be controlled and varied for communication purposes. Although the leading scientists of his day dismissed his work as too far-fetched to merit serious consideration, some dedicated themselves to vindicating Maxwell's theory. In 1864, Guglielmo Marconi succeeded in transmitting the first radio signals capable of being received at a separate location without the use of an interceding wire or cable.

The first practical application of Marconi's discovery was in ship-to-ship communication, thereby solving a predicament that had previously baffled the navies of the world. It was, in fact, the United States Navy that first coined the word *radio* in May of 1912, as a replacement for the over-used *wireless*, and which later coined the term *broadcast*. Ship-to-ship and ship-to-shore radio signals resulted in the saving of countless lives, though the most famous distress signal received was from the ill-fated *Titanic*.

After having proven itself as a device with practical applications, radio was quick to find a home on land as well as at sea. Although no precise date is available, it's generally conceded that KDKA, operating on an experimental basis out of Pittsburgh, was the first American-based radio station. Not long afterward, the first license to operate a regular radio broadcasting station was awarded to WBZ in Springfield, Massachusetts, on September 15, 1921.

During the following thirty years, radio underwent a staggering growth cycle. The prospect of instantaneous communication took America by storm, and by 1924, there were nearly 1,500 independent radio stations nationwide. These stations were almost entirely community oriented, with occasional experiments in joint broadcasting (usually to simplify the coverage of sporting events and presidential speeches).

On November 15, 1926, experimentation in networking took a giant leap into reality with the formation of the National Broadcasting Company (NBC), led by David Sarnoff (who, as a young man working at a radio transceiver, had been the one to first detect the distress signal from the *Titanic*). By 1928, NBC had acquired so many affiliates that it decided to divide its member stations into two divisions, called the Red and Blue Networks. In 1927, the Columbia Broadcasting System (CBS) opened its doors as a radio network.

The 1930s and 1940s have come to be known as the Golden Age of Radio. Around the nation, as families had once crowded about the hearth, they now huddled around the box, listening to the adventures of the Shadow, the antics of Benny and Costello and Fields and weekly suspense series such as *I Love a Mystery* and *Inner Sanctum*. These exciting days of radio are probably best described in the following excerpt from *Network at 50*, written by Norman Corwin, a man who shares with such giants as Arch Oboler and Orson Welles the distinction of being one of the greatest dramatists of radio's Golden Age.

> Years of the electric ear!
> The heavens crackling with report: far-flung, nearby, idle, consequential
> The worst of bad news and the best of good
> Seizures and frenzies of opinion
> The massive respiration of government and commerce
> Sofa-sitters taken by kilocycle to the ball park, the concert hall, the scene of the crime
> Dramas that let us dress the sets ourselves
> Preachments and prizefights
> The time at the tone, the weather will be, and now for a word
> The coming of wars and freeways
> Outcroppings of fragmented peace
> Singing commercials, and the Messiah.

Just as in early television, whose specter was already looming ominously on the horizon, there was always a certain adrenaline-filled frenzy to live radio. You could never be entirely sure that the program was going to go smoothly, as planned. In fact, about the only thing you could be sure of was that somehow, somewhere, something would go wrong. This probability was heightened by the fact that network programs were performed live not just once, but *twice a day*, first for the East Coast and then again, three hours later, for the West Coast. (It was also not uncommon for some of a show's cast and crew to go out for a few drinks between broadcasts, a situation that contributed greatly to the producer's anxiety.) There were also technical difficulties that had not yet been ironed out. Radios didn't have automatic limiters on them to crunch the sound like they do now.

When television made its inevitable appearance, many predicted it would mean the end of radio. And, in fact, this shiny new medium managed to steal away many of radio's greatest stars (Bob Hope, Jack Benny, George Burns and Gracie Allen, Amos 'n' Andy, Red Skelton, Ozzie and Harriet, and Kay Kaiser, to name but a few). Fred Allen was one of the few who found themselves unable to make the transition to television, which he called a medium "because it is neither rare nor well done." Many of the employees at the radio networks began wearing buttons that read "Help Stamp Out TV." But it was too late. As audiences turned more regularly to television for entertainment, the number of dramatic presentations on radio decreased. By the 1960s and 1970s, radio had returned to its original community-oriented status or was built around areas of specialization. There were all-news stations, all-rock stations and all-country or classical stations, but drama was difficult, if not impossible, to find.

While radio networks continue to exist (CBS, NBC, the Mutual Radio Network and others), their relationship to their member stations has changed considerably. The stations are largely independent of network control (except network-owned-and-operated stations); the role of the parent network has largely become that of providing hourly news reports or occasional special broadcasts. It is also possible for a single station to be affiliated with more than one network.

One very important change during this time has to do with what are known as "programming cycles." In the early years of radio, stations operated in half-hour and one-hour *cycles* (or blocks, as they were sometimes called). A cycle is the amount of time an average listener remains tuned in to a given station. Modern television also works in this fashion, programming shows in increments of thirty minutes. Bereft of long-form dramatic series, the programming cycles of radio stations have steadily decreased in length and now run anywhere from eight to twenty minutes, depending on the station's format. A good way of understanding the cycle concept is to listen to an all-news station, most of which repeat key stories at regular intervals. Most people tune in for the headlines or a few songs while driving or at home, then dive out again.

Starting in the late 1970s, audiences began showing a revived interest in old radiodrama and other forms of alternative radio programming. A few new dramatic programs were produced and found large audiences eagerly awaiting more. Some of this can be attributed to the fact that television's novelty had long since worn off, and that audiences were tired of seeing the same ideas recycled season after season. They wanted something *more*, programs they could participate in on a creative level, which is impossible in television since everything is "right there in front of you" and the imagination begins to stultify.

Unfortunately, the majority of radio stations around the nation have traditionally resisted the idea of resurrecting radiodrama, primarily because it means disrupting their established formats and programming cycles. It should be noted here that this attitude is held almost exclusively by commercial radio stations. Noncommercial, or public, radio stations, which generally program in longer blocks of time, are usually more receptive to radiodrama. National Public Radio in particular has had a long-standing commitment to the preservation and continuance of radiodrama as an art form.

Some commercial stations grudgingly responded to this new demand by rerunning Golden Age broadcasts with proven audience response, while others decided to take a chance on new programs. Invariably, however, many stations ran the programs late at night when their formats would be least disrupted . . . and fewer listeners were awake. This guaranteed lower ratings than might have been gained elsewhere, a fairly cynical move designed to reinforce the belief that there's no audience for radiodrama.

Despite this, by the early 1980s, radiodrama entered what many described as a Silver Age. New radiodrama productions were being undertaken on both a national and local basis. The national programs included *CBS Mystery Theater, Earplay, NBC's National Radio Theater, ZBS Media, Masterpiece Radio Theater* and *Enchantment Radio Theater*. Locally oriented excursions into radiodrama led to the creation of the National Radio Theater of Chicago, the Los Angeles Theater of the Ear (LATE) via KPFK-Los Angeles and a variety of others. ZBS Media (Rural Route 1, Box 1201, Fort Edward, New York 12828) has become one of the most prolific commercial radiodrama producers, selling both to stations and directly to consumers. Their programs include dramas of varying length, from five minutes to an hour or more. (The *Jack Flanders* and *Ruby* series of dramas represent some of the best work being done currently in the field and are highly recommended.) By creating programs of varying length, ZBS was able to work within the programming cycles of different radio stations, allowing for greater market penetration.

This revival of radiodrama was also assisted by the development of new technologies that allow for greater range and accuracy in sound effects.

Digital sampling and synthesizers have given producers greater latitude in the kinds of shows they can do, particularly in the realm of science fiction. Instead of having to fake the sound of fire (usually achieved by crackling wax paper next to the microphone), now one can buy, or download from various computer systems, the real sound of fire. What once required massive amounts of money and the full resources of a network radio operation can now be done affordably by just a few people.

But radiodrama has in general always been less expensive to produce than television. In 1978, my producer from *Alien Worlds*, Lee Hansen, commented (in what can best be termed a slight exercise in hyperbole), "Hell, we could've done *Star Wars* for a buck ninety-five." Ironically, starting in 1981, *Star Wars* and *The Empire Strikes Back* were both produced by Lucasfilm Ltd. in a twenty-six part series for National Public Radio and became one of that network's most expensive projects to date. (These radiodramas were made available on cassette starting in 1993 from the Highbridge Company, 1000 Westgate Drive, St. Paul, Minnesota 55114.) It also remains one of NPR's most successful programs, generating the biggest listener response in that network's history: 50,000 letters and phone calls in a single week. The show was heard by 750,000 listeners per episode and ended up adding 40 percent to NPR's overall audience.

By the 1990s, some of the bloom was off the rose, and some of the boom off the radiodrama, but the market does seem to have stabilized in terms of radio stations and expanded into other, newer areas, as we'll see later.

A LOOK AHEAD

Judging from current indicators, it does not seem as if the medium of radio will, like television, undergo any radical changes in the coming years . . . except in the following respects. Because of ever-increasing technology, the ability of radiodrama producers to make their programs sound authentic will continue to grow. Stereo effects and multichannel recorders, synthesizers, digital samplers and vocoders are daily becoming a bigger part of radiodrama production, and given the growing number of audiophiles in the United States, this certainly won't hurt the radiodrama field.

Radio as a medium is also undergoing a subdued revolution, thanks to the cable industry. Just as coaxial cables carry a large number of television channels, they transmit an impressive number of radio channels, too. Many of these stations are willing to experiment and to provide a variety of entertainment options. It's also less costly to operate a cable-only radio station than a broadcast station. As the number of stations increases, and the specialties of each become more distinct, it is only natural in the next few decades to expect a significantly higher number of stations providing opportunities for radiodrama.

One of the most promising developments lurking in the future of radiodrama is a distant relative of pay television. Several experimental systems have been undergoing testing in selected portions of the United States. The system allows the direct purchase of audio programs through the use of a cable decoder and tape recorder.

The system works in the following way: A given program, a spoken copy of the day's *Wall Street Journal*, a record or a dramatic presentation is scrambled and sent down through a cable to local subscribers. Each program is cablecast at a different time, usually late at night. The subscriber chooses what programs he wants to record, sets the decoder to receive only that program or programs and goes to sleep. The next morning, an audiocassette containing that program is ready for play.

The benefits of this system are enormous: It allows program collectors to put together an entire library of audiotapes. Since the decoder monitors which programs are recorded, at a given fee per program, royalties can be paid out of the purchase price to the producer, writer and cast of a given radiodrama. It is possible to develop programs only for this system, called *audiodramas*, that continue to feed back royalties in the same fashion as a published book.

Finally, over the last ten years, a whole new marketplace has opened up for radiodrama . . . or, more precisely, audio stories that use radiodrama techniques. Most major bookstores now carry extensive audio book sections. Initially, when these first appeared on the market, they consisted of nothing more than readings of current best-sellers or other novels by their authors or by actors. In some cases, music would be added or the occasional sound effect. But over time, the readings became more complex, utilizing sound effects in greater number and complexity and hired actors for various parts.

The lack of attention span that wounded radiodrama on broadcast radio is the same factor driving purchased audiodramas. People too busy to sit down and read a book now buy an audio version, plug it into the car stereo and listen to it on the drive to and from work. As the market share for audio books gets larger and more competitive, production values will continue to increase until the majority of audio books are virtually indistinguishable from radiodramas.

Radiodrama without the radio. Audiodramas. More generic in orientation, more commercial in their application. Already new works are being commissioned directly for the audiodrama market, and that field will only continue to grow in the coming decade.

For these and the other reasons mentioned at the start of this section, radiodrama can be expected to continue growing and expanding, once again becoming a viable part of the entertainment community. Although it will never again be as nationally important an entity as it was during the early days of radio, it will continue its growth as a source of artistic expression.

And freelancers, educated to the basic requirements of radiodrama, will be a very big part of that auditory renaissance.

Chapter Sixteen

The Art and Craft of Radiodrama Scripting

Before we can further discuss the where's and how's of radiodrama writing, the first obvious question is *why?* What benefits exist for the select few who sit behind their computers and struggle to paint pictures on the canvas of the mind's eye?

There are a lot of terrific things about radiodrama writing. As we mentioned earlier, it is still fairly accessible for relatively inexperienced freelancers. Whereas selling a television script involves more competition and will be influenced to varying degrees by your track record as a scripter, this is not necessarily true for radio scripting. There simply aren't enough people doing it to form a huge block of competitors. If you know the medium and the mechanics involved in putting a reasonable-sounding script together, it really doesn't matter what you've done in the past. That you can do it at all, and tell a good story within that medium, is the most important issue to a producer desperate for material.

To move away from the pragmatic for a moment, there is another, largely intangible benefit for radio scripters. Creatively speaking, radiodrama is probably the one medium most dependent on the writer's craft. In every other field of scriptwriting, there are creative loopholes. If a producer has a weak TV or film script, she can hold out the hope that the actor's visual presence will hold your attention or, in the case of comedy, rely more on sight gags than on harder-to-accomplish verbal humor. In some cases, a director's tricks, a performer's repertoire of attitudes or the sheer spectacle of a motion picture can save a less than salutary script.

But in radiodrama, there are no pictures to distract you, no sudden or dynamic camera moves, no fancy editing, no long, lingering close-ups of famous actors. If the story isn't there, if the dialogue doesn't sing . . . you're dead. In this field, you really have to work to keep the attention of your audience.

And yet, at the same time, that's the best thing about it. If your program is a winner, the lion's share of the credit rests on your ability as a writer. That is not meant to detract from the contributions of the cast members, the director, the composer, the engineers or the sound effects people. They play an important role in the quality of any produced radio program, and the absence of good people in any of these categories can cripple a good script. But it is the writer's words that create the characters and the world they live in and allow the audience to see everything that happens as clearly as if they were looking at film.

Television, stage, motion pictures . . . in each of these areas, there is a certain amount of forced collaboration, points of overlap between the different creative disciplines. But in radio, there's only a plurality of voices (for which inflections and pauses have been indicated in the script), the carefully assembled lines of dialogue and description (courtesy of the writer's imagination), the sound effects that help form a picture in the listener's mind (selected and inserted by the scriptwriter at crucial moments) and the music (for which tone and tenor have, once again, been indicated by you know who).

Because of this tremendous reliance on the script, radiodrama writers tend to have more control over the script than they would in another medium. After all, you're the one who hears the voices, who sees the room where the murder takes place and hears the music; you know the story and the characters better than anyone else. So there isn't much that happens to your script after it leaves your typewriter that you don't know about or have some input into. Whenever I've sold a radiodrama script, I have always been consulted about cast selection, script changes, the nature of the characters and so forth.

In some cases, when you are working with a major producer for the first time, you will even be flown to the studio so you can get a look at the facilities, meet the cast and be on hand for any last-minute script changes.

For those who may be put off by the more highly technical aspects of writing for television or film, radio is a wonderful medium for artistic expression. You don't have to worry about camera angles, transitions, limitations of budgets or sets or costumes. The vocabulary of radio is fairly simple, the process far from frightening in its complexity and budgets generally the least of your concerns. Your main concerns are story, dialogue, sonic imagery and characterization.

One slightly more tangible benefit is that selling a radiodrama script or two to a legitimate producer who is a Writers Guild signatory qualifies you to join the WGA, which for many constitutes a kind of benchmark, reaffirming one's status as a professional writer.

The final benefit of scriptwriting for radio is that it tends to pay fairly well, particularly if you get involved with a networked or syndicated series. Smaller programs can pay far less, of course, and some pay only in the experience you get as a budding scripter. As such, the rate of payment for a radiodrama script, depending on the length of the script, the nature of the series and whether it's a WGA signatory, can range from seventy-five dollars to several thousand dollars. So it can be something very much worth pursuing.

THE ART OF RADIODRAMA SCRIPTING

To begin writing radiodramas, one of the first things that you as a creative entity have to do is engage in a little self-reeducation. Radiodrama is an art form with requirements and eccentricities unique unto itself. While there are things you can do in radio that you simply couldn't do in television or film, there are also some things that can't be done in radio. You must, in essence, learn an entirely new set of dramatic cues and signals that serve to make the script comprehensible to someone who doesn't have your personal insight into the story.

To illustrate what's meant by this idea of reeducation, we'll look at a simple dramatic scene, as it might be written for film or television, and see what changes would have to be made to transfer the scene to the realm of radiodrama.

EXT. HOUSE—FRONT PORCH—NIGHT

GEORGE, a scholarly looking man in his late fifties, steps onto the porch, fumbles with his keys, then opens the front door and steps into the living room.

INT. HOUSE—LIVING ROOM—CONTINUOUS

George shuts the door, flicks on the light, and hangs his coat on a rack on the door. He turns, then stops. Sitting in a chair across the room, and facing him, is FRANK, a grim-looking, shabbily dressed hoodlum in his early thirties, a man who looks like he has had a long familiarity with the streets. He holds a .38 caliber pistol, pointing it carelessly at George.

                    FRANK
          Well, well. What's up, doc?

GEORGE
(seeing the gun)
What do you want?

FRANK
I think you know the answer to that. (with meaning)
How's Sally these days?

GEORGE
That's enough! Look, either you stay away from my
daughter, or—

He stands, advances, sputtering in rage.

FRANK
Or you'll what?

GEORGE
I'll kill you, I swear it!

FRANK
(laughing)
Right. You're gonna hurt me. What are you gonna do,
doc? You figure on turning into a man overnight?

George's face flushes; he is angry beyond words. He takes a step forward.

GEORGE
Why, you—

Before he can take another step, Frank pulls the trigger. George grasps his
chest, then falls to the floor, dead. Frank rises, checks for a pulse. Realizing
what he has done, he races out of the room and into the night outside the
house.

FADE OUT

Well, now . . . that seems a simple enough scene. Nothing confusing
about it at all. It's straightforward in what it tells us about the action and
the characters, and it certainly gets the story moving. You've probably seen
something similar to this a dozen times or more on television and film
screens.

But if you were to produce this scene, as written, for radio, you would
leave your listeners confused about who the characters are, what they're

like, where the action is taking place, and you would even mislead them about who shot whom!

Let's take it point by point.

Setting

Question: Where are we? Answer: George's house, of course. We can see that. But is it really that obvious when you take away the pictures? What information is present that tells an audience listening to the radio where all the action is taking place? Simply put, there ain't none. The scene could be taking place in an office, a large passenger cruiser or a log cabin for all the listener knows.

Your first obligation is to let your audience know where they are. One way to do this is by incorporating a narrator into your script. The purpose of a narrator is to establish location and setting with a minimum of confusion, to provide a sense of continuity between scenes, to reveal things that may or may not be known to the characters involved (a device generally frowned upon) and to assist in the transition from one scene to another. But you have to remember that a narrator is not always necessary. There are, in fact, many instances where you want to avoid a narrator altogether, since an omniscient commentator might give away too much, thereby putting a crimp into your script, particularly if it's a mystery.

There are two conditions under which it is desirable to use a narrator: when the program is part of a continuing series linked together by the presence of a narrator/host or when the set, location or logistical elements of your script are so complex that they can only be accurately conveyed by a narrator. The latter condition exists most often in radiodramas based on fantasy, science fiction, the metaphysical or the surreal where, for instance, it would be virtually impossible for the audience to visualize a setting on a planet or in a dimension they've never even heard of.

In any event, whenever you do use narration to set your scene, the scripted narration should be brief, brisk, vivid and very sharp. You should get in, set the stage and get out again as fast as possible. If you let your narrator sit back and pontificate on the characters, the plot or the ethical structure of the universe, you run the risk of letting your narrator become a character, which detracts from the story's characters. (Unless that's your intention. It's not uncommon in radio comedies to let the narrator assume a persona who sets the tone for the entire show.)

Given this situation, would it be desirable to use a narrator to facilitate the scene we witnessed earlier? Since it has not been established that the scene is part of a script for a continuing, narrated series, that rationale is out. So would the script benefit from the presence of a narrator? Probably not. The setting is nothing extraordinary, and you lose much of the suspense of the scene if the narrator simply tells the audience that George is about to find someone waiting for him in his living room, gun in hand. Better to let the listener discover that when George does.

No, your best bet here is to simply use the basic tools of the radio scriptwriter: sound effects and dialogue. So, how can we use these tools to establish the scene without getting corny? If this scene were taking place on a nuclear submarine, we'd have no problem at all. The sound effects would do all the work for us. If the scene were taking place in a hospital, the sound of a nurse's voice on the public address system could tell the listener where he is. If the characters were about to scale a mountain, you not only could use the sound effects of wind and snowshoes crunching on ice, you could also allow the characters to discuss the mountain, marveling at the grandeur and the terror of those high peaks.

In this instance, however, we simply have a man returning home at night. This complicates the matter considerably since there is no one readily identifiable sound associated with a house, and it would be rather silly for George to mutter to himself as he unlocked the front door, "Well, here I am, home at last."

What's required is subtlety and attention to detail. Think of the task as painting a picture with sound. What kinds of sounds would one encounter coming home late at night?

Crickets. Crickets are the most beloved bugs in the history of radio. The chirruping of a cricket tells a listener that the scene under way is taking place outdoors and that it's evening. The next step requires putting in a detail omitted from the film script because it was a given: How did George get home? As viewers, we can assume that he drove home. But here we can use the device to help set the scene.

So start with the sound of crickets. Then, we hear the sound of a car moving across a gravel road. The engine dies. The car door opens, then shuts. We hear a single set of footsteps move across the gravel, up a couple of wooden steps and stop. We hear the rattling of keys, a key being inserted in a door and the door opening and closing.

This, then, has established most of the needed information about the setting. Only one thing remains: to establish that this is George's home. Since *home* is a concept, it needs to be verbalized without being obtrusive. So one of the two characters needs to mention that tiny slice of information but without breaking character to do it. George is out of the question, for the reasons discussed before. That leaves us with Frank. Somehow, he has to establish that this is George's home, and given what we've seen of his character, he'll have to do it in a brash, not-entirely-complimentary fashion. The logical line would be a sarcastic "Welcome home, doc," possibly followed with, "Nice place you've got here."

And there we are. The flats have been painted, the scenery constructed, the stage set. It is important to remember, though, that you can't simply set the stage once, at the beginning of your script, and leave it at that. Throughout your script, you must continue to paint what are known in the radiodrama industry as "word pictures." How often and to what extent you do this is directly related to the number of different locations you intend to use in your script and how out of the ordinary they might be. To create word pictures, you turn once again to the devices of narration or character exposition in combination with sound effects. Just be sure your characters are not describing an everyday setting; nobody I know sits in her living room and, during a casual conversation, suddenly begins describing the room to a visitor—unless there is something special about the room that the visitor might not otherwise have noticed. And make sure that your sound effects can reasonably be achieved during production. I once saw a rejected script that used the following sound effect cue to set the scene: "SFX: Snow falling in a forest of elm trees."

To close out the discussion of setting, there are occasional circumstances where ambiguity actually adds a new dimension to your script. A good example of this would be a spy drama in which a person has been kidnapped at the opening of the script and is being held blindfolded at the kidnappers' headquarters. The listener and the protagonist share the sense of trying to figure out where they are and what's happening by the sound of it.

Later, after the prisoner escapes (they always escape) while being moved to a new location, it becomes necessary to go back and find the headquarters for some reason or another. Since the kidnappers never gave more than a few accidental hints about where they were keeping the prisoner, your protagonist now has to puzzle through all those sound effects—a train crossing, chickens squawking, a noon whistle at a factory and so forth—to try to determine where he was being held. In this way, your script has two basic plots: the kidnapping and the search for a hidden base, using only sounds as clues. It takes skill to pull off a script like this, however, so it's wise to wait until you have a solid understanding of more common techniques before attempting a tricky one.

As an exercise in setting, you might want to try to pick out the sound effects that would signal any given location. Picture yourself on a small boat or in a prison or at an electrical generating plant or at a street rally, and imagine what sounds you would hear while you were there. After a while, you'll notice there are generally one or two primary sounds that, more than anything else, will give the listener an immediate idea about where she is. These are the effects to include in your scripts.

Plot and Action

Like any other form of dramatic scriptwriting, a radiodrama must be *about* something. It must have a beginning, a middle and an end. There is a slight difference, however, in the types of stories required for radio. As a general rule, because of the nonvisual nature of radio, you'll find a minimum of heavy-action material: There are few car chases, slug fests and so forth. Such material may be appropriate for a visual medium, where you can see the hero clinging to the edge of a window ten floors up, but it often doesn't play well on radio. Which is one big reason why mysteries, suspense, comedy and science fiction programs have probably been the favorite genres for radiodrama writers and producers.

Radiodrama tends to be a cerebral medium. It highlights the interplay between characters, carefully constructs a delicate framework of suspense and tension and attempts to portray that which could not, or would not, be portrayed on network television or in film.

Which is one of the truly nifty things about radiodrama: You can do virtually anything the imagination conceives. For verification, I need only refer you to the great programs of the past. It has not been uncommon for radiodrama protagonists to travel to the planet Mars, to literally turn themselves inside out (an effect accomplished by slowly removing a surgeon's rubber glove right next to the microphone), to deal with an entire planet populated by superintelligent rats, to become invisible and walk among the streets clouding men's minds or to travel back and forth through time.

To further illustrate: During one of his radio specials, Stan Freberg emptied Lake Michigan, filled it with hot chocolate, then shoved a 500-foot mountain of whipped cream into it; at that point, the Royal Canadian Air Force appeared, towing a ten-ton maraschino cherry, which was dropped into the center of the whipped cream to the frenzied cheering of twenty thousand extras. He topped the exercise with the challenge, "Let's see you do *that* on television!"

The fact that you can toss aside the laws of probability (and in the foregoing example, common sense) does not mean that the radiodrama writer has a free hand to do *anything*. You may have an idea for the most incredible effect ever done in radio, but if it's not essential to the tale you're telling, forget it. Story, not effects, must always be the linchpin of your script.

Whatever your plot concerns itself with, one simple rule stands inviolate: Any action that takes place in your script must be capable of being visualized by the listener as accurately as possible. Sure, you may know what that sound effect signals, but if the listener shakes his head and says, "What happened? Did I miss something?" you're artistically dead in the water.

Take for example the scripted scene we examined earlier. Question: Who shot whom? Answer: It depends. If you saw the scene on television, the answer would be obvious: Frank shot George.

But if the event were produced for radio exactly as written, then the answer would again be obvious to the audience: George shot Frank.

Lest you conclude that the author is nuts, go back to the original scene and take a closer look at it. To start with, does any verbal exchange between the two characters indicate that one is holding a gun? No. Does a narrator announce its presence? Again, no. The first and only indication the audience has that a gun is present is the actual gunshot. So not only do we not know there's a gun in the room, we don't know who's holding it. And when is the gun finally fired? Right after Frank makes a snippy remark. George, his anger showing, shouts "Why, you. . . ." Then we hear a gunshot. Result: To the listener who hasn't seen the script, it appears that George, irritated by Frank's remark and angry at his presence, has pulled out a gun and shot him. This impression is further enhanced because no one speaks for the remainder of the scene. The listener would only become aware of the truth later, when Frank makes another appearance in another scene. Unfortunately, at that point the listener would probably undergo that one moment of confusion, "But I thought he was dead!" At that instant you lose the audience because they clearly sense that the writer has put together a sloppy script.

This little problem can be resolved simply by giving the audience sufficient subtle clues to pick up on what's going on, without making the listener conscious that this is going on.

Our first task is to establish that Frank is armed. Probably one of the oldest (and admittedly silliest) ways of doing this is to have the offended character say something to the effect of, "Frank! Where did you get that gun?" If you listen to any of the older radiodramas, you'll hear that line a lot. The problem with a line like that is that it doesn't fit naturally into a conversation. It's only there to establish that the other person is armed, after which the conversation continues toward its main point. After all, what is really the point of such a question in the real world? To get the other character to say, "Oh, this? Why, I picked it up at J.C. Penney's last Thursday after work. It has a nice recoil action. Would you like to hold it and see for yourself?"

So that route is definitely out. What's left? Well, as is the case with any form of drama, when in doubt, go straight for your character. The answer will invariably be found there.

Frank is your basic street-punk type. His courage comes out of the business end of a gun, and even then only when it's pointed at an unarmed victim. So he wouldn't utter the line, "You'll what?" in response to George's threatening tone, without something to back up the statement. Since this is an implied threat, it gives us an opening where we can wedge in the information about Frank's gun. This can be done with a sound effect and a bit of dialogue that actually helps to expand the plot a little.

The effect would consist of the sound of a pistol hammer being cocked, a move consistent with Frank's character. It underlines the threat.

Which brings us to the next step, a simple rule of dramatics that's true for every medium, but especially helpful in radiodrama: For every character action, there is an equal reaction from the other character(s). It's just physics transposed a bit, a little rudimentary logic. After all, if you were speaking to someone and that person pointed a gun at you and cocked the trigger, wouldn't it cause *you* to react in some way, if only with a pause? I should consider it very difficult to carry on business as usual when you're looking down the barrel of a .38 caliber interruption.

So George is bound to say something in reaction to the sight of Frank's gun. It is also necessary that he do so, since the sound of a gun being cocked is not quite sufficient in and of itself. It's altogether possible that the listener who has never been around guns may mistake the sound for a key turning in a door, or an old metal cigarette lighter being clicked. For our purposes, let's assume that George—a not altogether unaggressive character himself—would respond to the sight of a gun with, "Put that gun away."

Since that line interrupts the structure we established in the film scene, we must now alter Frank's lines to make everything fit together: He will respond, "No way, doc. Not until I have just a little more fun with Sally."

A final response from George, along the lines of "You lay your stinking hands on my daughter one more time, and I'll kill you, I swear it!" puts us right back on track again.

One other shorter way of handling the situation is that after George comes through the door (we hear it close), we hear the gun being cocked.

George says, "Who's there?" in response to the sound, which separates George from the sound, and since Frank is the only other person in the room, it helps point to the fact that Frank has the gun. And if Frank then steps forward (SFX: footsteps) and says, "One move and I'll blow your brains all over the wall," you've buttoned it down without in any way affecting your structure.

And there we have it. With a few added lines and a simple sound effect, we've not only established that Frank is armed, thereby making it clearer that it is he who does the shooting, but at the same time, we've also managed to convey a little more about Frank's character, or lack thereof.

Characterization

Establishing characterization in radiodrama can be a tricky business. If you write a country hick role for television, the producer simply puts out a call for character actors who look the part. The written lines get ranked second in primacy to the effect created by the performer's appearance and style of delivery. A good character actor can read the telephone book and make it sound convincingly countrified.

Naturally, that technique doesn't entirely hold in radiodrama. Admittedly, if you write a role for a country hick, a radiodrama producer will go out and find an actor skilled at backwoods accents. But there's more to the creation of such a character than an accent. A whole different way of speaking and thinking, varying rhythms and syntactical structure are involved, and while it's imperative at all times to trust your actors, you can't rely on them to bring out all the subtleties just through their delivery.

While it's important to make your dialogue sound authentic in any field of dramatics, particularly when you're dealing with regionalisms, this importance increases substantially when the only point of reference your audience has is the spoken word.

The beginning radio scripter must develop an ear for the way people speak and know what that manner of speech says about the person doing the talking. A speech pattern is like a fingerprint; no two are ever alike. A professor of literature, a car mechanic, an accountant, a professional model—even two people within the same family—each generally has her own particular method of speaking, which often gives the person's profession away.

But more than an occupation can be deduced from the way someone talks. The cadences, the pauses, the inflections, the choice of words, the inclusion or omission of certain phrases . . . all these tell us something about the speaker. Even if no overt attempt at identification is made during a radio program, the listener should be able to tell which of the characters is the street punk, which is the California surfer and which is the widow from the Midwest.

When writing accents from outside the continental United States, you've really got to do your homework. It's helpful if you have some grounding in the actual native language of that country because even if the character is speaking in English, very often the structural elements of the speaker's native language bleeds through into the English, flavoring and coloring it. There is, of course, the ever-present danger of going too far and turning your characters into stereotypes or, worse yet, unintentional caricatures. That's what I referred to earlier as the tricky part. It's a fine line to walk, and I'm afraid you won't find any shortcuts in this book on learning to walk that line. It's a skill that comes simply with trial and error, experience and the development of a good ear for dialogue.

Always listen carefully to people, even when they have nothing in particular to say (*especially* then, since the ability to speak while saying virtually nothing is a talent that can be applied to filler material meant simply to be entertaining).

In the case of our little scene before with Frank and George, both characters have a certain amount of contextual characterization built into their dialogue, more than enough for a visual medium. While it might also be sufficient for a radio script, it never hurts to push it a little for radio. In this case, Frank's lines could do with some more shading, something to point him a bit more toward the streets. We can, for example, take the line developed earlier, "Not until I have just a little more fun with Sally," and flavor it a bit, make it a little more informal, less grammatical. An alternative would be, "First, me and Sally, we're gonna have us a little fun, just like old times, y'know?"

This subtle change and others that can be plugged into the script heighten the menace of Frank's character, tell the audience more about his lack of education and generally help round him out. While it can be argued that this is only a trivial detail, it should be pointed out that a good radiodrama, like a painting, is composed of small, individually selected and deliberately placed brushstrokes, which, when perceived together, form a whole picture.

CRAFTING THE RADIODRAMA SCRIPT

One thing this book will not do is teach you how to come up with ideas for scripts. Ideas come out of your personal experience, angled just *so*, in such a way that it becomes drama. The only real consideration that must be given to the basis for your idea is whether it's a stand-alone drama or whether it's been written specifically as an episode for a continuing radio series, a topic we'll discuss in greater detail when we get to the chapter on "Marketing Your Radiodrama Script."

STRUCTURE

The best way to learn the basics of script structure is to read every script you can lay your hands on. When it comes to radiodrama, however, we run into a slight problem. Because the field slumped during the 1950s and into subsequent decades, books about and collections of radiodramas were published infrequently, if at all. Consequently, there aren't many books available on the subject. A close scrutiny of your corner bookstore will probably prove useless in your search unless it carries a large number of used books, in which case you may stumble upon one or two collections of radiodrama.

Public and university libraries will probably be your best bet in finding written, published scripts for radio. Some of the very best of these are the collections written by Norman Corwin, which, though often available in university libraries, are hard to track down on the open market. These publications include *Thirteen by Corwin*, *More by Corwin* and *On a Note of Triumph*, which contains the entire script for the famous nationwide broadcast aired on V-E Day. Other noteworthy resources include *Radio Sketches and How to Write Them* by Peter Dixon, a book first published in 1936 and, although somewhat out of date, remains a handy reference from a historical perspective, and *The Panic Broadcast*, by Howard Koch, a fascinating look at the events surrounding Orson Welles's infamous recreation of *The War of the Worlds*, including the entire script from that hysteria-provoking program. In addition, the radiodrama scripts for *The Hitchhiker's Guide to the Galaxy* have been recently published in book form, and *Flywheel, Shyster and Flywheel*—a popular collection of Marx Brothers comic radiodramas—remains fairly easy to find.

Happily, it is far less difficult to acquire actual recordings of radiodramas, classic and otherwise. Most reasonably sized record stores carry a full complement of old-time radio broadcasts, including episodes of *The Shadow*, *The Green Hornet*, *Inner Sanctum*, *I Love a Mystery*, *Buck Rogers* and many others, including such special, onetime programs as the aforementioned *On a Note of Triumph*. These recordings give you an idea of the types of shows that have been done in the past, how their effects were accomplished and the process by which the story was developed.

Contemporary radiodramas can be found through a variety of sources. As mentioned, the *Star Wars* radiodrama series is commercially available from the Highbridge Company, and many episodes from the SF series *Alien Worlds* can be obtained via the Mind's Eye. One of the most prolific producers of contemporary radiodrama is the ZBS Foundation/ZBS Media, which has produced adaptations of novels by North and South American writers, including Stephen King's *The Stand*, the Jack Flanders series of radiodramas, the eccentric, funny science fiction series *Ruby* and its successor, *Ruby 2*.

Finally, you should seek out radio stations in your community that either carry current radiodrama series or broadcast old radiodramas. Once you locate them, tape each broadcast and study it at your leisure.

During research, you'll discover that not all radiodramas are created equal. Depending on the writer, the nature of the program and the size of the budget, the construction of the programs will vary considerably from one to another. This is particularly true of the early broadcasts. In recent years, radiodrama structure has been standardized a little, particularly those radiodrama programs carried by commercial stations. We'll deal with non-commercial, or public, radio a little later. For the moment, we'll look at the individual components that make up a radiodrama, armed with the realization that while some series may omit one facet or another, all of them, to varying degrees, use the basic elements of script construction as presented here.

Prologue

This is the opening sequence of your script, wherein the characters and situations to follow are first introduced. In this sense, it is roughly equivalent to a teaser in television scripting. A prologue usually consists of a narrative introduction to the characters and the series itself, followed by a brief scene featuring those characters. A prologue, using this format, can accomplish a number of things, depending on your requirements. It can be used to show the day-to-day, mundane activities of your characters and thereby let the audience get a feeling for what the characters are like in circumstances other than the extraordinary ones that will follow. It can also be used to introduce the situation itself very vividly, along the lines of "Mount Everest has several thousand small ridges and individual cliffs, each suspended hundreds or thousands of feet above the snow-coated ground. Hanging from one of these is Jeremy Fastworth, who at this moment is wondering how many seconds of life he can reasonably expect to enjoy." You then cut to Jeremy himself. A prologue should get the listener's attention immediately. In this case, it should make the listener wonder who Jeremy Fastworth is, why he's on Mount Everest, how he got into his present predicament and how on earth he's going to get down again, short of a nasty run-in with gravitational physics. Like any good exercise in scriptwriting, it should make the audience want to stick around and find out what happens next.

Generally, depending upon the individual series, a prologue can run anywhere from one to three minutes and is usually organized in the following sequence:

- narrative introduction to the characters
- brief, scripted scene featuring the characters and/or their predicament
- narrative recap and invitation to stick around
- series theme music
- commercial break

Note: An exception to this rule is the series that chooses to put its theme music at the top of the prologue instead of the bottom. Again, this is one of those cases where it's essential to really know the series you're submitting to.

Acts

These are lengthier dramatic units that make up the body of your script. A half-hour program generally consists of three acts, with the first act around 5 minutes long, the second act approximately 10 minutes and the last act rounding out at anywhere from 7 to 9 minutes. You may have a minute or two of leeway, depending on how long your prologue is. When produced dry (without commercials added in), a half-hour radiodrama actually runs about 24 minutes.

One-hour programs can be a little tricky, depending on the series and whether or not it's being carried by a radio network. As a rule, there are four complete acts in an hour-long program, with each act running about 9 to 12 minutes. If this seems like a wide margin of error, there's good reason for it. Let's take, for example, the 1980s series CBS *Mystery Theater*, which was very popular for a number of years. Ostensibly, that series consisted of daily programs one hour in length. But actually, they're not. First, virtually any network breaks into the individual stations at the top of the hour for 10 minutes of news. So this already cuts 10 minutes out of the program. Second, for an hour-long program to show a profit, it has to include at least 10 minutes' worth of commercial advertisements, which decreases the total running time of your 60-minute program to a grand total of 40 minutes.

Surrounding an act are a narrative recap and/or a tie-back (discussed in more detail shortly); a series of dramatic scenes that are related in some fashion, preferably through the use of a plot; and a narrative comment at the end of the act.

Scenes

These dramatic subunits have caused more dissension among radio-drama producers than just about anything else. The controversy centers around the optimum length of any individual scene. Some producers see no reason why a single scene cannot last the entire act. Others shrink back in horror at that thought, some actually insisting that no single scene should ever run more than two minutes—shorter, if possible, because the contemporary radio audience is quick to change to another station. In the golden days of radiodrama, when there were only a few available networks, it was not uncommon to put the radio dial at the frequency for one of the networks and leave it there; but remote-control browsing, shorter attention spans and greater numbers of available radio stations have led to channel surfing here just as much as in TV.

My personal feeling is that the best radiodramas combine both long and short scenes. A long scene of, say, three plus minutes allows the audience to spend a little more time setting the stage and gives the scriptwriter more freedom in establishing solid characterizations. Interspersing these with short scenes of a minute or less helps keep the program moving and makes it seem to go by faster than it really does. This combination makes the most sense from a dramatic point of view because setting a mandatory and rather arbitrary length simply means that the writer will end up either padding some scenes (thereby making the action drag considerably) or cutting others (and thereby reducing the amount of possible characterization in that scene).

One of the most common errors made by novice radio scripters is the tendency to stick with the same location for each scene, with only the time element varying from scene to scene. Unless your script specifically calls for just one character—something that's very difficult to pull off—you will generally have a variety of characters and locations to play around with. Use that variety to your best advantage. If your script centers around the last will and testament of a dying man, for instance, go to his home and spend some time with the soon-to-be-deceased; then drift over to his office to listen in on his attorney and to the downstairs den and those who stand to inherit a substantial sum from his passage. This opens up a wealth of dramatic possibilities. You can show the dying man telling his attorney what he really thinks of his family. You can show how those family members act among themselves, backbiting and jockeying for position, and how they act in the presence of the patriarch, to whom they are uncommonly sweet. Not only does this pick up the action and increase the drama, it also saves you, the writer, a lot of cumbersome exposition. The dying man needn't give long, detailed descriptions of his relatives' true natures; it can be shown instead.

In assembling the scenes, many writers (myself included) tend to favor what is best described as a *circular approach*. In other words, as far as locations are concerned, you start with location A, then cut to B, then C, then back to B and finally again to A. You end up back where you started. In addition, you balance out each scene by making some short and others long.

Tie-backs

In those cases where a narrative recap is not expected to carry all the weight, a tie-back is used following a commercial to reintroduce the audience to the story. A tie-back takes place at the top of the second and subsequent acts and consists of the following: a brief, narrative summation of the previous act, right up to a highly dramatic moment; a replay of that moment as performed at the end of the prior act; and then a narrative introduction to the action about to take place.

A tie-back or some kind of narrative recap is often considered necessary because a commercial is an intrusive device that can break the continuity of your story. Devices such as these help bring the audience right back into your story and refresh their memories of the last dramatic scene. A tie-back usually takes less than one minute.

Hooks

Each act should end in such a fashion that, like a prologue, it makes the listener want to come back after the commercial break to find out what happens next. In addition, a hook works well from the standpoint of the producer. It forms a dramatic high point, the moment where the threat is issued, the music reaches a thundering crescendo and the narrator invokes the prospect of death, destruction or other unniceness.

Transitions

Any movement in time (past to present and back) or space (from one location to another) that serves to advance the plot is called a transition.

There are a number of ways to accomplish this. One is simply to throw a musical transition between two scenes. The catch with this technique is that in order to avoid having your audience wonder where you've taken them, the first few lines of dialogue following the musical transition should somehow indicate where we are and who's doing the talking, sometimes along the line of, "But George, do you really think it's a good idea to be prowling around father's office at night like this?"

Another useful technique is the use of a sound effect to accomplish your transition. An example of this would be having two characters discuss taking a plane to visit their uncle in Vermont; this is followed by the sound of an aircraft, which gradually fades down and under the dialogue that follows.

A third method, one that is steadily gaining more acceptance, is the use of a *cross-fade*, a technical term for overlapping the sounds of two different conversations, for instance, one fading down while the other fades in. This is similar to a dissolve in motion picture or television scripting.

Tracks

This is a term a radiodrama scriptwriter doesn't actually need to know but that comes in handy in understanding the process of producing a script. And it never hurts when a producer drops a phrase like "We're laying down the first track tomorrow" to be able to smile and know that he isn't going to be spiking rails all morning.

To *lay down a track* simply means to record something. A radiodrama is recorded and assembled in three stages. First comes a voice track for your dialogue. Next, the sound effects are recorded in the sequence in which they will be used. Then a music track is put together, and finally, all three tracks are mixed together and recorded onto a fourth, or "master track."

Parenthetical Directions

Since your audience can't see the actors shaking their fists or nodding their heads, there aren't a lot of directions you can give your cast in terms of physical action. All you can indicate is how the lines should be delivered. You can, for example, specify that the lines following your parenthetical direction should be spoken in an angry, sad, breathless, shocked or happy tone of voice. In many cases, if a line is to be delivered with a light touch, the direction given simply says, A *smile*.

I know that sounds peculiar, but don't laugh. You can hear a smile. Maybe it's subliminal, but there is a definite change in a speaker's tone of voice that occurs when the speaker smiles and means it. Try it yourself.

Snag yourself a volunteer and put her in one room while you go into another. Then deliver the same line or lines twice: once with a straight, sober face and the next time smiling in good humor. In most cases, the other person will be able to pick out which was which.

About the only other parenthetical directions for the actor's use are indications of time. If you want a certain line emphasized, you can flag it by calling for a beat or a pause right before the line. The only real difference between the two is that a pause is generally acknowledged to be a second or so longer than a beat.

Sound Effects

Another important element in a well-structured radio script is the proper use of effects, commonly abbreviated as SFX. Doors opening and closing, sirens, gunshots, ray guns and footsteps all fall under the heading of sound effects that, in conjunction with dialogue and narration, paint a mental picture of the events taking place. You should always choose your effects carefully, plug them in whenever and wherever they are actively needed (don't overload your script with them) and describe them as briefly as possible. For example, an indication for a door opening and closing would be written: SFX: DOOR OPENS/CLOSES. Two people walking on a gravel-covered driveway would be written: SFX: FOOTSTEPS ON GRAVEL × 2.

Vocal Effects

Anything done to alter an actor's voice to accommodate a need in the script is called a vocal effect, abbreviated as VFX. In most ordinary circumstances, there are only two vocal effects radio scripters will ever have to call for: a reverb and a filter effect.

Reverb is shorthand for reverberation. If your character is shouting in a cave, for instance, or in any other enclosed space, there normally would be some sort of echo or reverberation. This effect can be electronically duplicated in the studio.

A *filter* is used whenever you want to establish that your characters are speaking over the telephone. This is accomplished by electronically attenuating the voice of the actor who is supposed to be speaking through the telephone receiver, which effectively eliminates the lows of the voice and gives it the flat sound you normally get over the telephone.

If you want to get really artsy, you can use a filter to intercut from one speaker and location to another within the same scene. This is accomplished by alternating which voice gets filtered. It also helps if you can establish some kind of background noise behind one of the speakers. This makes the intercutting more audibly understandable because the background noise suddenly becomes louder when we cut to that speaker, whose voice also is no longer filtered.

Unusual vocal effects. Any vocal effects beyond those two are used infrequently. In science fiction radiodramas, a device called a vocoder is used to give a weird, alien texture to the speaker's voice. (A *vocoder* is basically an electronic synthesizer, the difference being that you're running a voice, instead of music, through it.) Other effects are often simply improvised. In *Alien Worlds*, a syndicated radiodrama series, my producer wanted to simulate the effect of two people speaking across space via a radio. But nothing seemed to give it an authentic texture. In the end, he solved the problem by purchasing a small CB radio set, with the transmitter in one studio, the receiver by a microphone in the control room and the second actor beside a standard microphone in a second studio, wearing a headphone that piped in the other voice. In order to do some intercutting, the producer had the actors exchange places and go through the scene again. Later he spliced together portions of each track, giving the effect of switching from one speaker to another as they communicated via radio.

In addition to these tried-and-true techniques, new audio production technologies are expanding the frontiers of radiodrama production. Digital sampling technology, which really came into its own in the 1980s and 1990s, allows producers to do nearly anything with voices and effects, combining wind sounds and voices and drums into a voice that one can play like a musical instrument; stereo and dolby surround technology allow the introduction of audio movement into what is otherwise a static format; new formats such as the Kunstkopf Binaural Sound System use microphones implanted into a human-shaped "head" to reproduce a three-dimensional audio "picture" with uncanny accuracy. New interfaces between computer software and audio technology will continue to change how the radiodrama of the future sounds.

FORMATS

Unlike telescripting, which utilizes four different script formats to accommodate differing technical requirements, there are only two standard radiodrama formats. Of those two, one is fading in popularity while the other rises. Since neither of these formats has a formal appellation, we will refer to them here as either blocked or indented.

The *blocked format* was modeled after the script format used in playwriting. This format was used during radiodrama's earliest years and is still in use today, although its popularity is decreasing. The advantage of using a blocked format is that it makes the dialogue easier to read since the lines are all double-spaced. The disadvantage is that the pages all look exactly the same: There's no indentation to mark the different portions of dialogue, and the pages thus have a tendency to blur together after a while, particularly during a live reading, and it can be difficult for an actor to find his place on the page again if he's been distracted. In addition, there are no provisions in the format for individual scene notations. There are only transitional devices, which can become confusing if there are a number of different scenes in your script.

Here, then, are the typographical requirements for a radiodrama script written in blocked form:

• NAMES are typed in all caps and appear 10 picas from the left edge of the page.

• Sound effects, music cues and transitional devices are all placed 10 picas from the left and are written in the following fashion, with each entry underlined: SOUND: A PAIR OF FOOTSTEPS; MUSIC: A DRAMATIC STAB; and TRANSITION: MUSIC or TRANSITION: SOUND OF AIRPLANE UNDER MUSIC.

• All dialogue appears between 23 and 75 picas and is written in upper- and lowercase letters. If there is more than one paragraph in a speaker's dialogue, the next paragraph is not indented. You simply move on to the next double-spaced line and continue.

• The first page of your script begins with the title of the series written in all capital letters in the center of the page, eight spaces from the top. The title is underlined, written in upper- and lowercase letters and appears two spaces below the series title, to differentiate between the name of the episode and the series in which it appears.

• The first actual line of your script begins ten lines below the episode title. Each page thereafter begins with the first line of dialogue eight spaces from the top of the page. The page numbers appear four spaces from the top at 75 picas.

• If a line of dialogue or any part of a speaker's line is carried over to the following page, it is indicated by writing (CONT'D) at the very end of the last line of dialogue appearing on that page. On the next page, (CONT'D) is written again in the space normally reserved for the first actual word of dialogue.

Having established the typographical parameters of a blocked script, we'll now take a look at how that translates into a typed page, after which we'll use the blocked format in bringing our scene between Frank and George to life.

And there we have it. In managing the transition from the largely visual to the exclusively auditory, we've now killed George off in both television and radio.

The *indented format* owes much of its development to two-column telescripting and looks very different from the blocked format. One reason

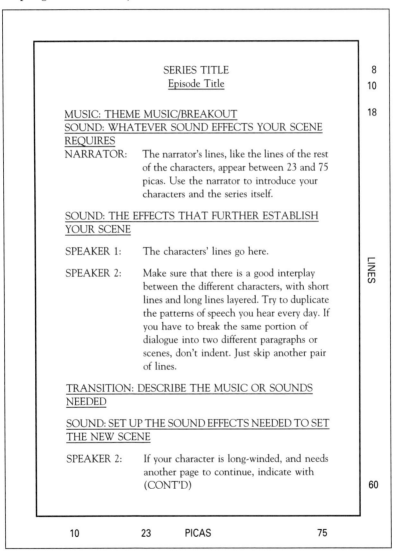

FIG. 9

why it seems to be becoming the industry standard is that it's simply easier to work with. The written material is clear, uncluttered, easy to read, far more efficient, times out to one minute a page more consistently than the blocked format and, well, it just looks niftier. The only real disadvantage to an indented format is that all the dialogue is single-spaced, and if your cast is limited to an unrehearsed reading, it might lead to a few slips. The

SERENDIPITOUS RADIO THEATER		8
The Confrontation		10
MUSIC: THEME MUSIC/BREAKOUT		18
SOUND: NIGHT NOISES, CRICKETS, AN OCCASIONAL OWL		
SOUND: A CAR PULLS INTO A GRAVEL-COVERED DRIVEWAY, STOPS		
SOUND: A CAR DOOR OPENS/CLOSES		
SOUND: A SINGLE SET OF FOOTSTEPS ON GRAVEL, THEN WOOD		
SOUND: KEY TURNING IN DOOR, DOOR OPENS/ CLOSES		
FRANK:	Welcome home, doc.	
GEORGE:	Frank?	
FRANK:	That's right. (BEAT) Nice little place you got here. Real nice.	
GEORGE:	What do you want?	
FRANK:	I think you know the answer to that. (WITH MEANING) How's Sally these days?	
GEORGE:	Now see here! Either you stay away from my daughter or I'll --	
SOUND: A PISTOL BEING COCKED		
FRANK:	Or you'll what ?	
GEORGE:	Put that gun away. If you think it'll do you any good, you're sadly mistaken.	
FRANK:	No way, doc. No, sir. At least, not (CONT'D)	60

LINES

10   23   **PICAS**   75

FIG. 10

typographical rules for an indented format are somewhat more complex than the blocked version and adhere to these dimensions:

- NAMES are capitalized and placed eight spaces from the left margin. An indication for a NARRATOR is also capitalized but placed at 13 picas.
- Dialogue, when spoken by any of the characters, is written in upper- and lowercase letters and appears between 35 and 75 picas. In order to

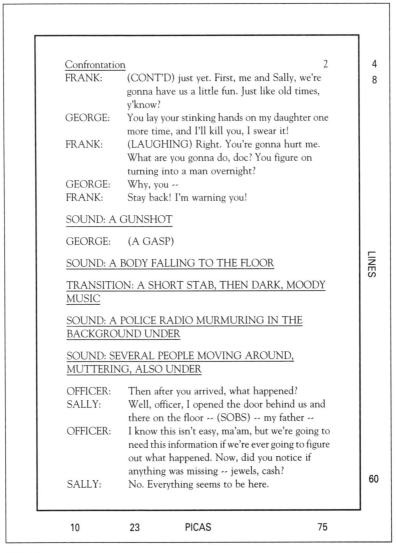

FIG. 11

separate it from the rest of the dialogue, narration is written in all caps.

• Sound effects are enclosed by parentheses, using a mixture of upper- and lowercase letters in a pattern like these: (SFX: PNEUMATIC DOOR opens right/closes) and (SFX: Single female FOOTSTEPS enter). The key here is to capitalize only the essential element(s) in your direction. If your script calls for several effects in a row, you single-space between each direction.

• Music cues are placed at 13 picas, blocked by parentheses, and written in standard uppercase and lowercase letters, as in (Dramatic Music Open) or (Theme Music Up and Out with a Flourish).

• Double-space between any given sound effect and any music cue.

• Triple-space between lines of dialogue from two different characters, between dialogue and sound effects and between dialogue and music cues.

• The first page begins with the series title capitalized, centered on the page, underlined and placed eight lines from the top of the page. The episode title appears three spaces lower, at eleven lines.

• The first actual line of the script begins seventeen lines from the top of the page.

• Acts and scenes are indicated and numbered in sequence. These indicators are placed at 8 picas, written in upper- and lowercase letters and are underlined. Two spaces below the act/scene indicator, you briefly describe the location, which is written in upper- and lowercase letters and blocked by parentheses. Single-space between the location description and a subsequent sound effect, and double-space between it and a music cue, should it follow immediately.

• Each subsequent page begins with the page number in the upper right-hand corner of the page, four spaces from the top at 75 picas. A condensed version of the title, preferably only one or two words, appears in all capital letters, four lines from the top at 8 picas.

• The act/scene indicator is also placed at the top of each subsequent page at 8 picas, eight spaces from the top of the page. This shows that the scene is continued onto the new page and would be written as Act 1, Scene 2 (cont). If your scene begins at the top of the page, then don't bother with the (cont). Three spaces below the act/scene indicator (eleven spaces from the top of the page) your first line of the script per se begins.

Chapter Seventeen

Marketing the Radiodrama Script

One of the first things that you as a radio scripter have to decide is whom you are going to write for, since this will greatly affect what and how you write. You should, for instance, decide whether you want to write for commercial or noncommercial (public) radio.

There are several advantages to writing for public radio. For one thing, it's easier than working with public television, which is generally closed to freelance scriptwriters unless you have the soul of a bookkeeper, the patience of a saint and your own source of funding. Public television is a mind-bogglingly complex system that, to quote radio scriptwriter Douglas (*Hitchhiker's Guide to the Galaxy*) Adams on a similar topic, requires proposals "signed in triplicate, sent in, sent back, queried, lost, found, subjected to public inquiry, lost again, and finally buried in soft peat for three months and recycled as firelighters." Public radio, on the other hand, offers a number of freelance opportunities with minimal bureaucratic red tape.

Another benefit of noncommercial radio is that you can tackle topics commercial radio wouldn't touch: metaphysical themes, political points of view, the problems of the handicapped and so forth.

A final point to remember about public radio is that a writer isn't firmly locked into a particular structure. Because there are no commercial interruptions, you can divide the script into a greater or lesser number of individual acts, and you need not work quite so hard at initially getting the listener's attention, since the basic public radio audience is familiar with radiodrama and willing to give it a chance to get started.

Commercial radiodrama producers are less readily visible but continue to produce material oriented to the needs of commercial stations. These include regular station breaks, shorter and snappier acts, with the radiodrama itself sometimes of short duration to fit better into drive times and other prime listening periods. Some radiodramas are three to five minutes in length. ZBS Media's *Ruby* was produced to be sold and broadcast by

AOR (Album Oriented Rock) stations in three-minute segments, roughly equal to many rock songs.

Once you've defined the general area you want to try for, the next step is to select a particular series. The best and most obvious way of doing this is to listen to whatever radiodrama series are carried in your vicinity. First, though, you've got to find them, which may be easy or rather difficult, depending on the circumstances.

Ideally, you should start by glancing through your local newspaper. Many daily papers carry radio log listings that provide information about what stations carry radiodrama and what times and days they're aired. Should this lead to a dead end, call up the reporter who normally covers television and radio, and find out if she knows offhand of any stations carrying radiodrama in your community. In most cases, such a person will generally be able to point you in the right direction. Should this also fail to pan out, you'll have to exercise a little ingenuity and work backward for a while. If you know that a radiodrama series is being carried on a particular network, track down who in your community is an affiliate of that network. If a series is syndicated rather than networked, your best bet is simply to write the series' main office (assuming you can find it), and ask for the list of stations carrying the program.

The last means of finding a radiodrama series open to freelancers is to check *Writer's Digest* magazine and *Writer's Market* on a regular basis. The former contains new listings published whenever they come in; the latter is updated yearly.

As you study your target series, start to analyze what it is you're hearing. Do you find that the same writer or writers generally write all the episodes? If so, there's a good chance the show is staff written. This doesn't mean you have no chance at all, but it does mean you should be prepared for a rougher ride.

Is it an anthology series, or does it utilize a set of running characters who populate each episode? If so, study the characters and make sure you catch all those little nuances of characterization in your own script.

Does the series revolve around a particular theme, such as mystery, science fiction, adventure or old West topics? If so, submit your script accordingly. Don't send a science fiction script to a producer who only wants dramas set in Nevada in 1897.

Does the program use a lot of special effects and music (the sure sign of a high budget) or a bare minimum? If it's the former, you have a lot more latitude in what you can call for in the script; if the latter, use restraint.

Is the program locally produced? Many are, and more are starting every day. Should this be the case, slant your script toward the community, with the script's action taking place at spots well known in that community. A sense of regionalism never hurts when dealing with local radiodramas.

Does the program have an "old radio" sound to it? If so, it's a fair bet the producer uses the blocked format. Another good indication is the producer having been in the business for a number of years, if you recognize his name from your research in old radio.

Is the series a Writers Guild signatory? If it is, then expect a little more resistance than you might encounter otherwise, since, as a rule, WGA signatories can use only Guild writers. However, they can use a non-Guild writer once provided he joins the Guild at that time—so don't give up hope. Most radiodrama series are not Guild signatories, which is good news for the beginning freelancer. Note: You can find out whether the series is a signatory by querying the producer or the WGA.

After you've answered these questions, you should have enough information to begin putting a few ideas together. As you do this, it's important to keep your developing ideas within the parameters of what your target series usually produces. Make sure that *you* are actively interested in the idea gestating somewhere in the back of your mind. If you're slipping a moral into it somewhere, be sure it's something you believe in. If you're just putting in a moral to be socially relevant, forget it. It'll sound preachy and obvious. At the same time, don't write something commercial only for the sake of writing something that will sell because that's how schlock is produced. Write what you know, what you believe in, what you want to write.

When you've finally settled upon an idea that looks good, go ahead and write a treatment (just as we did in "The Craft of Telescripting") and the first two acts of the actual script. Do not write more than that. Writing the first two acts gets you going, gets you well into the story and assures you that you will be able to finish it at a later date. You don't have to write more than that because in most instances the producer won't want to see more than the first two acts and a treatment for the whole program. Why put in that much time on something that, if she decides not to go with it, won't be produced?

When you've completed your first two acts and treatment, the next step is to contact the producer. This can be done simply by calling the local station that carries your target series and asking the program manager for the address of the production company and the producer's name (if it isn't mentioned during the regular broadcast). Armed with this final bit of information, you now come to the actual marketing of your script.

In brief, it's time to write your query letter.

A query letter to a radiodrama producer is similar to the query addressed to a television producer. It should state, in no more than a single page, your familiarity with and appreciation of the series, your knowledge of radiodrama formats and technical requirements, the fact that you have written two acts of a finished script and a treatment that covers the entire episode; and that you would appreciate the opportunity to send the script and treatment along for his examination on a speculative basis. Once again, do not put your concept into the query letter because of the possible threat to the producer of a plagiarism lawsuit. Not only that, the surest sign of an amateur is a letter that says basically "I've got this neat idea, here it is, now how much do you want to pay me?"

In closing your query letter, you might also want to inquire whether there is a preferred script format used by the show (be prepared for a retyping if so); and if a release form is required when submitting manuscripts (they usually are), would he please forward one for your use. Most radio release forms read the same as the general purpose one used in this book, so when you receive the release, you might want to check it against this one just to make sure what you're signing is legitimate.

When you finally hear from the producer, you will receive one of two answers: yes or no. No can mean no, we don't take freelance scripts; no, we're booked up right now and don't need any scripts for a while (in which case you should try again at a later date); or no, and we're not going to say any more than that, get what you can out of our form rejection letter. Those are the worst rejections, and should you receive a form rejection, stick it up on your dart board, think ill thoughts about the producer's lineage and move on to the next series.

Yes means yes, but don't get your hopes up. It means that you should send along your script and treatment, unless the producer specifically asks to see only the treatment, and wait as patiently as possible.

When the producer finally responds to your manuscript submission, there are a number of possible replies:

- A form rejection. Get your dart board out again.
- A not-quite-for-us rejection. This is an open door. Write to the producer, stating that you'd like to develop another idea and send it along, if that would not be an inconvenience. If she says that it is, then don't push the matter. If not, then go for it.

- An it-doesn't-quite-ring-true rejection with suggestions for improvement. Again, this is an open door. Write to the producer immediately, informing him you will rewrite your script to incorporate the suggestions made in his letter and then resubmit it. If he likes the general idea, he'll say OK. If not, and he still thinks you're just a little off target, he'll tell you to forget the original idea and develop another. Do so.

- A sorta-kinda rejection. This is where the producer says she likes your writing style, your flair for dialogue and characterization and suggests that although the present story is not quite right, she would be happy to look at another script. This is an even wider open door. Leap through it.

- A conditional acceptance. He likes the first two acts, and the treatment seems solid. So he will most likely suggest that you go ahead and finish the script on a speculative basis. If the rest of it lives up to the expectations raised by the first two acts, he'll buy it. If not, he'll probably buy the idea giving you story credit and suggest you try another script. Either way, you've got a sale.

- A complete acceptance. You receive a check in the mail for the first two acts and a few suggestions for the rest of the script, with the balance payable upon completion of the script. Your response: Photocopy the check, cash the original and go out to dinner with your significant other. Then get straight home and get to work because you've just been handed a marvelous opportunity.

Those are the parameters of response, from worst possible scenario to the best. If you get rejected, don't take it personally. Try again, or try elsewhere. If you get accepted, well, here are a few things you should know about and prepare yourself for.

First, be advised that most radiodrama scripts are purchased as a work for hire. This means the produced script is copyrighted in the name of the production company, and the company owns all the radio rights. Most work-for-hire agreements mention ancillary rights only briefly, and should you, for example, later desire to write a short story, play or telescript based on your radio script, there usually isn't much of a problem with this. In most instances, you need only secure the producer's permission, although occasionally, depending on the terms of your agreement, the producer may require a percentage or fee. This is, however, the exception to the rule.

What follows is the text of a standard work-for-hire contract. If your producer purchases scripts on such a basis (and, again, not all do), you will be asked to sign a contract similar to this one. If the particular agreement you receive specifically places all other rights beyond just the radio rights in the producer's hands, and if you would like to do a version of your story for another medium at a later date, then the best thing to do is simply tell this to your producer, and see if you can work out an amendment permitting you to pursue your intention. My own experience has indicated that in most instances both sides can be accommodated.

Here, then, is the text of a standard work-for-hire agreement for a purchased radiodrama script:

Assignment of Radio Rights

This Assignment is made and entered into as of this _____ *day of* _____ *, 19* _____ *by* _____ *(herein "Writer") and* _____ *(herein "Producer").*

WHEREAS, Producer is the sole creator of that certain original concept, format and idea for and the individual producer of a series of dramatic plays (hereinafter sometimes referred to severally, collectively and singly, as the context may require, as the "Program(s)"); and

WHEREAS, Producer has the exclusive license to use, deal in and exploit all, but only, the Radio Rights (as hereinafter defined) in and to the Program(s) (said Radio Rights include the right to produce, broadcast, advertise and exploit one or more radio programs or radio program series based on or suggested by the Program(s)); and

WHEREAS, Writer (has been and) currently is employed by Producer as a writer in connection with certain episodes of the Program (such episodes of the Program which Writer (has written or) may in the future write) are hereinafter referred to as the "Episodes," which Episodes are now and will in the future be works made for hire under the United States Copyright Act; and

WHEREAS, pursuant to the License Agreement, Producer owns and shall own all rights, titles, and interests of every kind and nature in, to, and with respect to the Programs, as aforesaid;

NOW, THEREFORE, for good and valuable consideration, receipt of which is hereby acknowledged, Writer agrees as follows:

1. Writer hereby assigns to Producer, with respect to his Radio Rights, all said rights, title and interest in, to and with respect to the Episodes, any and all thereof, and any and all parts thereof, including, without limitation, all material, works, writings, ideas, "gags," dialogue, and characters, written, composed, prepared, submitted or interpolated by Writer in and in connection with the writing, preparation and production of the Episodes (hereinafter sometimes referred

to severally, collectively and singly, as the context may require, as the "Material").

2. Writer acknowledges and agrees that, subject only to the Radio Rights licensed by Producer as aforesaid, Producer owns and shall own all the right, title, and interest in, to and with respect to the Episodes, the Program(s) and the Material, any and all thereof, and any and all parts thereof, all of which are automatically and shall automatically become the property of Producer.

3. Any and all of the rights assigned to Producer pursuant to this instrument shall be and are fully transferable and assignable by Producer, in whole or in part, without any restriction whatsoever.

4. Writer hereby represents and warrants that:

   (a) He has the full right and authority, subject to the Radio Rights licensed by Producer, as aforesaid, to transfer and assign all of his rights, title and interest in, to and with respect to the Episodes to Producer;

   (b) The Episodes are in all respects wholly original with Writer;

   (c) The exercise of any of the rights granted pursuant to this Agreement or the use of any or all of the Episodes or any parts thereof will not in any way infringe upon or violate the copyright, common law right, or literary, dramatic, or other rights, or constitute a libel, defamation, or invasion of the rights of privacy of, or unfair competition with any person, firm or corporation;

   (d) Subject to the Radio Rights licensed by Producer, as aforesaid, he has in no way assigned, conveyed, granted or hypothecated any rights of any kind or character in or to the Episodes, or any part thereof, to any person, firm or corporation other than Producer; and

   (e) He is not presently a member of any union, guild or any collective bargaining unit which will require any payments to be made by Producer for or on account of this Assignment (other than the payments made by Producer for Writer's services in connection with the Episodes as aforesaid).

5. Writer shall defend, indemnify and hold harmless Producer and Producer's assignees, successors and transferrees, and each of them, if any, from and against any and all claims, demands, damages, obligations, costs, expenses, liens, actions and causes of action (including attorneys' fees, whether or not litigation is actually commenced) of every kind and nature whatsoever, arising out of a breach or alleged breach of any of Writer's representations or warranties contained herein.

6. Writer acknowledges and agrees that the compensation paid to Writer by Producer shall be full and complete compensation for Writer's services in connection with the Episodes, and that Producer shall have no obligation whatsoever to pay Writer or any other person, firm or corporation on Writer's behalf (including, without limitation, any union, guild or other collective bargaining unit) any amounts for or in connection with the Episodes or any exploitation or use thereof. Further, Writer agrees that Producer has and shall have no obligation to utilize all or any part of the Episodes or to make, produce, release, distribute, advertise or exploit the Programs, the Episodes, or any other play or program based upon or which uses in any manner the Episodes or otherwise.

7. The provisions of this Agreement shall be binding upon Writer, his heirs, executors and administrators.

8. This Assignment shall be construed and interpreted pursuant to the law of the State of _____ .

9. This Agreement contains the full and complete understanding between the parties hereto, supersedes all prior agreements and understandings, whether written or oral, pertaining thereto, and cannot be modified except by written instrument signed by the parties hereto.

IN WITNESS WHEREOF, writer and Producer have executed this Assignment on the day and year first written above.

_____   _____

WRITER   PRODUCER

If that sounds extraordinarily complex, well, that's because it *is* extraordinarily complex. The upshot of it all, however, is simply this: that you wrote the episode, that you own all nonradio rights to it, that it won't get the producer dragged into a lawsuit of some sort and that the producer owns all radio rights to your script. This particular agreement is ideal, since it specifically deals only with the radio rights and thereby puts the writer in the position to someday turn out a version of the script in another medium. (This was the case with Arthur Kopit's *Wings*, which was commissioned as a radio play for the BBC and which later went on to become a considerable success on stage.)

The amount of money you are likely to receive from the sale of a radio-drama script can vary considerably. The range can go from $75 to $900 for a half-hour script and from $1,000 to $3,000 for a one-hour script. The extent of your payment is almost always a function of the overall budget for the series. If it's a national program, whether syndicated or networked, you can usually count on receiving a fairly substantial amount. If, on the other hand, the show is based at a local station (and there are more and more of these popping up daily), then the odds are pretty good your payment will be less. If the producer is a signatory to the Writers Guild, then there is a pre-existing formula for payment, credit placement and residuals, and the sale counts, however minimally, toward WGA membership.

The important thing to remember, though, is that at first, the amount of money isn't important. The essential thing is to get that first production under your belt. Once that's been done, and as you've learned more about radiodrama as an art form, then the more prepared you'll be and the easier it'll be to move on to the higher-paying markets.

In addition, after you've made your first sale, that same producer is likely to come to you again for more scripts and will often refer you to other producers while recommending your services to them. Remember, radiodrama writers are scarce, and when someone discovers a talented writer, it seems that everyone starts beating down her door for material, sometimes on rather short notice. I once had a producer wave a substantial amount of money in front of my nose for a radiodrama script, provided I could write the whole thing, from start to finish, in two and a half days. They needed it to fill a hole caused by another script that turned out to be unusable. He got his script.

Once the script has been sold, the agreements signed and the check deposited in your bank account, there come the usual revisions, discussions, debates over characterizations and cast members and so forth. You should participate in these and add your own suggestions as often as permitted, without getting obnoxious about the whole affair, and use the opportunity to learn what problems confront the producer and where you as a writer may be able to minimize them in the future.

Finally, for the scriptwriter who wants to learn as much as possible about radiodrama production, preferably from a hands-on perspective, there is one last alternative to consider.

Self-Production

As mentioned in the chapter on "Radiodrama Scripting," by the financial standards of television and film, radiodramas are relatively cheap to produce. Assuming you have written a script that does not call for a lot of complex effects and musical scores, it is altogether possible for you to produce your own script. The only ingredients you need to pull this off are the desire to do so, a few talented voices, a multitrack recorder, a tape editor, a good engineer, four or more microphones and a collection of sound and music effects records.

So let's take this one step at a time.

To start with, why would you want to produce your own script? For one thing, it familiarizes you with the problems any producer faces in giving life to a typewritten script. More than that, however, it gives you, as director/producer, complete control over the way your script is interpreted by the cast. It also lets you more fully understand the complete process of radio-drama production, giving you a better idea of the limitations of the medium. It is tremendously exciting. And it is of substantial help when you approach a producer of a syndicated or networked series. He feels more confident utilizing your services since you have established a foothold in the medium, and you have a finished dramatic tape to use as a sample of your work.

After you have decided to go ahead with your own production, you must confront two vital questions: Where will I record it, and who will I get to perform in it? Although those may seem like intimidating questions, the solutions really aren't that difficult.

If you want to spring for the drama yourself, you simply go to any recording studio in your area and tape there. Studio time, at its cheapest, goes for $35 to $75 per hour. (You supply your own recording tape.) If you have a cast that's properly rehearsed and you've already set up your sound effects and music cues in the correct order, you can be in and out of the studio rather quickly. For a half-hour script, you'll probably incur one hour to an hour and a half for the voice track, assuming you've properly rehearsed your cast; the time will expand if you haven't. After the tape has been edited—something you should do away from the studio, with the assistance of someone who knows the process and can help create a finished voice track—you go back in for another two hours or so and lay down the music and sound effects. Total time: three to four hours, again depending upon your state of preparedness.

(We'll get into the technical aspects of producing a radiodrama after we explore the different options for a tape location.)

If your plan is to do a whole series of radiodramas and syndicate them on a barter syndication basis (which we'll also explore later), you might be able to convince the studio to waive a recording fee altogether, provided you promise that if you get a series going after your initial production, you will continue to come to that studio with your business, thereby killing two birds with one microphone: You get a free demonstration tape, and the studio gets the prospect of a steady future customer. (You really have to be a fast-talker to pull this off, though.)

If you're not a fast-talker, and if you don't have the ready cash to spring on a production, don't despair. There is one remaining alternative: college radio.

College radio stations exist to provide students with experience in radio techniques, and it has been my experience that most of them welcome the opportunity to try something a little different. Since just about every college of substantial size has some sort of radio station (even if it only broadcasts over a two-block radius or through a cable system), you shouldn't have much difficulty finding one in your area. You will admittedly have to deal with college disc jockeys, who tend to be some of the most, ah, unique characters in the broadcasting industry, but at least you'll have a fair number of volunteers able and waiting to work on the project and a complete studio to work with.

To persuade a college radio station to go along with your project, simply contact the program manager/director (usually a student herself) and explain that what you have in mind is an educational opportunity. Moreover, it will be a credit on the resume of whoever helps out in the project, with said credit also given on the finished tape. Given that broadcasting is a hard industry to crack and that any credits whatsoever can help someone's prospects after graduation, you probably won't have much of a problem getting a go-ahead. You may, however, have to share producer credit with someone at the station since some college radio stations insist all productions be under the name of the students using its facilities.

After deciding where you are going to produce your script, the next step is to secure your cast members. Peculiar as this may sound, this is probably the least of your worries as a producer/director/writer.

To a performer, the single most important thing in the world is the chance to perform, to stretch his abilities, to learn and to acquire a credit or two that might prove helpful in future aspirations. For this reason, many aspiring actors are willing to perform for no pay at all in community theaters. You will find this to be the case with your radiodrama production as well. More so, in fact, since the end product of your combined labors will be a tape that the performers can then give to agents, directors and producers, whereas a credit in a local theater is basically an uninformative paper credit. So you can get a full cast of actors for your show (which should, however, use a minimum of performers) at virtually no cost. As a personal note, though, having worked with actors and having acted myself, I would highly recommend you dig up some sort of recompense for their labors. Paying for the gasoline they use to and from rehearsals is always a good gesture, and providing each cast member (free of charge) with a cassette recording of the finished show is not only desirable, but essential to keeping good relations with the theatrical community.

After securing your cast and the studio, the single most important element for the production of a decent-sounding radiodrama is the presence of a skilled engineer. I cannot overemphasize the importance of this person. This is the person who sits at the control board during your taping and should sit at the editing table after the taping, the person who makes the whole thing come together. You must work closely with the engineer to make sure you communicate exactly how the cast's voices should sound. If you want any electronic effects, like a filter or reverb effect, that can be done during production; communicate to the engineer when you want the voices to fade down or fade up and so forth. If you explain exactly what you want, and if you have a solid engineer, you'll generally get what you want.

The best way to secure a good engineer is to ask around at the studio or college station. Look for someone who can *react quickly*, who has worked on live broadcasts and who has some familiarity, however rudimentary, with radiodrama. When you've found such a person, work hard to persuade her to do the tape editing with you as well. If this turns out to be impossible, use the same criteria to find someone skilled at editing tape.

The ancillary equipment, microphones and such, comes with the facility you're using. As a rule, it doesn't take much equipment to produce a radiodrama. In fact, I once knew someone who put together a respectable twenty-minute production using a home multitrack recorder, a few microphones and a handful of friends who volunteered their services as performers and live sound effects people. The result was credible, if simplistic. I recommend this to you only if you happen to own a multitrack recorder, have a lot of talent as an engineer and come equipped with five arms and six eyes.

Finally, you have to secure your sound effects and music cues. This is also relatively easy. Assuming you've already written the script—a necessity—and you know what effects and music are called for in the script, as well as which ones can be done live as opposed to being edited in later, you need only pay a visit to your local, well-stocked record store and rummage through the sound effects records. Usually, you can find sounds that range from atomic blasts to fly buzzings and mood music intended for use in radio productions, and therefore free from royalty requirements. Warning: If you opt to use music from established sound tracks or commercial records, you run two risks. First, you risk the possibility that your listener, recognizing the cut, will be distracted by the memory. Second, should your production ever be aired over a commercial radio station, you may be dunned for royalties for using someone else's music in your show.

Having attended to all these production-oriented needs, you are now ready to undertake your first radiodrama production. To get started, I recommend the following sequence of events:

1. Select your cast carefully so that they sound like the people who inhabit your script. Choose them from local theater groups and from local colleges by placing audition notices.

2. Rehearse, rehearse, rehearse. Even though your cast will be able to use their scripts during the taping, it's absolutely essential that all the glitches are eliminated before you go into the studio. Each delay during taping will raise the cost of the production, and every flub must be removed during the editing process.

3. Time the script, and be prepared for rewrites. When you do a run-through of the script with your cast, have them put in the pauses needed by the sound effects and music cues the script calls for. It's necessary for you as the director to know exactly what's needed and how long each effect will run. If, after a complete reading, you find that the script runs too long, and you can't move the cast through it any faster, start cutting. Cut anything that isn't absolutely necessary to the action, and rewrite where possible those lines the cast members just can't say without tripping over their tongues. Rehearse until you can go through the entire script without a single slipup.

4. Tape the voice track. Go into the studio, explain to the engineer what you want and then start the tape rolling. Be ready for flubs, though, no matter how well prepared your cast might be. Remember, it's one thing to read a script in your living room, in the company of friends, and quite another to do the same thing staring at a microphone. Be patient with your actors. Instruct your cast members that if a mistake occurs, they should pause silently for two beats and the person with the flubbed line should back up one or two lines and start again. This eliminates the need to stop and then restart all the recording equipment.

Important note: Be sure the erring cast member goes back to a line that hasn't been "walked on" by someone else. By this, I mean if, in the first run-through, the previous line ended with two people speaking at once, it will severely handicap your efforts to put things together later when you discover you have two different versions of the same line: one with a single speaker, another with two.

5. Edit out the glitches in the voice track. Eliminate the overlong pauses, the stumbles, the flubbed words. This is done by playing the tape on an editing machine and, when you come to the piece of tape containing the error, simply cutting out that piece and splicing together the two remaining ends. When you've finished this, and as someone who's made his fair share of goofs at the editing machine let me reaffirm this, it's important to have a good editor working with you to time the finished tape. If it runs over, you'll have to go back and cut any spoken lines that can possibly be removed without ruining the tape or crippling the drama. It'll hurt, but do it.

6. Put your sound effects in their order of appearance in the script, and transfer them to tape. Do the same for your music cues. Then, when you go back into the studio, you have two options: First, you can record both the voice track and the sound effects onto a separate tape, cuing up each effect as needed, and then later, onto a fourth tape, lay in the music on top of the voices and effects. The problem with this is that each time you rerecord a voice, it loses some of its audio quality, and this step requires recording the same voice through two generations. The second option, should you have a really sharp engineer, is to lay both the sound effects and the music cues in simultaneously so that the voices have been recorded onto only one other generation of tape.

7. Have your finished tape transferred from reel-to-reel to cassette tape or DAT (Digital Audio Tape), and provide a copy to each of the cast members and the engineer, being sure that everyone's credit has been included on the tape.

8. Throw a party and relax. You're finished.

Well, sort of.

If your only intention was to produce a tape or two for your own experience and education and for use as a sample of your work, then your efforts stop here. If, however, you have big plans for your show and want to make a series out of it, you want to take the process one step further, into an arrangement known as *barter syndication*.

The principle behind barter syndication is this: You, as writer/producer, create a half-hour program that runs twenty-four minutes dry, thereby leaving six minutes for commercials. You then approach a sponsor, preferably one with a national product. You tell the sponsor that in return for underwriting the cost of production, he can have all six minutes' worth of commercials, which are then pressed on the record along with the radiodrama itself. In exchange, you syndicate the series to a substantial number of radio stations, which broadcast the program and commercials.

The benefits behind this are obvious: For the sponsor to purchase six minutes of airtime on all the stations that air the drama would cost far more than the cost of simply producing a half-hour show. He saves money, in other words. The participating radio stations get a strings-free radiodrama that they don't have to pay for. And finally, the writer/producer gets a salary, her show is syndicated and she has the financial capacity to move on to new projects.

This system works with half-hour, one-hour, and even five-minute radiodramas. (The latter are starting to come into prominence, usually as short comic sketches, but it remains to be seen whether the trend continues.)

Those of you who are less adventurous, yet wish to give this technique a whirl, might start with a brief program supported by a local sponsor.

Although barter syndication is usually something a writer/producer gets into only after having been in the radiodrama business for some time, it merits your attention because most of the new radiodrama programs coming down the audio pike these days appear to be functioning on a barter syndication basis, and it would profit anyone entering this business to be aware of this growing trend.

PART V

The Stage Play

Try to be original in your play and as clever as possible; but don't be afraid to show yourself foolosh; we must have freedom of thinking, and only he is an emancipated thinker who is not afraid to write foolish things. Don't round things out, don't polish—but be awkward and impudent. Brevity is the sister of talent. Remember, by the way, that declarations of love, the infidelity of husbands and wives; widows', orphans', and all other tears, have long since been written up.

—Anton Chekov

Chapter Eighteen

Writing for the Stage: Past, Present and Future

Playwriting is a field in which the writer's contribution is treated with the greatest amount of respect, wherein a talented writer can, in time, make a reasonable income from his words, and an arena that is currently providing ever more opportunities for beginning playwrights.

It's also a medium that requires muscles not usually exercised in other forms of scriptwriting. Its dimensions are different; the techniques used in one medium rarely apply to the other. Playwriting requires a new and revised mindset in order to be done properly . . . all of which will be examined in detail in the following pages.

First, though, while knowing something about where theater came from is less vital than it is for television writing or screenwriting, a brief excursion into the history of live drama is certainly worth our time.

THE HISTORY OF PLAYWRITING

The play, in all its varied forms, is probably the oldest vehicle for dramatic presentation in the history of civilization. Its origins stretch back to the dawn of mankind, when the hunters of nomadic tribes would return to the caves and, in mime and simple words, sketch out the events of the hunt, reenacting each kill for the rest of the tribe. Although primitive in form, all the elements of a play were there nonetheless: a stage, a flickering light, a story of life and death, an audience and a performer. Such have always been the bottom-line requirements of drama, and these basic elements endure.

As the centuries passed, drama became institutionalized. It was used as a means of conveying news from distant places, to mark the changing of seasons and phases of the moon; in time it merged with ritual and religion, and drama became the means whereby we could understand the activities of the gods.

Early Drama

Early drama probably reached its peak in Greece, where it was used to portray the passions of the gods and the foibles of human beings. Here, drama flourished under the capable hands of Aeschylus, Aristophanes and Sophocles, to name but a few. Even Aristotle took a few well-aimed shots at explaining precisely what drama was and how it should best be presented. He maintained that a play is a whole that has "a beginning, a middle and an end. A beginning is that which does not itself follow anything by causal necessity, but after which something naturally is or comes to be. An end, on the contrary, is that which itself naturally follows some other thing, but has nothing following it. A middle is that which follows something as some other thing follows it. A well-constructed plot, therefore, must neither begin nor end at haphazard."

What distinguished Greek drama was its use of such clearly defined plot devices as that distinct beginning, middle and end and the introduction of a chorus, which, being omnipresent and all-seeing, could pass on to the audience information that the characters themselves either did not yet know or did not know they knew. The chorus was also a handy device for some not-too-subtle moralizing at the play's conclusion.

With the fall of Greece, the flame of dramaturgy was given over to the Romans for safekeeping. Some historians speculate that the Roman empire embraced drama not out of aesthetic appreciation, but out of jealousy, anxious to prove that they were every bit as intellectual and artistically oriented as the Greeks. Plays were soon presented before the general public, and even in the hall of the various caesars. Interestingly enough, it was in the latter that political drama began playing an increasingly greater role. In many cases, productions were staged before Caesar's court that ridiculed the emperor's enemies and glorified his many conquests. From time to time, the players were even permitted to lightly—*very* lightly—satirize the emperor himself, although those who took the opportunity a little too much to heart soon found themselves considering the prospect of an immensely shortened lifespan.

In time, however, Rome also fell and largely took with it the form of the live play. Some forms of drama, including pantomime, were banned outright and their performers exiled by religious decree. Although it would continue to sprout up and enjoy a brief glory in the following centuries, the art of drama was still held in generally low esteem and was even dubbed by some "the Subversive Art." In China and Japan, though, theater enjoyed and continues—to varying degrees—a healthy life as part religious ritual, part cultural expression and part celebration.

The Age of Shakespeare

Unquestionably, drama in the English language underwent its greatest renewal in the late sixteenth and early seventeenth centuries. These were the years of William Shakespeare and Francis Bacon and England's famous Globe Theater. It can probably be argued that Shakespeare was the one person most responsible for legitimizing and popularizing the play with mass audiences. His dramas were tightly constructed and elegant in form; he worked with the blessings and financial support of the monarchy but maintained a constant affinity with the lower classes. He wrote of kings and battles, of star-crossed lovers, of madmen caught in the irresistible tide of Fate, of mistaken identities and enchanted midsummer evenings . . . all the things, in short, that the common people loved to hear about. His plays often ran three hours or longer because for many in his audience this was the only entertainment they would have for the month, and he wanted to give them their money's worth.

During the years that followed, dramaturgy, having established a firm foothold, continued to grow, frequently favored by the people and sanctioned by the government. In time, it gave us Goethe in Germany, Moliere in France and Cervantes in Spain. It is amusing to consider that even as drama became more institutionalized and more respectable with the passage of time, the performers were rarely given much social acceptance. An actor was generally held to be a person of low character and questionable morals; an actress was looked upon as possessing neither character nor morals, her station in life not very far removed from the street-corner prostitute.

All of which made for a fascinating paradox: It was quite fashionable to be seen at the theater, but to be seen on the town in the company of someone involved with the theater was likely to result in rumors and social repudiation.

This situation did not noticeably improve when drama made its leap across the Atlantic to the United States. More than one American mother during the eighteenth and nineteenth centuries joined in the age-old chant, "Better death or a convent for my daughter than a life in the theater!"

It's worth noting that playwrights were not *always* included in the community's roster of disreputable characters. Not all were deemed shady individuals. It was allowed that most were just alcoholics and the rest a bit odd, but basically harmless in the absence of sudden loud noises. While the majority of these characterizations had nothing to do with the reality of the theater, some of the more notable playwrights of the eighteenth and nineteenth centuries took them as license for extreme or colorful behavior, on the theory that if they're going to think you're crazy anyway, why not give them what they expect.

Happily, by the time the twentieth century arrived, those who chose to align themselves with the theater were no longer perceived as pariahs. In time, live theater became an integral and respected facet of American and European life. It inhabits the bright lights of Broadway and the ramshackle, fire-code-violating makeshift theater in small towns across the nation. At first largely dependent upon the works of Shakespeare and other European playwrights, American theater eventually found its own voice, and thus the world was given Eugene O'Neill, Thornton Wilder, T.S. Eliot, Lillian Hellman, Arthur Miller and Tennessee Williams, to name but a few.

THEATER TODAY

Today, virtually any community of moderate size has at least one repertory company, and other avenues of dramaturgy have arisen in the larger cities. This has, however, led to a certain theatrical stratification. Working from a playwright's perspective, American theater can be divided up into four categories, each of which arose out of the economic and cultural milieu surrounding and shaping the evolution of contemporary theater. The first is the small community theater or repertory company that produces low-budget plays that rarely require more than one or two sets, uses a small cast whose members tend to reappear in one production after another, stages its productions at irregular or limited intervals and frequently operates out of whatever structures are available at the moment—a church, a public auditorium or even a school auditorium. Such theaters tend to produce plays by established playwrights because they cannot sustain the economic risk of an untested play by an unknown or little-known playwright. In many cases, they operate on a shoestring budget, somehow surviving from one show to the next, limping along from Ibsen to Chekov to Shaw and, upon occasion, Ionesco. Although such operations offer little in the way of opportunity for new playwrights—except in the rare instance of a local competition for a new play—the contribution of these small theaters to American drama should never be understated because it is here that most performers cut their teeth on the acting profession.

One step up the ladder are the local theaters that are somewhat larger, work out of a single, stable house, offer a regular season and are capable of staging more elaborate productions. They frequently operate on a nonprofit basis, receiving some assistance from the city, the state or the federal government in the form of grants and subsidies. In most cases, these theaters offer the usual selection of conventional plays by established playwrights but are not entirely deaf to the entreaties of new voices, and from time to time—whenever their budgets permit the risk—they will stage a new play by an equally new, and often local, playwright.

Bridging these two venues, and yet always just outside and to the left of both of them, are the experimental theaters that make it a daily practice to fly in the face of convention. The seeds of contemporary and future drama are sown most prolifically here. These theaters operate out of a love that ignores the figures in the bank account and the threats of countless creditors. They are staffed by marginally paid executives and volunteers who in some cases literally live in the theater. They produce occasional classics (when the accounts drop too low), plays by exotic foreign playwrights, new works by local playwrights, experimental plays, socially relevant plays, staged readings, ethnic plays and whatever else they feel like producing. They are perplexing, impudent, outrageous, wholly accessible to anyone willing to invest time and effort, and enormously refreshing.

The final category consists of what some theatergoers rather snobbishly refer to as "legitimate theater," as if all the other theaters were somehow illegitimate. Included in this category are the large, well-established community theaters that stage a full season of elaborate productions, showcase theaters that feature national or regional touring companies exclusively and, of course, Broadway itself. The latter two tend to favor new works, but these plays are usually by established writers and have been proven at a variety of smaller theaters before making their big Broadway debut. In recent years, the emphasis on a Broadway premiere has been supplanted by tryouts on the West Coast, usually in Los Angeles and other major cities. But when and if the play succeeds on Broadway, it seems that suddenly all prior history outside New York is conveniently and permanently forgotten.

Naturally, there are some theaters and dramaturgic organizations that do not readily fall into these four categories. But in most instances, the aforementioned outlets comprise the bulk of contemporary American theater. In addition, there are a number of publishers who turn out countless plays, not a few by new playwrights, on a yearly basis.

So the opportunities are there, and the search for new material continues. One of the most frequently asked questions in theatrical circles is, "Where are all the new playwrights?"

Before that question can properly be addressed, however, it would behoove us to examine another question: Why write for the theater in the first place?

Chapter Nineteen

The Art and Craft of the Stage Play

THE BENEFITS OF PLAYWRITING

Besides being an exciting, powerful medium rich in history and tradition, there are several concrete factors that make playwriting an attractive prospect for scriptwriters. One of the foremost of these is the deep and abiding respect given by the cast and the director to the written word. It's a marvelous attitude that makes the very thought of rewriting a playwright's words beyond any serious consideration.

In television, film and radio scriptwriting, you as the writer are generally working for someone else, and that person therefore has the right to change anything in your script, a right that is frequently exercised, to varying degrees. But when you sit down in front of your computer and begin committing a play to paper, you are working for no one but yourself. As a consequence, the play must stand or fall entirely on its own merits. If it is worth producing, then those doing the producing are obligated to produce it as written. If there are many things in it that, in their estimation, don't work, then they can simply choose not to produce it. In some cases, the writer and director can choose to take a show on the road and work it out, modifying the parts that don't work. But in general, once committed, they produce it as written, though sometimes with some editing to keep the play within certain time constraints or to modify scenes that might prove too expensive or cumbersome to produce.

That's a very attractive arrangement. In the other media discussed in this book, the written words can be changed to accommodate the performer or the director, but in live theater, the cast members are charged with molding themselves to fit the work.

Concomitant with this benefit is the fact that playwrights are generally more respected by the lay public and the entertainment community than any other kind of scriptwriter. Because the other media involve so many perceived compromises and decisions by committee, a play is largely viewed as a vehicle for individual expression and is therefore considered—rightly or wrongly—to be a purer art form. Playwrights are more widely known by name than most writers for the other media. The most notable exceptions to this—Larry Gelbart and Paddy Chayefsky—had achieved a fair degree of success on the stage as well as on the screen or the television tube.

A third niceness is the eventual income to be derived from an even moderately successful play. This income comes from two primary sources: the published playbook and performance royalties. As for any published book, the author receives a certain percentage of the cover price, usually ranging from 5 to 10 percent. Most publishers also make it a point to turn over a percentage of the performance royalties—generally 25 percent or more of what they get—to the author. These payments can continue to come in for as long as the book remains in print, which effectively guarantees a steady income for many years to come.

It's also a nice feeling to look at your royalty check—broken down into performance and book fees—and, with a little division, figure out that your play, your words, have been given life in five, ten or fifteen theaters across the United States during the preceding six months.

A fourth advantage to playwriting is the greater freedom of expression available here than in most other media, particularly television, with only motion pictures coming close in terms of visual and verbal latitude. If the proper telling of your story requires nudity, profanity or references to peculiar sexual habits, you are free to include them in your script, as long as you remember that the racier the script, the less chance of production in the conservative American heartland.

Finally, you as the playwright have the marvelous opportunity to receive feedback from the audience and, in many instances, the cast itself. In the early stages of production, this enables you to tighten any sequences that don't work, and after it's been out in book form, to witness the reactions of an audience purely for your own satisfaction.

Before we can reap any of these benefits, however, it is incumbent upon us to first write the play. To do this requires an understanding of the art and the craft of playwriting and, along the way, an equal understanding of the ways in which plays differ from scripts for any of the other media we've discussed in this book.

THE ART OF THE STAGE PLAY

There are many creative steps to take before actually sitting down and writing a play. We will examine each of these considerations on an individual basis. But before we even begin to touch upon any of them, there is one criterion that must be addressed above all else: You must read and see as many different kinds of plays as possible. Such a prolonged study will tell you far more about playwriting than can possibly be conveyed in this or any other book.

Suggested Reading

What follows, then, is a list of plays that will probably be of greatest value to the scriptwriter who intends to discover what makes a really good play what it is. These are plays lurking in my own library that I make a point to reread at any given opportunity, learning a little more from each reading. Between them, you have a cross section of the various kinds of plays, from the comic to the tragic to the absurd and the classic.

- Samuel Beckett's *Waiting for Godot* (absurd)
- Christopher Fry's *The Lady's Not for Burning* (satire)
- Alan Ayckbourn's *The Norman Conquests* (comedy)
- Christopher Marlowe's *Dr. Faustus* (tragedy)
- Anton Chekov's *The Seagull* (tragedy)
- Peter Shaffer's *Equus* (psychological drama)
- Anthony Shaffer's *Sleuth* (thriller)
- Edward Albee's *A Delicate Balance* (social drama)
- Moliere's *The Misanthrope* (verse play)
- Jean Giraudoux's *The Enchanted* (light drama)
- Simon Gray's *Otherwise Engaged* (heavy drama)
- Harold Pinter's *Old Times* (heavy drama)
- Joe Orton's *Loot* (comedy)
- Tom Stoppard's *Arcadia* (drama with math)
- Steve Martin's *Picasso at the Lapin Agile* (comedy/satire)
- George Bernard Shaw's *Too True to Be Good* (satire)
- Arthur Miller's *Death of a Salesman* (drama/tragedy)
- Luigi Pirandello's *Six Characters in Search of an Author* and *The Man With the Flower in His Mouth* (surrealism)
- Israel Horowitz's *The Line* (farce)
- Jean Paul Sartre's *No Exit* (existentialism)
- Thornton Wilder's *Our Town* (light drama)
- William Shakespeare's *Two Gentlemen of Verona*, *A Midsummer Night's Dream*, *The Comedy of Errors*, *Julius Caesar*, *King Lear*, *Macbeth* and *Hamlet* (mixed bag)
- Bruce Friedman's *Steambath* (existentialism)

Although rather long, this list is by no means all-inclusive. There are many other plays that greatly deserve attention from any aspiring playwright. These include Jerome Lawrence's *Inherit the Wind*, Tennessee Williams's *The Glass Menagerie*, and the many plays of Ibsen, Cocteau and Ionesco. But the ones I've listed are those you might best profit from at first; each is an excellent example of the genre it represents. Thus, if you are of a surrealist or humorous bent, you would probably be well advised to go through the list picking out the plays in those categories and see how each playwright handled his theme.

Reading these plays will give you a healthy knowledge of the dramatic devices and techniques that have gone on to shape contemporary theater. Meanwhile, we'll take a look at the many elements that should be taken into consideration when beginning a stage play, particularly those that make writing plays different from scriptwriting for film and television.

Some Practical Considerations

Possibly the single most important thing to remember when writing a stage play is that you are dealing with an extremely restricted physical universe. In radio, using the stage provided by the imagination, you can go anywhere, anytime, as quickly as you like. A big-budget motion picture has less of a capacity for handling unusual or exotic settings, and television is even more restricted. But in live theater, you must make do with one stage, anywhere from one to four sets, a limited cast and a limited budget.

All this may seem rather obvious, but it's a point where many new playwrights run aground on the rocks of practicality. I've seen many playscripts that call for rapid-fire scene changes, with the action continuing throughout. In a film script, for instance, you could have a scene in which George, a frustrated and underpaid accountant, is at home with his wife, discussing his fear of asking for a raise. Finally resolved, he walks out the door. You then cut to the office, with George walking in through that door and confronting the boss. The action is continuous and accomplished by a simple cut. But in a stage version, such a direction would require stopping the action for anywhere from ten to fifteen minutes while the stage is reset for the office scene. As a consequence, you should try to accomplish as much in each scene as possible and only indicate scene changes when absolutely necessary. In film, we emphasized the importance of "opening up" the script visually, to include a variety of scenes in order to make the action interesting. In playwriting, you have to do just the opposite and "close down" the universe of your play to just the absolute essentials.

Also, remember that limiting the number of sets does not by any means limit the possibility for action. You can write a perfectly interesting and exciting play using a single set. In fact, some of the very best plays have been written just this way: *Sleuth*, *Waiting for Godot*, *The Line* and *Steambath* are all one-set plays. *The Norman Conquests* is unique in this respect because it consists of three individual plays, all taking place on the same weekend but each set in a different part of the same house. One play takes place in the dining room, another in the living room and the last in the garden. The remarkable thing about them is that each of the three plays can be seen individually, without having to see the other two (although I recommend seeing them all, just for the fun of it). Each play is vibrant, exciting and—most important—a whole unit unto itself.

To proceed along similar lines, here's another of those paradoxes-that-really-aren't-when-you-think-about-it. Although it is imperative to limit the physical universe of your play as much as you can, you as the playwright must be constantly aware of everything that is going on beyond that limited universe. Let's say that you've decided to write a play that is set entirely in the living room of a house. That's fine. But where is the house? Remember, you've got to be prepared to indicate dialects and mannerisms. So we now decide that it's in the southern part of the United States. Fine, but which part of the South? Each region is different. OK, so let it be set in Louisiana. When? The year is very important in terms of dress, social attitudes and so forth. At last, we decide that the play is set in the living room of a house in New Orleans in the year 1952.

Then, once so decided, you must remember your environment and maintain the atmosphere of that place and that time within the microcosm of your play. Always be mindful of the world that exists just outside the mock front door of your set because the world you have chosen to create onstage is a part of that exterior reality. Case in point: During a workshop, a student turned in a play set in Victorian England. Within seconds of looking it over, I noticed two critical errors. I illustrated the first by having some of the students read part of the play aloud without telling the listeners where or when it was set. They were then asked to guess at the time and location of the play. Nearly everyone guessed the present, somewhere in the United States, possibly the East Coast. He had not taken into consideration the different syntax, idiom and attitudes of the period. That was his first mistake. His second mistake was in having the protagonist and his fiancée behave in an openly affectionate manner—hugging, kissing, holding hands and so on—in the presence of casual friends. This is something that, to say the least, would have been severely frowned upon because of the repressive social customs of the Victorian era.

He had not, in short, done his homework. A play is built upon subtleties, and passing over them can be self-destructive. In contemporary England, for instance, one does not ride in an elevator, visit the rest room, go to a bar or call a friend. One rides a lift, visits the loo, drops by at a pub and rings someone up. They're small things, yes, but not paying attention to these details makes the entire work somehow ring false in the ears of the audience.

Another example: In a play of my own set in the first part of the twentieth century, in New York, I had a character call someone on the telephone by dialing the number. A critic who sat in on the performance took great pleasure in nailing me to the wall with the fact that direct dialing was not initiated in New York until five years after the date of the play's setting. Before then, the caller would tap on the telephone cradle, get the operator and ask for the correct exchange. Again, it was a trivial point, but as a reviewer myself, I can say that critics love to find such oversights and will nail you every time you ignore such details of daily life.

Since we're on the topic of time, it's worth noting that as a playwright you are actually dealing with four separate time zones, a situation that can lead to literary jet lag. These are *period time* (already discussed); *real time*, which is the time the audience actually spends sitting in their seats, also known as the running time; *story time*, the subjective time required to fully tell your story, which may be weeks, days, months or years; and finally, *dramatic time*, in which an hour is condensed into ten minutes, or a minute is expanded to fill an hour's real time. These distinctions are important to bear in mind when doing any jumping around in time. If the first half of your play is separated in story time from the second half by a period of ten years, you have to deal with the fact that the characters will not, in most cases, act and speak in the same way they did ten years before. They are not the same people. They have lived, changed, experienced joy and sadness and loss and success, have gone through the fire and returned again, perhaps not quite as naive—or even as cynical—as they once were. Your task as a playwright is to keep track of these changes, let them become evident through dialogue and, in time, explain them.

As a sidelight to this, having a person come back after ten years totally unchanged also tells the audience much about the kind of person he might be. The only people not changed by life are those who are unaware of it in the first place.

Certain concessions must also be made to real time. In a film, it is possible to show someone receiving an insult and then cut to a later scene where the person is venting rage at the remark, thereby eliminating the necessity of showing him working up the rage. This doesn't work on stage, however. It is difficult for an actor to go from happiness to anger in a split second (unless the person being portrayed is a psychotic, of course). From a pragmatic point of view, the actor is caught in the same real time as the audience and must, therefore, process through from one emotion to the other. Your task as a playwright is to provide the time and the dialogue for this transition.

So when you get ready to write your play, be sure you have a handle on its proposed length, the period you will be using as a background and the total time subjectively required to tell your story, always allowing sufficient time for the performers to process through from one emotion to another. I once had a student submit a play for critiquing in which all the emotional changes took place in another room of the house, while the actor was offstage, thereby—in the playwright's mind—taking care of the difficult task of processing through each new emotion. I handed it back and asked that the setting be changed to the other room. It was probably a lot more interesting in there.

There are other creative decisions that must be made before you can sit down and begin writing your play. You must decide whether your play will revolve around a certain theme or story or if it is a character study. Any play of quality will have all of these elements present, but in nearly every instance, one of the three is dominant.

Deciding clearly what your story is about will help keep you on track and help you avoid going off into territories not necessary to the dominant purpose of your play. Be careful, though, not to overemphasize any one of these elements. Having a certain theme is fine, provided it does not turn your play into a social or political tract. Story is essential, but it must not reduce your characters to limp two-dimensionality. Finally, you can write a wonderful character study, but if there isn't a story, something that will bring out that character and move the play along, then it will be rambling, purposeless and, generally, garden-variety dull.

Peter Shaffer's *Equus* is a good example of this principle. The story is based on a news clipping that Shaffer chanced upon, and the resulting play about a boy who blinds a stable full of horses was guided carefully by the facts in the case. This anchor in story is particularly useful when, as is the case with *Equus*, much of the story takes place in the shadowed realm of a disordered mind. It keeps the playwright from getting lost. Although the play slowly reveals why he did what he did, the entire thrust of the play remains what he did. The incidents of the story form the basis for everything that follows, and those events are the direct result of everything that went before.

You must also decide whom your play is really about. While there may be many different characters, all undergoing some changes in status or personality during the course of your play, there must always be one particular character who forms the focus of your play, and the play is really about this character. It needn't even be the character who has the most lines. But it is the most pivotal character.

For instance, while in the play *Romeo and Juliet* both of Shakespeare's star-crossed lovers share equal billing in the title and both have a roughly equal number of lines, the focus of the play is unquestionably Romeo. He is the active character, the one who makes the decisions; he chooses to fight Tybalt, kills him, decides to accept banishment, arranges for the couple's planned rendezvous and is the first of the two to die. Juliet is, by and large, the passive, reactive character. The same rule applies to Shakespeare's *Julius Caesar*. As matters develop, Caesar's time on the stage, both in corporeal and spiritual form, is very limited, and aside from his death (which affects him deeply), he does not change much for the remainder of the play. *Julius Caesar* is actually about Marc Anthony and the struggle between his conscience and his belief that what he is doing is right for Rome.

Beyond the other elements of drama that are universal and apply equally to film, television and the stage—a plot that moves the audience from point A to point B, rounded three-dimensional characters and a climax that resolves the story—the final element that serves to distinguish the stage play from any other form of scriptwriting concerns the question of action. The prospect of two people talking for half an hour on the movie screen or on a television show without any physical or visual action whatsoever is considered deadly. But conversation is the basic unit of drama. Drama deals in the currency of characterization; we do not attend a stage play to see a wide variety of special effects, death-defying stunts, bank robberies or car chases. We go to see a group of actors defining and exploring the human condition within the parameters set by the playwright.

While the action in a stage play may be physical—ranging from the Shakespearean swordplay of *Hamlet* to the life-and-death games of *Sleuth*—such activities are secondary to the dramatic underpinnings of the play as they relate to story, theme and character. In many cases, the action of a play can be purely emotional in nature. In other cases, what action is present is not always easily definable. Beckett's *Waiting for Godot*, with some interludes, is primarily about two people waiting in the desert for someone named Godot . . . who never arrives. In the end, they are a little more desperate, somewhat more desolate, but they decide that they will continue to wait. They are essentially unchanged. Yet the play remains a fascinating, convoluted work that takes the audience through a series of verbal and existential mazes, finally depositing them right back where everything started.

These are the creative considerations that you must labor over before beginning to write your play. The next step is to examine some of the purely practical difficulties confronting the playwright that can affect the act of dramatic creation.

THE CRAFT OF THE STAGE PLAY

If a newly written play is to go no farther than the desk drawer or that already stuffed-to-the-limit box at the bottom of the closet, there's really no need to concern oneself with the physical requirements of live theater. But if you want to see your work produced, it's a good idea to pay attention to some of the theatrical conventions. These can be divided into three parts: considerations of structure, performance and staging.

Structure

Somewhere along the line, someone discovered that audiences have an aversion to sitting in cramped theater seats for two or more hours straight, without the chance to stand up, stretch and walk around a bit. In addition, a play may call for several changes in story time that necessitate altering the stage, the set and the costumes, a time-consuming process during which the audience is left literally in the dark.

To avoid these situations, the playwright may either create a one-act play that is too brief to result in a general insurrection or a multiact play that has one or two intermissions built into its structure. Each of these presents different advantages and drawbacks.

The one-act play. The one-act play is theater in its sparest form. Because of its limited length—usually anywhere from twenty-five to as long as forty-five or even sixty minutes—it has little room for digression. Like a short story, it must contain only the most essential elements. It must tell its story, illustrate its characters, present its theme and get out quickly. In most instances, the action presented is continuous, with few—if any—changes in story time. It also puts a premium on telling the story with one set, a proviso that makes a lot of sense when you consider a set change can take as long as fifteen minutes. Looked at with a scriptwriter's sense of priorities, this is one fourth of the total time available to you as a playwright to tell your story, and in most instances, that quarter hour would be put to better use in moving your story forward than in moving furniture.

Because of its brevity, it's virtually impossible to cram a complex, many-layered plot into a one-act play. There simply isn't the time to develop it properly. As a result, most one-act plays present straightforward stories, emphasize the "slice of life" school of dramaturgy or are primarily character pieces. Israel Horowitz's *The Line* is a one-act play that illustrates the interactions of a group of very different people while they're waiting in a line for a very long time. It is a play produced frequently by colleges and universities because it's a brilliant example of what a writer can do with a brief play, a minimum of props and a collection of performers who are not averse to tossing, tumbling, falling, shouting and generally making just a whole lot of noise. Other one-act plays that say a lot with a little include William Saroyan's *Hello Out There* and Luigi Pirandello's *The Man With the Flower in His Mouth*.

The multiact play. The multiact play allows the writer to explore situations, themes and characters in far greater detail than is possible in a one-act play. Multiact plays consist of either two or three acts. Both run approximately the same length in real time, roughly two hours (or a little longer).

A two-act play has one intermission of fifteen or twenty minutes, meaning that the two acts run about fifty minutes apiece. A very intense drama may be divided into two acts to sustain the tension for as long as possible at one stretch.

A three-act play has two fifteen-minute intermissions, which thereby limits each act to thirty or thirty-five minutes. A clear majority of light dramas and nearly every comic play is of the three-act variety.

Whether using a two-act or three-act play format, it's a good idea to outline your play briefly before writing it. (An extensive treatment isn't usually necessary unless you're considering a very complex play.) You should be careful to keep the flow of the play moving, and layer in the small dramatic hooks or miniclimaxes evenly throughout the play, each act ending on a high note of tension or humor. Each small climax should build organically upon the one preceding it, cresting in the inevitable final climax of the play. It is necessary to layer evenly to avoid the problem of a finished play with a first and third act that are pure dynamite but a second act that could put an insomniac into a coma.

It's also a good idea to use these natural breaks in structure to facilitate changes in story time and/or setting. An intermission gives the stage crew sufficient time to change the set without breaking the attention of the audience. In addition, when the audience returns from the intermission, they—like the characters—have had a little interlude and can better accept the idea that time has elapsed in the story line.

A change in story time that does not require a change in setting can be done through the intercession of an intermission or may be integrated into the act by using a simple blackout to signal the transition in time. To further highlight the illusion of a transition, it's often a good idea to have different cast members onstage before the blackout and after the blackout or have the same characters doing different things in different parts of the room.

It's also helpful to remember that the program the audience receives prior to the curtain going up (or sideways) will explain how much time has transpired at each break, if any, and whether any transitions will be taking place during an act. This saves the playwright the heartbreak of having a character come out at the beginning of a new act, pat his chest, look around at the other characters and say, "Well, well . . . so it's been two weeks, has it? My, how time does fly."

Probably one of the greatest benefits of the three-act format is the immediate structuring that it gives to a play. Act one generally contains the information and dialogue needed to establish the characters, the situation, the goal(s) and the means that the characters intend to use in accomplishing their desires. Act two contains the complications and the actual steps taken toward reaching the set goals. Act three resolves the question—they either do or do not accomplish their task—and explores the consequences, if any.

For the writer just starting out in the theater, it's often wise to start with one-acts and work your way up from there. Not only will this give you the experience of working with characters in a limited dramatic format and learning the basic techniques of theater, but—as we'll see later in the chapter on marketing—you have a far better chance of getting a one-act play produced and responded to by a critical audience than you do a full-length play that has not benefited from production experience on your part.

Performance

One of the biggest adjustments in mindset a scriptwriter makes when writing a stage play concerns performers' bodies. You must train your ear to hear what your characters are saying and train your mind's eye to see what they are doing while they are speaking.

Example: In a film, you have two characters out on a boat talking. That's the only action in the scene. But it is not a static scene because the director can cut from one performer's face to the other, go from a tight shot to a long shot, pan the surrounding scenery and shoot over one or the other actor's shoulder. This turns an otherwise static conversation into an active part of the film.

You cannot, however, do this sort of thing on the stage. The actors are simply there, and it is up to you to find something for them to do while they're speaking. To have huge portions of your script comprised only of dialogue without the benefit of physical action is to effectively strap the performer to a chair or reduce her to aimlessly wandering around the room. Both of these options are boring.

Waiting for Godot emerges, once again, as an excellent example of dealing with performers caught in a potentially static situation. There are large blocks of the play that consist of the two main characters talking and simply waiting. But they are by no means inactive. They rush from one side of the stage to the other, scanning the horizon; they check and exchange hats; they check their shoes for pebbles; they hit one another. Thanks to Beckett's forethought, *Godot* is not only a fascinating, thought-provoking play, it is also a play that demands considerable physical effort on the part of the performers, a factor that further enhances the overall effect of the play.

One device that many new playwrights fall back on is called, informally, The Alcoholism Syndrome. It works like this: Every time a new character enters the room, character A fixes him a drink and continues to prepare new drinks whenever anyone runs out. This gives the performer a chance to walk around a bit and do something while the plot is being unveiled. At least, that's the rationale.

There are several problems with this, though. First of all, the sight of drinks passing from one person to another becomes rather tedious after a while. Second, this can be carried accidentally to ludicrous extremes. I once looked over a script and, after counting each drink the author forced the characters to consume, concluded that they all should have passed out in the middle of the second act. Finally, some consideration should be paid to the poor actors. Each time you see a character drink what passes for whiskey, he is actually drinking tepid, unsweetened tea that has probably been sitting there for hours. Imagine how you would feel after drinking stuff like that night after night, week after week.

Often, the problem is rooted in the fact that the playwright looks exclusively to dialogue to advance the plot, while viewing physical actions and mannerisms as something separate from the plot, something to be tossed in upon occasion to keep the audience from dozing off at a crucial moment. Nothing could be further from the truth. The body of the actor as it moves through space and the words the actor speaks are not separate. They both must work together to advance the plot by emphasizing one of the most essential elements of plotting—characterization. Remember, no one does anything without a reason, and that reason is directly related to who that person is, how she sees the world and her relationship to that world. All these character elements are demonstrated by what the characters say and how they behave. This requires that attention be paid to the little details and that you truly know your characters.

Take, for instance, a very poor character given a moment's shelter in the home of a very rich character. No doubt the poor character will be struck by the interior of the house and wander wide-eyed from painting to sculpture to the Ming vase on a pedestal over by the door. It's a simple character-based action, but then it snowballs. It leads to new lines, such as the poor character asking if the painting by the mantel is really an original Picasso. How does the rich character respond? Does he ignore the trappings of his lifestyle in deference to the evening paper's headlines? Or does he accompany the poor character from one objet d'art to another, explaining in detail how each piece was acquired and how much it cost? Either action tells the audience something about the character.

Good playwriting, like any other form of drama, is predicated upon the actions and reactions of characters, each with her own set of attitudes, goals and personal history. Whenever a writer ends up in some trouble while writing a script, it can usually be traced back to characterization. So if your character is fanatically neat, have her constantly tidying up the place and telling other characters where they may and may not rest their feet. It's certainly more sensible than having that character mention, "You know, I'm a fanatically neat person. Does that surprise you?" Because if it isn't already apparent, and it does come as a surprise to audience and other characters alike, then frankly, somebody has goofed—and it's nearly always the writer.

Another problem that aspiring playwrights must work around is the ever-present possibility of having one or more dead characters sitting about onstage. By this, I do not mean a character who has just been shot, stabbed, garrotted or run through by a sword. What I mean here is the character who for long periods of time has nothing whatsoever to say.

Example: Let's say you've written a scene for television or film in which three people are having a conversation. As it happens, though, two of the three do nearly all of the talking, while the third character looks on. While this is a less than optimal situation, it is not necessarily deadly. The director can do the scene largely in close-ups of the two people who are talking. In this way, although there is officially a dead character in the scene, the audience isn't as bothered as they might be because they don't see him.

But a dead character onstage is very definitely visible, even though she may wish she could vanish into the background or hide under a seat cushion.

Part of this problem is rooted in the fact that beginning scriptwriters often have a hard time handling scenes in which three or more characters are present simultaneously. Hence, a substantial number of plays by novice playwrights feature either just two characters or manage to handle more characters by having one leave shortly before the other enters so that even though the play may call for nine characters, there are never more than two or three onstage at the same time.

The solution to this comes in three parts. First, there's simple pragmatics: Make sure that every character onstage has at least one or two lines per page of script. Second, go back to the roots of your story, to characterization: What would people like those in your play be likely to say given such a situation?

Finally, study the dynamics of conversation. Ambrose Bierce once defined conversation as "A fair for the display of the minor mental commodities, each exhibitor being too intent upon the arrangement of his own wares to observe those of his neighbor." Although this may be just a little too cynical, it contains a grain of truth. During a conversation, we tend to listen to what the other person is saying until such time as the speaker hits upon a subject that we can relate to. Then, though we continue to listen to the speaker, we are already starting to frame our own verbal response. When an opening presents itself, we interject this observation, which then triggers off a similar response in someone else. It's also worth remembering that conversations are rarely cut and dried: In many instances, one person will talk over another, and a third person may start a comment, think better of it and withdraw. The best examples of such artfully handled conversations can be found in Ayckbourn's *The Norman Conquests*, Pinter's *Old Times* and other plays by these two brilliant writers.

Action and reaction. It's the basic law of physical science and the physics of drama. It's also the key element in improvisation, which emphasizes one performer actively listening to the other performer and then actively responding to something that the first person said. If you want to see the act of creative conversation taking place before your very eyes, find a local theater or club that features an improvisational troupe and attend a performance. You may even want to get together with a few friends, each picking a different role and occupation, and try it yourself. For that matter, a little experience onstage as an actor may prove beneficial to understanding the inner dynamics of acting.

Couldn't hurt.

Staging

The final greatest obstacle thrown into the path of beginning play-wrights—staging—is actually divisible into two different parts: the set, including furniture and props; and the movements of the performers in relation to the set. Since we've already touched on the subject of movement, we'll continue in that vein and examine the requirements of set design and direction last.

It's not uncommon for a writer, on attempting his first play, to suffer a kind of stage fright. Knowing that a character must be doing certain things, the question then becomes where shall she be when she is undertaking this certain action? Shall I have my character cross downstage or move upstage right? How does this affect the positioning of my other character? What is upstage and downstage?

Actually, it's not uncommon to get upstage, downstage, stage right and stage left confused. We as spectators, members of an audience, are used to looking at a stage from that perspective. But stage directions are written for use by the performer, not the audience. As a consequence, everything is reversed. Whenever doubt enters the scene, always imagine yourself standing on the stage and looking out at the audience, with the entire stage on a slight incline, tilting downward as you approach the audience, then rising as you retreat backward.

For slightly easier reference, the following diagram is offered.

Rear Curtain

Upstage Right	Upstage Center	Upstage Left
Right	Center	Left
Downstage Right	Downstage Center	Downstage Left

The Audience

Often, this confusion results from misinterpretation of the phrase, "She upstaged him." This can be taken to mean that by moving in front of him, she went upstage. But the correct interpretation of this is that, through her sudden move, she forced him into the upstage area and therefore into lesser visual prominence.

Once you've finally memorized the diagram, the best thing to do is put the information in the back of your mind and forget it, calling out the specific stage directions—known as *blocking*—only when absolutely necessary. As it turns out, overly specific blocking not only is not required, but frequently is unwanted.

When you're writing a script and you want a character to move downstage right, there should be a reason for it. The character doesn't just reach the indicated spot, hit his mark and stand there doing nothing—unless, of course, you've written a surreal, existentialist or otherwise metaphysical play in which, for instance, each part of the stage represents something. Your concern as a writer is to tell the characters what to do and where to go to accomplish that task. Therefore, a character crosses to the desk and picks up a gun or goes to the French windows and opens them or answers a knock at the front door. If you've established the approximate location of each part of the set—the desk, the windows, the door—then you don't need to dwell on specific blocking indications. In nearly every important instance, you need only describe what the character is doing. If you find yourself doing a lot of blocking, seriously ask yourself if it's all really necessary. Nine times out of ten, it won't be.

In addition, an author's attempts at blocking are frequently unwanted by the director. From a director's point of view, the author should only be concerned with the specific actions and movements that are necessary to advance the story. The subtle little physical relationships between the actors, the way they face one another, the way they stand or walk or gesture or talk . . . all these are within the exclusive province of the director—unless, again, it's in some way important to the story, at which point all bets are off.

The blocking can vary depending on the preferences of the director, the size and shape of the stage, the actors themselves and a variety of other factors. The director may choose to adapt the play to a theater-in-the-round format (in which case downstage right is whatever corner of the arena he *decides* is downstage right), may opt for the characters to play a scene nude or may have them hold a conversation while sitting in stiff-backed wooden chairs facing away from one another.

The task of the director is to interpret your script, contributing to it those physical touches that will—in the director's estimation—highlight certain aspects of the play and make the entire dramatic presentation a fluid, living thing. This is why a play can vary greatly in pacing and delivery when handled by two different directors who have conflicting attitudes about the play and about what makes good drama. There is, for instance, J.B. Priestley's play *An Inspector Calls* that has always been staged in a very conventional manner: a drawing room into which characters come and go. In 1995, a flurry of theatrical awards went to a new staging of the same play using vastly different and somewhat surrealistic staging techniques and production design, which opened the play up considerably. Same text, just a different idea on how to interpret that text.

The other area in which a playwright has some degree of input is in the creation of the set required by the play. The first part of any playscript is a description of the arena in which the action will take place: a bedroom, a den, a prison cell or what have you. In describing this location, it's sometimes possible to get carried away, writing in details that might look nice, but don't really have anything to do with the story or don't help to create the specific mood of the play. Chekov put the situation in the proper perspective when he remarked, "If there is a gun on the wall at the beginning of act one, then you'd best be sure that the gun has been fired by the end of act two."

Just as your story should be spare and to the point, so too should the props and sets that you require. In describing the set, you should write out what pieces of furniture and props are necessary, the period of time they should represent (1800s, early American settlers), the condition of said items and where they are in relation to one another, using the stage directions as required to get your point across. If lighting is an essential element to creating the correct mood, you should describe the kind you want: dim, moody, suggestive of night, bright and glaring, slightly gold or deeply blue. Beyond that, the set designer will come up with whatever else is easily available to help set the scene. The lighting director will create a subtle effect to also highlight the play.

One very practical reason for the sparcity of directions has to do with budgets. You can call for any number of extensive props, but if the theater hasn't the money to purchase them, the shop to make them or the clout to borrow them, some of these props will have to be dispensed with, and it's better to state up front which are necessary by virtue of their relation to the story than have someone make a mistake and not order an essential article. Or, more likely, decide not to produce the play because it's simply too expensive. The same applies to lighting if the theater has only a fixed lighting system or costumes if they have a small wardrobe budget and the story requires period costumes that are too expensive to acquire.

Not infrequently, some compromises may be called for. A toilet plunger painted black with two black cans and a string may have to suffice for a telephone circa 1918. The entire play might even be staged using large boxes covered with black cloth, bunched together in groups and in forms that *suggest* a table or a bed or a set of chairs. This is why, as a rule, you should try whenever possible not to make a given prop or effect the linch-pin of your play because if it's problematic, that may set it beyond the reach of those theaters that may want to produce your play but don't have the facilities or the budget to do so.

Since the portion of your script that contains staging information also includes a thumbnail description of your characters, be sure to make your descriptions as brief, to the point and generalized as possible. It's not neces-sary to spell out the character's hair color, the way his eyes flash in the sunlight, the way her nose perks up just a little at the end. The best person for the role—in the director's estimate—may have hair of some color other than what you have visualized or may vary in some other way. The best actor for the role may look nothing like what you imagined when you wrote the script but *performs* best and most believably. So the character description serves simply to give the director a rough idea of what the character is like. The rest of the character's personality will emerge through dialogue and action.

Bearing in mind all these points about movement, scene description and staging, let's take a look at an excellent example of a spare opening, one that contains all the information that is important to the director but does not get lost in a maze of complex stage directions. The following excerpt comes from the first page of *Table Manners* by Alan Ayckbourn, a part of the *The Norman Conquests* trilogy.

> The dining room. Saturday 6 P.M. A fine evening—sun streams through the large windows of the room. A solid table and four chairs. A sideboard. A window seat and a couple of additional upright chairs. The room is large and high-ceilinged and like the rest of this Victorian vicarage-type building, badly needs redecorating. ANNIE, in baggy sweater, jeans and raffia slippers enters with a flower vase of water. She thumps this down in the middle of the table, picks up the roses which lie beside it and drops them into the vase. She gives the whole lot a final shake and that, as far as she's concerned, concludes her flower arrangement. She is moving to the sideboard, about to lay the table when SARAH enters. She wears a light sum-mer coat and dress. She is breathless.

And that's the extent of it. It is, if anything, almost a simple inventory. It specifies what furniture is needed, what props (the vase and flowers), the type of clothing worn by the characters, the specific room, day and time. This gives the director the freedom to place the actors and the furniture anywhere he thinks would work best for that particular theater. Further, in this play, it doesn't matter so much what the characters look like as how they relate to one another, and that is something that develops slowly, within the play itself.

Should there be any specific requirements in terms of age, build and appearance that the characters should conform to, it is usually a good idea to write them together on a separate page and include them with the body of your script, a process we'll examine shortly.

The Playscript

You've decided upon your story, you know the characters as intimately as possible, you've roughly outlined your play in terms of what should happen during each act and you are now ready to sit behind the typewriter and begin writing and assembling your script. The only remaining questions are: What does a script look like; What should be included in it; and In what order? We'll take them one at a time, moving from the first page of your playscript to the last.

• The first and most obvious requirement is your title page. This is typed in the same way as the title page for a motion picture script. The only difference is that, instead of typing "An Original Screenplay by," you type "A One-Act Play by" or "A Play in Two Acts by" or "A Play in Three Acts by," with your name following directly below.

• The very next page is the play breakdown, which appears in this order: At 65 picas, four lines from the top of the page, is the page number, Roman numeral i. Four lines farther down the page, at eight lines, the title of the play is typed in all capital letters, underlined and centered on the page.

• Four lines below the title, at 20 picas, typed in all capital letters are the words ACT ONE. A series of ellipses move across the page to 45 picas, where you describe the day and date of act one. This is done for each subsequent act, triple-spacing between each line.

• If the acts are broken up by time jumps in story time, this is also indicated. If act one is divided into two scenes, then the first line of the page breakdown reads ACT ONE: Scene One, followed by the series of ellipses. ACT ONE: Scene Two appears two lines beneath the first line.

In some cases, retyping ACT ONE may be unnecessary, in which case the words Scene Two are typed beneath the words Scene One.

• At the bottom of the page, an inch from the end of the page, the approximate running time of the play is typed between 20 and 70 picas. When completed, your play breakdown should look something like the one below.

The next page—Roman numeral *ii*—contains the information concerning your characters.

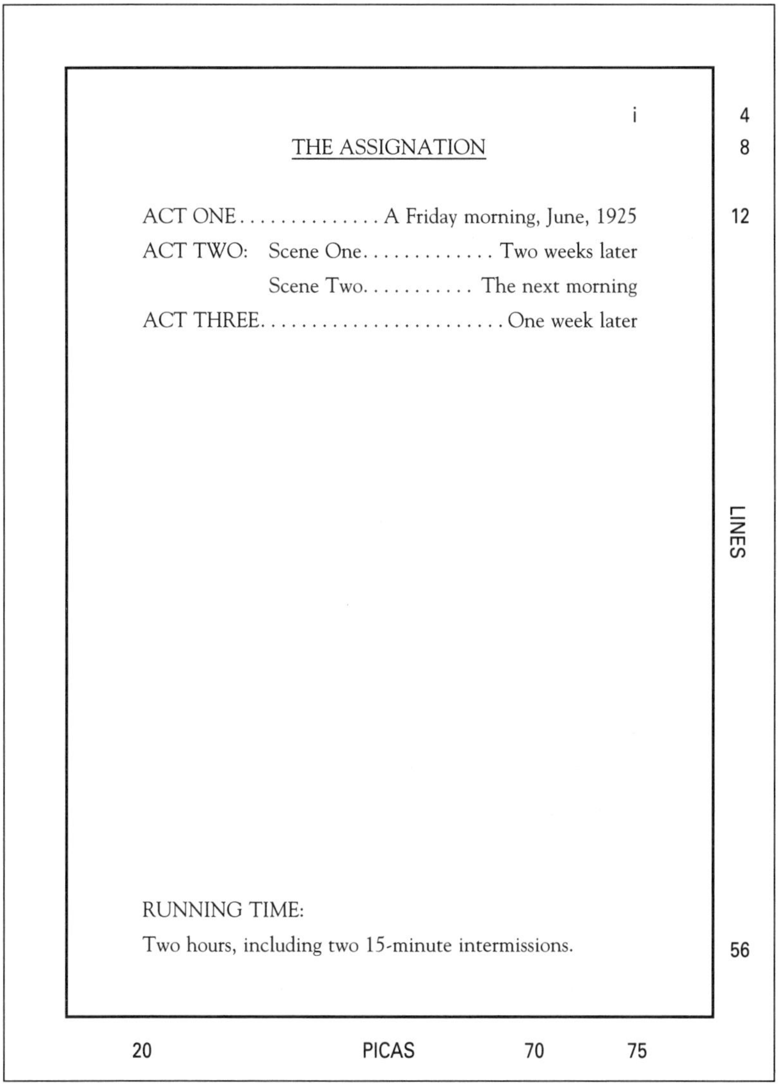

```
                                                         i        4

                        THE ASSIGNATION                           8


        ACT ONE.............. A Friday morning, June, 1925        12
        ACT TWO:   Scene One............. Two weeks later
                   Scene Two.......... The next morning
        ACT THREE...................... One week later




                                                              LINES




        RUNNING TIME:
        Two hours, including two 15-minute intermissions.        56


              20              PICAS            70      75
```

FIG. 12

• The words *Cast of Characters* appear centered on the page, eight lines from the top. Four lines farther down, you type the NAMES of each character in all capital letters, with a brief description of that character following. This information should be more or less centered on the page, using the longest line as a marker. The descriptions can be quite simple, as in this case:

> GEORGE, a heavy-set man in his thirties.
> JANE, his sister.
> FRANK, his best friend.

Or they can be quite elaborate, spelling out the characters and their backgrounds to a maximum of 65 to 70 picas across and several lines or more in length.

• The Setting, page *iii*, is typed in uppercase and lowercase letters, underlined in the center of the page, eight lines from the top. The body of your description begins four lines farther down, between 15 and 71 picas, with the first line indented five spaces.

• The actual playscript itself begins next, on Arabic numeral *1*. The title of the play is again typed in all caps eight lines from the top, centered. The words Act One appear in upper- and lowercase letters, centered and underlined, two spaces beneath the title.

• Four spaces beneath that, at fourteen lines, is the scene description. Even though you have described the setting on a separate page, you must include a brief, referential description at the beginning of each new act and scene, integrating the action with the scene description and including points of reference in every subsequent scene and act. Double-space between each line.

• The dialogue begins two lines below the last line of the scene description and is broken down as follows: The NAME of the character speaking is typed in all capital letters at 10 picas, followed by a colon, two spaces and then the actual line of dialogue. Each subsequent line of dialogue spoken by that person is indented five spaces, starting at 15 picas, always ending at roughly 75 picas (again this includes the picas to the left of the margin; if you're using the denoted 10 space margin, then it's 65 picas thereafter). The reason for this is simple: It causes the characters' names to stand out, making it easier for performers to find and mark their lines.

• Any emotive descriptions, expressions or directions for movement or action are bracketed by parentheses and typed in uppercase and lowercase letters. If the direction indicates an action to be taken while speaking, it is written within the lines of dialogue. An emotive direction, when used to immediately signal a mood change, is placed between the character's name and the first word of dialogue. It is written without the first letter being capitalized. If the direction appears between or outside of spoken lines, it is typed between 15 and 75 picas, parenthesized, and typed in upper- and lowercase letters. Whenever another character's name is used in a direction, the name should always be capitalized. If a character enters a room, the name and the word ENTERS is capitalized. Triple-space between dialogue and descriptions.

• If a line is carried over to another page, it is not necessary to write a continuation note on the last line appearing on the prior page, or to retype the character's name at the start of the next page. You simply type the remaining lines within the 15 and 75 picas. Each act ends with *Curtain Falls* centered at the page bottom.

As usual, whenever typographical directions are written out like this, they tend to sound more confusing than they really are. To illustrate this, we'll look at a few pages that use these typographical specifications.

Since we have pretty well covered what the first page of act one looks like, we'll take it from the first page of act two of a play which, for our purposes, we shall call *The Assignation*.

The Assignation was written with the intention of stressing the dialogue and interchanges, rather than complex action or elaborate stage directions. The action that *does* take place—running to the window, slamming the window, popping in and out of the room—is plot specific, meaning that it is intended either to advance the story (the glance out the window that tips Fenwood off) or reveal the nature of our characters (Fenwood's nervousness in the aforesaid popping in and out). The action as described does not preclude input from the director. For instance, in the section of dialogue where Jack warns Fenwood that he has three seconds to start making sense, a director can direct that line to be given from across the room, while Jack points a threatening finger. If another director wanted to make the scene a little more physical, he could have Jack grab Fenwood by his lapels and deliver the line nose-to-nose. This leaves the writer in control of the story and gives the director latitude in interpreting the mood and pace of the play.

The syntax, sentence structure, phrases and implied mannerisms are all written with the intent of sounding uniquely British, an attempt that—to refer back to the need for doing one's homework—necessitates a familiarity with English diction, currency, slang and so forth. Something of the plot structure is also intimated here. One may assume that act one set up the circumstances of the date, allowed Fenwood to mention his encounter with "the girl on the ship" and established Jack as the dominant social personality. Act two will, from all appearances, be the culmination of that scheme. The date will take place, and given this meeting's lackluster beginnings, it's doubtful that it will be pleasant. Act three, then, will proba-

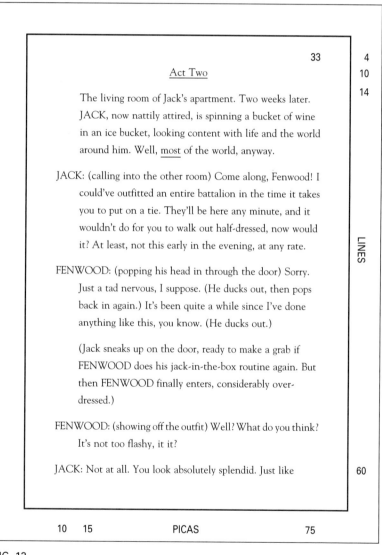

33   4

Act Two

10
14

    The living room of Jack's apartment. Two weeks later.
    JACK, now nattily attired, is spinning a bucket of wine
    in an ice bucket, looking content with life and the world
    around him. Well, <u>most</u> of the world, anyway.

JACK: (calling into the other room) Come along, Fenwood! I
    could've outfitted an entire battalion in the time it takes
    you to put on a tie. They'll be here any minute, and it
    wouldn't do for you to walk out half-dressed, now would
    it? At least, not this early in the evening, at any rate.

FENWOOD: (popping his head in through the door) Sorry.
    Just a tad nervous, I suppose. (He ducks out, then pops
    back in again.) It's been quite a while since I've done
    anything like this, you know. (He ducks out.)

    (Jack sneaks up on the door, ready to make a grab if
    FENWOOD does his jack-in-the-box routine again. But
    then FENWOOD finally enters, considerably over-
    dressed.)

FENWOOD: (showing off the outfit) Well? What do you think?
    It's not too flashy, it it?

JACK: Not at all. You look absolutely splendid. Just like

LINES

60

10   15   PICAS   75

FIG. 13

bly be designed to absolutely foul up any chance of the characters retaining their dignity and complicate matters even further before finally resolving all the loose strings in the relationships that may or may not bloom among the players.

Using the format demonstrated here, you should write approximately 90 pages in the case of a three-act play (30 pages per act), 100 to 105 pages

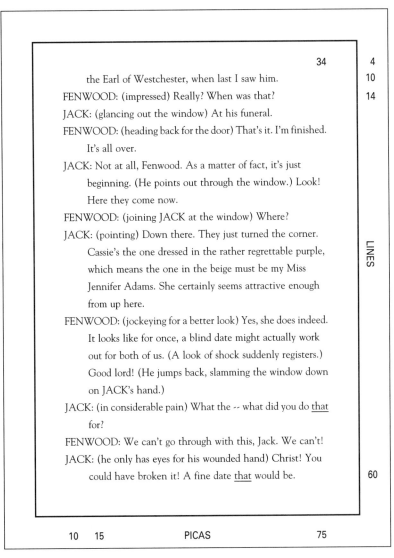

FIG. 14

for a two-act play (50 to 52 pages per act) or 20 to 50 pages in the case of a one-act play.

When you have finished writing your play, you should either read it aloud to yourself or find someone willing to read through it with you. Done properly, your play should time out to about one minute per page when performed aloud. During this process you should also endeavor to

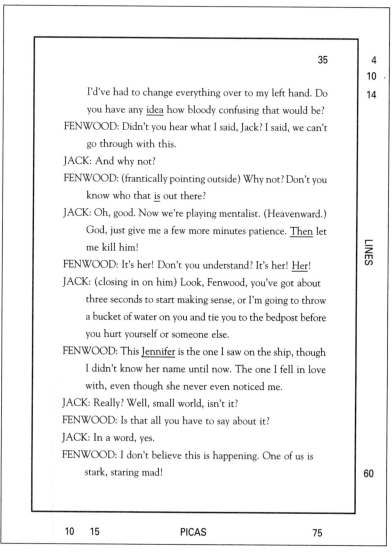

I'd've had to change everything over to my left hand. Do you have any <u>idea</u> how bloody confusing that would be?

FENWOOD: Didn't you hear what I said, Jack? I said, we can't go through with this.

JACK: And why not?

FENWOOD: (frantically pointing outside) Why not? Don't you know who that <u>is</u> out there?

JACK: Oh, good. Now we're playing mentalist. (Heavenward.) God, just give me a few more minutes patience. <u>Then</u> let me kill him!

FENWOOD: It's her! Don't you understand? It's her! <u>Her</u>!

JACK: (closing in on him) Look, Fenwood, you've got about three seconds to start making sense, or I'm going to throw a bucket of water on you and tie you to the bedpost before you hurt yourself or someone else.

FENWOOD: This <u>Jennifer</u> is the one I saw on the ship, though I didn't know her name until now. The one I fell in love with, even though she never even noticed me.

JACK: Really? Well, small world, isn't it?

FENWOOD: Is that all you have to say about it?

JACK: In a word, yes.

FENWOOD: I don't believe this is happening. One of us is stark, staring mad!

FIG. 15

look for lines that are difficult to say or are redundant within any given block of dialogue. Your play should be as trim and lean as possible.

At this point, if your script seems pretty solid, your next step is to make up some copies of the manuscript, with a good stiff cover sheet and backing sheet to make handling easier and to protect the manuscript during shipping. The cover sheet should be simple and to the point: the title and your

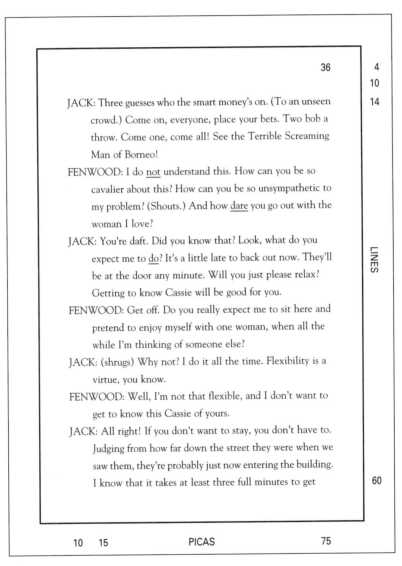

FIG. 16

name. You can use either regular typewriter type for this or use any of the commercial desktop publishing programs to create a cover page with a large and friendly typeface. Light gray or brown are usually good paper colors, and 25-pound bond is a good choice. More specific personal information (your phone number, agent, fax number) would more appropriately be appended to the title page that appears directly after the cover sheet. The

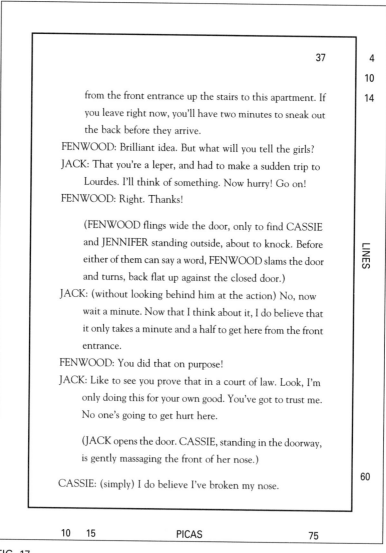

37   4

10

from the front entrance up the stairs to this apartment. If   14
you leave right now, you'll have two minutes to sneak out
the back before they arrive.

FENWOOD: Brilliant idea. But what will you tell the girls?

JACK: That you're a leper, and had to make a sudden trip to
Lourdes. I'll think of something. Now hurry! Go on!

FENWOOD: Right. Thanks!

(FENWOOD flings wide the door, only to find CASSIE
and JENNIFER standing outside, about to knock. Before
either of them can say a word, FENWOOD slams the door
and turns, back flat up against the closed door.)

JACK: (without looking behind him at the action) No, now
wait a minute. Now that I think about it, I do believe that
it only takes a minute and a half to get here from the front
entrance.

FENWOOD: You did that on purpose!

JACK: Like to see you prove that in a court of law. Look, I'm
only doing this for your own good. You've got to trust me.
No one's going to get hurt here.

(JACK opens the door. CASSIE, standing in the doorway,
is gently massaging the front of her nose.)

60

CASSIE: (simply) I do believe I've broken my nose.

LINES

10   15   PICAS   75

FIG. 17

entire package should also be copied on three-hole paper, bound with one-inch brass paper fasteners.

Now, at last, you have your completed playscript in hand and are ready for production. The question, though, is what does one do with a play once it's finished?

Chapter 20

Marketing the Stage Play

The One-Act Play

The steps taken in marketing your play depend entirely upon the type of play you've written: full-length or one-act. In most respects, the marketing approach for a one-act play is probably the most flexible, both in terms of production and publication. To start with, contact the dramatic arts departments of your local colleges and universities. Most college-level schools—including junior colleges—that have such departments invariably have directing classes as part of their theater arts curriculum. As it happens, the only way to learn how to direct is by following the same technique used when learning how to write: You do it. Because it would simply cost too much and take up too much time to assign each directing student a different full-length play, most colleges compensate by assigning directors the task of directing three or more one-act plays during a given semester. This frequently results in a new one-act play being produced on the college campus at least once or possibly twice a week during the academic year. Many of these one-act plays are selected from anthologies by established authors, mainly because they're easier to find.

But a growing number of drama programs encourage their students to seek out new works. Presenting an original play carries with it several benefits. It allows the student director to work with the author, which is unlikely or impossible in the case of a popular playwright. It forces the director to draw on her own ideas instead of simply copying past productions of a given play, a fact not lost on the instructors. Similarly, the instructor can't grade the play based on prejudices formed on the ways it has been interpreted in the past. A production of an original play from a local writer helps reinforce the college's interest in working with the community, and the publicity that results is never a bad thing. And finally, should the play go on to be successful, meaning that it continues to get produced and eventually published, the published book—as a courtesy—

usually lists where the play was first produced, which is, again, nice publicity for the college. The overall benefits of such a series of productions is so great, in fact, that many college drama departments require their directing students to exert every possible effort to make one of their three selected plays an original one-act by a new author.

What are the benefits of such a program to a playwright? First of all, it gets the play produced, which is itself something of an accomplishment. Ideally, it should permit the author to work with the director and in the process actually see how a play takes shape after it leaves the writer's hands. (Some colleges permit only limited interaction between writer and director, fearing that the director might rely too much on the writer's vision. I think this is foolish, but such is life.) It lets the author witness the reaction of an impartial audience to the content and style of the play. Since most audience members will probably be drama students themselves, you can count on getting a reasonably informed, critical audience. If something in the play doesn't work, you'll know it quickly. This can give you an excellent picture of the play's strengths and weaknesses, which can be addressed in any subsequent rewrites.

Along with the benefits, however, there are also some potential drawbacks. For one thing, there's rarely any money involved. The theory is that the production is its own reward, which, if you stop to think about it for a minute, is really a pretty fair assessment.

You should also be prepared, should you go this route, to separate the play from the performers and the director. In most instances, these students are still learning their craft, and it could well be that their combined efforts may not be equal to the quality of the play. (In remembering this, also bear in mind that it can work the other way around.) So if something doesn't work in the performance, ask yourself if the problem is the written word or the delivery, and revise accordingly. For this approach, the following steps are in order: First, find out which colleges in your area have one-act directing programs. You then have the option of either calling the department chairperson directly or putting your request into a query letter. (My own experience has been that a brief, straightforward telephone inquiry is preferred.) Explain to the chairperson that you are a playwright, you have recently completed a one-act play that doesn't require extensive set or production-oriented budgets and, if the department is open to original one-acts, you would like to submit the play to the director's program with the clear understanding that no royalties will be required. This last stipulation, by the way, also ensures that the copyright stays in your name. Be certain to find out what the parameters are when it comes to your desire to work with the director.

Should the door for a submission open up, package your script and send it off to the department head. Enclose a brief letter that restates the main points of your conversation and offers a promise of support and assistance to the director should any be desired and permitted.

When your play arrives, an announcement will be made to the directing students that an original play is available to anyone who wants to do it. It's possible that after going from one director to another, no one will want to direct it. But this should not be taken as a statement about the quality of the play. It could be that it just didn't excite that particular group of aspiring directors. If this is the case, and you really believe in the play, let it remain in the department's hands until the following semester, when a new group comes in. The odds are good that if the play has any quality whatsoever, someone will want to direct it.

Since no money is being paid and there is often no direct connection between the theater arts departments of different colleges, there is nothing wrong with submitting the play to a number of different departments. This only increases your chance of seeing your play produced. When one of the departments decides to produce the play, you can then either yank the script from the others or allow them to produce it as well. Whether you do or do not tell them that some other college is going to, or already has, produced the play is something only you can decide. The odds are that if you don't tell them, they probably won't find out. In most cases, it won't make any real difference.

To succeed as a writer, you must begin to snowball your credits and watch them grow, one into another. How big the original snowball might be almost doesn't matter and the venue doesn't matter. What does matter is that it is done. And this particular venue can be very productive.

If there aren't any colleges in your area with such a program, or if you simply prefer a production in a less academic environment, your attention should shift to community theaters.

A community theater can produce a one-act play in several ways. There is, for instance, what's known as a "showcase" production. It runs for one to three nights—usually over a weekend—and consists of several one-act plays by local playwrights, which may be bannered to the local public as "An Evening of One-Acts" or suchlike. The plays are often selected on the basis of how they differ in style, approach, theme and content. These productions are often limited to the smaller or medium-size community theaters and are built up into theatrical events. Both the theater and the playwrights benefit from such a production. An event of this type generates publicity, which in turn brings in audiences, which theaters need in order to survive. In addition, the theater can usually be confident that the brief run will enjoy at least a modest success. Those who aren't attracted by the event status will probably come because they happen to know the playwright or someone in the cast.

If the theme or approach of your play happens to coincide with a full-length play that the theater is planning to produce, it's altogether possible that your play could be presented as a "warm-up" for the main feature. This possibility is further increased if the full-length play is relatively brief.

Finally, if you live in a town with an experimental theater, or a large town that has a substantial, theatergoing community, other possibilities open up. Some local theaters have an after-theater-theater program, presenting a one-act play in the late evening hours as a follow-up to a full-length play. In many cases, plays chosen for this program are experimental or just a little too bawdy for the general public, so they are presented under a separate billing. In areas where the theatergoing community is large, some theaters offer a lunchtime theater program, presenting one-acts or, in some instances, improvisational performances at little or no cost.

Depending on the fiscal condition of the theater and its policy toward new playwrights, there may or may not be any payment. Some theaters set aside a certain percentage of the receipts from the performance to be divided between the playwrights and, on occasion, the performers. Note: The majority of small community theaters pay very little if anything to their performers. In some cases, the amount paid may amount to nothing more than carfare. Usually, the actors hold daytime jobs but want to act, if only to gain the experience they need to move on to better-paying acting jobs. Always be as nice to starving actors as your artistic integrity and patience will permit; they live just as close to the edge as writers do. Sometimes closer.

As with a college production, the greatest benefit to the writer is the production itself. But there are other advantages as well. Your play will be seen by the general public, rather than by a specialized group of students. Their reactions may be just a little more representative of other potential audiences as a result. It also gives you as a playwright more exposure to your community, establishing you in their minds as a talent to be reckoned with. Finally, there is every chance in the world that a production at a local theater will be reviewed by a community newspaper, and even though there are times when every playwright is convinced that the reviewer must have attended some other play than the one he wrote, reviews are desperately important. They are critical evaluations of your work by someone who sees a lot of theater and who is, presumably, educated in the art and craft of live drama. If the review is negative, it would be expedient to closely examine the portions of the play the reviewer took exception to. If you feel the reviewer had a point, you may want to look at that section again. If you disagree strongly, then don't change a word. If the review is complimentary, use it as a means of locating and reinforcing the strongest points of your play. In addition, a good review will be of great help in getting your play produced elsewhere or in getting it published.

Publication and production outside your community are the last outlets for the one-act play. Neither should be attempted unless your play has first been produced by someone—a college or community theater—or unless you're absolutely convinced about the quality of your play. In either event, your first step should be to consult the latest edition of *Writer's Market*, which contains a comprehensive listing of those interested in publishing or producing original one-act plays.

Some notes on both of these avenues:

It's very difficult, if not almost impossible, to get a one-act play published in book form, particularly if it hasn't been produced at least once. As a rule, most outlets for published plays are magazines that deal with the subject of drama. Some magazines feature one-act plays infrequently, and others regularly publish a new one-act as part of their format. There are also quarterly publications and other magazines that publish nothing but one-act plays. Some of these copyright the play in their own names, others copyright the work in the name of the author; most pay something to the author, and some make special provisions for royalties. The key benefit to having your play published is exposure. The only people who subscribe to such publications are those who are actively interested in drama and have at least a passing interest in reading and producing new plays.

A considerable number of theatrical organizations throughout the United States produce one-act plays. Some will take scripts that have not been produced at all in any workshop or showcase performances, while others prefer a script that has gone through these steps. Small theaters, community theaters, theater clubs and repertory companies that accept new material are listed in *Writer's Market* along with their current needs and preferences. Some of these theaters pay no royalties at all; others pay anywhere from 5 to 25 percent royalties or offer a single, specific sum for each performance, a dollar amount ranging from $10 to $100 or more each time the play is staged. When going through the current listings, it's important to find a target theater whose orientation is similar to the approach of your play. It would be fruitless, for instance, to send a surreal existentialist play to a dinner theater or to send a lighthearted comedy to an experimental theater that specializes in socially relevant productions.

When submitting a play to an outside producer, it's always a good idea to include in your query letter anything that uniquely qualifies you to write the play, and, of course, enclose a self-addressed, stamped envelope if you ever expect to see your script again. The waiting period following submission can be anywhere from two weeks to six months or more, depending on the size of the theater, the backlog of scripts and the possibility that the theater only operates during certain seasons.

The Full-Length Play

Contests and outside productions can sometimes be a big part of selling your full-length playscript, and the steps outlined for the one-act play apply equally to these.

One variance comes in the form of different publication possibilities. Because a full-length play is simply too long for a magazine to handle, it must be published in book form. The publishers who are open to new works fall under two categories.

First, there are the playbook publishers who specialize in children's plays exclusively. There are also those who handle only plays for junior and high school productions, religious-themed productions and so on. These markets are probably the easiest to crack and the ones most open to unproduced scripts. Writers interested in the juvenile market should be sure to include all the elements of plot, story and characterization because children can be the toughest critics of all. Most publishers in this area offer a royalty contract of 5 to 10 percent of the book rights and 15 to 25 percent of performance rights, and they generally copyright the play in the author's name. Under common-law copyright laws, the play remains in the author's name indefinitely. Once produced, though, you should take the steps to formally copyright the work, securing the forms from the U.S. copyright office. Some theaters insist on the play being formally copyrighted prior to production.

Publishers of contemporary adult plays for the community and legitimate theater market are often more selective of the plays they publish. There are also fewer of these around, which makes the market even more restrictive. Because of the risks of publishing an untested play in book form, a terrific financial undertaking, most publishers prefer to see a play that has been produced to good reviews at least once.

If the play has been produced earlier and seems like a good investment, a majority of established publishers will agree to a royalty contract such as that outlined above. If it hasn't, many of these publishers may only agree to publish the play provided they pay for it through an outright purchase. This minimizes their risk by cutting down on any money they have to pay out after the publication. All the royalties, both for performance and publication, belong to them. In time, even a barely adequate play, under this arrangement, will at least recoup the initial expenditures. But . . . if the play goes on to be a considerable success, you don't get a penny of the resultant money. And that is why it's so essential to have your play produced at least once at any of the theaters available through the published listings or at a local community theater.

Therefore, you should contact each of your community theaters by telephone and find out which of them are open to new playwrights with original scripts. Your best bet is with the middle-size theater group or an experimental theater. Many such theaters provide different kinds of outlets for original scripts. If the play is good enough and the budget permits, they can go ahead with a full-fledged production. As a rule, it will probably not be quite as elaborate as the staging of a well-known play. The budget for props and other equipment may be less, and the play may run for only three weeks instead of the usual five or six, but the important thing is the production itself. Again, depending on the theater's finances, there may or may not be any payment to the author.

There are other outlets besides a complete, extended production. A limited showcase production may be staged for one weekend, using the stage setting for another ongoing play. More and more theaters now are conducting "play discovery projects," in which new plays are solicited and staged in a readers' theater format. This eliminates props, costumes and blocking and instead relies on the verbal interpretive skills of the actors.

It is preferable, overall, to exert every possible effort to secure a local production before taking your play "on the road," so to speak. This gives you the opportunity to work with the cast, see the play come together and work out all the bugs before sending it to an outside theater. Remember, being a locally based playwright carries with it certain inherent advantages. Every theater likes to look at itself as a valid part of the community, responsive to the theatrical talents within that community. So even though two equally acceptable scripts may arrive in the hands of the theater's artistic manager or producing director or what-have-you, one from a local resident and one from another city or state, the local resident will always have the inside track. Mind you, though, that's when all things are equal. The ultimate question comes down to which is the better script, if either.

Finally, many community theaters hold contests in which area playwrights are invited to contribute a full-length play written around a certain theme—a play based on the history of the community or that utilizes a dramatic device not often seen in contemporary playwriting, such as the classic melodrama. If you feel comfortable with the requirements, then you might be well-advised to enter the competition. If not, keep the theater in mind for future submissions of original plays because the contest is an indication of the theater's openness to new material.

All of this pretty much sums up the state of the contemporary marketplace for original works by new playwrights. The question now, however, is what can be expected in coming years.

FORTHCOMING ATTRACTIONS IN THE THEATER

For the early part of the history of American theater, most—if not all— of the plays produced were by European or English playwrights. Then, gradually, American playwrights began to develop their own voices. Their works contained the scope of much of American culture. It was a process of defining what American theater was and, in that process, of discovering who we as a people were and are.

The 1990s are shaping up as a redirection of that process of definition. Or, more precisely perhaps, a refinement. The emphasis has moved from the multinational to the national and now to the local. A sense of regionalism has arisen in American theater, with the development of plays that are distinctly New York, Hollywood, Texan or even Oregonian in flavor. They take the monolithic block that is called American Culture and slice it into very thin segments so that we can see through it and, by understanding a part of it, better come to understand the whole.

With this continuing emphasis on communities, it seems likely that the interest of local theaters in playwrights from their area will not only persist but grow. The next decade, from all indications, will continue to put a premium on the discovery of new playwrights.

Nor is this emphasis only centered about regionalism. There is a growing demand for plays that deal with ethnic issues, with social issues, with the lives of women. Along with the feminist revolution of the 1960s, theatergoers discovered that women not only can act, but can also write, and they have their own stories to tell. For centuries, half the population has spoken with a muted voice or been interpreted through the words of men. This is changing, and it seems certain that just as minorities of all types have entered the world of playwriting and staked a claim of their own, so too will women playwrights be a vital force in American theater.

Which is not to say, however, that all plays and all playwrights should aim for stratification by region or ethnic background or sex. The greatest plays of all are those that are universal, that speak to all people of matters not confined to any one group—love, war, happiness and the quest for meaning in life.

Part of the stress on communities has also come through the slow deterioration of the bigger venues. On Broadway in New York, in Los Angeles, Chicago and other major cities, the cost of producing plays has become so exorbitant that the field threatens to collapse upon itself. Where once Broadway and off Broadway were frequent venues for dramatic or challenging plays, now the majority of productions are revivals of past successes, plays by names long established or plays considered relatively safe. New or original work has to slip in the back way, breaking in out of town in smaller markets until it has enough momentum to carry it into the larger venues.

The other wild card in the deck is the ongoing dilemma about public funding for the arts, which goes through periodic reexaminations in Washington, and in the 1990s, seems to foreshadow ominous times for arts groups, the National Endowment for the Arts and other support organizations.

The 1990s and the years beyond will probably not be any simpler than the years preceding them. If anything, they will be more complex. The quest to find out who we are will continue, and theater has always been a big part of that quest. It mirrors people. It says, "This is who we are today and how the world looks to us today." New voices that contribute to that vision of ourselves and the world will always be needed. Evidence of this can be found in the fact that although the economy of the 1980s and 1990s has become more difficult to deal with, more and more community theaters have arisen, and though still struggling, persist. There are no new or shattering developments in technology that will propel theater and playwrights into a golden era of opportunity. But neither is there anything sufficient to stop an art form that has been around for thousands of years. Theater has never been dependent on technology. It is, and will be, as it has always been, some words, a flat patch of ground to stand on, someone to move and give life to the words and the unending story of human beings trying to live in the world in the face of adversity, death, joy, love and loneliness and somehow come through it with dignity, courage and a belief in the greatness of the human being singular.

PART VI

The Business of Scriptwriting

The life of writing men has always been a bitter business. It is notoriously accompanied, for those who write well, by poverty and contempt; or by fatuity and wealth for those who write ill.

—Hillaire Belloc

Chapter Twenty-One

Warning Signs

When word got out that I would be revising this book for a new edition, readers of the original version began chiming in with suggestions. The one comment I got most frequently is best summarized in a note I received from one Blake Harris, who helps run a beginning screenwriter's support system on the GEnie national computer bulletin board system.

"If someone had told me how the system *really* works, and what traps to avoid, so that I believed it, I would have saved seven years of doing the wrong things. The more your revision can help to show what it's really like—life on the street so to speak—the more valuable it will be. Anything more you can add to your book which gives the real picture of life in the film business will make it more useful."

It was this note, along with others from beginning writers who had run across more than their share of barracudas and dead ends and disappointments that convinced me to add a chapter on warning signs—indications that the ripple in the water heading your way isn't the wake of a rescue ship but rather a shark fin.

The following is based on two sources: my own experiences and the many letters I've received from new writers over the ten years spent writing my column for *Writer's Digest*, which became my bellwether for detecting new ways of ripping off neophytes. Needless to say, what follows is strictly subjective opinion.

But if you fall for any of them after being warned, it's entirely your own fault. Don't say I didn't warn you.

AGENTS

If necessary, tattoo this on your forehead in reverse type so that you will see it every time you look in the mirror until you've got it memorized: No agent worth having charges a reading fee. Ever. I don't care what she says.

I don't care how well she says it, what extenuating circumstances are in play or how much she's "taking a chance" on you. If an agent asks you for a fee to read and/or critique your script, run—do not walk—to the nearest exit.

If you have never had a script sold or produced, it *may* be kosher for the agent to ask you to reimburse the cost of mailing and duplicating your scripts, but look at the fee carefully. If you can get the scripts copied elsewhere for less, then do so on your own. You should not be charged for phone calls, messenger service or the writing of letters.

Further, the agent should be a signatory to the Writers Guild of America, east or west. You can find out quickly enough if this is the case simply by calling the Guild at the numbers provided in this book. (If they've changed numbers, you can easily enough get the new numbers from Directory Assistance.) The agent should charge no more than 10 percent of any sales, and the agent gets *no* share in residuals.

You should also be careful to ascertain that someone who is representing himself to you as an agent really is an agent and not providing some ancillary or tangential service. There are, for instance, some people who claim to "market ideas," as an agent might. They claim to give producers synopses of scripts, either verbally or in writing, through any number of schemes. Sometimes they ask for fees in order to publish those ideas in book form. Other times, they claim to publish newsletters or arrange roundtables or send the ideas around electronically via modem or fax.

Invariably, these services cost money. Lots of it.

Now, you could very well pay these fees if you're of a mind to do so. Or you could take that money, convert it to one-dollar bills, pile it high on your coffee table and set fire to it. The end result will be very much the same.

PRODUCERS

If you want to be a doctor or a lawyer or a minister, you have to go through a specific regimen and get a license, which you hang on your wall. There is no similar method of gatekeeping when it comes to producers. *Anyone* can rent a small office just off Sunset Boulevard, call his company Magabazillion Productions or something equally big sounding and call himself a producer. It's that simple. But a producer can't produce, can't set up meetings with studios or networks or film stars until he has one vital commodity: a script.

You can be sure that if there's any way conceivable to get a script without having to pay for it, many producers are going to do so. There are some, of course, who are genuinely honest people, but for now let's focus on the not-so-honest ones.

Here are the three most common scams that less-than-legitimate producers tend to run on writers who don't know any better. Each begins with a phone call. . . .

Shopping Without a License

"Listen, Bobby, I just got finished reading your script, the one you sent in with that release form 'cause of the ad I ran in the *Reporters*. Great stuff. Love it. I think we can set this up with one of the majors, no problem. Maybe get a big star . . . I'm thinking maybe Stallone, maybe Willis . . . you like Willis? I like him too, good stuff.

"So anyway, what I wanna do is get it over to some friends I've got over at MGM first thing tomorrow. Yeah, I know it's fast, but my friend's got a three-picture deal, and he's got two locked down already. If we don't get in fast, he's gonna find something else. I also wanna get this to some other places, you know, spread out, get the best deal, maybe get an auction going. We can't rush this, though, so once they've got it, we have to give 'em time to read it, talk to *their* people, you know, the whole shebang. But I won't do this without your OK. If we can get the right people interested, we'll make a deal, option the script and get this puppy into production as fast as possible. How's that sound, Bobby?"

Terrible.

When a producer takes your script and brings it to a studio or network to try to get one of them to make a deal, the term for this is "shopping the script." Under WGA rules, a producer cannot shop your script unless and until he has optioned the property from you. He has to *pay* for the rights, usually for periods anywhere from three to six months in duration. This is important because every time a script of yours is shopped and rejected, that becomes a dead market for that script thereafter.

When a studio gets a script in-house, it's "covered," meaning someone there reads it and writes up a report on it. The executives sometimes read the script but more often just read the report, particularly if the report recommends against the property. Eventually the script is sent back, but the report remains. Usually you never even get to see it, and they won't give it to you if you ask. So if you come back there six months or a year later with the same script, they yank out the coverage, see that it was rejected, and that's the end of your script at that studio.

It's altogether possible for a script to be rejected because of the company it keeps; if it walks in the door accompanied by a producer who's unestablished or otherwise less than legitimate, that can taint the project. And six months later, nobody may remember exactly *why* the script was rejected, only that it was turned down . . . and that's a terrible degree of inertia to try to overcome.

So you've got a producer out there burning up markets, and while that producer's out shopping it around, you can't take it to anyone else. So it's only correct that you be paid at least a modest option fee in exchange. If the producer can't even afford to pull out one or two thousand dollars for an option and suggests a "free option" deal, he's not big enough to make any kind of deal in any event and should be avoided. And the producer will always try to rush you, to tell you that it has to go out *today* or you risk losing the deal.

Another phone call. . . .

It's Almost There

"It's a great script, Melanie. The bit with the chimpanzee detective . . . love it, love it, love it. I think it works as a first draft, but I think it needs just a little tweaking before we can take it any further. I'd love to kick it upstairs, but I know what these guys like and what they don't like, and there are a few things in here that'll red-flag it. So I've got some notes, just a few suggestions, most of which I think you'll agree with once you've heard them. If you could make these few changes, I think I'd have a better chance of getting it past the boys upstairs and making a deal. I'd love to go out on a limb and make a deal now, but they're really going to need to see if you can pull off what the script needs to make it work. Can I pencil you in for three on Tuesday?"

So let me see if I've got this straight: The script as a complete entity was good enough to get the producer excited, but he's not sure if you can do the *revisions?*

This is what's called a "free rewrite." It's a bad thing and should be avoided at all costs. Like the free option, it's also a violation of WGA rules. If the producer wants you to revise the script, he has to pay you to do so. Virtually every legitimate agent will tell you the same thing. A very few of them will say, "Well, now, let's not be hasty. Go and listen to what he has in mind. If the changes are huge or they violate what you had in mind for the script, then don't do it. But if the changes are minimal and help to get it sold, what's the harm?"

The harm is that you're working for someone without getting paid for it, you're now putting out two different versions of your script and you can go from producer to producer doing the same thing endlessly and never get a penny for all of your efforts. Sure, this is no harm for the agent, she isn't the one stuck with the typing.

Yet another phone call. . . .

The Check's (Eventually) in the Mail

"Jack, great news: We love the script, and we want to make a deal for it. Yeah, we're all very excited about it. Now, we've just about tapped out our development funds, so what I'd like to do is make this deal on a deferred payment basis. We're prepared to offer top dollar, payable the second we start principal photography. I'd like to wait until next quarter, when we'll get another shot in our development budget, but we think we can move this pretty fast. We'll put it all in writing."

DEFERRED PAYMENT

Translation: You'll never see a dime.

There are lots of other ways producers can trick you, too many to list and probably too ludicrous for anyone who hasn't been here a few years to believe. But most of them are subsets of these three. Always remember that anyone who says he's got a sure thing, doesn't; that if it sounds too good to be true, it probably *isn't* true; and that if the word *free* is used in any context other than a lunch provided by the producer, you're being taken for a ride. The only way to be sure is to drag an agent or a lawyer into the conversation, and no *legitimate* producer should object to that.

PLAGIARISM

At every workshop or seminar I've given on scriptwriting, the most common question is, "How do I protect my ideas from being stolen?"

The reality is that ideas are rarely, if ever, stolen; ideas, frankly, are a dime a dozen. Take the same idea, and give it to ten different writers, and you'll get ten different stories. What you have thought up has almost certainly been thought of by others; what matters is *execution*, the specifics of characterization and dialogue and plot turns. "Male meets female. Male falls in love with female. Pursues female against all odds. Finally dies for the sake of his love for female." Is this *Romeo and Juliet* or *King Kong?* Answer: yes.

It's been my experience that new scriptwriters worry about this area far too much. In the entire span of my career, I have only encountered three or four instances of plagiarism, usually of well-established stories by famous writers, committed by nonwriting producers or by neophyte writers who don't know any better or think nobody will notice. The lure of theft is largely determined by the perceived value of the item in question. That value is clear in scripts or stories by established writers, less so with new writers.

Nonetheless, the public perception of Hollywood producers as voracious creatures crouched and waiting to steal your ideas remains as an entrenched part of our culture. And this, combined with our transformation over time into a more litigious society, is one of the factors that has made it even more difficult for new writers to break in. Every new face in the door shoving a script into your hand is one more person who might turn around and sue you for plagiarism.

Nearly every hugely successful motion picture ends up with somebody either suing or threatening to sue. (Curious how they almost never sue over flops.) Steven Spielberg's *E.T.* was the subject of multiple lawsuits, all from different people, each of whom was absolutely convinced that he had taken her idea, even though there were three or four other people all saying exactly the same thing about *their* ideas. (All were found to be groundless in the end.)

When you've got nine thousand writers all throwing out ideas, and literally tens of thousands of aspiring writers out in the rest of the country doing the same, similarity of ideas, even to a seemingly outrageous extent, is inevitable. It's called *simultaneous creation*, and it happens all the time. You may have an idea you think is unique; you tell it to ten of your friends, and none of them have ever thought of anything like it. But now you put it on TV in front of scores of millions of people, and the odds are that *somebody* out there has had the same idea, and you can only hope and pray that this person has never sent your studio an unsolicited manuscript or published his story in some little magazine somewhere, or you're going to be on the receiving end of a subpoena.

All too often, I hear from people who write to me or pull me aside at seminars and say, "I sent my script to a TV show, and they sent it back, but three weeks later I saw *exactly* the same story on that show. They must've stolen it."

And here's why that notion is dangerously wrong. If you saw the episode three weeks later, then the episode had to have been filmed weeks or even months before your script ever arrived. It takes *time* to make a TV episode: two weeks to prepare for filming after you've got the script, one week to film it, two weeks to edit it, two to three more weeks to get it approved and scored, another week or two for any required special effects, another partial week to mix it all together and deliver it to the network, which likes to have its episodes two to three weeks prior to airdate. That's an average of *four months* before you ever see it on TV.

I repeat: *Ideas are commonplace*. When I was working on *The Twilight Zone*, four different writers came in one day and as part of their pitches, each of them presented the same basic idea. (It got pretty eerie after a while, let me tell you.) On every show I've ever worked on, the most frequently stated reason for saying no to a freelancer during a pitch of his story is "We're already doing that one."

I would be lying through my keyboard if I said plagiarism doesn't happen ever. It does happen, but it's rare, and if you get too caught up in that fear, you'll either never submit anything or create an unpleasant atmosphere for yourself and anyone you approach. That doesn't mean that you shouldn't take reasonable steps to protect yourself, however. Granted that the odds of ever actually being ripped off are about the same as being hit by lightning. Still every rainy season you manage to hear about *somebody* getting thumped by a thunderbolt. So here are some writing equivalents to not standing under a tree during a storm:

1. Register your script with the Writers Guild. (See chapter twenty-two on the WGA for specifics on how to do this.) As further evidence of the sheer amount of material out there, leading to inevitable duplication, the WGA registers no less than fifty thousand new scripts per year, every year. And that doesn't even begin to include the many scripts not registered, which are estimated to be two to three times that number.

2. Keep a precise log of which company has received your script, who within that company received it, when it was sent, when it was returned, what reasons were given and whether the package was opened.

3. Do yourself a favor and don't send unsolicited material to producers to begin with. Such packages can be unwittingly opened by the production staff, creating liability on the part of the producer. Always query first. If a package comes to me that looks like it might contain a script, and I don't recognize the name on the envelope, it's sent back unopened.

4. Don't send around ideas for stories or brief treatments. Nobody wants to look at them anyway. A script is a more detailed version of your story, and it's in the specifics that a case of plagiarism is made or lost.

5. If dealing with a producer whose reputation is unknown to you, con-tact the WGA's Signatory Department and ask if there have been any problems with this producer in the past, specifically if she is on the Unfair or Strike lists.

6. Somewhere in the middle of your script, make a tiny dot with a red pen in the bottom left-hand corner of the page, the part usually hidden by

the brads binding it together. When the script comes back, check that page; if the red dot is suddenly a black dot, it means this isn't your original script anymore but rather a copy. If someone made a copy of your script and kept the original without telling you, something's amiss.

Finally, unless you have real hard evidence to the contrary, try to give the studio or producer the benefit of the doubt. Because honestly and truly, it doesn't happen as often as you may think.

WORKSHOPS

Overall, workshops have the potential to be a good thing; they represent your first opportunity to put your words in front of a critical audience for their reaction. But workshops, particularly scriptwriting workshops, have a nasty tendency over time to become the end rather than the means to an end. After a while, you begin to know what does and doesn't gain acceptance in the workshop in terms of topics and approaches, and it often happens that writers begin writing for the other people in the workshop rather than using the workshop to find their own individual voices.

So a gentle warning to all those considering going into a script workshop: Never stay in any one workshop for more than one year, and never take more than two such prolonged workshops in any three-year period.

Additionally, be careful in your selection of a workshop. Make sure your instructor knows what he is talking about and has real credits. Read the descriptions, and, most important, read between the lines. "Baxter C. Hall has written over half a dozen screenplays, is a script consultant and has been an instructor with Miskatonic Living Workshops for the last ten years." Translation: Mr. Hall has almost certainly never sold anything and mainly subsists on teaching workshops, charging for his advice along the way.

"Dr. Cynthia Lebensraum is a psychological consultant to many of the leading networks and studios." Translation: a nonwriter, probably one of the psychobabble parasites who nickel-and-dime the networks. Run like hell.

For not much more than the price of the average novel, you can buy a copy of the Writers Guild of America, west, *Writers Guild Directory*, which lists all of its members, their credits and agencies. If you're going to take a workshop or class from someone who says she is a working professional in the field (and why would you take one from anybody else?), get the *Directory* and check her credits. Make sure she (1) exists and (2) is, preferably, in the area you're interested in. It will take ten minutes and save you months of grief.

The same applies to classes taught in theater or playwriting. The means of verifying credits isn't necessarily as easy—unless the instructor belongs to the Dramatist's Guild, which maintains lists of credits—but you should investigate nonetheless to the best of your ability. Remember, as a writer your resources are limited by time, energy and money; make sure you get the most out of your investments.

Finally, there are all of the others who will try to take advantage of you: the actor who wants a showpiece or one-person show and asks you to write it for him on the theory that you'll both share royalties when it takes off; the director with some credits who wants to "take you under her wing" to help you write her next movie (on a deferred payment basis, of course); and even other writers who want you to adapt their ideas into screenplays or theatrical plays, sharing the proceeds fifty/fifty. . . .

Glamour, real or perceived, attracts sharks, and the nature of showbiz in its many incarnations attracts more than its share of creeps. Thus you *must* go into this business with the absolute knowledge that at some point, you may be hustled. Whether or not you fall for it will depend on how careful you are and what you're willing to be gulled into believing. I'm not asking you to be cynical; I'm not saying you're naive. It may happen to you only once; it may happen to you a lot. But it *can* happen, and you need to be cautious and aware.

It's unfortunate that the field is such that a chapter like this is required, but the purpose of this book is to enable you to survive as a scriptwriter. If you're going to insist on going swimming, somebody should take the time to explain the concept of *sharks*.

Chapter Twenty-Two

The Writers Guild of America

THE HISTORY OF THE ORGANIZATION

The history of the Writers Guild of America can be traced back to 1912, when the Authors Guild was formed to protect the financial and creative interests of novelists, short story writers, nonfiction writers and others. A few years later, the Authors Guild merged with the Dramatists Guild and created the Authors League. In 1921, with the arrival of motion pictures, some of the League's members formed a social organization called the Screen Writers Guild, which functioned as a branch of the League and tried to improve—informally—the lives of writers working in the then-unregulated movie world.

It soon became apparent, however, that a social organization wasn't enough; a protective association to safeguard the rights and economic prospects of screenwriters was necessary. In 1936, the SWG reincorporated as an affiliate of the Authors League, much to the chagrin and annoyance of the film industry. Despite the resultant furor, the 1937 U.S. Supreme Court decision upheld the National Labor Relations Act, giving the SWG the right to act as a collective bargaining agent for screenwriters. The first collectively bargained contract between the studios and the SWG was signed in 1942. Flushed with victory but hopelessly disorganized and torn by internal dissension (a description that can just as easily describe the WGA of today), the SWG nonetheless went on to assist in the creation of a Radio Writers Guild in 1947 and a Television Writers Group in 1950.

In time, a collective bargaining structure divided between five different labor organizations became top-heavy and too compartmentalized, leading to confusion and duplication of effort. So starting in the 1950s, meetings were held in New York City between the leaders of the Authors Guild, the Dramatists Guild, the Television Writers Group, the Radio Writers Guild and the Screen Writers Guild in the hope of figuring some way out of the organizational quicksand in which they now found themselves.

The Writers Guild of America, founded in 1954, was to be the solution to the problem. One single agency would act as the bargaining force for all the professional screen, radio and television writers in the United States. Because the entertainment industry was then divided evenly between New York City for television and the West Coast for motion pictures, the Guild was divided in half, with the Mississippi River designated as the border between the two areas of jurisdiction.

Even though the industry has changed and most television production has moved out to the West Coast, the division in the WGA still continues today. The Writers Guild of America, East, Inc., is located at 27 West Forty-Eighth Street, New York, New York 10036, (212) 575-5060, and the Writers Guild of America, West, Inc., relocated in 1996 to newer and larger facilities at 7000 West Third Street, Los Angeles, California 90048-4329, (213) 951-4000. The bulk of WGAe members are radio scripters, soap-opera writers, those newswriters not already covered by other unions and some feature-film writers. The largest overall concentration of WGA members is on the West Coast, under WGAw jurisdiction.

By the beginning of the 1980s, the total membership of the WGA came to just under 7,000, with nearly 6,000 of these members located on the West Coast. As of 1994, the total roster is well in excess of 9,000 members.

This relatively small group of writers is responsible for virtually everything you see on television and in movie theaters and hear on a majority of radiodrama series. Anyone can become a member of the Writers Guild after having sold at least one script to television, film or radio as a non-Guild freelancer. Under the Taft-Hartley Act, which allows any nonunion individual to take part in a union activity on a limited basis, you can sell two scripts before having to join the WGA. But they will begin bugging you to join as an associate member as soon as the ink on your first contract has dried.

HOW THE WGA WORKS

After your second sale, either you join the Guild or you are proscribed from selling more scripts to any WGA signatory (though you're still free to sell to non-WGA signatory production companies). While most writers seem to have no problem with this, some have legitimate problems with the idea of unions or are sufficiently stubbornminded not to want to belong to *any* organization, particularly one that might support issues or ideas they may themselves not support. This has led to one of the more sensitive issues with the WGA and other labor unions, that of financial core membership. Because you are required to join the union, whether you want to or not, labor laws allow the member some latitude in the form that membership may take. Core membership means that your dues are slightly (make that *very* slightly) reduced, and you may work for non-Guild signatories, even work during a strike. But in exchange, you cannot vote in Guild elections, serve on any Guild committees or run for any Guild office, effectively leaving your fate in the hands of other people.

Membership in the Guild is not automatic. After you have made your sale(s), the WGA contacts you about becoming an associate or full member, depending on the nature of the sale, and sends you an application. The work you performed is then confirmed and evaluated, and your membership category is determined. You are then charged a fairly hefty initiation fee (roughly $900), and from then on you pay dues of $25 per quarter, plus 1 to 1.5 percent of all your earnings within Guild jurisdiction. (All figures are subject to change.)

And now for some hard, cold facts.

• Even with the growth in various markets outlined elsewhere in this book, 9,000 WGA members is a *lot* of people. There are generally more WGA members than work.

• On any given day, 50 percent of the WGA is out of work.

• Most WGA members earn less than an average elementary school teacher. Only about 2 to 5 percent earn six-figure yearly salaries or better. The average working TV freelance writer sells two to five scripts per year. Many sell fewer. Some sell more.

• I have been a WGA member since 1978. In all of that time, not one producer has ever asked me if I'm a member, so if you're hoping that membership will prove beyond doubt that you are a working writer or will somehow confer a threshold of status within the entertainment community, a password to all the right meetings . . . it won't.

• WGA leadership has frequently taken pains to point to the number of WGA members who won membership based upon one or two sales early on and who have not sold anything since. They thus argue that the total membership figure is somewhat inflated, given the presence of nonworking writers or writers whose main income is not derived from scriptwriting. Consequently, as the 1990s wore on, the WGA tightened its rules in an effort to ease out the nonworking writers in an attempt to create, in the words of Guild leadership, "a lean, mean machine."

• Most of the advances made by the WGA, considered by the industry to be the most militant of all the studio guilds, have been made through some long and bitter strikes. The 1988 strike lasted six months and cost many members their livelihood, careers and homes, losses that took years to recapture, if at all. So be prepared to pound the pavement.

Something you have to remember about the WGA is that it is composed of *writers*. Though that seems an obvious statement, it has to be repeated in order for you to truly understand one of the biggest problems with the WGA: Writers by nature tend to be creative, eccentric, freethinkers— that's just one at a time. Now put 9,000 of them in a room, many of them working in different fields, some as freelancers, others as writer/producer or writer/director hyphenates, with feature writers who may not understand or care about the problems of TV writers. The TV writers don't want to jeopardize their weekly checks by going out on strike for the benefit of sporadically employed feature writers.

The single biggest division in the WGA is between freelancers and hyphenates, since the latter at least nominally are part of management. This is particularly true during strikes, when you as a writer may support the issues at hand, but you're also a producer, and the network is looking at you to deliver the show on time, regardless. Writer/producers of con- science who don't break the line can sometimes find themselves out of a career. Nonetheless, in a show of solidarity and will, many did just that during the terrible strike of 1988.

The other freelancer/hyphenate hot spot centers on staff-written TV shows, which the former group believes limits the number of writers who can work. Many freelancers would like to develop some kind of quota system, encouraging or requiring producers to accept a certain percentage of non-staff-written scripts; producer/writers want to keep their options flexible and use whichever writers they think are *right* for their shows. Disagreements in this area have been known to turn quite ugly.

None of this is helped by the fact that in recent years, WGA leadership has tended to divide members between those who support Guild leader- ship's notions, regardless of whether they're right or wrong, and anybody who questions the established way of doing things. Disagreement is often characterized as disloyalty or as the harping of a "lunatic fringe" handy for rhetoric, attack and dead-catting come time for Board elections.

Matters are made even more complex by the fact that the WGA cannot act in isolation; decisions made between the WGA and the studios can trigger heated conflict between the WGA and other guilds, such as the Directors Guild of America (DGA).

For example: For over twenty years, one of the most bitterly controver- sial areas for writers and directors is the *possessary credit*. A possessary credit is what you see on the movie screen when it says "A Film by [insert name]" when that person (usually the director) did not actually write the film. The theory is that if you didn't write the film, you don't have the right to say it's by you. But it happens all the time.

Ironically, it's the WGA's own fault that this has become an issue. Originally, no such possessary credit was ever granted to a director who didn't also write his films. That was the agreement between the WGA and the studios. Then along came Alfred Hitchcock, whose films were so cohesive and uniquely his own that Universal Studios petitioned the WGA to allow him the use of the possessary credit, "A Film by Alfred Hitchcock." After thinking it over, the WGA finally decided to allow this, even called the agreement informally "The Hitchcock Clause," but admonished the studio to only use this on Hitchcock films.

But once you allow one such exception, the rest follow, and soon even first-time directors were plastering their names behind "A Film by," much to the dismay of screenwriters. Ever since then, the WGA has tried to renegotiate control over the possessary credit but has met with stiff resistance from the DGA, which says it violates their contract with the studios. The DGA threatens legal action every time the issue is raised, on the grounds that it "undermines the traditional role of the director," even though that "traditional role" didn't even *exist* prior to the Hitchcock Clause.

Membership in the Writers Guild promises neither success nor ultimate happiness. Though it hosts work-related seminars and helps to put writers together with agents or with older writers under mentor programs, the WGA does not actively find work for its writer members. While it holds lectures and panel discussions on various creative aspects of the writing business, it makes no pretensions to being a school for scriptwriters.

Ironically, one of the areas not represented by the WGA is the field of animation writing, which traditionally has been under the auspices of the Screen Cartoonists Guild. Starting in 1994, with the formation of a WGA subgroup called the Animation Writers Caucus, efforts were being made to bring animation writing under WGA jurisdiction. It's hoped that the complex legal maneuvering required for this will be accomplished by the year 2000.

If there is any single most troublesome aspect to the WGA, it is its tendency to function more like a club or fraternity than a union; there are cliques and inner circles, the favored (whose faces end up in articles in the Guild *Journal*) and the disfavored (who are kept as invisible as possible). Guild elections are noted for their nastiness and vituperation, where each person has to align with whatever clique he thinks will best serve his interests, and the majority of candidates are those handpicked by a small Guild committee looking for right-minded individuals. This situation has over recent years led many writers (and I will admit that I include myself in this) to opt out of Guild politics altogether and to have as little to do with the internal functioning of the Guild as possible.

But then there are always those who thrive in this kind of environment, who love organizing and campaigning and are willing to permit affronts in the goal of bettering the lives of other writers. And for them, the WGA may be the perfect home, noisy neighbors and all.

BENEFITS OF MEMBERSHIP

So why join the WGA? Well, because you have to and because sometimes it helps to be in the company of other writers who've been in the same position you're in. Most importantly, being in the Guild allows you to continue working as a scriptwriter for the majority of producers who are signatories to the Guild. Part of being a signatory means promising that they will not employ non-Guild members on any basis other than that permissible under the Taft-Hartley Act.

In addition, the Guild oversees all contracts with agents and producers, distributes residuals (albeit slowly), arbitrates proper determination of writing credits, provides a registration service open to Guild members and other writers and publishes a monthly *Journal* with marketing information, articles and other material useful to a scriptwriter.

The Guild creates a forum for meeting other writers, producers and directors on a social basis; provides a credit union, a group insurance plan and a pension plan; operates a film society; organizes committees that among other areas examine new technologies and support freedom of expression; and can lobby for the rights of freelance and minority writers.

But you don't have to be a WGA member to benefit from many of its programs. After selling just one script to a Guild signatory, the WGA collects and distributes your residuals even though you're not yet in the Guild. Also, any writer may take advantage of the Guild's script registration office.

Scripts for radio, television and motion pictures can be registered by sending one copy of the script and a small fee (check with the Guild for current fees, but as of 1994, registration fees were usually in the range of fifteen dollars) to the Writers Guild of America, West, Inc., Script Registration Office, 7000 West Third Street, Los Angeles, California 90048-4329. A registration number will be sent to you when the script is received. In theory, this number should appear in the lower left-hand corner of the title page, thus: WGAw Registration # _____ .

The operative phrase being *in theory*. There is some debate over whether or not that *should* be displayed. One side of the debate says that it puts the producer on notice that you're protected, that you've done your homework. They insist that producers have nothing to get exercised about in this. The other side of the debate says that putting the registration number on a script implies that you think the producer might steal your script and that this kind of atmosphere doesn't do much to endear the producer to your work.

Personally, I tend to side with the latter school of thought, but the important thing is that you *do* it; whether you choose to announce it is a decision you'll have to make at that time.

A current television market list—excerpted from the Guild *Journal*—can also be obtained from the Guild for a much smaller fee, sent to the same address, but you might be better served by subscribing to the *Journal* as a whole (another option open to nonmembers) for all the other information contained there.

The Writers Guild of America operates in affiliation with the Association of Canadian Television and Radio Artists (ACTRA) at 105 Carlton Street, Toronto, Ontario, M5B 1M2 Canada, (416) 363-6335; the Writers' Guild of Great Britain (WGGB), 430 Edgware Road, London, England W2 1EH, (01) 723-8074; and the Australian Writers' Guild at 197 Blues Point Road, North Sydney, NSW, Australia 2060, (61) 922-3856.

In addition to the main phone number given for WGAw earlier, there are other direct-dial numbers that may be of use to new scriptwriters. For agencies, call (213) 782-4502. Other departments are at the following extensions: Claims, 4663; Contracts, 4501; Credits, 4528; Legal Services, 4521; Library, 4544; Membership, 4532; Publications, such as the WGA *Journal*, 4542; Public Affairs, 4574; Script Registration, 4540; Residuals, 4503; and Signatories, 4514.

Chapter Twenty-Three

The Art of Getting and Keeping an Agent

The trap of established cliché: It's impossible to get an agent until you've reached a point in your career when you no longer need one.

The truth: Agents make 10 percent of what their clients earn. If a writer is a little crazy to think she can make a living by typing out black-on-white figments of imagination, someone else has to be even crazier to think he can make a living off 10 percent of the other person's income. It's the joke of the psychiatrist talking to two patients brought in from Central Park.

"Where do you live?" he asks one.

"I live under the stars and the heavens and the sky above."

"And where do you live?" the doctor asks the other patient.

"Next door to him."

That's the agent.

It's an insane job description, and therefore you can't blame agents for trying to inject at least a little sanity into the situation by minimizing their degree of risk. Consequently, agents take on two kinds of clients: established writers who are changing agencies or have just made their first major sale and clients who they genuinely believe have the talent, drive and persistence to become successful scriptwriters. Agents do not accept charity cases. They are not a public service company. They don't want to hear your tales of a hard life. They're there because the client has made money or may reasonably make them money in the future. Period.

So there's no truth to the notion that agents aren't interested in acquiring new scriptwriters. Their interest may vary across different agencies and, over time, even within the same agency, depending on how many clients they are currently handling, but the interest is there because the roster of clients is always changing. Agents and writers share one characteristic with the shark: As soon as they stop moving, they die. Many writers start with one agent, enjoy some success, then at the expiration of the contract move on to a bigger agent or simply retire.

Some writers change agents like others change socks, and if an agent doesn't have at least a few new talents on tap to fill the gap, then the real estate profession will find itself with yet another practitioner.

It's the law of supply and demand: The writer supplies the scripts, and the agent demands whatever she humanly can without being run out of town on a rail.

So agents need writers. Writers need agents. How do the two sides come together? The first step is to find an agent. A good, reliable, legitimate agent who does not happen to share any of the other characteristics of the shark except the need to keep moving. The problem is that there are literally hundreds of agents in the Los Angeles area alone. Some of them work out of lavish offices, some package stars and directors as well as writers, some are small but try very hard and some have offices built into the rear of a Ford station wagon or that go in and out with the tide in Santa Monica.

This may sound like exaggeration, but it isn't. My first agent had more or less retired from the business before I came into contact with him. He didn't choose to tell me this. I wrote sample scripts, sent them to him . . . and they sat fallow for the better part of a year. The second agent I engaged, whom I'll identify only as Carol, kept changing offices every month. She always had a reason for it, even made the reasons sound plausible enough for me to fall for the okeydoke. Never answered her phone, always let the machine get it. I would go by her office, which was often an apartment building, and she was never there ("out making deals" was her usual explanation). The day I found notices of eviction and a stack of bills in front of her door was the day I figured it was time to move on. Another wasted year.

(I was managing to work during this time, by the way, but always in situations where I had gotten the work myself, not through the agent.)

My third agent was with a big agency but wasn't really into the kinds of projects I wanted to do, and I often found myself shunted into second position, with her other clients taking more time and attention. No career guidance, no sales, nothing.

Finally, I lucked out with a smaller boutique agency that was and is very selective in its roster of clients—they have about sixty or seventy clients. My specific agents within this agency are the two owners of the company, handling different aspects of my work. I've been with them for about ten years now, and it's been a terrific relationship.

And that word—*relationship*—is key to our discussion. There are many good agencies out there, but just as there are many good dating possibilities out there, not everyone is suited to your needs and tastes. Somewhere out there is the perfect marriage. And somewhere out there is the marriage from hell. Unfortunately, no one, and no book, can tell you which is which. The only way you're going to find out who's your ideal date is to plunge into the field and be very selective.

THE HUNT

Agencies take certain steps to minimize their risk when selecting a client. Given the typical scenario above, how can you minimize your own risk in finding an agent?

First, you want an agent who's been around for a while, and be sure it's an agent who specializes in the marketing of scripts. There are a lot of good literary agents who can sell a book in two minutes but who simply don't or can't handle scripts. Sometimes they'll say that they can, but the truth is usually a different situation. When you see a New York address for an agent, for instance, investigate further and determine if this is someone who actually handles scripts (probably for the soap-opera or movie business since that's what's available on the East Coast) or if he's primarily a book agency with a contact on the West Coast who handles scripts. If the latter, move on because you may as well develop a relationship directly with a West Coast agent rather than have one more middleman between you and your potential buyers.

I have also seen script agency listings in places like Montana and Arkansas and Louisiana, and at the risk of profoundly annoying those companies (remember, this book is for your service, not theirs), I've never heard of any of them ever selling anything. Your best bet is to concentrate on someone in the Los Angeles area.

Any legitimate agency is bound to certain standards in terms of what it can charge a writer and the services it can provide in exchange. These regulations are specified in the Writers Guild of America Artists Managers' Basic Agreement, to which all of the major and minor agencies are signatories. Not only does this protect you by guaranteeing that the agency is reasonably legitimate, but it also has a long-term advantage. Let's say, for the moment, that you sign with a non-Guild signatory agent, and by gosh, she makes a sale for you. You then join the Writers Guild. The problem, though, is that writers can only be represented by Guild signatories after they join the Guild. Which simply means that the writer must now change agencies, a move that can be painful for both parties.

More important, though, the provisos of the WGA agent signatory contract are there to protect you against abuse. Under those provisos, an agent can only charge you 10 percent of any payments made to you while a client of that agency, and only in script areas. Some agencies will try to charge you anywhere from 12 to 15 percent. There are also rules about reading fees: They're not allowable.

If you're an absolutely new and uncredited writer, some agencies may ask you to contribute a percentage of their costs for copying and mailing your sample scripts. This, too, is frowned upon but is more of a grudgingly accepted practice. To make sure you're not taken, you can volunteer to make up script copies on your own (probably costing less than the agency's cost) or ask for hard-copy receipts and then contribute a percentage not to exceed 50 percent. You should not pay for agency phone calls. And if you're paying postage, you want to be sure to get complete reports on where the script has been sent and to whom.

Having a WGA signatory agent representing you will save you a great deal of time otherwise spent monitoring her behavior. It won't save you from all the drones out there (note that all of the agents I encountered earlier were WGA signatories), but it will at least help stack the odds more in your favor than would otherwise be the case; and if there should be a problem, the WGA can intervene on your behalf.

It's always a good idea to verify names and addresses before sending out query letters. An updated list is published periodically by the WGA and can be obtained for about two dollars even by nonmembers. (Note: Be sure to verify current fees with the WGA before sending anything.)

With this list in hand, the next step is to contact an agent. You may choose to wait until you've made your first sale, in which case it's much easier to find someone willing to represent you. You may also consider contacting an agent after you've had an offer but before concluding the sale, to provide additional inducement, since he'll be able to claim the 10 percent agency fee for handling the negotiation.

On the other hand, you may not want to wait until you've sold something. It's not a requirement. But you do have to have completed at least one, and preferably more, full-length film or television scripts. This is the only basis upon which an agent can determine whether to accept you as a client. If you approach an agent with the statement that you are interested in doing some scripts and that you will do one at some time in the future, or that you're considering one now but that you want to have an agent first, you'll get a rather rude response. Under those circumstances, an agent doesn't even want to know you exist.

"Nothing bugs me more than the person who calls and says, 'I'd like to be a scriptwriter, and I've got a lot of good ideas, but I'd really rather not bother actually writing the script until I've got an agent,' as though an agent were a guarantee of success," one agent told me. "The only guarantee of success is talent combined with persistence, and I can generally be certain that if someone comes at me with that kind of attitude, he hasn't got either of those qualities. Writing is work, just like anything else. There are no magic formulas, no miracles. If someone doesn't have the wherewithal to put together a script before I take him on as a client, the odds are good that he never will put together anything even remotely acceptable."

So let's start with the assumption that using the techniques provided in this book, combined with your own talent and imagination—you have now written a couple of scripts. Your next step is to contact one of the agents listed in the latest WGA agents list and inquire about the possibility of representation. Explain that you have written one or more complete scripts that are available for examination by the agent and are ready to be marketed. If you have a background in other areas of writing, from playwriting to newspaper reporting, be sure to include that information. If not, the less said the better. Some agencies will indicate in their listings that they take new clients only on the basis of personal recommendation. If you have such a connection, use it. If not, apply elsewhere. Don't waste valuable time chasing down false or unproductive leads.

Briefly describe your goals as a writer and what kinds of scripts you are most interested in writing. This is important because not all agents handle the same areas. Some prefer to work only with feature films or television movies, while others work closely with the producers of episodic television. Many, though, do cover all of these areas. Describe the script itself in broad strokes in only a paragraph or so. State in closing that if the agent would be interested in looking at the script, you would be happy to send it along and that, should the agent find the script of interest, you will be ready to come to Los Angeles for a meeting at his or her convenience. If you're not ready to make this step and initiate a personal meeting, you lessen the chances the agent will choose to represent you.

If the agency is not fully booked with clients, the odds are fair that you will eventually get a positive response. I use the word *eventually* for good reason. Agents can be maddeningly slow. Which is why you should send out your letters of inquiry in groups of ten to fifteen, not one at a time. It took one agent literally a year and a half to get back to me early on when I was still shopping. To simplify expenses, you should coordinate any positive responses so that you can hit Los Angeles and meet with all of them over a three- to four-day period, thus avoiding repeat trips. Prepare to be disappointed; this is a long and difficult process, and rejection can be painful. But if you stick with it, and the sample scripts have merit, you've got a fighting chance.

During the course of your meeting, the agent will again go over your goals, express any comments, praises, criticisms or reservations about the script, and then move the conversation into more casual areas. The agent will want to see how the two of you will get along, if you are open to advice and suggestions, how you react to criticism and so forth. Scriptwriting can be a temperamental business, so client-agent relationships are built upon mutual respect and trust. Consequently, you should never attempt to mislead your agent or do anything to endanger that mutual trust. Like any good relationship, once the bond of trust is shattered, it's almost impossible to reconstruct it.

If all the signs are right and each party understands exactly what is expected by the other, then a contract will be sent to you. Actually, you will get three separate contracts, all identical, each to be signed by yourself and the agent. One copy is for your records, a second copy stays with the agent and the third copy is filed with the Guild. Attached to the contract is a huge, bulky document called a "Rider W," which explains in detail the principles of the Basic Agreement so that both parties know precisely what their rights and responsibilities are.

All contracts used by the Guild signatories are exactly the same. If you decide to go with a non-Guild signatory, or if you do get a contract that differs from a standard agent-client agreement, check it against the one provided in the appendix for any unusual loopholes.

Once you've signed with an agency, what can you expect next?

Gradually, the agent will try to get your name and work known around town. Your scripts will be sent to producers doing projects along the lines of your submitted samples. You should not take this period to stop writing and wait for Hollywood to come knocking. Keep writing. Turn out more samples. The more your agent has to work with, the more diverse the samples, the greater your chance of hitting the right person. In addition, if a script is submitted to a major studio, it's "covered," meaning it's read and synopsized by a studio reader. That coverage stays in-house forever. Consequently, even though studio personnel change rather rapidly, if a reader gives your script a black mark, that's known the instant your script comes in and someone checks the logs. (Yes, this is unfair; many good scripts get a bad rap because one reader thought it was crummy. It's the way of the world.) Scripts can thus become old very quickly; they can't be sent back again to some places. All the more reason to continue to provide new samples.

During this time, your agent should be trying to steer you in the right direction with additional samples. A good agent gives gentle career advice without trying to move you into areas you really don't want to explore. Your agent should also be setting up whatever meetings are possible, which in the beginning will be few and far between. Many of them will be simple "get to know you" meetings. Remember, Hollywood is to some extent personality driven. Producers like to know they can work with someone. So even though a meeting may not end with an assignment, if the producer comes away from the meeting impressed and intrigued, you stand a good chance of being called in later for a more serious meeting.

Getting an agent also doesn't mean you should drop your own efforts at finding assignments, as outlined in this book. To tell you the absolute truth, most writers I know find that their agents only get them jobs about 20 percent of the time. The rest come through hard work, past credits, the gradual accumulation of contacts in the business . . . and sheer dumb luck. But in the beginning, an agent is a cachet, a guide, an inroad—proof that at least *someone* in the business thinks you've got what it takes. And that's unspeakably important.

One last thing.

Do not write me and ask for recommendations on agents. I won't provide them. For one thing, that's not my line of work; I'm not a matchmaker. Further, what I think might be a good agent may well be your idea of a personal hell. I state this plainly here because after this book was initially published, roughly one third of all the letters that came in were solicitations for agent recommendations.

Embarking on the search for an agent can be a long, slow, discouraging process. As you slog through it, remember that it's this way for everyone in the beginning. Just keep telling yourself this: At one time in his history, every selling writer went through a period where he didn't have any credits and didn't have an agent. Nonetheless, he persisted. And that is the key.

Patience, determination, direction and strength.

Good luck.

Glossary of Visual Terminology for Television and Film

The world of television and film scripting has its own unique language, and it is essential that anyone aspiring to write for these media fully understand this language. A knowledge of production terminology enables the scriptwriter to visualize the concept under construction in very specific terms and, equally as important, to communicate that concept in a way that can be immediately understood by anyone who reads the script.

The following is a list of the visual terms used most frequently in television and film production.

CAMERA DIRECTIONS

Background(B.G.). The area farthest from the lens of the camera that is still within clear visible range. This term is used to convey something happening away from the primary action. For example: "As Bob and Kathy speak, an elephant moves across the stage in the B.G."

Close shot. An indication for the camera to close in on a certain action, usually to emphasize the action and the way it relates to the plot. "As Robert drives, we see Fred removing a gun from his belt in a CLOSE SHOT."

Close-up. An indication for the camera to close in on an actor's expression—often just the face, other times including the whole head. A call for a close-up is indicated by the abbreviation CU and takes place when a dramatic moment needs to be emphasized or when you want to dwell on a character's reaction to an incident in your script. "Sherwood opens the box and finds a bomb inside. CU on Sherwood's reaction." (To clarify the difference between a close-up and a close shot, a close shot used in this scene would be handled thus: "Sherwood opens the box and finds a bomb inside. CLOSE SHOT on the bomb's timer ticking away the seconds.")

Exterior (EXT). A notation establishing that the action taking place is shot outside something—an office, a building, a spaceship. The notation EXT is used at the beginning of a scene along with the scene number (if needed), and a notation of time of day. "EXT. HOTEL—PARKING LOT—DAY."

Extreme close-up (ECU). Similar in intention to a basic close-up but more intense, with only the eyes and possibly a nose in the shot.

Frame. That portion of the scene visible to the camera and framed by its lens. (Think of it as a picture frame surrounding a portrait.) "As smoke rises from the manhole, Rick enters the frame."

Interior (INT). Similar to *Exterior* in purpose. Used to establish that the action being described takes place inside something. "INT. SUB-MARINE-CONTROL ROOM—NIGHT."

Long shot. An indication for the camera to be placed some distance from its subject(s). "In a LONG SHOT, Jeremy and Betty walk on the beach at sunset."

Medium shot. The happy medium between a close and a long shot. In most cases, you do not need to signal such a shot since most camera work is done in medium shots anyway. It is generally used to return the camera's perspective to normal after a close or long shot. "We return to a MEDIUM SHOT of Jeremy and Betty as they walk past a sign reading 'Beach Closed.' "

Pan. An indication for the camera to move in a steady horizontal line across the scene. "The camera PANS the faces of the mourners."

Shot. Same as *Frame.*

Stock footage. This tells the director that the scene can be realized using material already on film and in the camera from previous episodes. Many exteriors and car-driving sequences are stored on stock footage and plugged into a program when a similar scene is required, thereby saving the expense of reshooting the location all over again. "The ship steams away into the distance. STOCK FOOTAGE."

Swish-pan. Similar to a *Pan* but faster, with more dizzying effects. Frequently used to connote rapidity of movement.

Zoom. An indication for the camera to move from a long to a close or medium shot in the same take, "zooming" in on the subject. "Shooting over John's shoulder, the camera ZOOMS IN on the front window of the bank across the street."

Special Effects Shots

Aerial shot. An indication that the scene is to be shot from a great height, usually from a helicopter or airplane.

Crane shot. A camera shooting from a less dramatic height, in this case from a movable crane that can move from a face-on shot to a perspective looking down on the action.

Freeze-frame. A term used mostly in videotape, this means literally freezing the action on-screen. (Freeze-frames are widely used at the conclusion of situation comedies, with the end credits rolling over the frozen scene.)

Hand-held camera. This is a device used to increase the "you-are-there" sensation. The cameraman walks toward the scene with the camera hand-held instead of on wheels, and this gives the finished film a jerky, documentary feel that also follows the rhythm of actual footsteps. You often see this effect in detective mysteries—the camera is used to represent the point of view of a burglar about to break into someone's house. This would be written as, "EXT. HOUSE—THIEF'S P.O.V.—CAMERA HAND-HELD."

Insert. Any momentary aside or diversion from the body of the script, very much like a parenthetical statement in prose writing. If, during your scene, there is a man holding a box and you want to go to a close-up on the label of that box, you write "INSERT: CU ON THE LABEL ON THE BOX." You describe what's on the label, and then, to return to the body of the action, you simply write "BACK TO SCENE" two spaces below your insert.

Pixillation. A computerized process that omits two out of three frames of action, thereby creating a surreal, jumpy look. The effect is similar to that associated with a flashing strobe light at a discotheque. (Also used in film animation.)

Point of view (P.O.V.). This informs the reader that the scene is being filmed from the perspective of one of the characters. For an example of this, see *Hand-held camera.*

Series of shots. A montage of camera shots of different locations connected to create a certain impression, say, a father looking for his lost daughter. This would be written as "SERIES OF SHOTS: EXT. LOCATIONS—DAY AND NIGHT—SHOPS, STORES, OFFICES," followed by, on the next line, "Father goes from store to store, asking patrons if they have seen his daughter." This is a timesaving device and is usually shot without sound; a musical sound track might accompany the action.

Split-screen shot. This means just what it says—the frame is split down the middle, with each side displaying an action taking place at a different location. This is often used to show both sides of a telephone conversation. "INT. SPLIT-SCREEN—JOHN AND MARSHA ON THE TELEPHONE."

Slow motion. Slowing the action down in order to heighten the moment or—in parodies—to ridicule it.

Superimpose. To place one image over another.

Tracking shot. When your characters are walking along the beach, and the camera stays right beside them all the way, this is a tracking shot. The name came about because on rough or uneven terrain—such as a beach—wooden tracks are set down for the camera to roll upon.

Transitions

Blackout. An immediate darkening of the screen that does not signal the end of the script. Blackouts are frequently used in comedy sketches to signal the end of the sketch.

Cut to. The most common transition of all, to cut to one scene from another means that the transition is immediate, without break or blackout or fancy camera work in between.

Dissolve. This device moves us from one location to another by superimposing the first few seconds of the next scene over the last few seconds of the preceding one.

Fade-in. An indication that the script is now beginning. The term fade-in is used only once, at the very start of the manuscript.

Fade-out. Also used only once, this signals the conclusion of the script.

Intercutting. Signals important things happening in two distant locations at the same time. This means that the camera will cut back and forth from one location to the other during the scene. When you have established your primary scene and come to the location you want to cut back and forth from, you simply write the scene indication and description as you would otherwise and follow it with "Camera INTERCUTS between the two scenes."

Match cut. Let's say your character is reading about a grand opening at a new bank. The opening is announced in a newspaper headline, and the scene you want to cut to is of a banner draped over the front of the bank bearing the same words, in the same typestyle, with one overlapping the other as in a dissolve. This is called a match cut, meaning that one element in the second scene is identical in some fashion to an element of the same visual size in the preceding scene.

Solarization. The opposite of a blackout. The scene fills with light so that, eventually, nothing is visible but the light.

Sample Release Forms

In nearly every instance, a film, radio or television producer will specifically ask that a release form be signed by the person submitting a script for her examination and that the release be included with the script.

To facilitate this process a bit, two separate release forms are presented here for your use and convenience. The first is a short-form release generally favored by most television producers. The second is a somewhat longer release that can be used in a variety of circumstances, for television, film and radio.

If desired, you can simply Wite-Out the page numbers and other identifying marks that these pages contain and photocopy the forms as printed. Otherwise, you can just retype them and photocopy them onto $8\frac{1}{2}'' \times 11''$ pages.

When you approach a producer, be sure to mention that you possess a standard release form, but that if there is one preferred by his production company to please forward it along to you. When mailing your script, be sure to write the words RELEASE FORM ENCLOSED on the envelope to avoid having the package sent back unopened.

Program Material Release Form: Television

_____, 19 _____

Title and/or Theme of Material Submitted Hereunder: _____

Gentlemen:

I am today submitting to you certain program material, the title and/or theme of which is indicated above (which material is hereinafter referred to as the "program material"), upon the following express understanding and conditions.

1. I acknowledge that I have requested permission to disclose to you and to carry on certain discussions and negotiations with you in connection with such program material.

2. I agree that I am voluntarily disclosing such program material to you at my request. I understand that you shall have no obligation to me in any respect whatsoever with regard to such material until each of us has executed a written agreement, which by its terms and provisions will be the only contract between us.

3. I agree that any discussions we may have with respect to such program material shall not constitute any agreement expressed or implied as to the purchase or use of any of such program material which I am hereby disclosing to you either orally or in writing.

4. If such material submitted hereunder is not new or novel, or was not originated by me, or has not been reduced to concrete form, or if because other persons including your employees have heretofore submitted or hereafter submit similar or identical program material which you have the right to use, then I agree that you shall not be liable to me for the use of such program material and you shall not be obligated in any respect whatsoever to compensate me for such use by you.

5. I further agree that if you hereafter produce or distribute a television program or programs based upon the same general idea, theme, or situation, and/or having the same setting or background and/or taking place in the same geographical area or period of history as the said program material, then, unless you have substantially copied the expression and development of such idea, theme or situation, including the characters and story line thereof, as herewith or hereaf-

ter submitted to you by me in writing, you shall have no obligation or liability to me of any kind or character by reason of the production or distribution of such program(s), nor shall you be obligated to compensate me in connection therewith.

6. You agree that if you use any legally protectible portion of said program, provided it has not been obtained by you from, or independently created by, another source, you will pay me an amount that is comparable to the compensation normally paid by you for similar material or an amount equal to the fair market value thereof as of the date of this agreement, whichever is greater.

I acknowledge that but for my agreement to the above terms and conditions, you would not accede to my request to receive and consider the said program material that I am submitting to you herewith.

Very truly yours,

_____

_____

_____

Evaluation Agreement

Gentlemen:

I am submitting to you herewith the following material (hereinafter referred to as "said Material").

TITLE: _____

FORM OF MATERIAL
 Synopsis Screenplay   Radioplay
 Treatment Telescript   Other: _____

PRINCIPAL CHARACTERS: _____

_____

BRIEF SUMMARY OF THEME OR PLOT: _____

_____

_____

WGA REGISTRATION NO.: _____ NO. OF PAGES: _____

1. I request that you read and evaluate said material, and you hereby agree to do so, and you agree to advise me of your decision with respect to the material.

2. I warrant that I am the sole owner and author of said material, that I have the exclusive right and authority to submit the same to you upon the terms and conditions stated herein; and that all of the important features of said material are summarized herein. I will indemnify you of and from any and all claims, loss or liability that may be asserted against you or incurred by you, at any time, in connection with said material, or any use thereof.

3. I agree that nothing in this agreement nor the fact of my submission of said material to you shall be deemed to place you in any different position than anyone else to whom I have not submitted said material.

4. I understand that as a general rule you purchase literary properties through the established channels in the industry and not through a submission such as this. I recognize that you have access to and/or may create or have created literary materials and ideas which may be similar or identical to said material in theme, idea, plot, format or other respects. I agree that I will not be entitled to any compensation because of the use by you of any such similar or identical material which may have been independently created by you or may have come to you from any other independent source. I understand that

no confidential relationship is established by my submitting the material to you hereunder.

5. You agree that if you use any legally protectible portion of said material, provided it has not been obtained by you from, or independently created by, another source, you will pay me an amount that is comparable to the compensation normally paid by you for similar material or an amount equal to the fair market value thereof as of the date of this agreement, whichever is greater. If we are unable to agree as to said amount, or in the event of any dispute concerning any alleged use of said material or with reference to this agreement, such dispute will be submitted to arbitration.

6. I have retained at least one copy of said material, and I hereby release you of and from any and all liability for loss of, or damage to, the copies of said material submitted to you hereunder.

7. I enter into this agreement with the express understanding that you agree to read and evaluate said material in express reliance upon this agreement and my covenants, representatives and warranties contained herein, and that in the absence of such an agreement, you would not read or evaluate said material.

8. I hereby state that I have read and understand this agreement and that no oral representatives of any kind have been made to me, and that this agreement states our entire understanding with reference to the subject matter hereof. Any modification or waiver of any of the provisions of this agreement must be made in writing and signed by both of us.

9. If more than one party signs this agreement as submittor, the reference to "I" or "me" through this agreement shall apply to each party jointly and severally.

Very truly yours,

_____

Address

_____

City and State

_____

Telephone Number

_____

Signature

_____

Print Name

Accepted and Agreed to by

_____

Signature

Client-Agent Contract

1. I hereby employ you as my sole and exclusive literary agent for a period of _____ (not to exceed 7 years) from date hereof to negotiate contracts for the rendition of my professional services as a writer, or otherwise, in the fields of motion pictures, legitimate stage, radio broadcasting, television, and other fields of entertainment.

2. You hereby agree to advise and counsel me in the development and advancement of my professional career and to use reasonable efforts to procure employment and to negotiate for me, as aforesaid.

3. As compensation for your said services agreed to be rendered hereunder, I hereby agree to pay you a sum equal to ten percent (10%) of all moneys or things of value as and when received by me, directly or indirectly, as compensation for my professional services rendered or agreed to be rendered during the term hereof under contracts, or any extensions, renewals, modifications or substitutions thereof, entered into or negotiated during the term hereof and to pay the same to you thereafter for so long a time as I receive compensation on any such contracts, extensions, options or renewals of said contracts. It is expressly understood that to be entitled to continue to receive the payment of compensation on the aforementioned contracts after the termination of this agreement you shall remain obligated to serve me and to perform obligations with respect to said employment contracts or to extensions or renewals of said contracts or to any employment requiring my services on which such compensation is based.

4. I hereby agree that you may render your services to others during the term hereof.

5. In the event that I do not obtain a bona fide offer of employment from a responsible employer during a period of time in excess of four (4) consecutive months, during all of which said time I shall be ready, able, willing and available to accept employment, either party hereto shall have the right to terminate this contract by notice in writing to that effect sent to the other by registered or certified mail.

6. Controversies arising between us under the provisions of the California Labor Code relating to artists' managers and under the rules and regulations for the enforcement thereof shall be referred to the Labor Commission of the State of California, as provided in Section 1700.44 of the California Labor Code.

7. In the event that you shall collect from me a fee or expenses for obtaining employment for me, and I shall fail to procure such employment or shall fail to be paid for such employment you shall, upon demand therefore, repay to me the fee and the expenses so collected. Unless repayment thereof is made within forty-eight (48) hours after demand therefore, you shall pay to me an additional sum equal to the amount of the fee as provided in Section 1700.40 of the California Labor Code.

8. This instrument constitutes the entire agreement between us and no statement, promises or inducement made by any party hereto which is not contained herein shall be binding or valid and this contract may not be enlarged, modified or altered, except in writing by both the parties hereto; and provided further, that any substantial changes in this contract must first be approved by the Labor Commissioner.

9. You hereby agree to deliver to me an executed exact copy of this contract.

Dated _____

AGREED TO AND ACCEPTED BY:

[Talent Agency]	Name of Artist
[Address]	Address
[City and State]	City and State
[Social Security Number]	

Most agent-client contracts are signed for an initial period of one to two years, after which the contract must be renewed. One positive element of this contract is the four-month escape clause. Should the agent possess salable scripts but fail to sell them or secure other employment for you as a writer at a minimum level of $10,000, you can discharge the agent. This is particularly helpful when dealing with an agent who is not shopping your scripts around as much as possible. If the agent is exerting every possible effort, however, and something just hasn't clicked yet, you would be well advised to wait a while longer, perhaps as long as nine months or so. The benefit to the agent here is that if you as a writer fail to provide anything, or anything that is marketable, the agent can terminate the contract and move on to more rewarding clients.

Once you've secured representation, you should attempt to pick the agent's brain as much as you can without becoming an irritation. A good agent will provide a list of producers she has worked with before and can sell to again; can instruct you in the best way to "pitch" your particular idea; can tell you what is currently hottest in the marketplace; and can direct your energies into the areas where you stand the greatest chance of succeeding.

Although it's possible to go it alone (over 90 percent of all my script sales have been done without the benefit of an agent, although I do have one now—actually two, one on the East Coast and one on the West Coast) a good agent can be a powerful ally.

BABYLON 5
"The Coming of Shadows"
Show #209
Written by J. Michael Straczynski

CAST

CHARACTER	ACTOR
SHERIDAN	BRUCE BOXLEITNER
IVANOVA	CLAUDIA CHRISTIAN
GARIBALDI	JERRY DOYLE
DELENN	MIRA FURLAN
G'KAR	ANDREAS KATSULAS
LONDO	PETER JURASIK
DR. FRANKLIN	RICHARD BIGGS
VIR	STEPHEN FURST
REFA	WILLIAM FORWARD
CENTAURI EMPEROR	TURHAN BEY
CENTAURI PRIME MINISTER	MALACHI THRONE
CUSTOMS GUARD (#1)	BRYAN MICHAEL MCGUIRE
RANGER	FREDRIC LEHNE
KHA'MAK (NARN)	NEIL BRADLEY
NARN PILOT #1	KIM STRAUSS
NARN PILOT #2	JONATHAN CHAPMAN
ZACK ALLAN	JEFF CONAWAY

POST
| VOICE OF KOSH | ARDWRIGHT CHAMBERLAIN |

BABYLON 5
"The Coming of Shadows"
Show #209

SETS

INTERIOR
CENTAURI
     CENTAURI PALACE GRAND CHAMBER
BABYLON 5
     SHERIDAN'S OFFICE
     CUSTOMS AREA
     LONDO'S QUARTERS
     DOWNBELOW
     DOCKING BAY (CGI)
     G'KAR'S QUARTERS
     BLUE CORRIDOR
     SANCTUARY
     CENTRAL CORRIDOR
     GARDEN/ROTUNDA (CGI/COMPOSITE)
     ROTUNDA
     CREW CORRIDOR
     MEDLAB/HALLWAY BETWEEN INFIRMARY & MEDLAB
     NARN FIGHTER *
     ZOCALO
     NARN FIGHTER
     GARIBALDI'S OFFICE
     OBSERVATION DOME
     GREEN SECTOR HALLWAY
     COUNCIL CHAMBERS
     DELENN'S QUARTERS

EXTERIOR
SPACE
     NEAR CENTAURI PALACE
     CENTAURI CAPITAL
     JUMPGATE
     CENTUARI PRIME
     PLANETSIDE
     NARN CITY (CGI)/ANGLE ON PLANET

SHADOWMAN VESSELS
QUADRANT 14
NARN JUMPGATE
BABYLON 5—ESTABLISHING & TRANSITIONAL
    (CGI/COMPOSITE)
    SUN (CGI/COMPOSITE)
    STAR WITH HAND (CGI)
    JUMPGATE

BABYLON 5
"The Coming of Shadows"
TEASER

FADE IN:

EXT. SPACE—NEAR CENTAURI PRIME

A CENTAURI WARSHIP passes THROUGH FRAME, then we TILT AND PAN DOWN to the planet below. SUPERIMPOSE: Centauri Prime (Homeworld, Centauri Republic). The world is half in eclipse, half out. In the night regions, we should see, even from here, the light of cities along the coastlands in those areas free of clouds. PUSH IN and DISSOLVE THROUGH TO:

EXT. CENTAURI CAPITAL

A HIGH SHOT of the city, with art deco-like architecture, somewhere between the round skyscrapers of Buck Rogers and Empire's Cloud City. Green parks and open spaces, a nearby bay. Ostentatious, like all things Centauri. One item in particular catches our eye: a huge PALACE that rises out of the surrounding terrain. We PUSH IN on it.

INT. PALACE—GRAND CHAMBER

(Use newly acquired palace set.) START on a pair of double doors that OPEN to reveal a CENTAURI PRIME MINISTER. He is in his fifties or sixties, Earth-time, dignified, serious. He enters the huge room, which is spare, but elegant, white drapes hanging from the ceiling and arching across to the walls, where they tumble down along the sides of the walls. PAN AROUND to REVEAL the dominant feature in the room, which is an elevated throne. Like the rest of the room, it is simple but elegant; there is the sense that this throne has been around a long, long time. There's not much else in the place; it's really more of a receiving room than a functional room. FOUR white-veiled Centauri Women stand on either side of the throne, looking down, hands folded. On the throne is the CEN-TAURI EMPEROR, in his sixties or seventies, frail but dignified, eyes closed, hands folded in his lap. Most noticeably, he has little or no remaining hair.

The Prime Minister stops in front of the throne. Clears his throat. Nothing. Starts to do so again when:

EMPEROR

I'm not asleep.

And now his eyes open, and there is a small smile on his face. This is a good and gentle man.

PRIME MINISTER

My apologies, majesty. I meant no offense.

EMPEROR

Is everything ready?

PRIME MINISTER

Yes. The royal liner is standing by, and we have adequate warships for protection. They're prepared to set forth as soon as we arrive.

EMPEROR

As soon as I arrive. You will remain here.

PRIME MINISTER

I must protest—

EMPEROR

As I expected. But someone must remain here in case there's a crisis, and as my prime minister, you are next in the line of authority.

PRIME MINISTER

I wish you would change your mind. The doctors say your condition is delicate . . . the least stress—

EMPEROR

All the more reason to go now, while I still can. What remains of our empire stretches before me, and I would see it one more time before I die. What I must do cannot wait any longer.

He rises. The Women on either side move with him. One of them unfolds an ornate hairpiece. We don't need to see all of it, just enough to see what it is.

EMPEROR

No need for that. When you get as old as I am, the trap-pings of status don't mean as much as they used to. I sometimes think that our women are right to shave their heads and rise above such things.

PRIME MINISTER

Majesty—

EMPEROR

I will go among them as I am.
There is nothing more to discuss.

He stops, looks around at the room. Smiles, albeit sadly.

EMPEROR

Thank you for taking care of all this again while I sail beyond the sunset one last time. You've given the pilot our first destination?
(Prime Minister nods)
Good. You've always served me well, old friend, and I think sometimes I do not thank you as much as I should.
(beat)
Goodbye.

And with a smile, the Emperor moves toward the huge double doors, which part as he approaches. On the face of his Prime Minister, which wells with emotion, suspecting as we do, that he will never see his emperor again, we go to

EXT. BABYLON 5 - ESTABLISHING

Just a BEAT UNDER:

G'KAR
(vo)
This is absolutely intolerable!

INT. SHERIDAN'S OFFICE

SHERIDAN sits back, watching with some interest as a pacing, furious G'KAR goes through a display of anger that could take three years off your life just watching it.

G'KAR

This visit by the Centauri Emperor is completely unacceptable to my government! He is a monster, an aberration, a criminal! His family is directly responsible for

stripmining my world! His father personally ordered the
execution of a hundred thousand Narns!

SHERIDAN

But he <u>himself</u> did nothing, am I correct?

G'KAR

A technicality!

SHERIDAN

In fact, unless I'm mistaken, the current Emperor has
gone out of his way to offer your world concessions and
return lost territory—

G'KAR

<u>Stolen</u> territory!

SHERIDAN

Whatever. Look, I appreciate the fact that a hundred
years of blood isn't something you forget about overnight.
But the bottom line is that it's not my problem. This
station is open to everyone. If the Emperor wants to visit
Babylon 5, I think that's great. It raises our visibility, and
helps the folks back home think that maybe we're doing
some good.

Sheridan rises, moves toward G'Kar.

G'KAR

So you're going to allow this even over my objections.

SHERIDAN

(looks around)

Did I suddenly turn invisible or something? <u>Yes</u>, Ambassador, the Centauri Emperor will be allowed to come
aboard. If that bothers you, then I suggest you hide in
your quarters, stick your fingers in your ears and hum real
loud until it's over. Unless you'd like to try something as
breathtakingly rational as trying to open up a dialogue.
You're in a position to negotiate directly with the head
of the Centauri Republic, and you're wasting it on a
tantrum.

He's eye-to-eye with G'Kar. Finally, G'Kar sighs . . . and there is something fatalistic in his expression.

> G'KAR
>
> I shouldn't have expected you to understand, Captain.
> My mistake. I will not make it again.

G'Kar starts away when:

> SHERIDAN
>
> G'Kar . . . don't do something we'll both regret.

> G'KAR
>
> It's too late for that, Captain. Too late by far.

And with that, G'Kar exits, and we

FADE OUT.

<u>END TEASER</u>

ACT ONE

FADE IN:

EXT. BABYLON 5

Just a BEAT to establish, then:

INT. CUSTOMS AREA

A Human comes through customs, stopping beside one of the CUSTOMS GUARDS, who scans his card. This is a RANGER, one of those whom we've seen in the BG in prior episodes. As the Guard checks his identicard:

> CUSTOMS GUARD #1
> Back again, eh? That's three times this month.

> RANGER
> I do a lot of business here.

> CUSTOMS GUARD #1
> Anything I can help you with?

And then the Ranger looks OS.

HIS POV - GARIBALDI

as GARIBALDI moves THROUGH FRAME, talking to someone, although we can't hear him.

BACK TO SCENE

as the Ranger takes back his identicard.

> RANGER
> No, thank you. I've found what I'm looking for.

And with that, the Ranger moves off.

INT. LONDO'S QUARTERS

LONDO stands off to one side, listening, as REFA paces the room. VIR sits off to one side, listening with a subtle apprehension.

> REFA
> —and after the Emperor has made his speech, I've arranged for him to give you an audience. The whole thing will be recorded.

LONDO

Does he know what it's about?

REFA

He believes it's nothing more than a progress report on
your situation here. We've taken the liberty of writing
your speech for you.

He hands Londo a datacrystal.

REFA

I've had experts in psycholinguistics working on it for
weeks. It's perfect; fiery but dignified; elegant, but strong.
It outlines the decline of our government and our need
for change. It also makes a few predictions about what
will go wrong next with the economy, the military. . . .

LONDO

And these predictions, they will come true?

REFA

Already arranged.

Londo exchanges a glance with Vir, who looks down, away, wanting to be
anywhere else in the universe but in this room.

LONDO

Sabotage . . . ?

REFA

A word or two in the right ear, a critical food shipment
delayed . . . the method is unimportant. All that matters
is that when it comes true, the Emperor will look weak
and short-sighted, whereas we have our eyes on the
future.

Londo considers this, holding the datacrystal out and peering into its fac-
eted depths.

LONDO

You're asking quite a lot of me; after giving this speech,
I will not exactly be in favor with the Emperor and his
court.

> REFA
>
> True . . . for as long as he's alive. Which shouldn't be
> much longer. He's never quite recovered from the death
> of his son, and I'm told his health is fragile at best. When
> he passes, all that will remain is the memory that we
> were right. We must position ourselves to move in when
> the time is right. Image is everything, Mollari. Well, I'll
> leave you to study the speech. If you have any questions,
> you know where to find me.

And Refa exits. Londo slowly turns his attention from the datacrystal to
Vir.

> LONDO
>
> This conversation makes you uncomfortable?

> VIR
>
> Yes, it does.

> LONDO
>
> Then for once, we have something in common.
>   (beat)
> I am an old man . . . what is lost by trying? As the humans
> say, "Who dares, wins."

> VIR
>
> Who dares sometimes gets his head cut off and stuck on
> a pike.

Londo nods, understanding the stakes here, and closes his hand around
the datacrystal as we go to

EXT. SPACE - JUMPGATE

As the jumpgate opens, and the Centauri liner flashes out, accompanied
before and after by three Warship escorts.

INT. DOWNBELOW

The Ranger waits. It's a disreputable area, shadowed and isolated. He fits
right in. Then we HEAR footsteps. He straightens as a figure in a dark,
cowled robe approaches. With a subtle move, a long, thin-bladed knife
slides out of his sleeve and into his hand. He doesn't bare it, doesn't make
a threatening move, only waits.

The figure stops in front of him. Pulls back the cowl. It's DELENN. The Ranger relaxes slightly at the sight.

> DELENN
> Did you bring it?

He hands her a datacrystal.

> RANGER
> The message you were waiting for. I'm to tell you . . . it's from an old friend.
> (beat)
> What about the weapons?

> DELENN
> It is difficult. But I believe I can get you what you need.

EXT. BABYLON 5

The Centauri ships are parked alongside Babylon 5, too large to fit inside. A SHUTTLE emerges from the liner and moves toward the docking bay. We FOLLOW IT, then reverse into

INT. DOCKING BAY (CGI)

As the shuttle drops down into and through one of the bay doors toward the landing areas elsewhere.

INT. CUSTOMS AREA

The place has been cleared of all civilians. Security Guards line the entrances, and stand at attention beside the main door. Sheridan, Garibaldi, Ivanova and FRANKLIN are all there, still in dress uniforms. One of the Guards approaches Garibaldi, whispers to him. Garibaldi nods, and the Guard moves off.

> GARIBALDI
> (to Sheridan)
> He's in. The bay is secure.

> SHERIDAN
> Initiate Pomp and Circumstance, Commander.

She toggles her link, and the customs area fills with the CENTAURI AN-THEM. As the music plays, there's a BEAT, and then the doors open. The

Emperor enters, accompanied by two of the Veiled Women, as before, and a number of Centauri Elite Guards, who wear stylized, almost ancient or traditional looking helmets (not funny big hair helmets, regular looking).

He approaches Sheridan, stops, extends both hands.

> EMPEROR
> On behalf of the Centauri Republic, I offer the hands of friendship.

> SHERIDAN
> On behalf of the Earth Alliance, I accept.

They clasp at the forearms and slightly bow, then move apart as Sheridan introduces his staff. (As they're introduced, they bow slightly.)

> SHERIDAN
> This is my second, Commander Susan Ivanova . . . Chief of Security Michael Garibaldi . . . and Dr. Stephen Franklin, Chief of Staff of our Medlab facility.

> EMPEROR
> An honor. News of the work you are doing here has reached even into the Royal Palace on Centauri Prime. I am deeply moved by the knowledge that you would choose to stand in harm's way in the interests of peace.

> IVANOVA
> Thank you.

> SHERIDAN
> If you'd like to come this way, we can begin your tour.

> EMPEROR
> Yes, of course. . . .

They start out, Garibaldi hanging back, eyes all over the place, trusting nothing. The Emperor reaches out and, much to his surprise, touches Franklin's arm.

> EMPEROR
> Tell me, Doctor, have you seen much of the Vorlon . . . I believe his name is Kosh?

DR. FRANKLIN

No, no more than anyone else. He's always inside that encounter suit of his. Why?

EMPEROR

I have never seen a Vorlon before, in or out of his shell. Over the centuries we sent many expeditions into Vorlon space. None of them returned. I have heard many strange stories about them. . . .

SHERIDAN

Well, with any luck, Ambassador Kosh will attend the reception along with the other ambassadors.

EMPEROR

But you're not sure . . . ?

SHERIDAN

With Kosh, it's hard to be sure about much of <u>anything</u>.

And they head away.

INT. G'KAR'S QUARTERS

On the monitor appears another Narn, this one high in the government. Call him KHA'MAK. G'Kar is in his doublet.

KHA'MAK

The first circle of the Kha'ri have concluded their deliberations. After much debate, they have endorsed your plan.

G'KAR

Good.

KHA'MAK

G'Quan bless you and hold you in his hands. May he protect you from harm as you do what must be done.

G'KAR

When does the Kha'ri feel would be the best time?

KHA'MAK

The reception, just before he gives his speech. There will be greater exposure. Are you still prepared to go through with this?

G'KAR

Yes. It is a strange feeling to know, suddenly, that all of
the decisions in your life have brought you to this
place . . . that there is no longer doubt, or uncertainty.
The future now consists of only three probabilities.

And from a drawer or bureau or box, he removes a cloth-covered object . . .
a dagger, carven elaborately in Narn tradition. He raises it slowly,
slowly. . . .

G'KAR

I will stand . . . and I will turn . . . and I will strike. In
that moment the Emperor and I will both die . . . or he
will die and I will spend my life in prison . . . or I will
fail, and be killed. For the first time in my life, the path
is clear . . . the path is clear.

And the dagger is before his face, and we are CLOSE as we

FADE OUT.

<u>END ACT ONE</u>

ACT TWO

FADE IN:

EXT. BABYLON 5 (CGI/COMPOSITE)

PUSHING IN on the Sanctuary window, until we SEE the Emperor in the window, looking out into space.

INT. BABYLON 5 - BLUE CORRIDOR

Two Centauri Imperial Guards stand on either side of the door as Sheridan approaches with one of the Veiled Centauri Women. The Guards move together, blocking the door.

> SHERIDAN
> He asked to see me.

They look to the Veiled Woman, who nods. They move apart to permit admission. Sheridan approaches the door, which opens as he enters

INT. SANCTUARY

The Emperor stands, alone, looking at the stars, just as we last saw him. Sheridan enters, the door closes behind him.

> SHERIDAN
> Your majesty.

> EMPEROR
> Captain.

The Emperor hesitates, and Sheridan can see that there is something else. He approaches, coming up alongside the Emperor and looking out.

> EMPEROR
> May I ask you a question?

> SHERIDAN
> Depends on the question, I guess.

> EMPEROR
> Why are you here . . . in this place, in that uniform? Was
> it your choice, or were you pressed into service?

> SHERIDAN
> It was my choice. The planetary draft didn't start until
> the War, a few years later. I guess I wanted to serve some-

thing that was bigger than I was . . . maybe even make
a difference somewhere, somehow.
(beat)
I was thinking of your comment when you came aboard.
You seem very interested in why people chose to be here.

EMPEROR

It has occurred to me recently that I have never chosen
anything. I was born into a role that had been prepared
for me; I did as I was instructed; married who I was told
to marry; took up the role of emperor when my father
died; served as husband, father, ruler. . . . I did all I was
asked, because it never occurred to me to choose otherwise. And now, at the end of my life . . . I wonder what
might have been.

SHERIDAN

I think we all feel that way, from time to time. That's
why my father taught me to live each second as if it were
the last moment of my life. He said if you love, love
without reservation; if you fight, fight without fear. He
called it the way of the warrior.

EMPEROR

No regrets, then?

SHERIDAN

A few . . . but just a few. You?

EMPEROR

Enough to fill a lifetime.
(points to stars)
There was a time when all this was ours. So much has
been lost, so much forgotten . . . so much blood, so much
pain . . . for what, I wonder? The past tempts us, the
present confuses us, the future frightens us . . . and our
lives slip away, moment by moment . . . lost in the vast,
terrible, in-between.
(beat)
But there's still time to seize that last, fragile, moment . . .
and choose something better. To make a difference, as
you say. And I intend to.

The Emperor turns, and there is a light in his eyes, the look of a man who has seen beyond the edge of his life, to a dream beyond.

> EMPEROR
> I look forward to seeing you at the reception tonight, Captain. I think you will see something . . . most extraordinary.

And with that, the Emperor heads away. Sheridan watches him go, then glances back at the stars, as we go to

INT. CENTRAL CORRIDOR

As Garibaldi walks with a cluster of other Security Guards.

> GARIBALDI
> I want this whole section cleared, every entrance and exit checked and re-checked. They'll be coming down any second, and until then, nobody gets in without proper ID. I don't care if you recognize them by sight or not.

And he continues away. As he passes, we PAN ACROSS to a side entrance to the corridor, where we SEE the Ranger, watching, watching. . . .

INT. G'KAR'S QUARTERS

G'Kar is speaking to the monitor, which is recording his words (would be nice if we could see his words appearing on-screen in Narnish as he speaks). He idly touches the dagger atop his desk.

> G'KAR
> —I take this action without the knowledge or permission of my government. Neither should my aide, Na'Toth, be held accountable for my actions. The responsibility is mine alone. I ask that my remains, and my personal property, be sent back to Narn, to my family. My copy of the Book of G'Quan I leave to Na'Toth, in the hope of her eventual enlightenment.

He switches off the console. Sits back, closes his eyes.

INT. GARDEN/ROTUNDA (CGI)

PUSHING IN on the Rotunda which rises out of the Garden.

INT. ROTUNDA

The place is packed with Human VIPs, plus the following: Londo, Delenn, Refa, and in a separate cluster, Franklin, Sheridan, and Ivanova. There is much food and drink.

                    SHERIDAN
          So what's the deal on those veiled Centuari women that
          follow the emperor around?

                    IVANOVA
          Londo says they're telepaths, raised together since birth.
          They're linked 24 hours a day, no matter how far apart
          they are. What one sees, the others see. Traditionally,
          when the emperor leaves, two go with him, and two stay
          behind.

                    DR. FRANKLIN
          Interesting . . . it guarantees that he knows what's hap-
          pening at home, and keeps the royal court up to speed
          on what he's doing.

                    IVANOVA
          Did the Emperor tell you what this important speech is
          about?

                    SHERIDAN
          No, he just said it was important. I hoped that might be
          enough to bring out Ambassador Kosh; looks like I was
          wrong.

                    IVANOVA
          Too bad, considering what the Emperor said about the
          Vorlons. He might never get another chance to see one.
          But I suppose it was too much to hope for.

                    DR. FRANKLIN
          Speaking of too much to hope for . . . look who just
          walked in.

They turn, and there is G'Kar, who enters in full diplomatic dress. Sheridan approaches.

                    SHERIDAN
          Ambassador.

> ### G'KAR
> Captain.

> ### SHERIDAN
> I see you've changed your mind about opening up a
> dialogue.

> ### G'KAR
> I make no promises . . . but I will hear what he has to
> say.

> ### SHERIDAN
> That's all anyone could ask for.

With that, Sheridan moves away. G'Kar scopes out the room, looks to the raised platform where the Emperor will speak.

INT. CREW CORRIDOR

Garibaldi walks PAST CAMERA. A moment later, the Ranger also moves past camera. Following him

AROUND A CORNER

Suddenly Garibaldi grabs him, shoves him against the wall.

> ### GARIBALDI
> Okay, pal, you've got ten seconds to explain why you're
> following me.

> ### RANGER
> I need to talk to you.

> ### GARIBALDI
> About what?

The Ranger looks like he's about to answer when two other guards come on the run.

> ### GARIBALDI
> It's okay, I got him.
> > (to Ranger)
> Okay, you said you had to talk to me. About what?

But now the Ranger goes quiet. Looks away.

GARIBALDI

That's what I figured.

(to the Guards)

Take him down to holding and keep him there until the reception's over.

He turns the Ranger over to the Guards, who nudge him forward as we go to

INT. CENTRAL CORRIDOR

The place has been cleared. The Emperor, his Imperial Guards, and the Veiled Women move into the corridor, heading for the transport tubes at the other end.

INT. ROTUNDA - INTERCUT

Laughter, conversation, Londo and Refa off to one side, talking in hushed tones.

INT. CENTRAL CORRIDOR - INTERCUT

CLOSE on the Emperor coming into frame. CAMERA SLIGHTLY OVERCRANKED.

INT. ROTUNDA - INTERCUT

Delenn approaches G'Kar . . . but he sees her coming and angles away, his thoughts dark and obsessed.

INT. CENTRAL CORRIDOR

The Emperor, surrounded by his entourage, comes closer into frame . . . CAMERA SLIGHTLY OVERCRANKED . . . when he suddenly stops, clutches at his chest. Pain. The wind knocked out of him. His knees weaken. He goes down, clutching at one of the Veiled Women as he falls. One of the Veiled Women SCREAMS, all SLOW-SLOW-SLOW as

ECU - THE EMPEROR - SLOW MOTION

As his head comes to rest on the floor, unconscious.

INT. ROTUNDA

ON Sheridan and Delenn, talking, as Sheridan looks to

ANGLE - DR. FRANKLIN

Who gets a call on his link, speaks into it. We see sudden concern on his face, and he sprints for the door.

ANGLE - ON SHERIDAN

And from his look, he knows instantly that something is wrong, very wrong. PUSH IN as we GO TO

INT. CENTAURI PALACE

The Prime Minister sits on the throne, speaking softly with two Minbari and one Human, when the door opens. In come two of the Veiled Women, heads downcast. The Prime Minister stops dead when he sees them. They approach across the floor, coming to rest on either side of him. He looks from one to the other, and his hand covers his face in grief.

EXT. BABYLON 5 - TRANSITIONAL

With the Centuari warships and liner parked outside.

INT. MEDLAB

The Emperor is hooked up to a medbed, eyes closed, as Dr. Franklin enters. The two Veiled Women stand behind the bed, eyes downcast. Franklin goes to him, lightly touches his arm.

> DR. FRANKLIN
> Your majesty. . . .

Slowly, the Emperor's eyes open, find Franklin.

> DR. FRANKLIN
> I wish I'd known of your condition when you arrived. I
> could've done something . . . tried something . . .
> (beat)
> Your government is asking to have you transferred to
> your warship, I told them that moving you right now
> could be fatal. I want your permission to—

The Emperor raises a hand, softly, as if to say, "enough." In his eyes is resignation, he knows he has little time left. When he finally speaks, his voice is a whisper.

> EMPEROR
> There is something . . . more important than where I die.
> A message you must give for me.

DR. FRANKLIN

If it's important, perhaps one of your own people—

EMPEROR

No . . . if I did, the message might never be delivered. Listen to me, Doctor, listen carefully. . . .

And as Franklin leans in:

INT. LONDO'S QUARTERS

Refa paces, Londo and Vir also present.

REFA

This changes everything. We have to move quickly.

LONDO

I agree. I hear word of this has already reached homeworld.

REFA

Our competitors are mvoing into position, setting themselves up to ascend the throne the moment he dies. Before that happens we have to rise above the others . . . we must do something extraordinary, something unparalleled. . . .

LONDO
(realization)
He said . . . just pick a target . . .

REFA

I'm sorry . . . ?

Londo knows what he has to do . . . and he also knows the possible massive ramifications of what he is about to say. This must have weight to it. With the following words, the future is forever altered. Vir sees what's coming, like a man watching an accident in slow motion. Londo turns, moves off a bit.

LONDO

I believe there is a Narn colony on the border of Centauri space . . . Quadrant 14. . . .

VIR

Londo. . . .

> REFA

Colony . . . it's a listening post! They've been using it to spy on us for years! By all rights, that entire planet should be ours!

> LONDO

Then let us take it back.

This stops Refa cold. He studies Londo.

> REFA

Our military experts have told us the colony is armed to the teeth; we couldn't take it without a major assault. . . . We would lose thousands of lives. . . .

> LONDO

I will take care of it. Have your contacts in the military send an expedition to Quadrant 14.

> REFA

I can only guarantee a few ships—

> LONDO

It will be enough.

> REFA

I hope you know what you're doing, Mollari.

And Refa exits. Londo walks away from Vir.

> LONDO

Find Mr. Morden. Bring him here.

> VIR

Londo . . . don't do this.

> LONDO

I have no choice.

> VIR

Yes, you do! Londo, please, I know you don't listen to me, but I'm asking you, this once . . . don't do this. Once you start down this road there's no going back. You—

> LONDO

Do I have to go find him myself?

They're eye to eye. Finally, Vir sighs, shakes his head.

                    VIR
          No . . . I'll go. I'll go and I'll bring him here. And some-
          day, Londo, I will remind you of this conversation.
          Maybe . . . maybe then you'll understand.

And with that, Vir exits. When he's gone:

                    LONDO
               (half to himself)
          I understand just fine.
               (beat)
          By this time tomorrow, we will be at war with the Narn.
          May the Great Maker forgive me. . . .

And on Londo's pained, doomed expression, we

                                        FADE OUT.

                    END ACT TWO

ACT THREE

FADE IN:

EXT. BABYLON 5 - ESTABLISHING

The Centauri warships and liner still parked alongside. PUSH PAST
THEM to the station and DISSOLVE THROUGH TO:

INT. G'KAR'S QUARTERS

Where G'Kar is practically apoplectic speaking to the wall monitor, on
which we SEE the same Narn as before.

>   G'KAR
> I was ready . . . I had prepared myself . . . I had made my
> peace with the universe, put all my affairs in order. . . .
> I had the dagger in my hand . . . and he has the indecency
> to start dying on his own! Never in my entire life have
> I seen a case of worse timing! You'd think he could've
> waited a few more minutes before—

He's interrupted by the doorbell.

>   G'KAR
> Who is it?

>   DR. FRANKLIN
>   (os)
> Dr. Franklin.

>   G'KAR
> Maybe it's good news . . . with luck he's feeling better . . .
> all they have to do is prop him up for two minutes. . . .
> I'll call you back. Enter!

G'Kar toggles off. The door opens, and Franklin enters.

>   DR. FRANKLIN
> I just came from seeing the Centauri Emperor.

>   G'KAR
> How is the poor fellow? I was so looking forward to meet-
> ing him and opening up a dialogue.

> DR. FRANKLIN
>
> Funny, he was looking forward to meeting you, too. He
> had a message for you. Given his present condition, he's
> asked me to relay that message for him.

> G'KAR
>
> I have no time for threats—

> DR. FRANKLIN
>
> He wanted to say that he's sorry.

And this is the <u>last</u> thing G'Kar ever expected to hear. You could knock
him over with a feather.

> G'KAR
>
> What?

> DR. FRANKLIN
>
> He came all the way out here, risked his health, endan-
> gered his life, so he could stand beside a Narn, in neutral
> territory, and apologize . . . for all the things the Centauri
> have done to your people, for all the things his family
> did. He said, "We were wrong. We knew we were wrong
> when we were there and when we left, but we never said
> it. The hatred between our people can never end until
> someone is willing to say, 'I'm sorry,' and try to find a
> way to make it right again, to atone for our actions."

G'Kar sits heavily, astonished.

> DR. FRANKLIN
>
> He said it was the only choice he'd ever made in his
> life . . . and now that seems to have been taken away
> from him.

> G'KAR
>
> I had . . . I had no idea. . . .

> DR. FRANKLIN
>
> No, I'm sure you didn't . . . and maybe that's the biggest
> tragedy in the whole damned story.
>> (beat)
> Goodnight, Ambassador.

And with that, Franklin exits, leaving behind a stunned and shattered G'Kar.

EXT. BABYLON 5 - TRANSITIONAL

The station moves into eclipse, the sun fading.

INT. LONDO'S QUARTERS

Londo sits, asleep, a drink in his hand. PUSH IN on him, and DISSOLVE INTO:

START DREAM MONTAGE

The destruction of the monitoring station at Raghesh 3.

Londo in the coucil chambers from "Chrysalis."

> LONDO
> Keep this up, Ambassador, and soon you won't have a
> planet to protect.

EXT. SUN (CGI)

A red sun burns hot . . . and from the sun comes the specter of a dark hand, thousands of miles across, flames licking the edges, seeming to turn slightly and grasp (DO NOT USE A CGI CONSTRUCT FOR THE HAND; ROTOSCOPE A REAL HAND).

EST. CENTAURI PRIME

A quick shot, then:

DOWNSHOT - LONDO

Standing in the open air as he shields his eyes, looks up to the sky.

UPSHOT - THE SKY

As a squadron of full-scale Shadowmen vessels fly overhead.

INT. CENTAURI PALACE - GRAND CHAMBER

CLOSE on Londo as he bows to receive a simple crown, a loop of metal with a single gem in the front, over the forehead. The room is white, bright. Londo looks up

REVERSE

The same palace room is dark, splotches of red and black lighting, shadowed, the tapestries and veils torn, hanging.

ON LONDO

As he looks around . . . and he is a much older Londo, sitting on the throne, tired, his hair streaked with grey, a pallor in his face.

HIS POV - A DARK WALL

And we see slitted EYES seemingly peering out of nowhere in the darkness.

BACK ON LONDO

As he looks forward again.

REVERSE

G'Kar stands before Londo. G'Kar is older, and one eye is covered with a patch, his face marked by a scar.

EXT. STAR WITH HAND (CGI)

As the hand reaches fully out until it nearly touches us.

CLOSE - LONDO AND G'KAR

Their hands wrapped around one another's throats, face to face, on the floor, strangling the life out of one another.

INT. LONDO'S QUARTERS <u>END OF DREAM MONTAGE</u>

Londo awakes with a start, looks around.

> LONDO
> The time . . . what is the time . . . ?

He grabs a small clock, looks at it.

> LONDO
> It's begun.

Mollari rises, heads OS.

EXT. SPACE - PLANETSIDE

A Narn cruiser is silhouetted against the planet, with a number of other Narn ships and an orbiting Narn base nearby. Superimpose: <u>Narn Colony, Quadrant 14</u>.

ANOTHER ANGLE (CGI)

As three Shadowmen vessels PHASE INTO VIEW . . . and they come in FIRING.

ON THE STATION

As it's hit, ships zipping out of the way of the debris like bees.

THE BATTLE

A Ron Thornton special. Absolute carnage, worse by far than the assault on Quadrant 37.

INT. NARN FIGHTER

The NARN PILOT #1 REACTS to the OS BURST of light from the explosion.

> NARN PILOT #1
>
> By G'Lan. . . .
>> (beat)
> Break away! Break off!
>> (beat)
> Attack! All wings, attack!
>> (beat)
> Keep them away from the colony!
> Can't let them get past us!
>> (beat)
> Shrock, no . . . where are they coming from? What are they?!

Then, with almost all of his forces gone, he gives a long YELL, as his ship FIRES at the incoming shadow vessels . . . and we PUSH IN on his yell as red-blue LIGHT fills the screen, and his ship is destroyed.

EXT. NARN CITY (CGI)

Three-quarters shot, high-angle. We only SEE the Narn city for a moment as a BEAM suddenly arcs in from space and BLASTS it.

EXT. ANGLE ON PLANET

And where the beam struck, the planet ERUPTS in a blast that is similar in appearance to the volcanoes on Io: seen in silhouette, a geyser against space.

EXT. SPACE - SHADOWMEN VESSELS

As they finish blowing the last Narn ships to hell . . . and PHASE out of view.

INT. BABYLON 5 - ZOCALO

Londo walks with Refa, their voices low.

> REFA
>
> You're sure it's done?

> LONDO
>
> Yes. The Narns should be hearing about it soon. Our forces can move in at any time.

> REFA
>
> Then I'll have to move quickly. There's still one more thing I have to take care of back home . . . an obstacle to remove.

> LONDO
>
> What's that?

> REFA
>
> Better you don't know.

Refa heads quickly off. Londo, tired, starts to turn away when he HEARS:

> G'KAR
> (os)
>
> Mollari!

He turns to see G'Kar lumbering after him. Fearing the worst, Londo picks up his pace, heads for the transport tubes. The door closes before he can get to it, and G'Kar catches up to him.

> G'KAR
>
> You!

> LONDO
>
> I can explain everything—

> G'KAR
>
> I am going to buy you . . . a drink!

And he practically drags Londo to the bar, sits him down.

> LONDO
>
> I don't—I'm not sure I—

During the following, as what this is about dawns on Londo, his torment and discomfort grows exponentially.

> G'KAR
>
> Sit, Mollari. It's not everyday I get a revelation, you know. I've heard something that makes me think there may be hope for us after all. I'd believed your people capable of only murder and pain. But apparently there is still a spark of decency in your genetic code. It's not much of a foundation, I'll grant you that, but it's a start.

A pair of drinks are delivered. G'Kar takes one, hands the other to Londo.

> G'KAR
>
> I never thought I would be saying this, Mollari, but . . . to the health of your Emperor . . . and, perhaps, to your health as well.

He clicks Londo's glass. Londo is in terrible psychological pain, knowing what G'Kar doesn't know about what's coming.

> LONDO
>
> To the Emperor.
>   (beat)
> Thank you.

They drink. Londo wishes he were at the bottom of a deep hole somewhere.

EXT. QUADRANT 14

As several Centauri warships come out of jump, surrounded by a flurry of fighters.

WIDEN as they move through a cloud of debris . . . ruined Narn fighters, cruisers, absolute carnage.

EXT. NARN JUMPGATE

As it FLASHES, and out comes a dozen or so Narn fighters. They must emerge in a different direction than the Centauri cruisers, so they don't see them at first.

> NARN FIGHTER
> (vo)
We've lost the distress signal.

INT. NARN FIGHTER

NARN FIGHER #2 sits at the controls . . . devastated by what he sees.

> NARN FIGHTER #2
No . . . destroyed . . . all of it gone. . . . Who could have
done this? Who—

> NARN FIGHTER
> (vo)
Centauri warships detected! Closing fast!

> NARN FIGHTER #2
Centauri!? Alert homeworld! Prepare to attack!

> NARN FIGHTER
> (vo)
Sir, we're outnumbered! We don't have a chance!

> NARN FIGHTER #2
Then we die with honor!

EXT. SPACE

As the Narn fighters swing around, and begin heading toward the vastly
overwhelming Centauri forces. They haven't got a chance in hell.

INT. CENTAURI PALACE - GRAND CHAMBER

The Prime Minister walks the room, touches the throne, his thoughts far
away, concerned. Suddenly the room is plunged into darkness. He wheels
around.

HIS POV

Three or four Centauri stand silhouetted against the light of the doorway
behind them. We can see only their shapes.

> PRIME MINISTER
> (os)
Who is it? Who's there?

As one, they begin to move forward.

REVERSE - ON THE PRIME MINISTER

Backing away, but nowhere to go, as their shadows fall across him.

PRIME MINISTER

Guards! Guards!

CLOSE ANGLE

As a KNIFE pierces the Prime Minister's ribs. PAN UP QUICKLY to where his eyes are wide in pain . . . and yet somehow sad . . . as he slowly slides OUT OF FRAME.

LOW ANGLE SHOT

Shooting past the motionless Prime Minister, on the floor, to where the Silhouetted Figures move out of the room, their work completed.

INT. GARIBALDI'S OFFICE

A tired Garibaldi rubs his eyes as ZACK ALLAN enters.

ZACK ALLAN

The prisoner is asking to speak to you again.

GARIBALDI

C'mon . . . give me a break, you know the kind of day it's been.

ZACK ALLAN

He says it's important.

GARIBALDI

Okay . . . okay, fine, send him in.

Zack retreats OS. A moment later, the Ranger enters.

GARIBALDI

All right, you've got five minutes.

RANGER

I was sent to find you. I have a message.

He reaches toward a sleeve, and peels back a layer in which a datacrystal has been concealed. He holds it out to Garibaldi, puts it on the console.

RANGER

I believe it will explain everything.

Garibaldi hesitates for a moment, then picks up the crystal. Inserts it into a port.

                         GARIBALDI
          Play.

A BEAT . . . and on the monitor there suddenly appears the face of JEFFREY SINCLAIR. (PRODUCTION NOTE: This message from Sinclair has already been shot for playback.)

                         SINCLAIR
          Hello, old friend. It's been a while.

And on Garibaldi's stunned expression, we

                                             FADE OUT.

                         END ACT THREE

ACT FOUR

FADE IN:

INT. GARIBALDI'S OFFICE

As before. A stunned Garibaldi looks at the screen, on which we SEE Sinclair.

> SINCLAIR
> My job on the Minbari homeworld is more than just rep-
> resenting Earth. The President doesn't know about that
> part yet . . . and I don't think it'd be wise for you to tell
> him. There's a great darkness coming, Michael. Some of
> the Minbari have been waiting for it a long time. Prepar-
> ing for it. Others . . . don't believe it. They still think
> we're the enemy. We're not. And we have to get past
> that, or the darkness will overwhelm us all. So we're tak-
> ing steps to change that.

INT. OBSERVATION DOME

As Ivanova approaches Sheridan, her face grave.

> IVANOVA
> Captain . . . we just intercepted a message from the Narn
> Homeworld to Amabassador G'Kar.

> SHERIDAN
> I thought we didn't eavesdrop on our amabssadors.

> IVANOVA
> We don't. This was an open channel. I think they wanted
> us to hear it. The Centauri have launched a full-scale
> assault on a Narn colony in Quadrant 14.

> SHERIDAN
> Damn . . . .

INT. GARIBALDI'S OFFICE

As before. The messsage continues.

> SINCLAIR
> The bearer of this message is one of my Rangers.

ANGLE ON THE RANGER

Impassive, unmoved, listening.

> SINCLAIR
> (os)
> Some are Minbari, most are Humans. They've been
> drawn here to learn to work together, and prepare for
> the fight ahead.

BACK TO SCENE

As Garibaldi freezes the image.

> GARIBALDI
> That's right . . . when I saw you, I kept thinking I'd seen
> you before, but it wasn't you . . . just some others who
> were dressed pretty much the same.

> RANGER
> We've been here for almost two months, Mr.
> Garibaldi . . . keeping an eye on things. We are an army,
> small but growing.

> GARIBALDI
> An army needs weapons. Are they coming through here?

> RANGER
> No, but we do have friends here. That's all I can say for
> now.

Garibaldi glances back at the monitor, unfreezes the image.

> SINCLAIR
> Their job for now is to patrol the frontier, to listen, to
> watch . . . and return with reports too sensitive to entrust
> to regular channels. That means they'll be coming
> through Babylon 5 on a regular basis. They are my eyes
> and ears; where you see them, you see me.

INT. G'KAR'S QUARTERS

With G'Kar on the line with Kha'Mak.

KHA'MAK

The first reports from Quadrant 14 were confused.
They weren't sure who was attacking them. But the
returning fighters confirmed that Centauri warships
were leading the assualt.

G'KAR

What about our people? There were over a quarter million of us there.

KHA'MAK

There were . . . heavy casualties. Most of those killed
died in the first few minutes of the assault. As for the
survivors . . . you know how the Centauri are. Now that
they've taken control, I doubt we'll see any of them
again.
    (beat)
I don't understand how they could have wiped out our
defenses so quickly . . . I just don't understand it. I'll
report more when I learn it.

And Kha'Mak blips off the screen. G'Kar turns . . . and in his eyes is a rage
that is terrible to behold.

G'KAR

. . . I reached out my hand . . . and he betrayed me . . .
<u>he knew and he betrayed me</u>!

And he begins tearing up the place, throwing anything not tied down, a
HOWL of RAGE bellowing from somewhere deep inside.

INT. GARIBALDI'S OFFICE

As the message concludes:

SINCLAIR

In the name of our friendship, I ask that you give them
every courtesy and cooperation. I . . . I wish I could tell
you more, wish I could warn you . . . but the others don't
think it's time yet.
    (beat)
I hope to see you again soon, old friend. Until then, take
care. Stay close to the Vorlon. And watch out for shadows. They move when you're not looking at them.

And the image BLIPS off. Garibaldi sits back.

> GARIBALDI
> Well, I'll be a son of a—

Just then the console BEEPs at him. Coming out of it, he toggles it.

> GARIBALDI
> Yeah . . . ?

> ZACK ALLAN
> (vo)
> We've got a yellow alert in the ambassadorial wing! We
> need help, fast! It's G'Ka—

His voice is cut off.

> GARIBALDI
> Zack . . . Zack. . . .
> (toggles link)
> Station house to all security in Green Sector, yellow
> alert!

INT. GREEN SECTOR HALLWAY

Just as G'Kar picks up a Security Guard and THROWS him the length of
the hall and backhands two others. This hulking, lethal force of nature is
the Narn who fought against the Centauri before . . . enraged and feral,
crouched and looking for blood. He stalks ahead.

> G'KAR
> <u>MOLLARI . . . MOLLARI!</u>

He rounds a corner, and finds a line of armed Security Guards, PPGs aimed
and ready, and Sheridan standing in front of them. (Sheridan is <u>not</u> armed.)

> SHERIDAN
> That's far enough.

> G'KAR
> Mollari!

> SHERIDAN
> Go back to your quarters and no charges will be pressed.

G'Kar starts a step forward. The PPGs come up, aiming at him.

SHERIDAN

I mean it, G'Kar. You will go back to your quarters and
you will go back <u>now</u>.

G'Kar is in bloodlust mode . . . he speaks, but it's an effort. Sheridan slowly
approaches.

G'KAR

They're doing it to us . . . doing it to us again . . . I won't
let this happen . . . I won't let it happen again!

SHERIDAN

Then you're going to need all the help you can get, and
you can't do that if you're not here. Set one foot in
Ambassador Mollari's quarters and you'll either be dead
or gone. Either way it won't help your people.

G'KAR

They'll kill everyone! Don't you understand? They've
done it before! They'll kill everyone. . . .

SHERIDAN

Then you have to decide what's more important to you,
G'Kar . . . revenge, or saving the lives of your people?

He's now eye to eye with G'Kar. For a moment it looks like this could go
either way. Then G'Kar breaks eye contact . . . steps away toward a wall,
touches it, leans against it . . . and slides down, to the floor, hands covering
head, overwhelmed and torn by his emotions. One of the Guards starts to
come toward him, but Sheridan waves him off, feeling G'Kar's anguish.

SHERIDAN

No . . . leave him alone. Leave him alone. . . .

We LINGER for just a moment . . . on G'Kar . . . then go to

INT. MEDLAB

The Emperor, looking very much on his last legs, barely manages to open
an eye as Dr. Franklin runs a scanner over him, checking his signs. He
opens his mouth, works to say something. Nothing quite comes out.

DR. FRANKLIN

It's okay . . . easy . . . you should try to save your strength.
Is there anything you want?

> EMPEROR
> (softly, barely)
> I would very much . . . like to have seen . . . a Vorlon. . . .

Dr. Franklin nods, touches his arm gently, moves off. MOVE IN CLOSE on the Emperor, give it a BEAT. . . and a shadow falls over him. He looks up.

HIS POINT OF VIEW - KOSH

Looms over him.

BACK TO SCENE

As the Emperor reaches forth a hand to him.

> EMPEROR
> How will . . . this end?

> KOSH
> In fire.

INT. SHERIDAN'S OFFICE

Ivanova, Sheridan, and Garibaldi are gathered.

> IVANOVA
> What makes you think you can trust this source of yours?

> GARIBALDI
> Let's just say he comes highly recommended.

> SHERIDAN
> You're holding something back.

> GARIBALDI
> Yes, sir.

> SHERIDAN
> Why?

> GARIBALDI
> I gave my word.

> SHERIDAN
> Garibaldi . . . you're asking me to accept sensitive information without any idea where it comes from.
> (beat)
> I could order you to tell me.

GARIBALDI

And if I told you, you'd never be able to trust me with anything confidential, knowing that someone above you could order me to talk.

It's a good point. Sheridan finally sighs, relents.

SHERIDAN

All right. Go on.

GARIBALDI

Ever since New Year's, we've been hearing about some other major race on the prowl. My source tells me the rumors are true . . . and there may be some link to the Centauri Government. Who or what that link is, I don't know. But they're definitely getting support.

IVANOVA

And you think this other race was behind the assualt on Quadrant 14?

GARIBALDI

It's possible.

SHERIDAN

If it's true . . . they won't want that information to get out.

IVANOVA

What information? All we have here is supposition.

SHERIDAN

Sheridan's Rule #29: Always make your opponent think you know more than you really know.
          (beat)
If your source is right, we may be able to play a bluff.

INT. MEDLAB

Refa, Londo, the Veiled Women, Dr. Franklin, and the Imperial Guard are gathered around the Emperor's bed. He doesn't have far to go.

DR. FRANKLIN

I repeat: This is completely inappropriate; he's in no condition to—

> REFA

He is the Emperor . . . and the good of our people comes first. If he could, he would tell you so himself. This cannot wait.

> (to Emperor)

Your Majesty. . . .

Slowly, the Emperor slits open his eyes.

> REFA

Majesty . . . we have wonderful news. We have retaken the Narn colony in Quadrant 14. It fell within a matter of hours, and not one of our people was hurt or killed in the process. All of Homeworld is rejoicing . . . we are again what we should be. All we lack is your blessing.

The Emperor tries to speak, but nothing comes only, barely a whisper. Refa lowers his head, to listen, but with a frail hand, the Emperor nudges him away. Looks to Londo, on the other side.

Londo lowers his head, his ear barely an inch from the Emperor's lips. A few words emerge . . . then he simply stops. Londo rises, slowly. Looks to Dr. Franklin, who runs a scanner over him.

> DR. FRANKLIN

He's dead.

Refa looks to Londo.

> REFA

What did he say?

> LONDO

He said . . . continue . . . take my people back . . . to the stars.

The two Veiled Women exchange a glance, and exit.

INT. HALLWAY BETWEEN INFIRMARY/MEDLAB

The Veiled Women exit, followed a moment later by Londo and Refa. They wait until they're more or less alone, then:

> REFA

Mollari . . . what did he say . . . really?

                                LONDO
He said . . . that we are both damned.

                                REFA
                             (considers)
Well . . . it's a small enough price to pay . . . for
immortality.

And with that, Refa walks away.

INT. G'KAR'S QUARTERS

G'Kar sits in the darkness as the door opens, and Sheridan enters. He
approaches the motionless G'Kar.

                              SHERIDAN
Ambassador.
                             (nothing)
We think we have an idea how we can help. I've called
a council meeting. I hope you'll come. I think it's important that you be there.

No reply from G'Kar. Sheridan starts out, when he turns at:

                               G'KAR
Sheridan.
                              (beat)
I will attend.
                              (beat)
Thank you . . . for stopping me.

Sheridan nods, and exits. As G'Kar closes his eyes, go to

EXT. BABYLON 5

A transitional shot, to get us into

INT. COUNCIL CHAMBERS

Present: Londo, Delenn, Sheridan, Kosh. No G'Kar.

                              SHERIDAN
Ambassador Mollari . . . what about the Narn civilian
population? I'm told there are over a quarter million of
them at the colony. Will you let them return to the Narn
homeworld?

LONDO

I'm afraid we can't do that. But I'm sure my government
will find some productive activity for them.

DELENN

Forced labor camps . . .

Just then, they turn. G'Kar stands silently in the door. Even Londo can't
bring himself to meet G'Kar's gaze. Slowly, with dignity, G'Kar moves to
his seat on the Council.

LONDO
(awkward now)
Simple retraining. We have no desire to misuse anyone.

SHERIDAN

Ambassador. Would you like to make an opening
statment?

G'Kar shakes his head. No. Sheridan looks to Londo.

SHERIDAN

I should mention that I've just received permission from
my government to send observers to the colony. Their
job will be to monitor the treatment of the Narn civilian
population.

LONDO

They're not welcome.

SHERIDAN

Well, we're sending them anyway. Unless you'd like to
try shooting down an Earthforce transport . . . and personally, I'd advise against it. My people aren't looking
for another war . . . but they don't take kindly to being
shot at.
(beat)
Our observers will assess the situation, interview the survivors, and put together a full report . . . including as
much as they can find out about just how the colony was
conquered so quickly. I think we'd all be interested to
know how you did this, Ambassador. . . .

SHERIDAN (CONT'D)

And trust me, if our observers go there, they <u>will</u> find out.

The latter is a definite warning to Londo, and its meaning is not lost.
Londo considers, then:

LONDO

I believe . . . I believe I may be able to convince my
government to allow the colony's civilian population to
leave the area, and return safely to the Narn homeworld
as a gesture of good will. This would remove the need
for observers from Earth, wouldn't you agree, Captain?

SHERIDAN

Under those conditions . . . yes. I'm sure your . . . goodwill
effort will be appreciated for what it is, Ambassador.

Londo smiles. Sheridan smiles back. Both knowing the high stakes game
they're playing.

DELENN

The Minbari Government is willing to provide trasporta-
tion for the Narn, if that is agreeable to both parties.

LONDO

Absolutely.

DELENN

(to G'Kar)
Ambassador G'Kar?

G'Kar nods. He's got something on his mind.

SHERIDAN

Is there something else?

G'KAR

(nods, then:)
Before coming here, I received a communique from my
government. For a hundred years, the Centauri occupied
our world, devastated it. We swore we would never let
that happen again.

G'KAR (CONT'D)

This attack against our largest civilian colony has in-
flicted terrible damage and loss of life. They have crossed
a line we cannot allow them to cross. As a result . . . two
hours ago my government officially declared war against
the Centauri Republic.
>   (beat)
Our hope for peace is over. We are now at war . . . we
are now at war.

And on the stunned expression of the Council members, we

FADE OUT.

<u>END ACT FOUR</u>

TAG

FADE IN:

EXT. BABYLON 5 - ESTABLISHING

As the Centauri warship and liner move away from the station.

INT. OBSERVATION DOME

Ivanova is at her post as Sheridan enters.

> IVANOVA
> Centauri vessels are heading for the jumpgate . . . taking
> the Emperor home.

> SHERIDAN
> Godspeed.

> IVANOVA
> Did you notify Earth Central about the declaration of
> war?

> SHERIDAN
> (nods)
> They're obviously concerned, but they know it takes time
> to build up a full-scale interstellar war; both sides have
> to assign ships, develop strategies, create supply lines. . . .
> I figure we'll have some border skirmishes for the next
> few months before it builds to total war. With luck, we
> can negotiate this out before it reaches that stage.

> IVANOVA
> I don't know. . . . This time the Centauri have outside
> help, and for all we know, they could be ready for total
> war <u>now</u>.

> SHERIDAN
> Leave it to you to find the black cloud behind every silver
> lining, Commander.

> IVANOVA
> That's my job, sir.

EXT. JUMPGATE

As the Centauri ships depart.

INT. LONDO'S QUARTERS

Refa, Londo and Vir are present.

> ### REFA
> —and the unfortunate death of the Prime Minister, so soon after the Emperor, has had the effect of tilting the balance of power back home. Several competing families have been neutralized, leaving the Emperor's nephew to claim the throne . . . a young man who feels as we do about the future.

> ### LONDO
> And the declaration of war?

Refa moves toward the door.

> ### REFA
> This threat has only put our new Emperor more squarely on our side. If the Narns want a war, we will give it to them. And then some.
> (beat)
> For the first time in a hundred years, Ambassador, our people are on the right track again. And we have you to thank for it. You will find the new Emperor's gratitude most . . . rewarding. Good day, Mollari.

Refa exits. As the door closes, Londo turns to find Vir's eyes on him.

> ### VIR
> I'm surprised . . . you could've asked to be named to the royal court. It would've put you in the position to become emperor yourself someday. That is what you want, isn't it?

FLASHBACK REPRISE

QUICK CUTS: As Londo is crowned . . . is old . . . and at the last of his life, is locked in mortal combat with G'Kar.

BACK TO SCENE

As Londo shakes off the memory.

> LONDO
>
> No . . . I have no desire to be emperor. A coronation is nothing more than a sign to assassins that a new target has been set up on the firing range. I prefer to work from behind the scenes. . . . The reward is nearly as great, and the risk far, far less.

And Londo moves past Vir, who looks very dubious about this entire enterprise.

INT. CUSTOMS AREA

As Garibaldi walks the Ranger toward customs.

> GARIBALDI
>
> —so I want to thank you again for your help. You may have saved the lives of a quarter million Narns.

> RANGER
>
> Then you will give us the cooperation we need?

> GARIBALDI
>
> On one condition. I want you to keep me informed on what you and the other Rangers hear out there. We've got a shooting war on our hands, and we can use all the information we can get.

> RANGER
>
> Consider it done . . . if you keep our presence here a secret.

> GARIBALDI
>
> You got a deal.
> (Ranger starts off)
> Oh . . . one last thing. Aside from me, does anybody else know you're here?

> RANGER
>
> Just one other.

And the Ranger heads away.

INT. DELENN'S QUARTERS

As she enters a datacrystal into the viewer. Sinclair's face appears on the monitor.

>   SINCLAIR
>   Hello, old friend.

And we PUSH IN on her face, as we

                                        FADE OUT.

           THE END

INDEX